there's nothing in this
i'm tired of this
turn on the lights, you people.

MODERN SHORT BIOGRAPHIES

FLORENCE NIGHTINGALE

From an engraving in the Harvard College Library made from the original painting by Chappel

MODERN SHORT BIOGRAPHIES

Edited by

MARSTON BALCH, PH.D.
Assistant Professor of English
Tufts College

NEW YORK
HARCOURT, BRACE AND COMPANY
1935

PRINTED IN THE UNITED STATES OF AMERICA
BY QUINN & BODEN COMPANY, INC., RAHWAY, N. J.

TO

G. C. B.

PREFACE

Biography needs no special pleading today, as it did fifteen years ago. It has come honestly by its wide favor and against considerable opposition taken its place alongside of history, fiction, drama, painting, sculpture, and music as an integral species of human expression. But to select one aspect of biography and present it for perhaps the first time as a literary *genre* calls for some explanation.

This anthology seeks to illustrate the varied contemporary achievement in what may properly be termed the "short biography" by means of eighteen whole and representative examples from the pens of some of its most successful practitioners. As biography has gained importance its authors have taken precedence over their subjects, so that we hear less about a new life of Byron or Wellington, more about a new book by M. Maurois or Mr. Guedalla. The emphasis in this collection is accordingly upon writers and treatment rather than upon subjects and content, and autobiographies are neither included nor considered. But since modern biography's strongest points are its human and literary interests, the present pieces may be hoped to justify themselves to the common reader.

The book is aimed primarily to serve the student, who has already come to recognize biography as a great humanizing agent but has rarely been invited to explore it as a special type of literature; and it is designed to satisfy a widely observed want in several departments of academic study. This collection finds a natural place in freshman composition courses, where six or eight weeks may well be devoted to biography and where the need of both varied reading and suitable models is unfulfilled by the few longer works now available to the student at a small cost. It may be used also in advanced courses where the technique of composition is examined and practiced already in the short-story, the essay, and the one-act play, but not yet in the short biography. In the study of contemporary literature, whether general or specifically English, it may serve to represent the leading biographers by unabridged works that are thoroughly characteristic of their views and methods. For these three special purposes, besides that of giving the ordinary reader pleasure and information, the selections have all been carefully tested by the editor not only in college but in school and not only with freshmen in composition courses but with senior students of literature, and have proved stimulating in a high degree. It may be added, as a sidelight, that the test works just as effectively in the opposite direction as an index of the reader's own intellectual curiosity and alertness, of his apprehension of the biographer's great task and the degree of his success as a "weigher of souls" and a master of letters.

Since a general history of biography is yet to be written and much vagueness and misunderstanding beclouds the subject—despite the excellent studies of Professor Waldo H. Dunn, Mr. Harold Nicolson, M. André Maurois, and others to which the editor is greatly indebted—a summary review is given in the Introduction of the development of biography as a whole and of the short biography in particular from the beginning to the present time. To supplement this and to furnish the reader just entering upon this fresh field with all the facts that may help him toward intelligent judgments, the individual prefatory notes have been made as informative as possible without, it is hoped, prejudicing his mind or dulling his interest; and further material for his independent study is suggested at the end of the book. Save for three or four slight shifts to improve the reading order, the biographies are chronologically arranged and dated according to their original publication.

The obligations incurred by every anthologist are many; they are particularly heavy where the material is all new. The editor wishes to acknowledge his indebtedness to the following authors and publishers who have courteously permitted the reprinting of these short biographies:

D. Appleton-Century Company, Inc., for "The Sorrows of the Young Werther," from *Mape: The World of Illusion*, by André Maurois, translated from the French by Eric Sutton, copyright D. Appleton-Century Company, Inc., 1926; also for "Aunt Mary Emerson," by R. F. Dibble, published in *The Century Magazine*, July 1926, under the title, "She Lived to Give Pain," copyright D. Appleton-Century Company, Inc. Used by permission of the publishers.

Isabel Butchart, for "Margaret Baxter," from *Other People's Fires*, published by Sidgwick and Jackson, Ltd., London, 1924.

Robert M. Coates, for "Blind . . . Deaf . . . Dumb," reprinted by arrangement with the editors from *The New Yorker*, January 25, 1931.

Coward-McCann, Inc., for "An Adventurer Out of the West," from *Lonely Americans*, by Rollo Walter Brown, copyright, 1929, by Coward-McCann, Inc., New York.

Philip Guedalla, for "The Stepfather of the United States: H. M. George III," from *Fathers of the Revolution*, copyright, 1926, by Philip Guedalla, published by G. P. Putnam's Sons, New York and London.

Harcourt, Brace and Company, Inc., for "Florence Nightingale," from *Eminent Victorians*, by Lytton Strachey, copyright, 1918; for "James Boswell," from *Portraits in Miniature*, by Lytton Strachey, copyright, 1931; for "Miss Ormerod," from *The Common Reader*, by Virginia Woolf, copyright, 1925; for "Leeuwenhoek," from *Microbe Hunters*, by Paul de Kruif, copyright, 1926; for "Leonardo da Vinci," from *Genius and Character* by Emil Ludwig, translated from the German by Kenneth Burke, copyright, 1927. Used by permission of the publishers.

Harper and Brothers, for "The Wife of Abraham Lincoln," from *Wives*, by Gamaliel Bradford, copyright, 1926. Reprinted by permission of and arrangement with Harper and Brothers, publishers, New York.

Glenn Hughes, for "William Congreve," by Bonamy Dobrée.

Copyright, 1929, by Glenn Hughes, editor of the University of Washington Chapbooks, Seattle. Also in *As Their Friends Saw Them*, published by Jonathan Cape, Ltd., London, 1933.

J. G. Lockhart, for "Talleyrand," from *The Peacemakers, 1814-1815*, by J. G. Lockhart, published by G. P. Putnam's Sons, New York, 1934.

F. L. Lucas, for "The Perfect Letter-Writer," from *Studies French and English*, published by Cassell and Company, Ltd., London, 1934.

Macmillan and Company, Ltd., London, for "Young Weston," from *The Pageantry of Life*, by Charles Whibley, first published by William Heinemann, London, 1900.

Gilbert Seldes, for "Hammerstein the Extravagant," reprinted from *Harper's Magazine*, July 1932, copyright, 1932, by Harper and Brothers.

The editors of *The Yale Review*, for "Hindenburg," by Harold Nicolson, reprinted from the Summer 1931 *Yale Review*, copyright Yale University Press.

The editor is also grateful to the following authors, who have not only given their consent to reprint their biographies but have supplied valuable information upon their professional views and methods: Mr. Rollo Walter Brown, Mr. Robert M. Coates, Mr. Bonamy Dobrée, Mr. Philip Guedalla, Mr. J. G. Lockhart, Mr. F. L. Lucas, Herr Emil Ludwig, M. André Maurois, Mr. Harold Nicolson, Mr. Gilbert Seldes, and Mrs. Virginia Woolf; to his former students at Harvard and Radcliffe Colleges and the Phillips Exeter Academy, whose candid criticism helped in the selection of the contents; and to Miss Mildred M. Vroom of the Davis Library, Exeter, and Mr. Walter B. Briggs, Mr. E. L. Gookin, and Mr. R. H. Haynes of the Harvard College Library, who have lightened the labor. The friendly coöperation of all these persons, as well as of others who are obliged to remain nameless, has made the shaping of this book a happy and stimulating enterprise.

M. B.

Exeter, New Hampshire
August 1934

CONTENTS

ILLUSTRATIONS

INTRODUCTION

I. BIOGRAPHY

"Geography is about maps;
Biography is about chaps."

IF THE second line of Mr. Chesterton's waggish couplet had always been scrupulously observed, the reader might have been spared the paragraphs that follow. But biography, which has been written for over two thousand years and which grew in the last century into a major literary industry, is still today only an infant art mainly because it has *not* always been about "chaps." It has given us human statues and gargoyles—monumental abstractions, that is, of the Father of His Country, the Captain of Industry, the Empire Builder, the Loving Parent, the Patriot, the Saint, all wool and a yard wide; and less dull but equally far-fetched grotesques of their opposites, the Sinner, the Scoundrel, the Renegade, the Patriot Off His Pedestal. It has painted no end of historical panoramas. It has recorded ranks, posts, pedigrees, ceremonies, and worldly attainments. It has even taught us lessons, valuable lessons, in history, religion, morality, science, art, and business. It has at different times dealt with almost everything *except* real flesh-and-blood individuals as they actually lived. And even its most trustworthy books have so frequently been unreadable that biography has come down to our day a literature with a few prodigious masterpieces but with virtually no general artistic tradition.

It has had from the first a constant struggle to get and keep its independence. Originating in the natural desire to commemorate the dead and thus in some measure to prolong life, it has been made to serve the ends of all manner of writers before reaching the status of a separate literary art. The digressions, to be sure, were easy. From the expanded epitaph of a famous man to a heroic and half-mythical chronicle of his career, or to a moral lesson drawn from his example, or to an analysis of his works, or to a history of his party or his times—these are but short steps, yet they invariably lead away from the main theme, the man himself. Thus, between Plutarch in the first century and Strachey in the twentieth, most of the authors capable of shaping the standards and directing the aims of biography have been diverted by one force or another to the production of sermons or panegyrics, diaries or letters, romances or memoirs, annals or histories, or to the collection of documents.

In the main, the older biography came under the influence of two prototypes, the four Gospels of the *New Testament* and the forty-six *Parallel Lives* of Plutarch. The chronicles of the life of Christ were the model for numberless medieval saints' lives and many modern eulogistic narratives written for the reader's moral edification. While this panegyric tradition, springing straight from the commemorative instinct and the impulse of reverence—*de mortuis nil nisi bonum*—has given us some fine prose, it has been bad for biography. As a man rises to the stature of a hero his virtues become more and more easy to multiply and magnify, his vices more and more difficult to reveal or even perceive, and his inward conflicts and failures are hidden by the glamour of his outward triumphs. He is no more a man, but a type, a picture of excellence, all light and no shadow. Since we cannot see ourselves in him, even his merits soon fail to impress us; and biography finds itself merged in religion or philosophy or ethics because the hero-worshipper has forgotten that, as the First Lord in *All's Well* (IV. iii) says,

> "The web of our life is of a mingled yarn, good and ill together: our virtues would be proud if our faults whipped them not; and our crimes would despair if they were not cherished by our virtues."

Plutarch the Boeotian (46-120 A.D.) knew the truth of this measure of character, and for this reason his impact upon world biography has been more beneficial than that of the church fathers. He knew, moreover, how to use these contradictions in ascertaining a man's true nature: "Nor is it always in the most distinguished achievements that men's virtues or vices may be best discerned; but very often an action of small note, a short saying, or a jest, shall distinguish a person's real character more than the greatest sieges or the most important battles." His *Parallel Lives* of eminent Greeks and Romans set the standard of most of the biographical writing, especially on the Continent, from the sixteenth century on. The familiar structural pattern of life-narrative followed by character analysis and summary, still seen in conventional works, is his. To Plutarch's *Lives*, too, as well as to the earlier *Lives of Illustrious Men* of Cornelius Nepos (c. 99-24 B.C.) and the later *Lives of the Twelve Caesars* of Suetonius (2nd century A.D.), the *Lives of the Philosophers* of Diogenes Laertius (3rd century A.D.), and the *Lives of the Sophists* of Philostratus (c. 170-245 A.D.), must go the credit for instituting the collective biography, which in all countries has been a useful contributor to literature. If we except Xenophon's sketchy *Memorabilia* of Socrates (c. 390 B.C.), it was left for Plutarch's Roman contemporary, Tacitus, in the *Life of Agricola* (c. 98 A.D.), a measured tribute to his father-in-law, to write the first important single biography. While Plutarch himself holds that the substance of his books is not national history but human careers and characters, the writing of a man's life was obviously still regarded in classic times as a part of ethical and historical instruction, "an opportunity," as Sir Edmund Gosse says, "for celebrating, in his person, certain definite moral qualities. It was in these, and not in the individual characteristics of the man, that his interest as a subject of biography resided." A few things had been learned about technique, but the emancipation of the art was yet far off.

One may safely leap the fifteen hundred years from Plutarch to the Renaissance with only a few backward glances at books of special note. Besides the homiletical lives of saints that appeared in every Christian country, one should notice the *Life of Charlemagne* by the Frankish scholar and diplomatist, Einhard (c. 770-

840), and the *Life of Alfred* by the Welsh monk, Bishop Asser (d. 909)—intimate memoirs by faithful companions. Six hundred years later a notable series of portraits gave the poet and chronicler Fernán Pérez de Guzmán (1378-1460) the nickname, the Spanish Plutarch, and another brought fame to Hernando del Pulgar. Nearly all the medieval chroniclers gave biographical information and some wrote with imagination, style, humor, and an immense curiosity, clearly foreshadowing the *Memoirs* of Philippe de Comines (1445-1509).

With the Revival of Learning came a demand for compilations of facts, recollections, and anecdotes about famous people which gave rise to several biographical dictionaries and to such collective works as *The Lives of the Most Excellent Italian Architects, Painters, and Sculptors* (1550) by Giorgio Vasari and the vivacious *Fair and Gallant Ladies*, and *Illustrious Men and Great Captains* by the French courtier Brantôme (1540-1614). In England it is William Roper's charming life of his father-in-law, Sir Thomas More, and George Cavendish's lively study of his master, Cardinal Wolsey, both written about 1557 but printed much later, which mark the beginnings of genuine biography. The most celebrated addition to life-writing in the sixteenth century, however, was undoubtedly the *Memoirs* of the artist, Benvenuto Cellini (1501-71), printed in 1730, a monument of self-revelation and an Italian classic of universal and lasting popularity. Yet, save as it occasioned frank and realistic portraiture and gave material to objective writers, autobiography remained necessarily apart from the main stream.

The seventeenth century, with a splendid foundation to build on, might have contributed immeasurably to the art had not the potential biographers been taken up with the fashionable writing of dramas, essays, romances, histories, characters, criticisms, and *chroniques scandaleuses*. As it was, although nothing was achieved in the first half of the century, the second half is remarkable for the development in France of the biographical dictionary and in England for the appearance of several new talents. To offset in some degree the bad effect upon biography of the Theophrastian "character," or abstract type-sketch, popularized during the later years of Shakespeare's life by Hall, Earle, and Overbury in advance of La Bruyère, we have Edward Hyde, first Earl of Clarendon (1609-74), illustrating his *History of the Rebellion* with a gallery of lively literary portraits and John Aubrey (1626-97), with the true instinctive comprehension of the value of personal details but without the ability to fit them into a balanced narrative, compiling his *Minutes of Lives.* Passing over such diaries as Pepys's, such fascinating letters as Dorothy Osborne's, and such gossipy volumes as the *Memoirs of the Count de Gramont* by Anthony Hamilton—all good material for lives—, we may notice the frank and modest autobiography of Lord Herbert of Cherbury (1583-1648); the well-written reminiscences of the exuberant and adventurous Lady Fanshawe (1625-80); the curious but uninviting memoirs of Colonel John Hutchinson, written by his widow Lucy between 1664 and 1671; and the candid, blue-stocking memoirs (1656) of Margaret Lucas, Duchess of Newcastle, together with her honest life of the Duke, her husband (1667). Finally, as a sign of the limited reach and grasp of seventeenth century biography, we come to Walton's *Lives* and Sprat's *Cowley.* Izaak Walton, author of *The Compleat Angler,* is called "the pioneer of deliberate English biography" by virtue of his studies of Donne, Wotton, Hooker, Herbert, and Sanderson, published between 1640 and 1678. Too deeply impregnated with the Christian virtue of meekness and too neglectful of his subjects' real importance to satisfy the modern reader with realistic and full-bodied pictures, Walton nevertheless knew how to shape such material as he chose to use into impressive narratives, familiar, occasionally witty, yet modest and quiet in tone, sprinkled with imaginary conversations and ballasted with original letters. Yet if the *Lives* were popular and influential, so, too, unluckily, was the *Life of Cowley* (1668). For while Walton was a gentle, retiring soul, the aggressive Dr. Thomas Sprat had a certain ecclesiastical and literary authority in England, and when he chose to enter the field with a frosty and impersonal life of the late reigning poet, presented in the form of a letter and purposely denuded of every human element, he revived, as Mr. Nicolson says, the old tradition of the "discreet" biography, which was to have such a baneful influence upon the Victorians. One thing more the century added to the art—its name; for before 1660 the word "biography" and its cognates are not known to have been used. It remained for a later generation to produce the first masterpiece.

The Restoration Age in England, so rich in drama and criticism, so meagre in biography, cast its shadow over the first quarter of the eighteenth century, but not without some benefit to life-writing. In the words of Mr. Nicolson: "Inevitably the essay on contemporary manners, the novel of contemporary life, exercised a powerful and durable effect upon the development of English biography. They revived our national talent for realism, they gave an important stimulus to curiosity and sympathy, they created a habit of psychological observation, they enormously increased the numbers of the reading public, and they gave that public a very definite taste for detail."

At the same time there was growing up across the Channel a genuine biographical tradition among the French. There, where since the beginning of the fifteenth century many of the most active and distinguished warriors, courtiers, churchmen, and historiographers, from Chastellain (1415-75) and Comines to Brantôme and the Cardinal de Retz (1614-79), had written a succession of skillful narratives and portraits, memoir-writing now began to be the studied occupation of persons of culture and leisure; and we have, besides the famous volumes of Madame de Sévigné (1626-96) and Madame de Maintenon (1635-1719), the finished literary portraits or *Historiettes* of Tallemant des Réaux (1619-92). But these few out of the many authors were hardly more than prefacing the immensely varied and valuable output of the eighteenth century which made France the nation richest in memoirs and most advanced in the art of objective portraiture. Before Boswell was born or even Johnson had left Oxford, the Duc de Saint-Simon (1675-1755) was rivaling Tacitus in the striking, adroit language and the brilliant, sustained characterizations of his vast work. Voltaire, the leading man of letters in Europe, turned out several studies which, if they do not rank high today for scholarship, are at least models of lucid narrative.

Literary salons were generating whole schools of sophisticated young biographers and circulating their ideas and their manuscripts. Of these it needs only to name the memoirs of Bachaumont (1690-1771) of the first part of the century and Madame de Staël (1766-1817) of the last to suggest the wealth of this literature. Finally, one must mention Lytton Strachey's high praise of his own masters, "the Fontenelles and Condorcets, with their incomparable *éloges,* compressing into a few shining pages the manifold existences of men." Neither the memoirs nor the academic eulogies were strictly biographies in the modern sense, of course, but they all shared significantly in the development of the art.

Before we come to the signal masterpiece of English, if not of all, biography, let us take account of the works which had first to prepare the ground. The encyclopedic biography, a fund of information rather than an artistic medium, finally appeared in England in the *Biographia Britannica* (1747-60), the *Biographia Dramatica* (1764, etc.), and other such compilations. Popular taste for sensational lives was whetted by Daniel Defoe's quasi-fictitious biographies of three criminals, "the Highland Rogue," *i.e.*, Rob Roy (1723), Jack Sheppard (1724), and Jonathan Wild (1725), as well as by Edmund Curll's innumerable *Eminent Persons*, Captain Alexander Smith's *History of the Lives of the Most Noted Highwaymen, Footpads, Housebreakers, Shoplifters, Etc.* (1715), and dozens of other underworld chronicles, or "Grub Street biographies," as Addison termed them, leading up to *The Newgate Calendar* (1774, etc.). What Samuel Pepys would have set down in his shorthand *Diary* the actor-dramatist Colley Cibber spread out in the quarrelsome and talkative *Apology for His Life* (1740). Three breezy and unusually interesting studies of his brothers by the lawyer Roger North, written about 1714 and printed in 1742-44, are now taken by Mr. Nicolson, on account of their "humour, frankness, and great graphic and dramatic skill," to be an important link between Aubrey and Boswell. When in 1744 appeared Dr. Johnson's *Life of Mr. Richard Savage*, subsequently included in his *Lives of the Poets* (1777-81), pure biography in England had at last found its master.

Johnson, who confessed that "the biographical part of literature . . . is what I love most," seems to draw together in these short studies all the essentials of candor, of sympathetic comprehension, of dramatic actuality, of narrative power, of stylistic excellence toward which his predecessors had only been groping. "To the minute selection of characteristical circumstances," Boswell notes, "for which the ancients were remarkable, he added a philosophical research, and the most perspicuous and energetick language." He made his poets *live*. Yet even more important to the development of biography than these examples is his authoritative exposition of its principles. In the *Rambler* and elsewhere he repeatedly assailed the sham ethics of the "discreet" writer and proclaimed the necessity of telling the truth: "If a man is to write *A Panegyrick*, he may keep vices out of sight; but if he professes to write *A Life*, he must represent it as it was." Again: "If we owe regard to the memory of the dead, there is yet more respect to be paid to knowledge, to virtue and to truth." As for method, "The business of the biographer is often to pass slightly over those performances and incidents which produce vulgar [*i.e.*, popular] greatness, to lead the thoughts into domestick privacies, and display the minute details of daily life, where exteriour appendages are cast aside, and men excel each other only by prudence and by virtue." The trouble is, he goes on, that "biography has often been allotted to writers, who seem very little acquainted with the nature of their task, or very negligent about the performance. They rarely afford any other account than might be collected from publick papers, but imagine themselves writing a life, when they exhibit a chronological series of actions or preferments; and have so little regard to the manners or behaviour of their heroes, that more knowledge may be gained of a man's real character, by a short conversation with one of his servants, than from a formal and studied narrative, begun with his pedigree and ended with his funeral."

Meanwhile, Henry Fielding, in pseudo-biographical novels, bombarded the rising sentimentalism of his day and Oliver Goldsmith extolled the merits of the craft in his well-written lives of Voltaire (1759) and Parnell (1770). To Johnson's pioneering work, also, William Mason, a minor poet and dramatist, added, in *The Life and Letters of Gray* (1774), the effective example of incorporating private correspondence into narrative and so letting the subject, as he says, "become his own biographer." Although Mason was no model of accuracy or impartiality and the "life-and-letters" method which he consciously initiated has done on the whole as much evil as good, his book was a necessary step to Boswell and to the later progress of the art.

By far the greatest single biographical achievement in any country down to our time is James Boswell's *Life of Samuel Johnson* (1791). So much nonsense has circulated about this classic—that it made Dr. Johnson famous; that, being long and without chapter divisions, it is formless and dull; that it can only be appreciated in fragments; that its author was nothing more than an "inspired idiot"—that every student of biography and general literature should hasten to obtain a correct and immediate impression by the only possible recourse, reading it himself. The *Life* is, to be sure, a *tour de force* unlikely ever to be duplicated. It is the fruit of the very fortunate meeting of two singular individuals, the one an extraordinarily fit subject, the other an unusually adept author, the complement and supplement of one another in temper and ability. But it was far from being an accident. Long before Johnson strolled into Thomas Davies's bookshop in Drury Lane on Monday the 16th of May, 1783, and met his future biographer, Boswell had begun training himself to hold intelligent interviews with celebrities, to retain the language and tone of long conversations, to take copious and accurate notes, to verify every source of knowledge, to analyze and appraise difficult material, to narrate events and depict features tellingly, and to give life and order and movement to the reconstruction of human careers. In the years that followed he zealously continued this discipline all over Europe. He became versed in Johnson's own theory of biography. "I cannot conceive," he says, "a more perfect mode of writing any man's life, than not only relating all the most important events of it in their order, but interweaving what he privately wrote, and said, and thought; by which mankind are enabled as it were to see him live, and to 'live o'er each scene' with him, as he actually advanced through the several stages of his life." Boswell's vast work, finished in the face of untold obstacles and even of deliberate opposition in the last miserable years of his life, comes close to realizing this ideal. "It was not merely," as Mr. Nicolson says, "that Boswell perfected the annotative and the analytical methods of biography. His great achievement is that he combined them with the synthetic. He was able, by sheer constructive force, to project his detached photographs with such continuity and speed that the effect produced is that of life." He does not, like the modern biographer, give us the conflicts of purposes, the heights and depths of his subject's temperament, but, as Mr. Osbert Burdett points out, like the Dutch artist Teniers, he gives us all the small external details. Artfully artless in the Anglo-Saxon manner, with little appearance of plan or proportion, the book fulfills the promise of Aubrey, Walton, Mason, and North and is a handsome tribute to the inspiriting touch of Samuel Johnson.

Such a happy union of subject and author cannot, of course, recur very frequently, and England waited nearly fifty years before its like was seen again. Meanwhile, after the controversy over Boswell's ethics and an urbane vogue of French models had died down, the *Life of Johnson* became everybody's ideal and a deluge of "lives" began to pour from the presses. "Of late years," wrote John Watkins in 1821 in the preface to his *Universal Biographical Dictionary*, "thanks to the officious zeal of friendship, and the active industry of literary undertakers, biographical memoirs have become as multitudinous, prolix, and veracious as epitaphs in a country churchyard." The most memorable pre-Victorian works are Robert Southey's *Nelson* (1813) and *Wesley* (1820), Thomas Moore's *Letters and Journals of Lord Byron* (1830), and John Gibson Lockhart's *Life of Sir Walter Scott* (1838). As indicating the new trends, though, one should not overlook such books as Scott's own *Life of Dryden* (1808), a painstaking attempt to re-create the whole political and cultural background of his subject's life and works; Monk's *Life of Richard Bentley* (1830), one of the earliest documentary reconstructions beneath which for a century to come British bookshelves were to sag; Macaulay's short biographical studies; and the amazing and original *Imaginative Biography* of Egerton Brydges (1834). The *Nelson* and *Wesley*, though infected too much with the blandness of Walton, are smooth, simple, and straightforward narratives for a time when the contrary qualities were beginning to gain the ascendant. Moore, through his intimacy with Byron and his possession of the poet's own unique memoirs, which he destroyed, had an exceptional opportunity and responsibility, and made an honest attempt to meet the test. But the *Letters and Journals*, while lively reading and an invaluable source, falls far short of Boswell and can only be said to stand for the triumph of friendship over biography.

Lockhart's *Scott*, on the other hand, is generally conceded to rank very near the *Life of Johnson* for vividness, frankness, and wealth of document and characterization. "I have endeavoured," Lockhart states, after the example of Boswell, "to lay before the reader those parts of Sir Walter's character to which we have access, as they were indicated in his sayings and doings through the long series of his years—making use, whenever it was possible, of his own letters and diaries rather than of any other materials;—but refrained from obtruding almost anything of comment. It was my wish to let the character develop itself." And it does, through seven large volumes! This very magnitude, in fact, seems to be, when all disputants have rested, the only important defect in the work. Lockhart possessed all the materials a biographer could hope to have, including Scott's own autobiographical fragment composed in 1808. He had, too, a quality soon to become outmoded in England, the bravery to "touch the few darker points," as he calls them, of his father-in-law's life and character. He shows a mastery of cumulative construction on a very wide scale, and even, it must be allowed, an uncommon dramatic sense and power of selection. He lacked Boswell's ability to report conversation; yet this talent, indispensable at Mrs. Thrale's, was less in demand, as Mr. Nicolson suggests, in capturing the personality of the energetic Laird of Abbotsford coursing his hounds. He does not excel in prose style, and is often actually heavy; but the defect is compensated somewhat by his inexhaustible supply of concrete details skillfully placed to give freshness and reality to all but the most ponderous chapters.

"How delicate, decent is English biography, bless its mealy mouth! A Damocles sword of *Respectability* hangs forever over the poor English Life-writer (as it does over English Life in general), and reduces him to the verge of paralysis. The English biographer has long felt that if in writing his Man's Biography, he wrote down anything that could possibly offend any man, he had written wrong. The plain consequence was, that, properly speaking, no biography whatever could be produced." So said Thomas Carlyle, praising Lockhart, as if in answer to the accusing question he had already put in 1832: "How comes it that in England we have simply one good Biography, this *Boswell's Johnson;* and of good, indifferent, or even bad attempts at Biography, fewer than any civilized people?" For hardly had the *Life of Scott* appeared when the violent attacks upon Lockhart's "disloyalty" showed that a new generation was already in command of the field. Indeed, for many years now British writers were to be actuated not by intellect, humor, and common sense, but by emotion. They were to feel the oppressive duty to honor the dead either in elegiac volumes like Dean Stanley's *Life of Thomas Arnold* (1844) and Mrs. Gaskell's *Life of Charlotte Brontë* (1857); or in such an "unrhymed heroic poem" as Carlyle's own *Life of John Sterling* (1851); or in the promising *Life of Sir Walter Raleigh* by Edward Edwards (1868); or in scholarly studies like G. H. Lewes's *Goethe* (1855) and G. O. Trevelyan's *Macaulay* (1876); or in vast reconstructional histories like Carlyle's *Frederick the Great* (1858-65), J. R. Seeley's *Life and Times of Stein* (1878), and David Masson's *Life of Milton and History of His Time* (1859-80); or in numerous short critical compendiums like John Morley's "English Men of Letters Series" (1877-) or in Leslie Stephen's *Dictionary of National Biography* (1882-). Valuable as most of these conscientious works are for some purposes, they represent a period when, in England and America, at least, the comic spirit and the free artistic impulse, which are the soul of pure biography, lay frozen.

Even the appearance in 1882-84 of the nine volumes of James

Anthony Froude's honest and unsentimental *Life of Carlyle*, a genuine reaction from emotion toward objective psychological truth, could not stay the flood of Victorian panegyric. The *Carlyle* was a landmark in the development of the art in England, as we now see, because it loosed for the first time in biography the springs of irony and satire, which had formerly flowed only in fiction, drama, and verse. But Froude, who was savagely assailed as a faithless friend and executor, became such a universal abomination in Anglo-Saxondom that his contemporary influence was slight indeed. And although a few other books, such as Morley's lives of *Rousseau* (1873), *Gladstone* (1903), and others and A. V. G. Allen's *Life and Letters of Phillips Brooks* (1900) employed faithfully the Mason-Boswell-Lockhart method, they show no technical advance.

Biography had by this time become a veritable industry. The flow of "lives," "lives and times," "lives and letters" of successful persons was enormous. Not only rulers, noblemen, bishops, and men of letters, but travelers, politicians, business men, and ordinary citizens were now embalmed in print. Almost anybody of attainments or means could be assured a favorable volume to his memory, and Andrew Lang scarcely exaggerated when he wrote:

> "For now a dentist cannot die
> And leave his forceps as of old
> But o'er him, e'er his bones be cold,
> Begins the vast biography."

If nobody else would do it, he wrote it himself, so that from Gibbon and Franklin to the present the stream of autobiography is equally earnest and incessant. In lands less touched by Victorianism, tradition and popular favor helped sustain the art. But in England and America and to some extent everywhere, while history, fiction, and poetry had their innings, biography struggled pitiably through its outs.

Dare one imagine, taking a long view, the heights to which it might have risen by 1900 had it from the first enlisted such vigorous minds as Chaucer, Montaigne, Marlowe, Shakespeare, John Webster, Chapman, Molière, Defoe, Congreve, Fielding, Lessing, Fanny Burney, Jane Austen, Balzac, Hugo, Flaubert, Zola, Browning, Meredith, Hardy, and Bernard Shaw? The vision is dazzling.

What biography had actually accomplished by 1900 makes a very different picture. After the exceptional achievement of Boswell it had learned to apply accurate methods of historical investigation to the gathering, weighing, and assembling of large masses of facts. The passion for full, concrete details and the sincere desire to be truthful had resulted in Lockhart's *Scott* and Froude's *Carlyle*. Besides these English masterpieces, a sturdy tradition of literary excellence had produced in France the superb portraits of Sainte-Beuve (1804-69) and a great many longer lives of high, if not of supreme, quality. Little by little, through the reiteration of experienced writers like Thomas Carlyle, John Morley, and Edmund Gosse, the line was being drawn between the provinces of history and biography, "between the fortunes of the community and the exploits, thoughts, and purposes of the individual who had so marked a share in them"; and one notes also, perhaps as an effect of Romanticism, perhaps as a reflection of the novelists' minute analysis and interpretation of character, an increasing subordination of a man's words and works to the essential qualities of the man himself. While still groping for a satisfactory definition, biography, in the hands of politicians, historians, scientists, poets, painters, and philosophers, had widened and consolidated its hold upon the reading public. It had not yet created a recognized profession; it was scarcely an acknowledged art; its full potentialities had not been guessed; it was still helpless before a fluctuating public taste. But it needed only the impetus of the new intellectual dispensation just coming into view at the turn of the century to launch it surely on its destined way.

II. MODERN BIOGRAPHY

"The surface of life all at once is torn apart and one reads bare soul."

—Sainte-Beuve

At some time during the decade preceding the World War the gathering forces of the scientific spirit aroused in the mid-nineteenth century wrought a notable change in the complexion of human thought which was to have profound reverberations in the field of biography. What were these forces? What was this change? How did it affect the literature we are studying?

We have already seen evidence of the improvement in methods of research; we have noted the growing taste for exactitude and order in all scholarly work. In men of science especially, but not exclusively, there was also a compelling passion for observation in itself, for noticing things which easily escape attention and studying them carefully. This constant and habitual delight in examining things led normally, as the various sciences branched and matured, to the minute and systematic analysis of every particle and aspect of matter, from atoms to stars, from amoeba to man. The universal stimulation of curiosity was directed, in the best minds, by the pure, abstract love of truth, so admirably expressed by Charles Darwin: "For myself I would . . . take higher ground, for I believe there exists, and I feel within me, an instinct for truth, or knowledge, or discovery, of something the same nature as the instinct of virtue, and our having such an instinct is reason enough for scientific researches without any practical results ever ensuing from them."

But very practical and impressive results did ensue from them. For this spirit of free inquiry, once loosed upon a world governed mainly by traditions, clashed inevitably with the established beliefs, customs, standards, conduct, and literature of society—and inevitably won. Naïve at first, then courageously militant, it battered the ancient conventions. Skeptical, inductive, relentlessly experimental, it invaded the spheres of the natural sciences and demonstrated life to be evolutionary, mobile, complex. It renovated psychology and ethics, decreeing the old categories of good and evil to be relative, not absolute, and showing man himself to be at once a product and a stream of infinitely various forces. It touched art and, seizing upon its passionate interest in contemporary life and manners, first produced Naturalism out of Romanticism, then, in Impressionism, stirred the revolt against classic canons of beauty and modes of composition.

Having broken down popular interdictions and taboos, the revolutionary movement was not long in seeking out literature. "The first signs of it," says Virginia Woolf, "are recorded in the books of Samuel Butler, in *The Way of All Flesh* (1903) in particular; the plays of Bernard Shaw continue to record it." Mr. Harold Nicolson sees its effect on biography in Sir Edmund Gosse's *Father and Son* (1907). One may detect it also in the early reviews of Lytton Strachey lately reprinted in *Characters and Commentaries*. In America it was noted in Gamaliel Bradford's unconventional studies of Lee (1912) and other venerable figures. Fiction, always the most responsive literary medium, supplies abundant evidence of it; poetry, too. Everywhere the intellect was unshackling itself from the old moral conceptions, from the conventions of "good taste" and "respectability," from the blind and comfortable optimism of the nineteenth century. "The Victorian biographer," Mrs. Woolf reminds us, "was dominated by the idea of goodness. Noble, upright, chaste, severe; it is thus that the Victorian worthies are presented to us. The figure is almost always above life-size in top-hat and frock-coat, and the manner of presentation becomes increasingly clumsy and laborious." Suddenly the smug propriety is shattered. Here is a British author of an autobiographical novel satirizing his parents for rearing him in the stuffy atmosphere of Dr. Arnold's Public School System. And here is another book, published anonymously but, as it turns out, by one of the most highly esteemed men of letters, past middle life, depicting coolly, realistically, and with alarming detachment, "as a genuine slice of life" and "a diagnosis of a dying Puritanism," his long, tragic clash of will with his father. Here, too, is a brilliant young Cambridge graduate publishing as book reviews in left-wing periodicals devastatingly ironical studies of eighteenth century men and women. And again, here is an American, obsessed with the indecorous analysis of human souls, examining under a strong light the characters of his country's staple heroes. Truly, the old order was changing.

The War completed this intellectual upheaval, and when it was over a disintegrated literary world awoke to find the art of biography an established fact. Early in 1918 appeared Strachey's *Eminent Victorians* and three years later, *Queen Victoria.* With matchless irony and finality the old era was sent to its grave with the same phrases that sounded the advent of the new. Presently in England, America, Germany, France, and other lands consonant voices arose, new names and titles appeared in the bookshops. One heard of Gamaliel Bradford's psychographs, of Van Wyck Brooks's *Ordeal of Mark Twain*, of Emil Ludwig's *Goethe*, of Frank Harris's *Oscar Wilde*, of Lord Charnwood's *Lincoln*, of André Maurois's *Ariel*, of Harold Nicolson's *Verlaine* and *Tennyson* and *Byron*, of Philip Guedalla's *Second Empire*, of Thomas Beer's *Stephen Crane*, of R. F. Dibble's *Strenuous Americans*—of a whole new galaxy of unconventional biographies, long and short. Nearly everything about them was different from works of the old familiar kind. They were briefer, more unified in theme, more dramatic in construction, more original and striking in expression; they treated their subjects as men rather than as heroes; they employed anecdotes, but as clues to character, not as padding; they read like novels; they seemed meant to be enjoyed rather than studied; in a word, they were interesting.

Needless to say, they caused no little pain and confusion in conservative minds. Strachey, Ludwig, Maurois, and the other authors were attacked and lampooned from several quarters. Hero-worshippers resented what they considered the abuse of their heroes; scholars launched accusations of slipshod methods and faulty and insufficient documentation; historians accused them of betraying their ancient craft into the hands of dilettanti; while some of the elder critics, at a loss to classify such manifold strange writings, tried safely to belittle them with such epithets as "unpleasant," "maliciously clever," "iconoclastic," "experimental," "ephemeral."

Here and there, to be sure, in their zeal to be novel and different, authors went to excess and deserved sober rebuke. Some, reacting too violently from the solid Victorian document, took the unwarranted liberty of inventing talk or rearranging events to "improve" the picture, or else, impatient of stubborn facts and determined to make their own interpretation prevail, constructed that anomaly, the "fictional biography." Others exploited the post-war taste for humanizing the great by indiscriminate idol-smashing or by the simpler method of smearing the old white-wash with tar and feathers—the "true life" or "de-bunking" biography—or by openly courting the market for sensational reading. Still others pressed the study of personality so far as to throw performance into obscurity, giving us a scientist without science, a statesman without statecraft, a poet without poetry; or, in their humorless will to psychoanalyze their subject no matter how remote in time, lost perspective and the saving touch of common sense. These were the more radical expressions of a lusty new movement which, while they required curbing, were useful as signs of its trends and warnings of its dangers.

But the reading public frankly liked the best of the new books and asked for more, and the output has increased ever since. From being a mere handmaid of history biography has become in a few years the popular rival of fiction, an acknowledged department of literature employing some of the best minds of the age and manifesting itself in many fascinating aspects. What biography is today, now that it has won its ground and settled down to cultivate it, what it is trying to do, and how it is doing it, are questions we must now attempt to answer.

Biography, as we understand it today, may be defined as "the faithful portrait of a soul in its adventures through life" (Sir Edmund Gosse); or as "the imaginative interpretation of a human life" (Lewis Mumford); or as "the study and presentment of a human character, with its contradictions and its failures, with its inner conflict of aim and impulse and its outer struggle between circumstance and temperament" (Osbert Burdett); or simply as "the history of the lives of individual men as a branch of literature" (*Oxford English Dictionary*).

This modern conception goes beyond that of Plutarch and Dryden and Johnson—"the writing of particular men's lives"—and lays the stress upon aims and methods never consistently realized until our day. It underscores portraiture, interpretation, presentment. When we say, for instance, that biography is "the history of the lives of individual men as a branch of literature," we mean, as Mr. Nicolson explains, that it must be "a truthful record of an individual and composed as a work of art"—not a figment of the imagination, nor a panegyric of the dead, nor the chronicle of an epoch, nor a *tableau vivant*, nor a fabric of science. It must, of course, be scrupulously based on historical and psychological knowledge scientifically arrived at. It must take full account of the subject's background, of his environment, and of what he said and did, but only in so far as they shed light upon his developing character. It must give a faithful picture of the man's person and an honest interpretation of his personality as expressed in his career. And to provide the kind of pleasure we demand from a piece of literature it must be shaped and suffused, not by invention, but by a lively re-creative imagination and set forth in a satisfying artistic form.

An art with such high standards demands unusual qualities of its practitioner. It requires, first of all, *sensitiveness* to enter into and interpret another man's soul. As Emil Ludwig puts it, "This venture of conjuring up on the canvas the spirit of one long passed away and making him seem to live again before us and breathe, desire, fear, can only be undertaken by one who in his own breast cherishes those human emotions from which is born the tonic chord of every life." It calls also for *intuitive insight and experience* to apprehend the all-important spirit motivating the act, "to disentangle what a man says from what he thinks, . . . to pierce beneath the protective crust of pride and reserve." It asks of the writer *tolerance and a well-tempered understanding* to keep his portrait undistorted by bias or prejudice, by antipathy or favor. It demands *imagination* to revive the physical and spiritual features in a convincing semblance of reality. It exacts, besides the patience and ability to gather and appraise the infinite morsels of knowledge that make up every reconstruction of the past, a superior *skill in selection*, a fine discernment of those truths which will best transmit personality. To re-create bygone scenes and figures, to reanimate the stubborn facts of a man's or woman's whole existence with movement, proportion, climax, requires a *dramatic sense* equal to that of the playwright and novelist, if not greater; while to present this life in such form and language that the reading itself will be a beautiful and thrilling experience calls for *literary powers* of the first order.

Even when an author possesses all these talents in a high degree he has still to determine for himself the method best suited to the portraiture of his particular subject. For this step of the way there is no ready-made formula, since human character is his quarry and the qualities and experiences of no two individuals fit the same terms. His method will very likely come, if it come at all, from the peculiar nature of the man he is trying to depict and from his reactions to him. Of this man, the biographer realizes, he cannot know everything. For truth, especially psychological truth, is notoriously relative and elusory. Whether his study be as brief as Aubrey's or as long as Froude's, whether he draw his Disraeli, like M. Maurois, in a small book of three hundred pages or, like Monypenny and Buckle, in half a dozen volumes each twice that length, the whole truth is yet to be uttered. Joyce's *Ulysses* has taught him that. Moreover, he has so much material at hand that he cannot even tell all he knows and yet satisfy his sense of form. Form—that is the crux of his problem and the clue to its solution. For the biographer knows that proportion, after all, is more illuminating than masses of detail, that "contradiction is the salt of character," and that the life of a portrait depends upon the amount of contrast. He will therefore study the proportion of light and shadow, of strength and weakness in his character, the proportion of outward behavior and expression to inner feelings and purposes in his career, the proportion of formative development to mature achievement, the proportion of the stable elements of his personality to the impulsive or accidental variations from that norm. On the basis of these contrasts he will plot the curve of the man's life, determine the point of view from which he can best interpret it, the details of character and incident that will give it the correct perspective. When he does this he is selecting, and out of his selection will emerge his method and mode of writing.

The technical methods of modern biographers, both in portraiture and in narrative, are too many to enumerate, but they are almost invariably based upon the selection of details dictated by the subject and the author's interpretation. In portraiture a great deal has been learned from the painters, who attempt no photographic reproduction with equal detail in figure and background but throw high lights upon the revealing traits and leave the rest dark. "Like my master, Rembrandt," says Herr Ludwig, "from whom I have derived more knowledge of the chiaroscuro in the human soul than from all the poets, I try to give only the bare essentials of costume, so that art and eye may concentrate on the face which emerges from the shadow." Lytton Strachey, rebelling against a rooted tradition of panegyric which had painted its heroes as stock types of this or that virtue, and determining to convert the Angel of Mercy back into Florence Nightingale, the Christian Soldier back into General Gordon, the Queen back into the woman Victoria, the scientist-essayist-Lord Chancellor back into Francis Bacon, selected those contrasting traits (recorded in the sources but usually omitted from the official lives) which humanize the person, make him alive, tangible, three-dimensional. Then, to emphasize these natural contradictions he touched up with a vivid anecdote an unnoticed absurdity here or cast a high light of irony upon an incongruity there and showed us the essential character as he saw it: in Miss Nightingale, the demon of work; in Gordon, the frenzied enthusiast; in Victoria, the ingenuous but self-willed girl, the gloomy widow, the fairy Titania; and in Bacon, the serpent. That this was dangerously near caricature Strachey's lesser imitators have shown; but in 1918 hyperbole was needed to level the entrenchments of Puritanism, and the extraordinary success he achieved is proof enough of his skill and judgment. Instead of a symbol, M. Maurois is inclined to search out and underscore a *leitmotif* or dominant rhythm to express the particular cast and tone of his subject's life. In Shelley this is water; in Disraeli, flowers. Thus every biographer, according to his discernment of the character before him, will evolve his own mode of portraiture.

In the construction of the narrative the modern biographer leans more toward the novelist, the playwright, the cinema scenarist. No reader of *Queen Victoria* and *Elizabeth and Essex* can fail to note Strachey's dramatic conception of those life-stories. As in a Shakespearean "history" or a novel by Thomas Hardy, one follows the main characters through the inevitable rise and fall, the exposition, complication, climax, resolution, and catastrophe to the final setting-to-rights. Strachey's one stage piece was a failure, but an interesting play was made (and produced on Broadway) of scenes assembled from his *Victoria*, while *Elizabeth the Queen* and other recent plays on that monarch's life probably owe not a little to his dramatic instinct. Herr Ludwig, who was a dramatist for many years and who has produced a trilogy of plays on the life of Bismarck and assisted in the filming of his *Napoleon*, finds that all his biographies fall of themselves into five- or three-act form. M. Maurois, with an artist's strong predilection for design, was admittedly attracted to the study of Shelley, Disraeli, and Byron partly by an inherent curve, a "natural composition," a "mysterious symmetry" in their lives which decided the pattern of his narrative. In the massing of details Mr. Guedalla prefers a sequence of great historical scenes, a pageant panorama in the cinematographic manner, full of people and movement. Herr Ludwig, on the other hand, concentrates on the individual figure. "Does one ever demand of a portrait that it should include a landscape, the view of a town or group, such as naturally belongs to it? Neither can I reproduce the whole environment, for my aim is to keep to a single volume, and seeing that 700 pages about Napoleon and 1,300 about Goethe are very little, I can draw only the most important features of the background; the frame allows for no more." Incidental names he omits, and, instead of giving dates, reminds us frequently of the subject's age. In the modern biography, which begins with a person's birth and ends with his death, pedigrees and family connections are usually left out, save only when, as in the opening chapter of *Queen Victoria*, they contribute an incident to the human drama. Now and then by cinematographic "flashes" Herr Ludwig and Mrs. Woolf have been able to condense a life-story into a series of separate impressionistic episodes, fragmentary but revealing. A more frequent method is to foreshorten the narrative by throwing into bold relief certain significant aspects or periods, as in *The Queen and Mr. Gladstone* by Mr. Guedalla, *The Soul of Samuel Pepys* by Bradford, and M. Bernard Faÿ's *Franklin, the Apostle of Modern Times*, or in Mr. Nicolson's *Byron, the Last Journey* (where the additional use of the novelist's "stream of consciousness" technique realistically fills out the retrospective portrait), and Mr. Carl Sandburg's *Abraham Lincoln, the Prairie Years*. The adoption of some such point of view is especially needful, we shall see, in the strictly short biography, which is itself another way of treating the life. These are all technical problems which the biographer must solve for himself. He may be relieved of some of the labor of research by the documents of scholars; his work remains, as M. Maurois attests, "a very delicate task, which depends upon a sense of artistic perception much more than upon scientific method."

The fundamental secret of all true biography, as of art, is selection, interpretation. There is no such thing as a "complete life" of a man, in the sense of a book that tells everything, any more than there is a complete statue or a complete oil painting. A "definitive biography" may gather into a volume or two, or into ten or a dozen if need be, the known "facts" about his public and private career; but the man's character, the soul of his life and work, the real significance of his earthly existence, will require and challenge interpretation again and again so long as his memory is deemed important to any portion of mankind. This is why in late years we have had so many new lives of figures we had long thought familiar and dull but now find curiously strange and fascinating. The modern biographers have reinterpreted them to us in terms that arouse our interest and delight. Many of these persons who had been commemorated in eloquent thick volumes fifty or a hundred years ago are only now for the first time being revealed to the world in the guise of life. As there have been many paintings and sketches of interesting men and women, so may we look to have many biographies, which will be valuable to the world in the measure of their authors' powers of interpretation and presentment.

To be sure, modern biography, like modern music, poetry, architecture, and plastic and decorative arts, must bear full blame for the merely "modernistic" excesses perpetrated in the unrestraint of our time and full responsibility for clearing its main stock of these bastard growths. The critics will see to that. "It is now possible," wrote the late George Saintsbury in 1929, "to find studies in biography, specifically described as 'new' or 'modern,' which contain nothing but the impertinence of youth to maturity or the obtuseness of stupidity to achievement." Lytton Strachey, as the leading spirit of the movement, has been roundly and repeatedly censured for the faults of his example. But was it not so with Boswell, even with Lockhart, and is not that the fate of leaders everywhere? Already in 1928, in his admirable Cambridge lectures, M. Maurois was warning, "A bad Victorian biography is a formless mass of ill-digested matter; a bad modern biography is a book of spurious fame animated by a would-be ironic spirit which is merely cruel and shallow." Since then, as in the other arts, the pruning which every healthy tradition must continually perform upon itself has got well under way. "De-bunking," "fictional," "psychoanalytical," as applied to biography, have already become opprobrious terms, and we hear much less of the books they describe than we did ten years ago. The groundwork having been done, the authors are now busy developing the untold potentialities of their new art.

For biography has been raised at last to this status, and like the other arts it will be advanced by the independent genius of its artists. The conventional work, to be sure, will not cease to be produced. The scholarly documentation will always have its place, nowhere more helpfully than in the service of writers whose special talents fit them for interpretation and composition; and students will always need the benefits of sound biographical compendiums and dictionaries. Even the life-eulogy will doubtless fulfill some useful purpose. But strict biography, the art of combining truthful portraiture with skilled and impersonal presentment, still in its infancy, will grow and flourish. In the past fifteen years authors have devised, or adapted from other arts—since fiction, drama, poetry, painting, and biography have mingled much of late—, many new ways of telling life-stories. Is it not likely that in the future they will bring forth more? Another generation may find itself less concerned with psychological analysis than ours, but it can scarcely be less interested in people. For if the proper study of mankind is man, the appeal of biography is universal.

III. MODERN SHORT BIOGRAPHY

"To preserve . . . a becoming brevity—a brevity which excludes everything that is redundant and nothing that is significant—that, surely, is the first duty of the biographer."

—LYTTON STRACHEY

In the preceding portions of this essay we have reviewed the history of biography with special reference to modern developments. We now focus our attention upon one of these developments; not because it claims any superior importance of its own, but because it has never been specifically studied before and because it enjoys certain privileges and calls for certain technical treatments peculiar to itself.

All biography was in the beginning short biography. From Plutarch to Samuel Johnson the customary length of "lives" is something between that of Strachey's *Eminent Victorians* and his *Portraits in Miniature*. Indeed, we may credit James Boswell with inventing the single objective "life" in several volumes. Before the *Life of Johnson* these works are brief from sheer paucity of material; after that they are long from sheer profusion. For the Victorian scholars learned to combine such industry and minuteness in research that a book was not finished until every letter was examined, every source tapped; but few of them acquired even the rudiments of selection.

These, of course, are broad generalities, yet they are in the main true. Tacitus has been admired for the "succinctness and compressed beauty" of his style, Plutarch and Vasari and Walton are restrained by the arbitrary limits of their plans; but scandalmongers like Suetonius, Brantôme, and Tallemant des Réaux tell everything they dare to print, while Aubrey teases us with a paragraph on Shakespeare or fascinates us with forty pages on Locke, according to the wealth of his notebook. When we come to Voltaire's *Charles XII*, *Peter the Great*, and *Molière*, and to Johnson's *Savage* and the other *Poets*, we are well into the century in which literary style is hardly less than a fetish and when even the extensive memoirs of the Duc de Saint-Simon are separable into strings of dazzling individual portraits. It should be remembered, moreover, that as Johnson's *Lives* were prepared as prefaces to successive volumes of *The Most Eminent English Poets*, Sainte-Beuve's *Portraits Littéraires* and *Causeries de Lundi* appeared in a newspaper column, and thus both had brevity forced upon them.

At the same time that documentary works expanded from one volume by Mason to four by Boswell, to seven by Lockhart, to nine by Froude, a converse tendency found expression in short essays and lectures. In England these were usually quite as much critical as biographical and seem to have derived principally from Johnson, or perhaps Walton. Thus we have Allan Cunningham's *Lives of the Most Eminent British Painters* (1829); Macaulay's essays contributed to the *Edinburgh Review* and the *Encyclopaedia Britannica* (1825-42), some of the most brilliant parts of which, however, according to the latter authority, "are adapted and sometimes almost literally translated from Saint-Simon"; Carlyle's book-review essays on Goethe, Burns, Scott, and others (1828-38); Thackeray's *Lectures on the English Humorists of the Eighteenth Century* (1861); Matthew Arnold's *Essays in Criticism* (1863); R. W. Emerson's *Lectures and Biographical Sketches* (1863); R. L. Stevenson's *Familiar Studies of Men and Books* (1882), Augustine Birrell's *Obiter Dicta* (1887), and many more —nearly all composed of an account of the subject's life followed by an examination of his works. This scheme was convenient enough to be adopted almost universally for "student biographies" and dictionaries, but it could scarcely have been inspired by the artistic instinct.

The real forerunner of modern short biography is not Johnson nor Walton nor even Plutarch, but Charles Augustin Sainte-Beuve (1804-69). In bulk and range his forty volumes of portraits, with their seven or eight hundred separate studies of men and women, transcend anything of the kind done before or since;

while we have it on the authority of his constant disciple, Gamaliel Bradford, that they are of prime importance also in achievement: "He is by far the richest and most varied exponent of the practice, if not of the principles of modern biography, and his influence, his method, and his spirit thoroughly permeate the work not only of his French followers, Scherer, Brunetière, Gaston Boissier, but even, more perhaps than they themselves realize, the admirable accomplishment of such later masters as Mr. Strachey, Herr Ludwig, and M. Maurois." Like the Englishmen named above, he did not class himself and was not generally considered as a biographer, but as a critic; unlike them, he held that the aim of criticism is "to go straight at the author under the mask of the book." Consequently his weekly portraits, the best known of which being the *Causeries de Lundi* (*Monday Chats*), are almost purely biographical in the modern sense, brief lives beginning at birth and ending at death, combining psychological insight of a rare penetration with an easy narrative movement. The nineteenth century English essayist could be detached when criticizing a book, but let him turn to the author and the manacles of "propriety" clamped upon his pen hand. The Frenchman—and we might add to our list Stendhal (*Haydn, Mozart*, 1814), Michelet (*Femmes de la Revolution*, 1854), and Figuier (*Vies des Savants Illustres*, 1870), among others—felt as free as the modern writer. And we do well to keep in mind this French source of the short biography, since of the seventeen authors represented in this book the editor can vouch for the familiarity of all but three with the biographical literature of that nation.

With Sainte-Beuve's example in mind, then, let us come at once to our own times and consider briefly the main aspects of this type of writing before passing to the pieces themselves.

We have seen that one of the distinguishing features of modern biographers is their strong predilection for the form and spirit of the novel and the drama as contrasted with those of history, which dominated the Victorians, and that their books tend to keep to the corresponding proportions and length, now and then running into sizable trilogies, but ordinarily taking the shape of the single volume readable in an evening or two. Curiously enough, just as the twentieth century novelists and playwrights multiplied and perfected the short-story and the one-act play, contemporary biographers have been quick to cultivate the condensed "life" of from two to twenty thousand words. Some of these brief lives have appeared first as expanded book-reviews, Lytton Strachey and Mrs. Woolf practicing this particular mode for many years before either was heard of as a biographer. Others are prefaces to collected works. Most of them come out as contributions to weekly or monthly periodicals. Since they are nearly all written by the authors of full-length works, the opportunities for comparison and contrast are very rich indeed.

Like the other literary types, the short biography has grown up in response to special practical and artistic demands. First, the writer, like Sainte-Beuve, may desire to treat many figures, instead of the few which would occupy a lifetime if handled on a large scale. Human character being his objective, he wishes to examine and reconstruct it in as many and diverse manifestations as he can. Secondly, like Plutarch, he sees that certain people fall naturally into such homogeneous or contrasting groups as may illustrate a still wider cross-section of humanity. Thirdly, he has learned that interesting results can be obtained by subjecting chosen groups of persons to similar biographical treatment and noting their individual differences. Fourthly, he finds the short piece best for re-creating the lives of obscure persons hardly permitting or meriting an extended work. Finally, being an artist and wishing to escape all conventional limitations, he turns to the short biography to experiment with original or borrowed literary forms.

That the result is very far from the standard Victorian essay with its monotonously inartistic separation of narrative and criticism will be seen in the eighteen studies of the present collection. Though classifiable in different ways, they illustrate more than a dozen varieties of treatment in the synthesis of narrative, analytical, critical, and descriptive elements. According to the base or dominant element in the fusion, represented in this book are (1) direct narrative ("Florence Nightingale"); (2) character analysis or psychograph ("The Wife of Abraham Lincoln"); (3) narrative followed by character analysis ("Hammerstein the Extravagant"); (4) narrative with progressive character analysis ("Leonardo da Vinci," "Talleyrand," "An Adventurer Out of the West"); (5) character analysis with some narrative ("James Boswell," "Blind . . . Deaf . . . Dumb," "Aunt Mary Emerson"); (6) narrative with surprise ending ("The Sorrows of the Young Werther"); (7) narrative and criticism combined ("The Perfect Letter Writer"); (8) narrative and exposition combined ("Leeuwenhoek"); (9) narrative with cumulative description ("Hindenburg"); (10) retrospective narrative ("The Stepfather of the United States"); (11) narrative in "epic" sequence ("Young Weston"); (12) episodic narrative ("Miss Ormerod"); (13) narrative framed in a narrative ("Margaret Baxter"); (14) character analysis and criticism through dialogue ("William Congreve"); and want of room alone prevents the inclusion of other forms, such as double and group portraits and parallel lives, which biographers are continually devising or reviving to suit their purposes. Concentration upon the person has made the short biography infinitely more interesting to us than the Macaulayan and Carlylean essay, and the extension of Sainte-Beuve's ideals of portraiture by letting the subject speak for himself in modes adapted from the short-story, the drama, the interview, the letter, the diary, and the conversation, has brought forth a thriving new literature and revealed a brilliant gallery of authors.

No one will suppose that because the short biography is short it is easy to create. While it does not ordinarily, like the full-length work, invite or require much original research, it offers special difficulties on the side of portraiture. A portrait painter is always drawn by two divergent forces: he must catch the likeness of his sitter and yet make his portrait a work of art. This our author must accomplish by the most skillful touches, since in his small space every detail counts. If he draws with photographic fidelity, he will produce a flat, featureless picture. If he intensifies his subject's characteristic qualities, as the painter does, he risks making a caricature. If, like the novelist, he gives a complete and finished image, he may defeat his own ends, "for human characters are obscure and puzzling, and some loose ends convey this oddity best." Too much character analysis will render the picture static; too much incident will make the career seem unnaturally swift and crowded. A true, vivid, and graceful presentment within his narrow frame—this is what is wanted.

Perhaps it is just these problems which make modern short biography particularly attractive not only to authors of longer lives but to writers of fiction, poetry, and drama, who relish the challenge of creative art, as the following pieces suggest. At all events, having played its part in establishing the new branch of literature, it remains today one of biography's most favored manifestations.

CHARLES WHIBLEY

Although Charles Whibley, who was born in 1859, died as lately as 1930, this story of Francis Weston was in print in that delightful volume, *The Pageantry of Life*, as early as 1900, a full generation before our other short biographies were written. Yet, quite typical of its author's whole literary work, it is essentially "new" in both spirit and treatment and may serve as a foreshadowing of the radical changes that biography was soon to undergo. For Whibley brought an inexhaustible gusto and curiosity to the study of human nature as revealed in old books without being in the slightest degree bookish. While he developed his gifts of insight and expression in advance of modern psychological aids and twentieth century literary modes, it is a safe wager that few of his many biographies of gentlemen and statesmen, of dandies, writers, and ragamuffins will be superseded in our day.

As Mr. T. S. Eliot says in his memoir on Whibley (Oxford University Press, 1931), "he had a particular sympathy with–and a particular gift for explaining and making sympathetic to his readers–" just those classes of people. He had, besides, "as the first condition of being interesting," "the tact to choose only those subjects in which [he was] really interested, those which [were] germane to [his] own temper." Hence his lively *Book of Scoundrels* and his *Studies in Frankness*–for he had a "fearless sincerity"; also his *Literary Portraits* (1904), anticipating and even stealing the thunder of more recent biographies of Rabelais, Montaigne, Robert Burton, and Casanova. *Essays in Biography* (1913) may be profitably compared with *The Common Reader* of Virginia Woolf; while his two series of *Political Portraits* (1917 and 1923) are a standing challenge to historical biographers of the modern school. Add Whibley's *American Sketches* (1908), his *Literary Studies* (1919), his Introductions to the Tudor Translations, and his longer lives of Thackeray (1903), of William Pitt (1906), of Swift (1917), and the charming *Lord John Manners and His Friends* (1925), and we begin to comprehend the topography of the regions which his mind so intensely and so realistically inhabited.

"He used suitably," Mr. Eliot informs us, "a quill pen, but composed rapidly in a small fine hand and made very few *ratures* or corrections." For, nourished on the great historical and political writers of his own country, perfectly at home among the prose masters of France, and possessing great conversational powers, Whibley, like Lytton Strachey and André Maurois, developed early a technique and style perfectly expressive of and congenial with his own individuality.

Three years before his death Whibley married a daughter of the late Sir Walter Raleigh, man of letters and Professor of English Literature at Oxford.

"Not aspiring to any literary dictatorship or pontificate, or to academic or extra-academic honours"–though, M.A. of Cambridge and Honorary Fellow of Jesus College, he was conferred the degree of LL.D. by both Edinburgh and St. Andrew's Universities–Whibley appears altogether human in his books. His mind, as we see instantly from "Young Weston," was not an abstract but an imaginative and concretely visualizing mind. When he wished to commend the style of another writer, we are told, he said that it had *life* in it. Certainly there is *life* in the following narrative. Whibley leads us with the greatest ease and assurance to the tennis courts and palaces of Henry the Eighth and, without loading us with dates and names, revives an extremely human young man from the dust of four centuries.

YOUNG WESTON

THE KING, missing his stroke, stumbled clumsily upon the tennis-court; and, gathering up his heavy frame with difficulty, strode sullenly within. "Your Grace," cried young Weston, chuckling that another game was his, "Your Grace shall take your revenge with the dice-box." But Henry, enraged no less at his waning skill than at the loss of his money, threw not a word at his smiling favourite, who gazed imperturbable at the retreating corpulency.

Young Weston chuckled again. Though scarce sixteen he rode upon the full tide of fortune. Admitted, at an age when most boys linger at school, to the friendship of his Sovereign, he was secure that neither extravagance nor indiscretion could check his progress. A hundred advantages were his: his open brow, his clear blue eye, his burnished hair compelled admiration, and at Court he was already a famous breaker of hearts. His loose-knit frame united the suppleness of youth with the assured strength of manhood; and, as no exertion seemed too great for him, he undertook the most desperate adventure with a light heart and a lighter hand. He was an easy master of all sports, nor was there a single game of chance whereat his golden luck did not pursue him. To see him on horseback was to think of Alexander and Bucephalus, and though neither his weight nor his lack of judgment permitted him at a single chase to tire ten steeds, he rode as hard and as straight as the King himself. At tennis he knew not his equal in Europe, and, as he never played without backing his skill, a comfortable income was assured him in a world of gamblers. A courtier born, he assumed that all the elegances of a refined life were his proper birthright, and he was already an exquisite, when he left Surrey, under the Cardinal's august protection, to take office in the King's household. A ribbon awry, an ill-cut doublet were a lasting offence to him; the taste and ambition of childhood had taught him to be dainty in his dress; and he was a leader of fashion when most of his fellows were content with the fusty uniform of school or college.

No wonder, then, he dreamed his career a march of triumph; no wonder he believed his charm invincible. Mine, said he to himself, is the genius of success. He would royster and gamble through life, winning all those hearts which he chose to assail, and as much money as should equip him nobly for the most gallant enterprise. His childish vanity persuaded him to hope that he would bend even the stubborn King to his will, and the monarch's displeasure at another lost game irked him not a whit. The scene of the tennis-court was as common as sunrise, and the revenge with the dice-box ever doubled the debt. For all his extravagance, for all his ambition of beautiful things, of jewels, books, and pictures, he had small fear of an empty pocket, and he sunned himself in the favour of heaven with the pride and carelessness of some bright-plumaged bird. Moreover, he accepted his happiness without the least touch of vulgar surprise: after all he enjoyed no more splendour than that for which his childhood had prepared him.

His father, as became a travelled gentleman who had witnessed the brilliancy of the Cloth of Gold, was familiar with the art and luxury of France and of that fair country which lay beyond the

Alps. He had built amid the hills of Surrey a mansion which would not have outraged the taste of an Italian nobleman. And Francis, for all his sixteen years, could carry back his memory to the growing magnificence of Sutton Place. He had seen the doorways framed with their dainty pilasters; he had seen the delicate *amorini* chiselled upon the lintels; he had witnessed the honour that attends the acquisition of a treasure which is not only beautiful but fashionable. To Sutton had thronged the great nobles of England; there they had marvelled at the fantasy of Sir Richard Weston; there they had applauded his cultured, exotic taste. They had even condescended, while acclaiming the courage of the innovator, to steal the design for the enlargement of their own glory. The King himself had honoured the new house with his presence and approval; there was no courtier whom Wolsey had destined more generously for distinction than the master of Sutton. And young Weston left his home to assume the duties of a Royal Page with no danger of the ruin that follows a sudden aggrandisement.

When the boy arrived in London—it was in 1526—Henry was no longer the handsomest monarch in Europe. Not even the most genial Ambassador, in that spirit of content which is bred of a good dinner and 8,000 ducats won in a day, could assert that his play at tennis was "the prettiest thing in the world to see." His encroaching corpulency was fast driving him to the familiar aspect of a fat man with a small mouth. His plumped cheeks were thrusting his bead-like eyes still further into his head. Though yet an ardent sportsman, he sat heavily upon his horse, and was rather a spectator than a combatant at joust and tourney. His thirty-six years had impaired neither his learning nor his courage, but, in the words of the historian, his accomplishment soon became cunning, his bravery fell into cruelty. Though his wolfish character had not yet declared itself, though he had not yet come forth a Sadic monster with an immitigable taste for matrimony, a Gilles de Rais with a quenchless passion for another lawful spouse, he was already deeply committed to the cruel intrigue which was the tardy undoing of the blameless, foolish Catharine. The Bishops of England were even now busy with argument and excuse; the Cardinal's devotion was engaged in the persuasion of Rome; and Henry's own casuistical brain had at last discovered, by the light of Anne Boleyn's eyes, "a certain scrupulosity that pricked his conscience." He was Bluebeard, indeed, employing hypocrisy for bloodshed, but resolved, if the simpler method failed, not to shrink from the headsman's axe.

Such was the monster against whose will and cunning young Weston pitted his boyish intelligence. And the boy's charm and skill gave him an immediate advantage. For Henry was a tireless gambler; even in that distant time, when his father destined him for an archbishopric, and it was his amiable custom to say five masses in a day, he could resist neither the card-table nor the dice-box, and in Francis Weston he met an opponent whose skill was as great as his recklessness. There was no game at which this cynic of sixteen would not encounter his Sovereign, and so expert were his hand and eye that he ever came off victorious. Yesterday it was tennis, tomorrow it might be bowls, every day it was dice or imperial. And extravagant as Weston was in dress and finery, in all the luxury which belongs to the life of palaces, for a while he had small difficulty in making the King pay for his magnificence. Henry, moreover, despite his brutality, loved or feared a successful antagonist. Just as he reverenced Wolsey for the astuteness and obstinacy which outwitted his master, so he admired the stripling who defeated him in the tennis-court, and won his money across the table, to the rattle of the dice. In truth, the King was never tired of rewarding the boy's superiority; he would lend him money at the slightest embarrassment, he would give him presents in recompense for his sport and energy, and for ten years he was resolute to procure him profit and advancement. Thus young Weston passed from London to Greenwich, from Greenwich to Hampton, enjoying whatever there was of splendour and gaiety in life, a favoured guest at the twin Courts of Cardinal and King.

His father had sent him to London with a headful of worldly precepts, which Francis was astute enough never to forget. Now, Sir Richard Weston, an ancient intriguer, and friend of Wolsey, was among the first to foresee the rise of the Boleyns, and to the

Boleyns, cunning and ambitious, he commended his cunning and ambitious son. Sir Thomas Boleyn's grandfather, a Lord Mayor, had gifted him with the comfort of wealth, and distinguished connections had insisted that for him a brilliant career should be crowned with a peerage. There was nothing he would not sacrifice for the honour and advancement of an upstart house, and he had the wit to perceive the value of culture in the unequal battle. Culture, he recognised, is seldom so seductive as when it is exalted by the patronage of fashion, and learning had never been more fashionable than under the Eighth Henry. Thus were politics and intelligence inextricably mixed, as in our own day, and though the more ancient houses still reserved an exclusive respect for their horses and dogs, those with a keener eye upon their immediate advancement were quick to approve the newly discovered classics, and to babble of ancient Greece with a kind familiarity.

To his children it was then that Sir Thomas looked for his own advancement. One and all they were accomplished in the sport and knowledge of the day. If they were rather fashionable than erudite, they were scrupulously and intelligently in the movement, and they possessed the dash and assurance which proceed from a not too sensitive superiority. With them the revival of learning was a commonplace: they had dipped into *Utopia;* they appraised the achievement of Erasmus and Colet with a glib counterfeit of scholarship. The vogue of the minute compelled a knowledge of Latin and French, and at all points they thought themselves the King's equals, and the Cardinal's masters. Their wealth and confidence procured them an obedient following; every licence was granted to their pride and learning; and before long there grew up a tiny Court within the Court, wherein Anne Boleyn was a mimic queen, and all her friends and worshippers paid a willing reverence. Already the young Lord Percy had been disinherited for venturing upon an adoration, which Anne, not foreseeing the King's pleasure, had more than half reciprocated; and Henry, thus forced into an admission of his love, had declared his passion, proclaiming—after his wont—his motive honourable. Nor need the proudest Sovereign have shrunk from paying her homage, for Anne Boleyn was the most accomplished woman of her age: she had spent five years in the Court of the Reine Claude; she had learned all the wit and sprightliness that Marguerite of Valois had to teach; with an intellectual courage, rare even at this epoch of revolution, she had mastered the theological speculation of her time, and she would confute the most erudite of prelates and cardinals with a bland smile of innocence.

Henry, then, whose love of casuistry was irresistible, found a perpetual delight in the society of this lady, whose stockings were at least stained with blue, and who, while she captivated him with her wit, dazzled him with her person. For beauty, though it might elude the passer-by, was none the less seductive. A delicate brunette, she charmed rather by life and expression than by any formal regularity of feature. "Briefly," says Lord Herbert of Cherbury, "it seems the most attractive perfections were eminent in her." And if she sat her down to music, there was none so insensible, he would withhold a willing worship. "When she composed her hands to play," again it is the historian who speaks, "and voice to sing, it was joined with that sweetness of countenance that three harmonies concurred." The King, at any rate, fell a ready victim to her "perfections"; and when, echoing Elizabeth Woodville, she declared that, if she were not of birth high enough to be his Queen, she was still too well born to be his mistress, he redoubled the ardour of his suit, addressed her letters of passionate regret—which, forgetful of his middle-class ferocity, he signed with a heart—and urged his Cardinal to hasten the divorce.

Thus Anne Boleyn was a Queen in reverence, if not in name, and it was to her fortunes that young Weston attached himself. In her circle he, too, babbled of the learning that was new, and openly defied the tyranny of Popes and Legates. Ever hopeful of Catharine's downfall, her friends looked to the time when Anne should sit upon the throne, and when Wolsey, who had prospered them all, should be stripped of a power that grew impertinent. Thus they clutched the wine-cup of life with both hands, and left not a few poor dregs to attest their draught. They gambled and spent the gold their luck brought them with an extravagance which terrified those for whom Henry VII was yet a tradition; they talked with a daring and a certainty which appeared infamous to a society educated in the strictest obedience to authority; they rode, they jousted, they killed the hart with a skill which lent a glory to their courage and their pride. Living on terms of perfect familiarity with the tyrant who frowned upon them all, they treated him with a monstrous levity, and won his money or witnessed his discomfiture in happy disregard of his Sadic temper.

Of this society Francis Weston was instantly a leader: his father's taste in architecture had placed him on a pinnacle; the quickness of his own talent had confirmed the distinction. There was no pleasure whereto he was not impelled by his joyous temperament: not even the philosophy of Anne Boleyn's salon checked his enthusiasm for sport, and the King continued to pay dearly for his favourite's skill. But with the years his extravagance increased; a scanty patrimony hardly supported the necessities of life, and even his unrivalled luck was insufficient to sustain a growing weight of debt. No resource was left but a wealthy marriage, and he was scarce twenty when he entered upon a tiresome and profitable alliance. The King smiled approval, and for a demure present gave the bridegroom £6 13*s*. 4*d*. handsomely tied up, one supposes, in red tape. But before long Weston found the heiress a hindrance to his preferment at Court, and, with the cynical indifference that was his characteristic, he banished her to Sutton, and pursued afresh his career in that brilliant world of wit and extravagance, wherein the lightest bond was unendurable.

His moment of triumph arrived when the King proclaimed the marriage with Catharine a blasphemy, and crowned Anne Boleyn with so reckless a splendour as should atone for her years of equivocal sovereignty. On all sides were heard the sound of cannonades, the fountains ran wine, "white, claret, and red"; wherever the progress was stayed, there was prepared a lordly pageant. At Gracechurch Apollo and the Muses Nine, sitting upon Mount Parnassus, were appropriately revealed to the learned Queen; at the Conduit a sumptuous show of the Three Graces flattered the royal beauty. Nor did this memorable day end with an empty spectacle: there was none of the circle that was not instantly advanced; titles were freely distributed among the Boleyns, and young Weston became—at twenty-two—a Knight of the Bath. Wolsey was dead, killed by an implacable intrigue, and Weston and his friends believed that, with Cromwell to aid, the King would prove the willing slave of their greed and ambition. The Court, freed from the frowning tragedy of Catharine, became yet gayer and more refined; and, if the King glutted his taste for blood, if the head of Sir Thomas More fell under the axe, the favourites thought their own necks safe, and still enjoyed the fruits of a fashionable culture.

But Weston and the Queen, in their hatred of Wolsey, had removed the single statesman who might have controlled the savagery of the King, and it was this treachery that, at last, ensured their ruin. Meantime, a bitter quarrel divided the Queen's own family: my Lord of Norfolk was indignant that Anne's father, a new-made Earl, should be preferred before himself in the King's counsels, while the wife of George Boleyn, the most cultured wit and poet of them all, hated her sister-in-law as fiercely as she despised her elegant husband.

So the dissension became noisier and more vulgar; the restraints of prudence and learning were flung aside, and the Court was troubled perpetually by the paltry jealousies of angry women. Weston, less from loyalty, one is sure, than from an imperfect foresight, espoused the cause of the Queen, and thus unwittingly prepared his own death. The King, tired of wit, wearied, maybe, with the unprofitable sports of dice and tennis, determined that he would endure no longer the domination of the party his inclination had created. Anne, thought he, had proved somewhat amiable in her favours; and, though no breath of scandal touched her character, she amused herself too freely, for the taste of the British Bluebeard, with the attentions of the troubadours who thronged the Court. Moreover the King had fallen virtuously in love with Jane Seymour, and, since he preferred murder before the mere suspicion of adultery, he had determined, at a single blow, to rid himself of a wife who no longer pleased him, and to save the money which he daily squandered in the tennis-court.

But even he, though no restraint fettered his will, must find occasion for this fresh brutality. He could not in cold blood kill a virtuous and accomplished lady, whom he had loved through years of wooing and honoured with a share of his throne. Yet the desire of Jane Seymour was not to be denied, and the prim and bloodthirsty husband eagerly watched his opportunity. The opportunity came at a tourney; the Queen's brother and young Weston were in the lists, and the Queen in the innocence of her heart, and careless with the excitement of the joust, let her handkerchief flutter down between the combatants. One of them, said the King, picked it up and pressed it to his guilty lips, and on the morrow the Queen and her friends were involved in an infamous charge of adultery. Murder should have been enough to satisfy the dour temper of the corpulent monster, but he preferred to invent, in hypocritical self-justification, an array of shameful accusations. The trial was proclaimed with an indecent haste; the Queen's own uncle presided to ensure his niece's punishment; and, though to flatter the King even at the moment of death one miscreant pleaded guilty, six heads fell that Henry might satisfy his lust without infringing the first law of domestic respectability.

Francis Weston was involved in the common ruin of his cultured set, though the evidence, furnished forth by an interested prosecution, was sufficient for acquittal. The Queen, said the youth's detractors, had reproached him with paying too instant a suit to Margaret Shelton, a Maid of Honour, and with neglecting the poor heiress whom he had made his wife. "He replied," urged the voice of malice, "that he loved one in her house better than both. And the Queen said: 'Who is that?' 'It is yourself.' And she defyed him." There is the simple statement, and it was for this, guiltless and uncorroborated, that the most brilliant courtier of his age died a disgraceful death. As in life he had borne himself with a gay lightheartedness, so he gave his head with complete dignity and a noble reserve. He incriminated none; he spoke no word of praise or blame; he asserted his innocence, and after condemnation declined to part his lips in protest or confession; he even forbore to add one word in favour of the pardon which was asked; and he died owing the butcher who had slain him forty-six pounds, so that even from beyond the grave he won a last victory over his Royal master.

His debts amounted to the goodly sum of £925 *7s. 2d.* and with the gambler's thrift he made his last petition for their discharge. "Father and mother and wyfe," he wrote with a pathetic dignity, "I shall humbly desyre you for the salvacyon of my sowle to dyschardge me of this bill, and to forgyve me of all the offences that I have done to you. And in especyall to my wyfe, whiche I desyre for the love of God to forgive me, and to pray for me, for I beleve prayer wyll do me good. Goddys blessing have my chylderne and meyne.[1] By me a great offender to God." The schedule which then follows, the last document written by the courtier's hand, is a fitting farewell to a life of pleasure. To Browne, the draper, he owed fifty pounds; to "my lorde of Wylshyre," the father of the murdered Queen, forty pounds in angels; to Bridges, "my taylor," twenty-six pounds; to "parson Robynson" (the sporting parson existed even in the sixteenth century), sixty-six pounds; and most moving of all, "to a pooer woman at the Tennes play for bawles I cannot tell howe muche."

"To a pooer woman at the Tennes play for bawles I cannot tell howe muche." Where shall one find a dying speech so eloquent and appropriate? After this forethought, you are not surprised to know, on the faith of an eye-witness, that "he died very charitably." And if no better sportsman ever held a racket, so no more careless a gentleman was ever sacrificed to the lust and intrigue of a virtuous monarch. Truly his memory was writ in water. No sooner had his head fallen from his shoulders than he was forgotten of his friends. The King wore white for a day, and on the morrow married Jane Seymour, whose beauty had been the death-warrant of all. And Sir Richard Weston showed so chivalrous a contempt for his son's martyrdom that he did not for a single hour interrupt his obsequious friendship for the King. But his century knew no courtier so picturesque as Francis Weston, and you contemplate his career with the satisfaction that, if he lost his head, he yet compelled his patron and his murderer to pay handsomely for a pitiful lack of skill at "tennes, dyce, and imperiall."

[1] Meyne: household, retinue [Edit.].

LYTTON STRACHEY

Lytton Strachey did not invent the art of biography, but he captured biography for art. "The art of biography," he wrote in 1918 in the preface to *Eminent Victorians*—that page or two which sounded the note of the new school—"seems to have fallen on evil times in England. . . . With us, the most delicate and humane of all the branches of the art of writing has been relegated to the journeyman of letters; we do not reflect that it is perhaps as difficult to write a good life as to live one. Those two fat volumes, with which it is our custom to commemorate the dead—who does not know them, with their ill-digested masses of material, their slipshod style, their tone of tedious panegyric, their lamentable lack of selection, of detachment, of design?" Today, who *does* know them? Who, at least, without a qualifying adjective—"documentary," "exhaustive," "monumental," "official"—will now call them "biography" and place them on the same shelf with *Queen Victoria?* In the flood of biographical writing which has poured forth in response to that invitation, the material has frequently been quite as ill-digested, the style quite as slipshod, as before. But it has been different. For this change Strachey was, of course, by no means wholly responsible, but he was indubitably the spokesman.

By birth, education, and personal endowment Giles Lytton Strachey was well equipped to lead his generation to a new goal in letters. Born in 1880, he enjoyed the initial advantage of coming from an intellectual and literary family. His father was a general and Indian administrator; his mother, an author and brilliant aristocrat. He was, like Virginia Woolf, related to some of his most prominent countrymen, past and present. Educated mainly in France, he became "one of those rare Englishmen who know French from the inside." At Trinity College, Cambridge, he was known as a poet, and in his fourth year won the Chancellor's medal for English verse. He was unusually mature. Some of the essays and reviews from those years, as collected in his posthumous volume, *Characters and Commentaries* (1933), prove that at twenty-one he had already perfected the dazzling, ironical prose style that made his later fame.

For some years, buried in the country, he did nothing but walk and read —read French and eighteenth century English works. Mr. H. A. L. Fisher, who contracted for his first book, *Landmarks of French Literature* (1912), found him "a sensitive, ungainly youth, awkward in his bearing, and presenting an appearance of great physical debility, as if he had recently risen from the bed of an invalid. His voice was faint and squeaky. . . . The long red beard . . . was a thing of the future. He was very silent, but uncannily quick and comprehending." The *Landmarks* displays an extraordinary power of assimilation and compression and a rare gift of lucid and telling phrase. It was followed by five more years of reading, with occasional reviews in periodicals.

Strachey did not serve in the War, being both physically unfit and rationally skeptical. But in February 1918, when it might have been supposed that the reading public had other affairs to occupy them, he managed to secure a publisher for a group of four short biographies; and when the conflict ended, the general revulsion against the old era and the universal eagerness for the new were found to be fittingly expressed in the pages of *Eminent Victorians*. Here was an ironical revaluation of the past age. Here were wit, style, erudition. Here historical characters in a hundred different aspects were fused into rounded, coherent portraits as convincing and alive as any creations of fiction. The book captivated the public taste and inspired a legion of imitators.

Meanwhile, Strachey plunged into masses of nineteenth century documents, and for three years read, digested, selected, and wrote to produce, in 1921, *Queen Victoria*. This too was a new thing. This three-hundred-page narrative was "not just a life of Victoria that happened to be a work of art, but a work of art that happened to be a life of Victoria." And in that distinction lies the secret of true biography. In style, treatment, construction, and creative purpose it is so far from the old "Life and Times" and "Life and Letters" that everybody, even Strachey's detractors, realized that a new "high" in literature had been reached. It was a triumphant demonstration of the modern principle.

In 1922 appeared *Books and Characters*, a collection of brilliant essays and reviews, mostly on eighteenth century figures; in 1925, a sparkling lecture on Pope. By this time Strachey, in his Berkshire retreat, was immersed in the English sixteenth century, to which his romantic impulse had led him. The result of these years of labor was *Elizabeth and Essex* (1928), swifter, more highly colored, more dramatic than anything he had done before, a *tour de force* which, if it has not pleased all historians, has set them a very high standard of writing and research. Then he turned again to the short biography that had always attracted him and in the delightful *Portraits in Miniature* (1931), distilled into terse and sprightly thumb-nail sketches, briefer and more mellow than the former ones, a score of miscellaneous lives and much ripe comment on his own profession. He died in 1932, and left the field to his successors.

Master though he assuredly was of his art, Strachey was not invulnerable.

He was attacked repeatedly for his acidity, for occasional inaccuracy of fact, for his *clichés* and too regular purple patches. Most of the criticism, though, has been rightly leveled at his many imitators, who too easily caught the manner but missed the substance. While prophecy is always dangerous, we may safely say that until the future brings a change of temper to the world Lytton Strachey will remain, for literature at least, the biographer's biographer.

He never married, but he enjoyed in the Bloomsbury Group the most congenial and stimulating friendships possible to a man who preferred the eighteenth century to his own yet led the vanguard of the twentieth in English letters. There is significance in the fact that he dedicated his *Victoria* to his friend Virginia Woolf—who returned the honor in *The Common Reader*—and his *Portraits* to Max Beerbohm. Like theirs, his books have indeed been "few, but roses."

To extract the fullest pleasure from "Florence Nightingale," which is probably the best of the *Eminent Victorians*, one should know the legend it destroys and the saccharine flavor of the older biographers. The contrast is striking. Their "lives," moreover, all virtually stop with the Nurse's return from Scutari; Strachey insists on the entire career. It is not that he admires Miss Nightingale less, but that he despises her biographers more. This attitude results in his making her somewhat more of a tigress than she was; yet the whitewash had to be removed before we could even guess the true image of the woman.

In the sketch of James Boswell (*Portraits in Miniature*) Strachey describes the character and career of one of his own chief literary ancestors. Yet it is not the author of the *Life of Johnson* we see here, but the queer, tormented soul of the man himself. More complete biographies on the small scale may be found of Hume and Gibbon in the same volume. This one is chosen to show how Strachey frequently made a book review the occasion for a life.

FLORENCE NIGHTINGALE

EVERYONE knows the popular conception of Florence Nightingale. The saintly, self-sacrificing woman, the delicate maiden of high degree who threw aside the pleasures of a life of ease to succour the afflicted, the Lady with the Lamp, gliding through the horrors of the hospital at Scutari, and consecrating with the radiance of her goodness the dying soldier's couch—the vision is familiar to all. But the truth was different. The Miss Nightingale of fact was not as facile fancy painted her. She worked in another fashion, and towards another end; she moved under the stress of an impetus which finds no place in the popular imagination. A Demon possessed her. Now demons, whatever else they may be, are full of interest. And so it happens that in the real Miss Nightingale there was more that was interesting than in the legendary one; there was also less that was agreeable.

Her family was extremely well-to-do, and connected by marriage with a spreading circle of other well-to-do families. There was a large country house in Derbyshire; there was another in the New Forest; there were Mayfair rooms for the London season and all its finest parties; there were tours on the Continent with even more than the usual number of Italian operas and of glimpses at the celebrities of Paris. Brought up among such advantages, it was only natural to suppose that Florence would show a proper appreciation of them by doing her duty in that state of life unto which it had pleased God to call her—in other words, by marrying, after a fitting number of dances and dinner-parties, an eligible gentleman, and living happily ever afterwards. Her sister, her cousins, all the young ladies of her acquaintance, were either getting ready to do this or had already done it. It was inconceivable that Florence should dream of anything else; yet dream she did. Ah! To do her duty in that state of life unto which it had pleased God to call her! Assuredly she would not be behindhand in doing her duty; but unto what state of life *had* it pleased God to call her? That was the question. God's calls are many, and they are strange. Unto what state of life had it pleased Him to call Charlotte Corday, or Elizabeth of Hungary? What was that secret voice in her ear, if it was not a call? Why had she felt, from her earliest years, those mysterious promptings towards . . . she hardly knew what but certainly towards something very different from anything around her? Why, as a child in the nursery, when her sister had shown a healthy pleasure in tearing her dolls to pieces, had *she* shown an almost morbid one in sewing them up again? Why was she driven now to minister to the poor in their cottages, to watch by sick-beds, to put her dog's wounded paw into elaborate splints as if it was a human being? Why was her head filled with queer imaginations of the country house at Embley turned, by some enchantment, into a hospital, with herself as matron moving about among the beds? Why was even her vision of heaven itself filled with suffering patients to whom she was being useful? So she dreamed and wondered, and, taking out her diary, she poured into it the agitations of her soul. And then the bell rang, and it was time to go and dress for dinner.

As the years passed, a restlessness began to grow upon her. She was unhappy, and at last she knew it. Mrs. Nightingale, too, began to notice that there was something wrong. It was very odd; what could be the matter with dear Flo? Mr. Nightingale suggested that a husband might be advisable; but the curious thing was that she seemed to take no interest in husbands. And with her attractions, and her accomplishments, too! There was nothing in the world to prevent her making a really brilliant match. But no! She would think of nothing but how to satisfy that singular craving of hers to be *doing* something. As if there was not plenty to do in any case, in the ordinary way, at home. There was the china to look after, and there was her father to be read to after dinner. Mrs. Nightingale could not understand it; and then one day her perplexity was changed to consternation and alarm. Florence announced an extreme desire to go to Salisbury Hospital for several months as a nurse; and she confessed to some visionary plan of eventually setting up in a house of her own in a neighbouring village, and there founding "something like a Protestant Sisterhood, without vows, for women of educated feelings." The whole scheme was summarily brushed aside as preposterous; and Mrs. Nightingale, after the first shock of terror, was able to settle down again more or less comfortably to her embroidery. But Florence, who was now twenty-five and felt that the dream of her life had been shattered, came near to desperation.

And, indeed, the difficulties in her path were great. For not only was it an almost unimaginable thing in those days for a woman of means to make her own way in the world and to live in independence, but the particular profession for which Florence was clearly marked out both by her instincts and her capacities was at that time a peculiarly disreputable one. A "nurse" meant then a coarse old woman, always ignorant, usually dirty, often brutal, a Mrs. Gamp, in bunched-up sordid garments, tippling at the brandy-bottle or indulging in worse irregularities. The nurses in the hospitals were especially notorious for immoral conduct; sobriety almost unknown among them; and they could hardly be trusted to carry out the simplest medical duties. Certainly, things have changed since those days; and that they *have* changed is due, far more than to any other human being, to Miss Nightingale herself. It is not to be wondered at that her parents should have shuddered at the notion of their daughter devoting her life to such an occupation. "It was as if," she herself said afterwards, "I had wanted to be a kitchen-maid." Yet the want, absurd, impracticable as it was, not only remained fixed immovably in her heart, but grew in intensity day by day. Her wretchedness deepened into a morbid melancholy. Everything about her was vile, and she herself, it was clear, to have deserved such misery, was even viler than her surroundings. Yes, she had sinned—"standing before God's judgment seat." "No one," she declared, "has so grieved the Holy Spirit"; of that she was quite certain. It was in vain that she prayed to be delivered from vanity and hypocrisy, and she could not bear to smile or to be gay, "because she hated God to hear her laugh, as if she had not repented of her sin."

A weaker spirit would have been overwhelmed by the load of such distresses—would have yielded or snapped. But this extraordinary young woman held firm, and fought her way to victory. With an amazing persistency, during the eight years that followed her rebuff over Salisbury Hospital, she struggled and worked and planned. While superficially she was carrying on the life of a brilliant girl in high society, while internally she was a prey to the tortures of regret and of remorse, she yet possessed the energy to collect the knowledge and to undergo the experience which alone could enable her to do what she had determined she would do in the end. In secret she devoured the reports of medical commissions, the pamphlets of sanitary authorities, the histories of hospitals and homes. She spent the intervals of the London season in ragged schools and workhouses. When she went abroad with her family, she used her spare time so well that there was hardly a great hospital in Europe with which she was not acquainted, hardly a great city whose slums she had not passed through. She managed to spend some days in a convent school in Rome, and some weeks as a "Sœur de Charité" in Paris. Then, while her mother and sister were taking the waters at Carlsbad, she succeeded in slipping off to a nursing institution at Kaiserswerth, where she remained for more than three months. This was the critical event of her life. The experience which she gained as a nurse at Kaiserswerth formed the foundation of all her future action and finally fixed her in her career.

But one other trial awaited her. The allurements of the world she had brushed aside with disdain and loathing; she had resisted the subtler temptation which, in her weariness, had sometimes come upon her, of devoting her baffled energies to art or literature; the last ordeal appeared in the shape of a desirable young man. Hitherto, her lovers had been nothing to her but an added burden and a mockery; but now— For a moment, she wavered. A new feeling swept over her—a feeling which she had never known before, which she was never to know again. The most powerful and the profoundest of all the instincts of humanity laid claim upon her. But it rose before her, that instinct, arrayed—how could it be otherwise?—in the inevitable habiliments of a Victorian marriage; and she had the strength to stamp it underfoot.

> I have an intellectual nature which requires satisfaction [she noted], and that would find it in him. I have a passional nature which requires satisfaction, and that would find it in him. I have a moral, an active nature which requires satisfaction, and that would not find it in his life. Sometimes I think that I will satisfy my passional nature at all events. . . .

But no, she knew in her heart that it could not be. "To be nailed to a continuation and exaggeration of my present life . . . to put it out of my power ever to be able to seize the chance of forming for myself a true and rich life"—that would be a suicide. She made her choice, and refused what was at least a certain happiness for a visionary good which might never come to her at all. And so she returned to her old life of waiting and bitterness.

> The thoughts and feelings that I have now [she wrote] I can remember since I was six years old. A profession, a trade, a necessary occupation, something to fill and employ all my faculties, I have always felt essential to me, I have always longed for. The first thought I can remember, and the last, was nursing work; and in the absence of this, education work, but more the education of the bad than of the young. . . . Everything has been tried, foreign travel, kind friends, everything. My God! What is to become of me?

A desirable young man? Dust and ashes! What was there desirable in such a thing as that? "In my thirty-first year," she noted in her diary, "I see nothing desirable but death."

Three more years passed, and then at last the pressure of time told; her family seemed to realise that she was old enough and strong enough to have her way; and she became the superintendent of a charitable nursing home in Harley Street. She had gained her independence, though it was in a meagre sphere enough; and her mother was still not quite resigned: surely Florence might at least spend the summer in the country. At times, indeed, among her intimates, Mrs. Nightingale almost wept. "We are ducks," she said with tears in her eyes, "who have hatched a wild swan." But the poor lady was wrong; it was not a swan that they had hatched; it was an eagle.

II

Miss Nightingale had been a year in her nursing-home in Harley Street, when Fate knocked at the door. The Crimean War broke out; the battle of the Alma was fought; and the terrible condition of our military hospitals at Scutari began to be known in England. It sometimes happens that the plans of Providence are a little difficult to follow, but on this occasion all was plain; there was a perfect co-ordination of events. For years Miss Nightingale had been getting ready; at last she was prepared—experienced, free, mature, yet still young—she was thirty-four—desirous to serve, accustomed to command: at that precise moment the desperate need of a great nation came, and she was there to satisfy it. If the war had fallen a few years earlier, she would have lacked the knowledge, perhaps even the power, for such a work; a few years later and she would, no doubt, have been fixed in the routine of some absorbing task, and moreover, she would have been growing old. Nor was it only the coincidence of Time that was remarkable. It so fell out that Sidney Herbert was at the War Office and in the Cabinet; and Sidney Herbert was an intimate friend of Miss Nightingale's, convinced, from personal experience in charitable work, of her supreme capacity. After such premises, it seems hardly more than a matter of course that her letter, in which she offered her services for the East, and Sidney Herbert's letter, in which he asked for them, should actually have crossed in the post. Thus it all happened, without a hitch. The appointment was made, and even Mrs. Nightingale, overawed by the magnitude of the venture, could only approve. A pair of faithful friends offered themselves as personal attendants; thirty-eight nurses were collected; and within a week of the crossing of the letters Miss Nightingale, amid a great burst of popular enthusiasm, left for Constantinople.

Among the numerous letters which she received on her departure was one from Dr. Manning, who at that time was working in comparative obscurity as a Catholic priest in Bayswater. "God will keep you," he wrote, "and my prayer for you will be that your one object of Worship, Pattern of Imitation, and source of consolation and strength may be the Sacred Heart of our Divine Lord."

To what extent Dr. Manning's prayer was answered must remain a matter of doubt; but this much is certain, that, if ever a prayer was needed, it was needed then for Florence Nightingale. For dark as had been the picture of the state of affairs at Scutari, revealed to the English public in the despatches of the *Times* correspondent and in a multitude of private letters, yet the reality turned out to be darker still. What had occurred was, in brief, the complete break-down of our medical arrangements at the seat of war. The origins of this awful failure were complex and manifold; they stretched back through long years of peace and carelessness in England; they could be traced through endless ramifications of administrative incapacity—from the inherent faults of confused systems to the petty bunglings of minor officials, from the inevitable ignorance of Cabinet Ministers to the fatal exactitudes of narrow routine. In the inquiries which followed it was clearly shown that the evil was in reality that worst of all evils—one which has been caused by nothing in particular and for which no one in particular is to blame. The whole organisation of the war machine was incompetent and out of date. The old Duke had sat for a generation at the Horse Guards repressing innovations with an iron hand. There was an extraordinary overlapping of authorities, an almost incredible shifting of responsibilities to and fro. As for such a notion as the creation and the maintenance of a really adequate medical service for the army—in that atmosphere of aged chaos, how could it have entered anybody's head? Before the war, the easy-going officials at Westminster were naturally persuaded that all was well—or at least as well as could be expected; when someone, for instance, actually had the temerity to suggest the formation of a corps of army nurses, he was at once laughed out of court. When the war had begun, the gallant British officers in control of affairs had other things to think about than the petty details of medical organisation. Who had bothered with such trifles in the Peninsula? And surely, on that occasion, we had done pretty well. Thus the most obvious precautions were neglected, the most necessary preparations put off from day to day. The principal medical officer of the army, Dr. Hall, was summoned from India at a moment's notice, and was unable to visit England before taking up his duties at the front. And it was not until after the battle of the Alma, when we had been at war for many months, that we acquired hospital accommodation at Scutari for more than a thousand men. Errors, follies, and vices on the part of individuals there doubtless were; but, in the general reckoning, they were of small account—insignificant symptoms of the deep disease of the body politic—the enormous calamity of administrative collapse.

Miss Nightingale arrived at Scutari—a suburb of Constantinople, on the Asiatic side of the Bosphorus—on November 4th, 1854; it was ten days after the battle of Balaclava, and the day before the battle of Inkerman. The organisation of the hospitals, which had already given way under the stress of the battle of the Alma, was now to be subjected to the further pressure which these two desperate and bloody engagements implied. Great detachments of wounded were already beginning to pour in. The men, after receiving such summary treatment as could be given them at the smaller hospitals in the Crimea itself, were forthwith shipped in batches of two hundred across the Black Sea to Scutari. This voyage was in normal times one of four days and a half; but the times were no longer normal, and now the transit often lasted for a fortnight or three weeks. It received, not without reason, the name of "the middle passage." Between, and sometimes on the decks, the wounded, the sick, and the dying were crowded—men who had just undergone the amputation of limbs, men in the clutches of fever or of frostbite, men in the last stages of dysentery and cholera—without beds, sometimes without blankets, often hardly clothed. The one or two surgeons on board did what they could; but medical stores were lacking, and the only form of nursing available was that provided by a handful of invalid soldiers, who were usually themselves prostrate by the end of the voyage. There was no other food beside the ordinary salt rations of ship diet; and even the water was sometimes so stored that it was out of reach of the weak. For many months, the average of deaths during these voyages was seventy-four in the thousand; the corpses were shot out into the waters; and who shall say that they were the most unfortunate? At Scutari, the landing-stage, constructed with all the perverseness of Oriental ingenuity, could only be approached with great difficulty, and, in rough weather, not at all. When it was reached, what remained of the men in the ships had first to be disembarked, and then conveyed up a steep slope of a quarter of a mile to the nearest of the hospitals. The most serious cases might be put upon stretchers—for there were far too few for all; the rest were carried or dragged up the hill by such convalescent soldiers as could be got together, who were not too obviously infirm for the work. At last the journey was accomplished; slowly, one by one, living or dying, the wounded were carried up into the hospital. And in the hospital what did they find?

Lasciate ogni speranza, voi ch'entrate: the delusive doors bore no such inscription; and yet behind them Hell yawned. Want, neglect, confusion, misery—in every shape and in every degree of intensity—filled the endless corridors and the vast apartments of the gigantic barrack-house, which, without forethought or preparation, had been hurriedly set aside as the chief shelter for the victims of the war. The very building itself was radically defective. Huge sewers underlay it, and cess-pools loaded with filth wafted their poison into the upper rooms. The floors were in so rotten a condition that many of them could not be scrubbed; the walls were thick with dirt; incredible multitudes of vermin swarmed everywhere. And, enormous as the building was, it was yet too small. It contained four miles of beds, crushed together so close that there was but just room to pass between them. Under such conditions, the most elaborate system of ventilation might well have been at fault; but here there was no ventilation. The stench was indescribable. "I have been well acquainted," said Miss Nightingale, "with the dwellings of the worst parts of most of the great cities in Europe, but have never been in any atmosphere which I could compare with that of the Barrack Hospital at night." The structural defects were equalled by the deficiencies in the commonest objects of hospital use. There were not enough bedsteads; the sheets were of canvas, and so coarse that the wounded men recoiled from them, begging to be left in their blankets; there was no bedroom furniture of any kind, and empty beer-bottles were used for candlesticks. There were no basins, no towels, no soap, no brooms, no mops, no trays, no plates; there were neither slippers nor scissors, neither shoebrushes nor blacking; there were no knives or forks or spoons. The supply of fuel was constantly deficient. The cooking arrangements were preposterously inadequate, and the laundry was a farce. As for purely medical materials, the tale was no better. Stretchers, splints, bandages—all were lacking; and so were the most ordinary drugs.

To replace such wants, to struggle against such difficulties, there was a handful of men overburdened by the strain of ceaseless work, bound down by the traditions of official routine, and enfeebled either by old age or inexperience or sheer incompetence. They had proved utterly unequal to their task. The principal doctor was lost in the imbecilities of a senile optimism. The wretched official whose business it was to provide for the wants of the hospital was tied fast hand and foot by red tape. A few of the younger doctors struggled valiantly, but what could they do? Unprepared, disorganised, with such help only as they could find among the miserable band of convalescent soldiers drafted off to tend their sick comrades, they were faced with disease, mutilation, and death in all their most appalling forms, crowded multitudinously about them in an ever increasing mass. They were like men in a shipwreck, fighting, not for safety, but for the next moment's bare existence—to gain, by yet another frenzied effort, some brief respite from the waters of destruction.

In these surroundings, those who had been long inured to scenes of human suffering—surgeons with a world-wide knowledge of agonies, soldiers familiar with fields of carnage, missionaries with remembrances of famine and of plague—yet found a depth of horror which they had never known before. There were moments, there were places, in the Barrack Hospital at Scutari, where the strongest hand was struck with trembling, and the boldest eye would turn away its gaze.

Miss Nightingale came, and she, at any rate, in that Inferno, did not abandon hope. For one thing, she brought material succour. Before she left London she had consulted Dr. Andrew Smith, the head of the Army Medical Board, as to whether it would be useful to take out stores of any kind to Scutari; and Dr. Andrew Smith had told her that "nothing was needed." Even Sidney Herbert had given her similar assurances; possibly, owing to an oversight, there might have been some delay in the delivery of the medical stores, which, he said, had been sent out from England "in profusion," but "four days would have remedied this." She preferred to trust her own instincts, and at Marseilles purchased a large quantity of miscellaneous provisions, which were of the utmost use at Scutari. She came, too, amply provided with money—in all, during her stay in the East, about £7,000 reached her from private sources; and, in addition, she was able to avail herself of another valuable means of help. At the same time as herself, Mr. Macdonald, of the *Times*, had arrived at Scutari, charged with the duty of administering the large sums of money collected through the agency of that newspaper in aid of the sick and wounded; and Mr. Macdonald had the sense to see that the best use he could make of the *Times* Fund was to put it at the disposal of Miss Nightingale.

I cannot conceive [wrote an eye-witness], as I now calmly look back on the first three weeks after the arrival of the wounded from Inkerman, how it could have been possible to have avoided a state of things too disastrous to contemplate, had not Miss Nightingale been there, with the means placed at her disposal by Mr. Macdonald.

But the official view was different. What! Was the public service to admit, by accepting outside charity, that it was unable to discharge its own duties without the assistance of private and irregular benevolence? Never! And accordingly when Lord Stratford de Redcliffe, our Ambassador at Constantinople, was asked by Mr. Macdonald to indicate how the *Times* Fund could best be employed, he answered that there was indeed one object to which it might very well be devoted—the building of an English Protestant Church at Pera.

Mr. Macdonald did not waste further time with Lord Stratford, and immediately joined forces with Miss Nightingale. But, with such a frame of mind in the highest quarters, it is easy to imagine the kind of disgust and alarm with which the sudden intrusion of a band of amateurs and females must have filled the minds of the ordinary officer and the ordinary military surgeon. They could not understand it; what had women to do with war? Honest Colonels relieved their spleen by the cracking of heavy jokes about "the Bird"; while poor Dr. Hall, a rough terrier of a man, who had worried his way to the top of his profession, was struck speechless with astonishment, and at last observed that Miss Nightingale's appointment was extremely droll.

Her position was, indeed, an official one, but it was hardly the easier for that. In the hospitals it was her duty to provide the services of herself and her nurses when they were asked for by the doctors, and not until then. At first some of the surgeons would have nothing to say to her, and, though she was welcomed by others, the majority were hostile and suspicious. But gradually she gained ground. Her good will could not be denied, and her capacity could not be disregarded. With consummate tact, with all the gentleness of supreme strength, she managed at last to impose her personality upon the susceptible, overwrought, discouraged, and helpless group of men in authority who surrounded her. She stood firm; she was a rock in the angry ocean; with her alone was safety, comfort, life. And so it was that hope dawned at Scutari. The reign of chaos and old night began to dwindle; order came upon the scene, and common sense, and forethought, and decision, radiating out from the little room off the great gallery in the Barrack Hospital where day and night the Lady Superintendent was at her task. Progress might be slow, but it was sure. The first sign of a great change came with the appearance of some of those necessary objects with which the hospitals had been unprovided for months. The sick men began to enjoy the use of towels and soap, knives and forks, combs and tooth-brushes. Dr. Hall might snort when he heard of it, asking, with a growl, what a soldier wanted with a tooth-brush; but the good work went on. Eventually the whole business of purveying to the hospitals was, in effect, carried out by Miss Nightingale. She alone, it seemed, whatever the contingency, knew where to lay her hands on what was wanted; she alone could dispense her stores with readiness; above all she alone possessed the art of circumventing the pernicious influences of official etiquette. This was her greatest enemy, and sometimes even she was baffled by it. On one occasion 27,000 shirts sent out at her instance by the Home Government, arrived, were landed, and were only waiting to be unpacked. But the official "Purveyor" intervened; "he could not unpack them," he said, "without a board." Miss Nightingale pleaded in vain; the sick and wounded lay half-naked shivering for want of clothing; and three weeks elapsed before the Board released the shirts. A little later, however, on a similar occasion, Miss Nightingale felt that she could assert her own authority. She ordered a Government consignment to be forcibly opened, while the miserable "Purveyor" stood by, wringing his hands in departmental agony.

Vast quantities of valuable stores sent from England lay, she found, engulfed in the bottomless abyss of the Turkish Customs

House. Other ship-loads, buried beneath munitions of war destined for Balaclava, passed Scutari without a sign, and thus hospital materials were sometimes carried to and fro three times over the Black Sea, before they reached their destination. The whole system was clearly at fault, and Miss Nightingale suggested to the home authorities that a Government Store House should be instituted at Scutari for the reception and distribution of the consignments. Six months after her arrival this was done.

In the meantime she had reorganised the kitchens and the laundries in the hospitals. The ill-cooked hunks of meat, vilely served at irregular intervals, which had hitherto been the only diet for the sick men were replaced by punctual meals, well-prepared and appetising, while strengthening extra foods—soups and wines, and jellies ("preposterous luxuries," snarled Dr. Hall)—were distributed to those who needed them. One thing, however, she could not effect. The separation of the bones from the meat was no part of official cookery: the rule was that the food must be divided into equal portions, and if some of the portions were all bone—well, every man must take his chance. The rule, perhaps, was not a very good one; but there it was. "It would require a new Regulation of the Service," she was told, "to bone the meat." As for the washing arrangements, they were revolutionised. Up to the time of Miss Nightingale's arrival the number of shirts which the authorities had succeeded in washing was seven. The hospital bedding, she found, was "washed" in cold water. She took a Turkish house, had boilers installed, and employed soldiers' wives to do the laundry work. The expenses were defrayed from her own funds and that of the *Times;* and henceforward the sick and wounded had the comfort of clean linen.

Then she turned her attention to their clothing. Owing to military exigencies the greater number of the men had abandoned their kit; their knapsacks were lost for ever; they possessed nothing but what was on their persons, and that was usually only fit for speedy destruction. The "Purveyor," of course, pointed out that, according to the regulations, all soldiers should bring with them into hospital an adequate supply of clothing, and he declared that it was no business of his to make good their deficiencies. Apparently, it was the business of Miss Nightingale. She procured socks, boots, and shirts in enormous quantities; she had trousers made; she rigged up dressing-gowns. "The fact is," she told Sidney Herbert, "I am now clothing the British Army."

All at once, word came from the Crimea that a great new contingent of sick and wounded might shortly be expected. Where were they to go? Every available inch in the wards was occupied; the affair was serious and pressing, and the authorities stood aghast. There were some dilapidated rooms in the Barrack Hospital, unfit for human habitation, but Miss Nightingale believed that if measures were promptly taken they might be made capable of accommodating several hundred beds. One of the doctors agreed with her; the rest of the officials were irresolute: it would be a very expensive job, they said; it would involve building; and who could take the responsibility? The proper course was that a representation should be made to the Director-General of the Army Medical Department in London; then the Director-General would apply to the Horse Guards, the Horse Guards would move the Ordnance, the Ordnance would lay the matter before the Treasury, and, if the Treasury gave its consent, the work might be correctly carried through, several months after the necessity for it had disappeared. Miss Nightingale, however, had made up her mind, and she persuaded Lord Stratford—or thought she had persuaded him—to give his sanction to the required expenditure. A hundred and twenty-five workmen were immediately engaged, and the work was begun. The workmen struck; whereupon Lord Stratford washed his hands of the whole business. Miss Nightingale engaged two hundred other workmen on her own authority, and paid the bill out of her own resources. The wards were ready by the required date; five hundred sick men were received in them; and all the utensils, including knives, forks, spoons, cans and towels, were supplied by Miss Nightingale.

This remarkable woman was in truth performing the function of an administrative chief. How had this come about? Was she not in reality merely a nurse? Was it not her duty simply to tend to the sick? And indeed, was it not as a ministering angel, a gentle "lady with a lamp" that she actually impressed the minds of her contemporaries? No doubt that was so; and yet it is no less certain that, as she herself said, the specific business of nursing was "the least important of the functions into which she had been forced." It was clear that in the state of disorganisation into which the hospitals at Scutari had fallen the most pressing, the really vital, need was for something more than nursing; it was for the necessary elements of civilised life—the commonest material objects, the most ordinary cleanliness, the rudimentary habits of order and authority. "Oh, dear Miss Nightingale," said one of her party as they were approaching Constantinople, "when we land, let there be no delays, let us get straight to nursing the poor fellows!" "The strongest will be wanted at the wash-tub," was Miss Nightingale's answer. And it was upon the wash-tub, and all that the wash-tub stood for, that she expended her greatest energies. Yet to say that is perhaps to say too much. For to those who watched her at work among the sick, moving day and night from bed to bed, with that unflinching courage, with that indefatigable vigilance, it seemed as if the concentrated force of an undivided and unparalleled devotion could hardly suffice for that portion of her task alone. Wherever, in those vast wards, suffering was at its worst and the need for help was greatest, there, as if by magic, was Miss Nightingale. Her superhuman equanimity would, at the moment of some ghastly operation, nerve the victim to endure and almost to hope. Her sympathy would assuage the pangs of dying and bring back to those still living something of the forgotten charm of life. Over and over again her untiring efforts rescued those whom the surgeons had abandoned as beyond the possibility of cure. Her mere presence brought with it a strange influence. A passionate idolatry spread among the men: they kissed her shadow as it passed. They did more. "Before she came," said a soldier, "there was cussin' and swearin', but after that it was as 'oly as a church." The most cherished privilege of the fighting man was abandoned for the sake of Miss Nightingale. In those "lowest sinks of human misery," as she herself put it, she never heard the use of one expression "which could distress a gentlewoman."

She was heroic; and these were the humble tributes paid by

those of grosser mould to that high quality. Certainly, she was heroic. Yet her heroism was not of that simple sort so dear to the readers of novels and the compilers of hagiologies—the romantic sentimental heroism with which mankind loves to invest its chosen darlings: it was made of sterner stuff. To the wounded soldier on his couch of agony she might well appear in the guise of a gracious angel of mercy; but the military surgeons, and the orderlies, and her own nurses, and the "Purveyor," and Dr. Hall, and even Lord Stratford himself could tell a different story. It was not by gentle sweetness and womanly self-abnegation that she had brought order out of chaos in the Scutari Hospitals, that, from her own resources, she had clothed the British Army, that she had spread her dominion over the serried and reluctant powers of the official world; it was by strict method, by stern discipline, by rigid attention to detail, by ceaseless labour, by the fixed determination of an indomitable will. Beneath her cool and calm demeanour lurked fierce and passionate fires. As she passed through the wards in her plain dress, so quiet, so unassuming, she struck the casual observer simply as the pattern of a perfect lady; but the keener eye perceived something more than that—the serenity of high deliberation in the scope of the capacious brow, the sign of power in the dominating curve of the thin nose, and the traces of a harsh and dangerous temper—something peevish, something mocking, and yet something precise—in the small and delicate mouth. There was humour in the face; but the curious watcher might wonder whether it was humour of a very pleasant kind; might ask himself, even as he heard the laughter and marked the jokes with which she cheered the spirits of her patients, what sort of sardonic merriment this same lady might not give vent to, in the privacy of her chamber. As for her voice, it was true of it, even more than of her countenance, that it "had that in it one must fain call master." Those clear tones were in no need of emphasis: "I never heard her raise her voice," said one of her companions. Only, when she had spoken, it seemed as if nothing could follow but obedience. Once, when she had given some direction, a doctor ventured to remark that the thing could not be done. "But it must be done," said Miss Nightingale. A chance bystander, who heard the words, never forgot through all his life the irresistible authority of them. And they were spoken quietly—very quietly indeed.

Late at night, when the long miles of beds lay wrapped in darkness, Miss Nightingale would sit at work in her little room, over her correspondence. It was one of the most formidable of all her duties. There were hundreds of letters to be written to the friends and relations of soldiers; there was the enormous mass of official documents to be dealt with; there were her own private letters to be answered; and, most important of all, there was the composition of her long and confidential reports to Sidney Herbert. These were by no means official communications. Her soul, pent up all day in the restraint and reserve of a vast responsibility, now at last poured itself out in these letters with all its natural vehemence, like a swollen torrent through an open sluice. Here, at least, she did not mince matters. Here she painted in her darkest colours the hideous scenes which surrounded her; here she tore away remorselessly the last veils still shrouding the abominable truth. Then she would fill the pages with recommendations and suggestions, with criticisms of the minutest details of organisation, with elaborate calculations of contingencies, with exhaustive analyses and statistical statements piled up in breathless eagerness one on the top of the other. And then her pen, in the virulence of its volubility, would rush on to the discussion of individuals, to the denunciation of an incompetent surgeon or the ridicule of a self-sufficient nurse. Her sarcasm searched the ranks of the officials with the deadly and unsparing precision of a machine-gun. Her nicknames were terrible. She respected no one: Lord Stratford, Lord Raglan, Lady Stratford, Dr. Andrew Smith, Dr. Hall, the Commissary-General, the Purveyor—she fulminated against them all. The intolerable futility of mankind obsessed her like a nightmare, and she gnashed her teeth against it. "I do well to be angry," was the burden of her cry. How many just men were there at Scutari? How many who cared at all for the sick, or had done anything for their relief? Were there ten? Were there five? Was there even one? She could not be sure.

At one time, during several weeks, her vituperations descended upon the head of Sidney Herbert himself. He had misinterpreted her wishes, he had traversed her positive instructions, and it was not until he had admitted his error and apologised in abject terms that he was allowed again into favour. While this misunderstanding was at its height an aristocratic young gentleman arrived at Scutari with a recommendation from the Minister. He had come out from England filled with a romantic desire to render homage to the angelic heroine of his dreams. He had, he said, cast aside his life of ease and luxury; he would devote his days and nights to the service of that gentle lady; he would perform the most menial offices, he would "fag" for her, he would be her footman—and feel requited by a single smile. A single smile, indeed, he had, but it was of an unexpected kind. Miss Nightingale at first refused to see him, and then, when she consented, believing that he was an emissary sent by Sidney Herbert to put her in the wrong over their dispute, she took notes of her conversation with him, and insisted on his signing them at the end of it. The young gentleman returned to England by the next ship.

This quarrel with Sidney Herbert was, however, an exceptional incident. Alike by him, and by Lord Panmure, his successor at the War Office, she was firmly supported; and the fact that during the whole of her stay at Scutari she had the Home Government at her back, was her trump card in her dealings with the hospital authorities. Nor was it only the Government that was behind her: public opinion in England early recognised the high importance of her mission, and its enthusiastic appreciation of her work soon reached an extraordinary height. The Queen herself was deeply moved. She made repeated inquiries as to the welfare of Miss Nightingale; she asked to see her accounts of the wounded, and made her the intermediary between the throne and the troops.

Let Mrs. Herbert know [she wrote to the War Minister] that I wish Miss Nightingale and the ladies would tell these poor noble, wounded, and sick men that *no one* takes a warmer interest or feels *more* for their sufferings or admires their courage and heroism *more* than their Queen. Day and night she thinks of her beloved troops. So does the Prince. Beg Mrs. Herbert to communicate these my words to those ladies, as I know that *our* sympathy is much valued by these noble fellows.

The letter was read aloud in the wards by the Chaplain. "It is a very feeling letter," said the men.

And so the months passed, and that fell winter which had begun with Inkerman and had dragged itself out through the long agony of the investment of Sebastopol, at last was over. In May, 1855, after six months of labour, Miss Nightingale could look with something like satisfaction at the condition of the Scutari hospitals. Had they done nothing more than survive the terrible strain which had been put upon them, it would have been a matter for congratulation; but they had done much more than that; they had marvellously improved. The confusion and the pressure in the wards had come to an end; order reigned in them, and cleanliness; the supplies were bountiful and prompt; important sanitary works had been carried out. One simple comparison of figures was enough to reveal the extraordinary change: the rate of mortality among the cases treated had fallen from 42 per cent. to 22 per thousand. But still the indefatigable lady was not satisfied. The main problem had been solved—the physical needs of the men had been provided for; their mental and spiritual needs remained. She set up and furnished reading-rooms and recreation-rooms. She started classes and lectures. Officers were amazed to see her treating their men as if they were human beings, and assured her that she would only end by "spoiling the brutes." But that was not Miss Nightingale's opinion, and she was justified. The private soldier began to drink less, and even—though that seemed impossible—to save his pay. Miss Nightingale became a banker for the army, receiving and sending home large sums of money every month. At last, reluctantly, the Government followed suit, and established machinery of its own for the remission of money. Lord Panmure, however, remained sceptical; "it will do no good," he pronounced; "the British soldier is not a remitting animal." But, in fact, during the next six months, £71,000 was sent home.

Amid all these activities, Miss Nightingale took up the further task of inspecting the hospitals in the Crimea itself. The labour was extreme, and the conditions of life were almost intolerable. She spent whole days in the saddle, or was driven over those bleak and rocky heights in a baggage cart. Sometimes she stood for hours in the heavily falling snow, and would only reach her hut at dead of night after walking for miles through perilous ravines. Her powers of resistance seemed incredible, but at last they were exhausted. She was attacked by fever, and for a moment came very near to death. Yet she worked on; if she could not move, she could at least write; and write she did until her mind had left her; and after it had left her, in what seemed the delirious trance of death itself, she still wrote. When, after many weeks, she was strong enough to travel, she was to return to England, but she utterly refused. She would not go back, she said, before the last of the soldiers had left Scutari.

This happy moment had almost arrived, when suddenly the smouldering hostilities of the medical authorities burst out into a flame. Dr. Hall's labours had been rewarded by a K.C.B.—letters which, as Miss Nightingale told Sidney Herbert, she could only suppose to mean "Knight of the Crimean Burial-grounds"—and the honour had turned his head. He was Sir John, and he would be thwarted no longer. Disputes had lately arisen between Miss Nightingale and some of the nurses in the Crimean hospitals. The situation had been embittered by rumours of religious dissensions, for, while the Crimean nurses were Roman Catholics, many of those at Scutari were suspected of a regrettable propensity towards the tenets of Dr. Pusey. Miss Nightingale was by no means disturbed by these sectarian differences, but any suggestion that her supreme authority over all the nurses with the Army was in doubt was enough to rouse her to fury; and it appeared that Mrs. Bridgeman, the Reverend Mother in the Crimeas, had ventured to call that authority in question. Sir John Hall thought that his opportunity had come, and strongly supported Mrs. Bridgeman—or, as Miss Nightingale preferred to call her, the "Reverend Brickbat." There was a violent struggle; Miss Nightingale's rage was terrible. Dr. Hall, she declared, was doing his best to "root her out of the Crimea." She would bear it no longer; the War Office was playing her false; there was only one thing to be done—Sidney Herbert must move for the production of papers in the House of Commons, so that the public might be able to judge between her and her enemies. Sidney Herbert with great difficulty calmed her down. Orders were immediately dispatched putting her supremacy beyond doubt, and the Reverend Brickbat withdrew from the scene. Sir John, however, was more tenacious. A few weeks later, Miss Nightingale and her nurses visited the Crimea for the last time, and the brilliant idea occurred to him that he could crush her by a very simple expedient—he would starve her into submission; and he actually ordered that no rations of any kind should be supplied to her. He had already tried this plan with great effect upon an unfortunate medical man whose presence in the Crimea he had considered an intrusion; but he was now to learn that such tricks were thrown away upon Miss Nightingale. With extraordinary foresight, she had brought with her a great supply of food; she succeeded in obtaining more at her own expense and by her own exertions; and thus for ten days, in that inhospitable country, she was able to feed herself and twenty-four nurses. Eventually the military authorities intervened in her favour, and Sir John had to confess that he was beaten.

It was not until July, 1856—four months after the Declaration of Peace—that Miss Nightingale left Scutari for England. Her reputation was now enormous, and the enthusiasm of the public was unbounded. The Royal approbation was expressed by the gift of a brooch, accompanied by a private letter.

> You are, I know, well aware [wrote Her Majesty] of the high sense I entertain of the Christian devotion which you have displayed during this great and bloody war, and I need hardly repeat to you how warm my admiration is for your services, which are fully equal to those of my dear and brave soldiers, whose sufferings you have had the *privilege* of alleviating is so merciful a manner. I am, however, anxious of marking my feelings in a manner which I trust will be agreeable to you, and therefore send you with this letter a brooch, the form and emblems of which commemorate your great and blessed work, and which I hope you will wear as a mark of the high approbation of your Sovereign!

"It will be a very great satisfaction to me," Her Majesty added, "to make the acquaintance of one who has set so bright an example to our sex."

The brooch, which was designed by the Prince Consort, bore a St. George's cross in red enamel, and the Royal cypher surmounted by diamonds. The whole was encircled by the inscription, "Blessed are the Merciful."

III

The name of Florence Nightingale lives in the memory of the world by virtue of the lurid and heroic adventure of the Crimea. Had she died—as she nearly did—upon her return to England, her reputation would hardly have been different; her legend would have come down to us almost as we know it today—that gentle vision of female virtue which first took shape before the adoring eyes of the sick soldiers at Scutari. Yet, as a matter of fact, she lived for more than half a century after the Crimean War; and during the greater part of that long period all the energy and all the devotion of her extraordinary nature were working at their highest pitch. What she accomplished in those years of unknown labour could, indeed, hardly have been more glorious than her Crimean triumphs; but it was certainly more important. The true history was far stranger even than the myth. In Miss Nightingale's own eyes the adventure of the Crimea was a mere incident—scarcely more than a useful stepping-stone in her career. It was the fulcrum with which she hoped to move the world; but it was only the fulcrum. For more than a generation she was to sit in secret, working her lever: and her real life began at the very moment when, in the popular imagination, it had ended.

She arrived in England in a shattered state of health. The hardships and the ceaseless effort of the last two years had undermined her nervous system; her heart was pronounced to be affected; she suffered constantly from fainting-fits and terrible attacks of utter physical prostration. The doctors declared that one thing alone would save her—a complete and prolonged rest. But that was also the one thing with which she would have nothing to do. She had never been in the habit of resting; why should she begin now? Now, when her opportunity had come at last; now, when the iron was hot, and it was time to strike? No; she had work to do; and, come what might, she would do it. The doctors protested in vain; in vain her family lamented and entreated, in vain her friends pointed out to her the madness of such a course. Madness? Mad—possessed—perhaps she was. A demoniac frenzy had seized upon her. As she lay upon her sofa, gasping, she devoured blue-books, dictated letters, and, in the intervals of her palpitations, cracked her febrile jokes. For months at a stretch she never left her bed. For years she was in daily expectation of Death. But she would not rest. At this rate, the doctors assured her, even if she did not die, she would become an invalid for life. She could not help that; there was the work to be done; and, as for rest, very likely she might rest . . . when she had done it.

Wherever she went, in London or in the country, in the hills of Derbyshire, or among the rhododendrons at Embley, she was haunted by a ghost. It was the spectre of Scutari—the hideous vision of the organisation of a military hospital. She would lay that phantom, or she would perish. The whole system of the Army Medical Department, the education of the Medical Officer, the regulations of hospital procedure . . . *rest?* How could she rest while these things were as they were, while, if the like necessity were to arise again, the like results would follow? And, even in peace and at home, what was the sanitary condition of the Army? The mortality in the barracks was, she found, nearly double the mortality in civil life. "You might as well take 1,100 men every year out upon Salisbury Plain and shoot them," she said. After inspecting the hospitals at Chatham, she smiled grimly. "Yes, this is one more symptom of the system which, in the Crimea, put to death 16,000 men." Scutari had given her knowledge; and it had given her power too: her enormous reputation was at her back—an incalculable force. Other work, other duties, might lie before her; but the most urgent, the most obvious of all was to look to the health of the Army.

One of her very first steps was to take advantage of the invitation which Queen Victoria had sent her to the Crimea, together with the commemorative brooch. Within a few weeks of her return, she visited Balmoral, and had several interviews both with the Queen and the Prince Consort. "She put before us," wrote the

Prince in his diary, "all the defects of our present military hospital system and the reforms that are needed." She related the whole story of her experiences in the East; and, in addition, she managed to have some long and confidential talks with His Royal Highness on metaphysics and religion. The impression which she created was excellent. "Sie gefällt uns sehr," noted the Prince, "ist sehr bescheiden." Her Majesty's comment was different—"Such a *head!* I wish we had her at the War Office."

But Miss Nightingale was not at the War Office, and for a very simple reason: she was a woman. Lord Panmure, however, *was* (though indeed the reason for that was not quite so simple); and it was upon Lord Panmure that the issue of Miss Nightingale's efforts for reform must primarily depend. That burly Scottish nobleman had not, in spite of his most earnest endeavours, had a very easy time of it as Secretary of State for War. He had come into office in the middle of the Sebastopol campaign, and had felt himself very well fitted for the position, since he had acquired in former days an inside knowledge of the Army—as a Captain of Hussars. It was this inside knowledge which had enabled him to inform Miss Nightingale with such authority that "the British soldier is not a remitting animal." And perhaps it was this same consciousness of a command of his subject which had impelled him to write a dispatch to Lord Raglan, blandly informing the Commander-in-Chief in the Field just how he was neglecting his duties, and pointing out to him that if he would only try he really might do a little better next time. Lord Raglan's reply, calculated as it was to make its recipient sink into the earth, did not quite have that effect upon Lord Panmure, who, whatever might have been his faults, had never been accused of being supersensitive. However, he allowed the matter to drop; and a little later Lord Raglan died—worn out, some people said, by work and anxiety. He was succeeded by an excellent red-nosed old gentleman, General Simpson, whom nobody has ever heard of, and who took Sebastopol. But Lord Panmure's relations with him were hardly more satisfactory than his relations with Lord Raglan; for, while Lord Raglan had been too independent, poor General Simpson erred in the opposite direction, perpetually asked advice, suffered from lumbago, doubted, his nose growing daily redder and redder, whether he was fit for his post, and, by alternate mails, sent in and withdrew his resignation. Then, too, both the General and the Minister suffered acutely from that distressingly useful new invention, the electric telegraph. On one occasion General Simpson felt obliged actually to expostulate.

I think, my Lord [he wrote], that some telegraphic messages reach us that cannot be sent under due authority, and are perhaps unknown to you, although under the protection of your Lordship's name. For instance, I was called up last night, a dragoon having come express with a telegraphic message in these words, "Lord Panmure to General Simpson–Captain Jarvis has been bitten by a centipede. How is he now?"

General Simpson might have put up with this, though to be sure it did seem "rather too trifling an affair to call for a dragoon to ride a couple of miles in the dark that he may knock up the Commander of the Army out of the very small allowance of sleep permitted him"; but what was really more than he could bear was to find "upon sending in the morning another mounted dragoon to inquire after Captain Jarvis, four miles off, that he never has been bitten at all, but has had a boil, from which he is fast recovering." But Lord Panmure had troubles of his own. His favourite nephew, Captain Dowbiggin, was at the front, and to one of his telegrams to the Commander-in-Chief the Minister had taken occasion to append the following carefully qualified sentence–"I recommend Dowbiggin to your notice, should you have a vacancy, and if he is fit." Unfortunately, in those early days, it was left to the discretion of the telegraphist to compress the messages which passed through his hands; so that the result was that Lord Panmure's delicate appeal reached its destination in the laconic form of "Look after Dowb." The Headquarters Staff were at first extremely puzzled; they were at last extremely amused. The story spread; and "Look after Dowb" remained for many years the familiar formula for describing official hints in favour of deserving nephews.

And now that all this was over, now that Sebastopol had been, somehow or another, taken, now that peace was, somehow or another, made, now that the troubles of office might surely be expected to be at an end at last—here was Miss Nightingale breaking in upon the scene, with her talk about the state of the hospitals and the necessity for sanitary reform. It was most irksome; and Lord Panmure almost began to wish that he was engaged upon some more congenial occupation—discussing, perhaps, the constitution of the Free Church of Scotland—a question in which he was profoundly interested. But no; duty was paramount; and he set himself, with a sigh of resignation, to the task of doing as little of it as he possibly could.

"The Bison" his friends called him; and the name fitted both his physical demeanour and his habit of mind. That large low head seemed to have been created for butting rather than for anything else. There he stood, four-square and menacing, in the doorway of reform; and it remained to be seen whether the bulky mass, upon whose solid hide even the barbed arrows of Lord Raglan's scorn had made no mark, would prove amenable to the pressure of Miss Nightingale. Nor was he alone in the doorway. There loomed behind him the whole phalanx of professional conservatism, the stubborn supporters of the out-of-date, the worshippers and the victims of War Office routine. Among these it was only natural that Dr. Andrew Smith, the head of the Army Medical Department, should have been pre-eminent—Dr. Andrew Smith, who had assured Miss Nightingale before she left England that "nothing was wanted at Scutari." Such were her opponents; but she too was not without allies. She had gained the ear of Royalty—which was something; at any moment that she pleased she could gain the ear of the public—which was a great deal. She had a host of admirers and friends; and—to say nothing of her personal qualities—her knowledge, her tenacity, her tact—she possessed, too, one advantage which then, far more even than now, carried an immense weight—she belonged to the highest circle of society. She moved naturally among Peers and Cabinet Ministers—she was one of their own set; and in those days their set was a very narrow one. What kind of attention would such persons have paid to some middle-class woman with whom they were not acquainted, who possessed great experience of army nursing and had decided views upon hospital reform? They would have politely ignored her; but it was impossible to ignore Flo Nightingale. When she spoke, they were obliged to listen; and, when they had once begun to do that—what might not follow? She knew her power, and she used it. She supported her weightiest minutes with familiar witty little notes. The Bison began to look grave. It might be difficult—it might be damned difficult—to put down one's head against the white hand of a lady.

Of Miss Nightingale's friends, the most important was Sidney Herbert. He was a man upon whom the good fairies seemed to have showered, as he lay in his cradle, all their most enviable gifts. Well born, handsome, rich, the master of Wilton—one of those great country-houses, clothed with the glamour of a historic past, which are the peculiar glory of England—he possessed, besides all these advantages, so charming, so lively, so gentle a disposition that no one who had once come near him could ever be his enemy. He was, in fact, a man of whom it was difficult not to say that he was a perfect English gentleman. For his virtues were equal even to his good fortune. He was religious—deeply religious: "I am more and more convinced every day," he wrote, when he had been for some years a Cabinet Minister, "that in politics, as in everything else, nothing can be right which is not in accordance with the spirit of the Gospel." No one was more unselfish; he was charitable and benevolent to a remarkable degree; and he devoted the whole of his life with an unwavering conscientiousness to the public service. With such a character, with such opportunities, what high hopes must have danced before him, what radiant visions of accomplished duties, of ever-increasing usefulness, of beneficent power, of the consciousness of disinterested success! Some of those hopes and visions were, indeed, realised; but, in the end, the career of Sidney Herbert seemed to show that, with all their generosity, there was some gift or other—what was it?—some essential gift—which the good fairies had withheld, and that even the qualities of a perfect English gentleman may be no safeguard against anguish, humiliation, and defeat.

That career would certainly have been very different if he had never known Miss Nightingale. The alliance between them, which had begun with her appointment to Scutari, which had grown closer and closer while the war lasted, developed, after her return, into one of the most extraordinary of friendships. It was the friendship of a man and a woman intimately bound together by their devotion to a public cause; mutual affection, of course, played a part in it, but it was an incidental part; the whole soul of the relationship was a community of work. Perhaps out of England such an intimacy could hardly have existed—an intimacy so utterly untinctured not only by passion itself but by the suspicion of it. For years Sidney Herbert saw Miss Nightingale almost daily, for long hours together, corresponding with her incessantly when they were apart; and the tongue of scandal was silent; and one of the most devoted of her admirers was his wife. But what made the connection still more remarkable was the way in which the parts that were played in it were divided between the two. The man who acts, decides, and achieves; the woman who encourages, applauds, and—from a distance—inspires:—the combination is common enough; but Miss Nightingale was neither an Aspasia nor an Egeria. In her case it is almost true to say that the rôles were reversed; the qualities of pliancy and sympathy fell to the man, those of command and initiative to the woman. There was one thing only which Miss Nightingale lacked in her equipment for public life; she had not—she never could have—the public power and authority which belong to the successful politician. That power and authority Sidney Herbert possessed; the fact was obvious, and the conclusion no less so: it was through the man that the woman must work her will. She took hold of him, taught him, shaped him, absorbed him, dominated him through and through. He did not resist—he did not wish to resist; his natural inclination lay along the same path as hers; only that terrific personality swept him forward at her own fierce pace and with her own relentless stride. Swept him—where to? Ah! Why had he ever known Miss Nightingale? If Lord Panmure was a bison, Sidney Herbert, no doubt, was a stag—a comely, gallant creature springing through the forest; but the forest is a dangerous place. One has the image of those wide eyes fascinated suddenly by something feline, something strong; there is a pause; and then the tigress has her claws in the quivering haunches; and then—!

Besides Sidney Herbert, she had other friends who, in a more restricted sphere, were hardly less essential to her. If, in her condition of bodily collapse, she were to accomplish what she was determined that she should accomplish, the attentions and the services of others would be absolutely indispensable. Helpers and servers she must have; and accordingly there was soon formed about her a little group of devoted disciples upon whose affections and energies she could implicitly rely. Devoted, indeed, these disciples were, in no ordinary sense of the term; for certainly she was no light task-mistress, and he who set out to be of use to Miss Nightingale was apt to find, before he had gone very far, that he was in truth being made use of in good earnest—to the very limit of his endurance and his capacity. Perhaps, even beyond those limits; why not? Was she asking of others more than she was giving herself? Let them look at her lying there pale and breathless on the couch; could it be said that she spared herself? Why, then, should she spare others? And it was not for her own sake that she made these claims. For her own sake, indeed! No! They all knew it! it was for the sake of the work. And so the little band, bound body and soul in that strange servitude, laboured on ungrudgingly. Among the most faithful was her "Aunt Mai," her father's sister, who from the earliest days had stood beside her, who had helped her to escape from the thraldom of family life, who had been with her at Scutari, and who now acted almost the part of a mother to her, watching over her with infinite care in all the movements and uncertainties which her state of health involved. Another constant attendant was her brother-in-law, Sir Harry Verney, whom she found particularly valuable in parliamentary affairs. Arthur Clough, the poet, also a connection by marriage, she used in other ways. Ever since he had lost his faith at the time of the Oxford Movement, Clough had passed his life in a condition of considerable uneasiness, which was increased rather than diminished by the practice of poetry. Unable to decide upon the purpose of an existence whose savour had fled together with his belief in the Resurrection, his spirits lowered still further by ill-health, and his income not all that it should be, he had determined to seek the solution of his difficulties in the United States of America. But, even there, the solution was not forthcoming; and when, a little later, he was offered a post in a government department at home, he accepted it, came to live in London, and immediately fell under the influence of Miss Nightingale. Though the purpose of existence might be still uncertain and its nature still unsavoury, here, at any rate, under the eye of this inspired woman, was something real, something earnest: his only doubt was—could he be of any use? Certainly he could. There were a great number of miscellaneous little jobs which there was nobody handy to do. For instance, when Miss Nightingale was travelling, there were the railway-tickets to be taken; and there were proof-sheets to be corrected; and then there were parcels to be done up in brown paper, and carried to the post. Certainly he could be useful. And so, upon such occupations as these, Arthur Clough was set to work. "This that I see, is not all," he comforted himself by reflecting, "and this that I do is but little; nevertheless it is good, though there is better than it."

As time went on, her "Cabinet," as she called it, grew larger. Officials with whom her work brought her into touch and who sympathised with her objects, were pressed into her service; and old friends of the Crimean days gathered round her when they returned to England. Among these the most indefatigable was Dr. Sutherland, a sanitary expert, who for more than thirty years acted as her confidential private secretary, and surrendered to her purposes literally the whole of his life. Thus sustained and assisted, thus slaved for and adored, she prepared to beard the Bison.

Two facts soon emerged, and all that followed turned upon them. It became clear, in the first place, that that imposing mass was not immovable, and, in the second, that its movement, when it did move, would be exceedingly slow. The Bison was no match for the Lady. It was in vain that he put down his head and planted his feet in the earth; he could not withstand her; the white hand forced him back. But the process was an extraordinarily gradual one. Dr. Andrew Smith and all his War Office phalanx stood behind, blocking the way; the poor Bison groaned inwardly, and cast a wistful eye towards the happy pastures of the Free Church of Scotland; then slowly, with infinite reluctance, step by step, he retreated, disputing every inch of the ground.

The first great measure, which, supported as it was by the Queen, the Cabinet, and the united opinion of the country, it was impossible to resist, was the appointment of a Royal Commission to report upon the health of the Army. The question of the composition of the Commission then immediately arose; and it was over this matter that the first hand-to-hand encounter between Lord Panmure and Miss Nightingale took place. They met, and Miss Nightingale was victorious; Sidney Herbert was appointed Chairman; and, in the end the only member of the Commission opposed to her views was Dr. Andrew Smith. During the interview, Miss Nightingale made an important discovery: she found that "the Bison was bullyable"—the hide was the hide of a Mexican buffalo, but the spirit was the spirit of an Alderney calf. And there was one thing above all others which the huge creature dreaded—an appeal to public opinion. The faintest hint of such a terrible eventuality made his heart dissolve within him; he would agree to anything—he would cut short his grouse-shooting—he would make a speech in the House of Lords—he would even overrule Dr. Andrew Smith—rather than that. Miss Nightingale held the fearful threat in reserve—she would speak out what she knew; she would publish the truth to the whole world, and let the whole world judge between them. With supreme skill, she kept this sword of Damocles poised above the Bison's head, and more than once she was actually on the point of really dropping it. For his recalcitrancy grew and grew. The *personnel* of the Commission once determined upon, there was a struggle, which lasted for six months, over the nature of its powers. Was it to be an efficient body, armed with the right of full inquiry and wide examination, or was it to be a polite official contrivance for exonerating Dr. Andrew Smith? The War Office phalanx closed its ranks, and fought tooth and nail; but it was defeated: the Bison was bullyable.

> Three months from this day [Miss Nightingale had written at last] I publish my experience of the Crimean Campaign, and my suggestions for improvement, unless there has been a fair and tangible pledge by that time for reform.

Who could face that?

And, if the need came, she meant to be as good as her word. For she had now determined, whatever might be the fate of the Commission, to draw up her own report upon the questions at issue. The labour involved was enormous; her health was almost desperate; but she did not flinch, and after six months of incredible industry she had put together and written with her own hand her "Notes affecting the Health, Efficiency, and Hospital Administration of the British Army." This extraordinary composition, filling more than eight hundred closely printed pages, laying down vast principles of far-reaching reform, discussing the minutest details of a multitude of controversial subjects, containing an enormous mass of information of the most varied kinds—military, statistical, sanitary, architectural—was never given to the public, for the need never came; but it formed the basis of the Report of the Royal Commission; and it remains to this day the leading authority on the medical administration of armies.

Before it had been completed the struggle over the powers of the Commission had been brought to a victorious close. Lord Panmure had given way once more; he had immediately hurried to the Queen to obtain her consent; and only then, when her Majesty's initials had been irrevocably affixed to the fatal document, did he dare to tell Dr. Andrew Smith what he had done. The Commission met, and another immense load fell upon Miss Nightingale's shoulders. Today she would, of course, have been one of the Commission herself; but at that time the idea of a woman appearing in such a capacity was unheard of; and no one even suggested the possibility of Miss Nightingale's doing so. The result was that she was obliged to remain behind the scenes throughout, to coach Sidney Herbert in private at every important juncture, and to convey to him and to her other friends upon the Commission the vast funds of her expert knowledge—

so essential in the examination of witnesses—by means of innumerable consultations, letters, and memoranda. It was even doubtful whether the proprieties would admit of her giving evidence; and at last, as a compromise, her modesty only allowed her to do so in the form of written answers to written questions. At length the grand affair was finished. The Commission's Report, embodying almost word for word the suggestions of Miss Nightingale, was drawn up by Sidney Herbert. Only one question remained to be answered—would anything, after all, be done? Or would the Royal Commission, like so many other Royal Commissions before and since, turn out to have achieved nothing but the concoction of a very fat blue-book on a very high shelf?

And so the last and the deadliest struggle with the Bison began. Six months had been spent in coercing him into granting the Commission effective powers; six more months were occupied by the work of the Commission; and now yet another six were to pass in extorting from him the means whereby the recommendations of the Commission might be actually carried out. But, in the end, the thing was done. Miss Nightingale seemed indeed, during these months, to be upon the very brink of death. Accompanied by the faithful Aunt Mai, she moved from place to place—to Hampstead, to Highgate, to Derbyshire, to Malvern—in what appeared to be a last desperate effort to find health somewhere; but she carried that with her which made health impossible. Her desire for work could now scarcely be distinguished from mania. At one moment she was writing a "last letter" to Sidney Herbert; at the next she was offering to go out to India to nurse the sufferers in the Mutiny. When Dr. Sutherland wrote, imploring her to take a holiday, she raved. Rest!—

I am lying without my head, without my claws, and you all peck at me. It is *de rigueur, d'obligation*, like the saying something to one's hat, when one goes into church, to say to me all that has been said to me 110 times a day during the last three months. It is the *obbligato* on the violin, and the twelve violins all practise it together, like the clocks striking 12 o'clock at night all over London, till I say like Xavier de Maistre, *Assez, je le sais, je ne le sais que trop*. I am not a penitent; but you are like the R. C. confessor, who says what is *de rigueur*. . . .

Her wits began to turn, and there was no holding her. She worked like a slave in a mine. She began to believe, as she had begun to believe at Scutari, that none of her fellow-workers had their hearts in the business; if they had, why did they not work as she did? She could only see slackness and stupidity around her. Dr. Sutherland, of course, was grotesquely muddle-headed; and Arthur Clough incurably lazy. Even Sidney Herbert . . . oh, yes, he had simplicity and candour and quickness of perception, no doubt; but he was an eclectic; and what could one hope for from a man who went away to fish in Ireland just when the Bison most needed bullying? As for the Bison himself he had fled to Scotland, where he remained buried for many months. The fate of the vital recommendation in the Commission's Report—the appointment of four Sub-Commissions charged with the duty of determining upon the details of the proposed reforms and of putting them into execution—still hung in the balance. The Bison consented to everything; and then, on a flying visit to London, withdrew his consent and hastily returned to Scotland. Then for many weeks all business was suspended; he had gout—gout in the hands, so that he could not write. "His gout was always handy," remarked Miss Nightingale. But eventually it was clear even to the Bison that the game was up, and the inevitable surrender came.

There was, however, one point in which he triumphed over Miss Nightingale. The building of Netley Hospital had been begun, under his orders, before her return to England. Soon after her arrival she examined the plans, and found that they reproduced all the worst faults of an out-of-date and mischievous system of hospital construction. She therefore urged that the matter should be reconsidered, and in the meantime building stopped. But the Bison was obdurate; it would be very expensive, and in any case it was too late. Unable to make any impression on him, and convinced of the extreme importance of the question, she determined to appeal to a higher authority. Lord Palmerston was Prime Minister; she had known him from her childhood; he was a near neighbour of her father's in the New Forest. She went down to the New Forest, armed with the plans of the proposed hospital and all the relevant information, stayed the night at Lord Palmerston's house, and convinced him of the necessity of rebuilding Netley.

It seems to me [Lord Palmerston wrote to Lord Panmure] that at Netley all consideration of what would best tend to the comfort and recovery of the patients has been sacrificed to the vanity of the architect, whose sole object has been to make a building which should cut a dash when looked at from the Southampton river. . . . Pray, therefore, stop all further progress in the work until the matter can be duly considered.

But the Bison was not to be moved by one peremptory letter, even if it was from the Prime Minister. He put forth all his powers of procrastination, Lord Palmerston lost interest in the subject, and so the chief military hospital in England was triumphantly completed on unsanitary principles, with unventilated rooms, and with all the patients' windows facing northeast.

But now the time had come when the Bison was to trouble and to be troubled no more. A vote in the House of Commons brought about the fall of Lord Palmerston's Government, and Lord Panmure found himself at liberty to devote the rest of his life to the Free Church of Scotland. After a brief interval, Sidney Herbert became Secretary of State for War. Great was the jubilation in the Nightingale Cabinet; the day of achievement had dawned at last. The next two and a half years (1859-61) saw the introduction of the whole system of reforms for which Miss Nightingale had been struggling so fiercely—reforms which make Sidney Herbert's tenure of power at the War Office an important epoch in the history of the British Army. The four Sub-Commissions, firmly established under the immediate control of the Minister, and urged forward by the relentless perseverance of Miss Nightingale, set to work with a will. The barracks and the hospitals were remodelled; they were properly ventilated and warmed and lighted for the first time; they were given a water supply which actually supplied water, and kitchens where, strange to say, it was possible to cook. Then the great question of the Purveyor—that portentous functionary whose powers and whose lack of powers had weighed like a nightmare upon Scutari—was taken in hand, and new regulations were laid down, accurately defining his responsibilities and his duties. One Sub-Commission reorganised the medical statistics of the Army. Another established—in spite of the last convulsive efforts of the Department—an Army Medical School. Finally the Army Medical Department itself was completely reorganised; an administrative code was drawn up; and the great and novel principle was established that it was as much a part of the duty of the authorities to look after the soldier's health as to look after his sickness. Besides this, it was at last officially admitted that he had a moral and intellectual side. Coffee-rooms and reading-rooms, gymnasiums and workshops were instituted. A new era did in truth appear to have begun. Already by 1861 the mortality in the army had decreased by one half since the days of the Crimea. It was no wonder that even vaster possibilities began now to open out before Miss Nightingale. One thing was still needed to complete and to assure her triumphs. The Army Medical Department was indeed reorganised; but the great central machine was still untouched. The War Office itself—!—If she could remould *that* nearer to her heart's desire—there indeed would be a victory! And until that final act was accomplished, how could she be certain that all the rest of her achievements might not, by some capricious turn of Fortune's wheel—a change of Ministry, perhaps, replacing Sidney Herbert by some puppet of the permanent official gang—be swept to limbo in a moment?

Meanwhile, still ravenous for more and yet more work, her activities had branched out into new directions. The army in India claimed her attention. A Sanitary Commission, appointed at her suggestion, and working under her auspices, did for our troops there what the four Sub-Commissions were doing for those at home. At the same time, these very years which saw her laying the foundations of the whole modern system of medical work in the army, saw her also beginning to bring her knowledge, her influence, and her activity into the service of the country at large. Her *Notes on Hospitals* (1859) revolutionised the theory of hospital construction and hospital management. She was immediately recognised as the leading expert upon all the questions involved; her advice flowed unceasingly and in all directions, so that there is no great hospital today which does not bear upon it the impress of her mind. Nor was this all. With the opening of the Nightingale Training School for Nurses at St. Thomas's Hospital (1860), she became the founder of modern nursing.

But a terrible crisis was now fast approaching. Sidney Herbert had consented to undertake the root and branch reform of the War Office. He had sallied forth into that tropical jungle of festooned obstructiveness, of intertwisted irresponsibilities, of crouching prejudices, of abuses grown stiff and rigid with antiquity, which for so many years to come was destined to lure reforming ministers to their doom.

> The War Office [said Miss Nightingale] is a very slow office, an enormously expensive office, and one in which the Minister's intentions can be entirely negatived by all his sub-departments, and those of each of the sub-departments by every other.

It was true; and, of course, at the first rumour of a change, the old phalanx of reaction was bristling with its accustomed spears. At its head stood no longer Dr. Andrew Smith, who, some time since, had followed the Bison into outer darkness, but a yet more formidable figure, the permanent Under-Secretary himself, Sir Benjamin Hawes—Ben Hawes the Nightingale Cabinet irreverently dubbed him—a man remarkable even among civil servants for adroitness in baffling inconvenient inquiries, resource in raising false issues, and, in short, a consummate command of all the arts of officially sticking in the mud. "Our scheme will probably result in Ben Hawes's resignation," Miss Nightingale said; "and that is another of its advantages." Ben Hawes himself, however, did not quite see it in that light. He set himself to resist the wishes of the Minister by every means in his power. The struggle was long and desperate; and, as it proceeded, it gradually became evident to Miss Nightingale that something was the matter with Sidney Herbert. What was it? His health, never very strong, was, he said, in danger of collapsing under the strain of his work. But, after all, what is illness, when there is a War Office to be reorganised? Then he began to talk of retiring altogether from public life. The doctors were consulted, and declared that, above all things, what was necessary was rest. Rest! She grew seriously alarmed. Was it possible that, at the last moment, the crowning wreath of victory was to be snatched from her grasp? She was not to be put aside by doctors; they were talking nonsense; the necessary thing was not rest but the reform of the War Office; and, besides, she knew very well from her own case what one could do even when one was on the point of death. She expostulated vehemently, passionately: the goal was so near, so very near; he could not turn back now! At any rate, he could not resist Miss Nightingale. A compromise was arranged. Very reluctantly, he exchanged the turmoil of the House of Commons for the dignity of the House of Lords, and he remained at the War Office. She was delighted. "One fight more, the best and the last," she said.

For several more months the fight did indeed go on. But the strain upon him was greater even than she perhaps could realise. Besides the intestine war in his office, he had to face a constant battle in the Cabinet with Mr. Gladstone—a more redoubtable antagonist even than Ben Hawes—over the estimates. His health grew worse and worse. He was attacked by fainting-fits; and there were some days when he could only just keep himself going by gulps of brandy. Miss Nightingale spurred him forward with her encouragements and her admonitions, her zeal and her example. But at last his spirit began to sink as well as his body. He could no longer hope; he could no longer desire; it was useless, all useless; it was utterly impossible. He had failed. The dreadful moment came when the truth was forced upon him: he would never be able to reform the War Office. But a yet more dreadful moment lay behind; he must go to Miss Nightingale and tell her that he was a failure, a beaten man.

Blessed are the merciful! What strange ironic prescience had led Prince Albert, in the simplicity of his heart, to choose that motto for the Crimean brooch? The words hold a double lesson; and, alas! when she brought herself to realise at length what was indeed the fact and what there was no helping, it was not in mercy that she turned upon her old friend.

Beaten! [she exclaimed]. Can't you see that you've simply thrown away the game? And with all the winning cards in your hands! And so noble a game! Sidney Herbert beaten! And beaten by Ben Hawes! It is a worse disgrace . . . [her full rage burst out at last] . . . a worse disgrace than the hospitals at Scutari.

He dragged himself away from her, dragged himself to Spa, hoping vainly for a return of health, and then, despairing, back again to England, to Wilton, to the majestic house standing there resplendent in the summer sunshine, among the great cedars which had lent their shade to Sir Philip Sidney, and all those familiar, darling haunts of beauty which he loved, each one of them, "as if they were persons"; and at Wilton he died. After having received the Eucharist he had become perfectly calm; then, almost unconscious, his lips were seen to be moving. Those about him bent down. "Poor Florence! Poor Florence!" they just caught. ". . . Our joint work . . . unfinished . . . tried to do . . ." and they could hear no more.

When the onward rush of a powerful spirit sweeps a weaker one to its destruction, the commonplaces of the moral judgment are better left unmade. If Miss Nightingale had been less ruthless, Sidney Herbert would not have perished; but then, she would not have been Miss Nightingale. The force that created was the force that destroyed. It was her Demon that was responsible. When the fatal news reached her, she was overcome by agony. In the revulsion of her feelings, she made a worship of the dead man's memory; and the facile instrument which had broken in her hand she spoke of for ever after as her "Master." Then, almost at the same moment, another blow fell upon her. Arthur Clough, worn out by labours very different from those of Sidney Herbert, died too: never more would he tie up her parcels. And yet a third disaster followed. The faithful Aunt Mai did not, to be sure, die; no, she did something almost worse: she left Miss Nightingale. She was growing old, and she felt that she had closer and more imperative duties with her own family. Her niece could hardly forgive her. She poured out, in one of her enormous letters, a passionate diatribe upon the faithlessness, the lack of sympathy, the stupidity, the ineptitude of women. Her doctrines had taken no hold among them; she had never known one who had *appris à apprendre;* she could not even get a woman secretary; "they don't know the names of the Cabinet Ministers—they don't know which of the Churches has Bishops and which not." As for the spirit of self-sacrifice, well—Sidney Herbert and Arthur Clough were men, and they indeed had shown their devotion; but women—! She would mount three widow's caps "for a sign." The first two would be for Clough and for her Master; but the third, "the biggest widow's cap of all"—would be for Aunt Mai. She did well to be angry; she was deserted in her hour of need; and, after all, could she be sure that even the male sex was so impeccable? There was Dr. Sutherland, bungling as usual. Perhaps even he intended to go off, one of these days, too? She gave him a look, and he shivered in his shoes. No!—she grinned sardonically; she would always have Dr. Sutherland. And then she reflected that there was one thing more that she would always have—her work.

IV

Sidney Herbert's death finally put an end to Miss Nightingale's dream of a reformed War Office. For a moment, indeed, in the first agony of her disappointment, she had wildly clutched at a straw; she had written to Mr. Gladstone to beg him to take up the burden of Sidney Herbert's work. And Mr. Gladstone had replied with a sympathetic account of the funeral.

Succeeding Secretaries of State managed between them to undo a good deal of what had been accomplished, but they could not undo it all; and for ten years more (1862-72) Miss Nightingale remained a potent influence at the War Office. After that, her direct connection with the army came to an end, and her energies began to turn more and more completely towards more general objects. Her work upon hospital reform assumed enormous proportions; she was able to improve the conditions in infirmaries and workhouses; and one of her most remarkable papers forestalls the recommendations of the Poor Law Commission of 1909. Her training school for nurses, with all that it involved in initiative, control, responsibility, and combat, would have been enough in itself to have absorbed the whole efforts of at least two lives of ordinary vigour. And at the same time her work in connection with India, which had begun with the Sanitary Commission on the Indian Army, spread and ramified in a multitude of directions. Her tentacles reached the India Office and succeeded in establishing a hold even upon those slippery high places. For many years it was *de rigueur* for the newly appointed Viceroy, before he left England, to pay a visit to Miss Nightingale.

After much hesitation, she had settled down in a small house in South Street, where she remained for the rest of her life. That life was a very long one; the dying woman reached her ninety-first year. Her ill-health gradually diminished; the crises of extreme danger became less frequent, and at last, altogether ceased; she remained an invalid, but an invalid of a curious character—an invalid who was too weak to walk downstairs and who worked far harder than most Cabinet Ministers. Her illness, whatever it may have been, was certainly not inconvenient. It involved seclusion; and an extraordinary, an unparalleled seclusion was, it might almost have been said, the mainspring of Miss Nightingale's life. Lying on her sofa in the little upper room in South Street, she combined the intense vitality of a dominating woman of the world with the mysterious and romantic quality of a myth. She was a legend in her lifetime, and she knew it. She tasted the joys of power, like those Eastern Emperors whose autocratic rule was based upon invisibility, with the mingled satisfactions of obscurity and fame. And she found the machinery of illness hardly less effective as a barrier against the eyes of men than the ceremonial of a palace. Great statesmen and renowned generals were obliged to beg for audiences; admiring princesses from foreign countries found that they must see her at her own time, or not at all; and the ordinary mortal had no hope of ever getting beyond the downstairs sitting-room and Dr. Sutherland. For that indefatigable disciple did, indeed, never desert her. He might be impatient, he might be restless, but he remained. His "incurable looseness of thought," for so she termed it, continued at her service to the end. Once, it is true, he had actually ventured to take a holiday; but he was recalled, and he did not repeat the experiment. He was wanted downstairs. There he sat, transacting business, answering correspondence, interviewing callers, and exchanging innumerable notes with the unseen power above. Sometimes word came down that Miss Nightingale was just well enough to see one of her visitors. The fortunate man was led up, was ushered, trembling, into the shaded chamber, and, of course, could never afterwards forget the interview. Very rarely, indeed, once or twice a year, perhaps, but nobody could be quite certain, in deadly secrecy, Miss Nightingale went out for a drive in the Park. Unrecognised, the living legend flitted for a moment before the common gaze. And the precaution was necessary; for there were times when, at some public function, the rumour of her presence was spread abroad; and ladies, mistaken by the crowd for Miss Nightingale, were followed, pressed upon, and vehemently supplicated—"Let me touch your shawl,"—"Let me stroke your arm"; such was the strange adoration in the hearts of the people. That vast reserve of force lay there behind her; she could use it, if she would. But she preferred never to use it. On occasions, she might hint or threaten; she might balance the sword of Damocles over the head of the Bison; she might, by a word, by a glance, remind some refractory minister, some unpersuadable viceroy, sitting in audience with her in the little upper room, that she was something more than a mere sick woman, that she had only, so to speak, to go to the window and wave her handkerchief, for . . . dreadful things to follow. But that was enough; they understood; the myth was there—obvious, portentous, impalpable; and so it remained to the last.

With statesmen and governors at her beck and call, with her hands on a hundred strings, with mighty provinces at her feet, with foreign governments agog for her counsel, building hospitals, training nurses—she still felt that she had not enough to do. She sighed for more worlds to conquer—more, and yet more. She looked about her—what was there left? Of course! Philosophy! After the world of action, the world of thought. Having set right the health of the British Army, she would now do the same good service for the religious convictions of mankind. She had long noticed—with regret—the growing tendency towards free-thinking among artisans. With regret, but not altogether with surprise: the current teaching of Christianity was sadly to seek; nay, Christianity itself was not without its defects. She would rectify these errors. She would correct the mistakes of the Churches; she would point out just where Christianity was wrong; and she would explain to the artisans what the facts of the case really were. Before her departure for the Crimea, she had begun this work; and now, in the intervals of her other labours, she completed it. Her *Suggestions for Thought to the Searchers after Truth among the Artisans of England* (1860), unravels, in the course of three portly volumes, the difficulties—hitherto, curiously enough, unsolved—connected with such matters as Belief in God, the Plan of Creation, the Origin of Evil, the Future Life, Necessity and Free Will, Law, and the Nature of Morality. The Origin of Evil, in particular, held no perplexities for Miss Nightingale. "We cannot conceive," she remarks, "that Omnipotent Righteousness would find satisfaction in *solitary existence*." This being so, the only question remaining to be asked is, "What beings should we then conceive that God would create?" Now, He cannot create perfect beings, "since, essentially, perfection is one"; if He did so, He would only be adding to Himself. Thus the conclusion is obvious: He *must* create *im*perfect ones. Omnipotent Righteousness, faced by the intolerable *impasse* of a solitary existence, finds itself bound, by the very nature of the case, to create the hospitals at Scutari. Whether this argument would have satisfied the artisans was never discovered, for only a very few copies of the book were printed for private circulation. One copy was sent to Mr. Mill, who acknowledged it in an extremely polite letter. He felt himself obliged, however, to confess that he had not been altogether convinced by Miss Nightingale's proof of the existence of God. Miss Nightingale was surprised and mortified; she had thought better of Mr. Mill; for surely her proof of the existence of God could hardly be improved upon. "A law," she had pointed out, "implies a lawgiver." Now the Universe is full of laws—the law of gravitation, the law of the excluded middle, and many others; hence it follows that the

Universe has a lawgiver—and what would Mr. Mill be satisfied with, if he was not satisfied with that?

Perhaps Mr. Mill might have asked why the argument had not been pushed to its logical conclusion. Clearly, if we are to trust the analogy of human institutions, we must remember that laws are, as a matter of fact, not dispensed by lawgivers, but passed by Act of Parliament. Miss Nightingale, however, with all her experience of public life, never stopped to consider the question whether God might not be a Limited Monarchy.

Yet her conception of God was certainly not orthodox. She felt towards Him as she might have felt towards a glorified sanitary engineer; and in some of her speculations she seems hardly to distinguish between the Deity and the Drains. As one turns over these singular pages, one has the impression that Miss Nightingale has got the Almighty too into her clutches, and that, if He is not careful, she will kill Him with overwork.

Then, suddenly, in the very midst of the ramifying generalities of her metaphysical disquisitions there is an unexpected turn, and the reader is plunged all at once into something particular, something personal, something impregnated with intense experience—a virulent invective upon the position of women in the upper ranks of society. Forgetful alike of her high argument and of the artisans, the bitter creature rails through a hundred pages of close print at the falsities of family life, the ineptitudes of marriage, the emptinesses of convention, in the spirit of an Ibsen or a Samuel Butler. Her fierce pen, shaking with intimate anger, depicts in biting sentences the fearful fate of an unmarried girl in a wealthy household. It is a *cri du cœur;* and then, as suddenly, she returns once more to instruct the artisans upon the nature of Omnipotent Righteousness.

Her mind was, indeed, better qualified to dissect the concrete and distasteful fruits of actual life than to construct a coherent system of abstract philosophy. In spite of her respect for Law, she was never at home with a generalisation. Thus, though the great achievement of her life lay in the immense impetus which she gave to the scientific treatment of sickness, a true comprehension of the scientific method itself was alien to her spirit. Like most great men of action—perhaps like all—she was simply an empiricist. She believed in what she saw, and she acted accordingly; beyond that she would not go. She had found in Scutari that fresh air and light played an effective part in the prevention of the maladies with which she had to deal; and that was enough for her; she would not inquire further; what were the general principles underlying that fact—or even whether there were any—she refused to consider. Years after the discoveries of Pasteur and Lister, she laughed at what she called the "germ-fetish." There was no such thing as "infection"; she had never seen it, therefore it did not exist. But she *had* seen the good effects of fresh air; therefore there could be no doubt about them; and therefore it was essential that the bedrooms of patients should be well ventilated. Such was her doctrine; and in those days of hermetically sealed windows it was a very valuable one. But it was a purely empirical doctrine, and thus it led to some unfortunate results. When, for instance, her influence in India was at its height, she issued orders that all hospital windows should be invariably kept open. The authorities, who knew what an open window in the hot weather meant, protested, but in vain; Miss Nightingale was incredulous. She knew nothing of the hot weather, but she did know the value of fresh air—from personal experience; the authorities were talking nonsense and the windows must be kept open all the year round. There was a great outcry from all the doctors in India, but she was firm; and for a moment it seemed possible that her terrible commands would have to be put into execution. Lord Lawrence, however, was Viceroy, and he was able to intimate to Miss Nightingale, with sufficient authority, that he himself had decided upon the question, and that his decision must stand, even against her own. Upon that, she gave way, but reluctantly and quite unconvinced; she was only puzzled by the unexpected weakness of Lord Lawrence. No doubt, if she had lived today, and if her experience had lain, not among cholera cases at Scutari but among yellow-fever cases in Panama, she would have declared fresh air a fetish, and would have maintained to her dying day that the only really effective way of dealing with disease was by the destruction of mosquitoes.

Yet her mind, so positive, so realistic, so ultra-practical, had its singular revulsions, its mysterious moods of mysticism and of doubt. At times, lying sleepless in the early hours, she fell into long strange agonised meditations, and then, seizing a pencil, she would commit to paper the confessions of her soul. The morbid longings of her pre-Crimean days came over her once more; she filled page after page with self-examination, self-criticism, self-surrender. "O Father," she wrote, "I submit, I resign myself, I accept with all my heart this stretching out of Thy hand to save me. . . . O how vain it is, the vanity of vanities, to live in men's thoughts instead of God's!" She was lonely, she was miserable. "Thou knowest that through all these horrible twenty years, I have been supported by the belief that I was working with Thee who wert bringing everyone, even our poor nurses, to perfection,"—and yet, after all, what was the result? Had not even she been an unprofitable servant? One night, waking suddenly, she saw, in the dim light of the night-lamp, tenebrous shapes upon the wall. The past rushed back upon her. "Am I she who once stood on that Crimean height?" she wildly asked—" 'The Lady with a lamp shall stand. . . .' The lamp shows me only my utter shipwreck."

She sought consolation in the writings of the Mystics and in a correspondence with Mr. Jowett. For many years the Master of Balliol acted as her spiritual adviser. He discussed with her in a series of enormous letters the problems of religion and philosophy; he criticised her writings on those subjects with the tactful sympathy of a cleric who was also a man of the world; and he even ventured to attempt at times to instil into her rebellious nature some of his own peculiar suavity. "I sometimes think," he told her, "that you ought seriously to consider how your work may be carried on, not with less energy, but in a calmer spirit. I am not blaming the past. . . . But I want the peace of God to settle on the future." He recommended her to spend her time no longer in "conflicts with Government offices," and to take up some literary work. He urged her to "work out her notion of Divine Perfection," in a series of essays for *Frazer's Magazine*. She did so; and the result was submitted to Mr. Froude, who pronounced the second essay to be "even more pregnant than the first. I cannot tell," he said, "how sanitary, with disordered intellects, the effects of such papers will be." Mr. Carlyle, indeed, used different language, and some remarks of his about a lost lamb bleating on the mountains having been unfortunately repeated to Miss Nightingale, all Mr. Jowett's suavity was required to keep the peace. In a letter of fourteen sheets, he turned her attention from this painful topic towards a discussion of Quietism. "I don't see why," said the Master of Balliol, "active life might not become a sort of passive life too." And then, he added, "I sometimes fancy there are possibilities of human character much greater than have been realised." She found such sentiments helpful, underlining them in blue pencil; and, in return, she assisted her friend with a long series of elaborate comments upon the Dialogues of Plato, most of which he embodied in the second edition of his translation. Gradually her interest became more personal; she told him never to work again after midnight, and he obeyed her. Then she helped him to draw up a special form of daily service for the College Chapel, with selections from the Psalms, under the heads of "God the Lord, God the Judge, God the Father, and God the Friend,"—though, indeed, this project was never realised; for the Bishop of Oxford disallowed the alterations, exercising his legal powers, on the advice of Sir Travers Twiss.

Their relations became intimate. "The spirit of the twenty-third psalm and the spirit of the nineteenth psalm should be united in our lives," Mr. Jowett said. Eventually, she asked him to do her a singular favour. Would he, knowing what he did of her religious views, come to London and administer to her the Holy Sacrament? He did not hesitate, and afterwards declared that he would always regard the occasion as a solemn event in his life. He was devoted to her; though the precise nature of his feelings towards her never quite transpired. Her feelings towards him were more mixed. At first, he was "that great and good man,"—"that true saint, Mr. Jowett"; but, as time went on, some gall was mingled with the balm; the acrimony of her nature asserted itself. She felt that she gave more sympathy than she received; she was exhausted, she was annoyed, by his conversation. Her tongue, one day, could not refrain from shooting out at him. "He comes to me, and he talks to me," she said, "as if I were someone else."

V

At one time she had almost decided to end her life in retirement, as a patient at St. Thomas's Hospital. But partly owing to the persuasions of Mr. Jowett, she changed her mind; for forty-five years she remained in South Street; and in South Street she died. As old age approached, though her influence with the official world gradually diminished, her activities seemed to remain as intense and widespread as before. When hospitals were to be built, when schemes of sanitary reform were in agitation, when wars broke out, she was still the adviser of all Europe. Still, with a characteristic self-assurance, she watched from her Mayfair bedroom over the welfare of India. Still, with an indefatigable enthusiasm, she pushed forward the work, which, perhaps, was nearer to her heart, more completely her own, than all the rest—the training of nurses. In her moments of deepest depression, when her greatest achievements seemed to lose their lustre, she thought of her nurses, and was comforted. The ways of God, she found, were strange indeed. "How inefficient I was in the Crimea," she noted. "Yet He has raised up from it trained nursing."

At other times she was better satisfied. Looking back, she was amazed by the enormous change which, since her early days, had come over the whole treatment of illness, the whole conception of public and domestic health—a change in which, she knew, she had played her part. One of her Indian admirers, the Aga Khan, came to visit her. She expatiated on the marvellous advances she had lived to see in the management of hospitals, in drainage, in ventilation, in sanitary work of every kind. There was a pause; and then, "Do you think you are improving?" asked the Aga Khan. She was a little taken aback, and said, "What do you mean by 'improving'?" He replied, "Believing more in God." She saw that he had a view of God which was different from hers. "A most interesting man," she noted after the interview; "but you could never teach him sanitation."

When old age actually came, something curious happened. Destiny, having waited very patiently, played a queer trick on Miss Nightingale. The benevolence and public spirit of that long life had only been equalled by its acerbity. Her virtue had dwelt in hardness, and she had poured forth her unstinted usefulness with a bitter smile upon her lips. And now the sarcastic years brought the proud woman her punishment. She was not to die as she had lived. The sting was to be taken out of her: she was to be made soft; she was to be reduced to compliance and complacency. The change came gradually, but at last it was unmistakable. The terrible commander who had driven Sidney Herbert to his death, to whom Mr. Jowett had applied the words of Homer, ἄμοτον μεμαυῖα—raging insatiably—now accepted small compliments with gratitude, and indulged in sentimental friendships with young girls. The author of "*Notes on Nursing*"—that classical compendium of the besetting sins of the sisterhood, drawn up with the detailed acrimony, the vindictive relish, of a Swift—now spent long hours in composing sympathetic Addresses to Probationers, whom she petted and wept over in turn. And, at the same time, there appeared a corresponding alteration in her physical mould. The thin, angular woman, with her haughty eye and her acrid mouth had vanished; and in her place was the rounded bulky form of a fat old lady, smiling all day long. Then something else became visible. The brain which had been steeled at Scutari was indeed, literally, growing soft. Senility—an ever more and more amiable senility—descended. Towards the end, consciousness itself grew lost in a roseate haze, and melted into nothingness. It was just then, three years before her death, when she was eighty-seven years old (1907), that those in authority bethought them that the opportune moment had come for bestowing a public honour on Florence Nightingale. She was offered the Order of Merit. That Order, whose roll contains, among other distinguished names, those of Sir Laurence Alma Tadema and Sir Edward Elgar, is remarkable chiefly for the fact that, as its title indicates, it is bestowed because its recipient deserves it, and for no other reason. Miss Nightingale's representatives accepted the honour, and her name, after a lapse of many years, once more appeared in the Press. Congratulations from all sides came pouring in. There was a universal burst of enthusiasm—a final revivification of the ancient myth. Among her other admirers, the German Emperor took this opportunity of expressing his feelings towards her. "His Majesty," wrote the German Ambassador, "having just brought to a close a most enjoyable stay in the beautiful neighbourhood of your old home near Romsey, has commanded me to present you with some flowers as a token of his esteem." Then, by Royal command, the Order of Merit was brought to South Street, and there was a little ceremony of presentation. Sir Douglas Dawson, after a short speech, stepped forward, and handed the insignia of the Order to Miss Nightingale. Propped up by pillows, she dimly recognised that some compliment was being paid her. "Too kind—too kind," she murmured; and she was not ironical.

JAMES BOSWELL

It would be difficult to find a more shattering refutation of the lessons of cheap morality than the life of James Boswell. One of the most extraordinary successes in the history of civilization was achieved by an idler, a lecher, a drunkard, and a snob. Nor was this success of that sudden explosive kind which is frequent enough with youthful genius—the inspired efflorescence of a Rimbaud or a Swinburne; it was essentially the product of long years of accumulated energy; it was the supreme expression of an entire life. Boswell triumphed by dint of abandoning himself, through fifty years, to his instincts. The example, no doubt, is not one to be followed rashly. Self-indulgence is common, and Boswells are rare. The precise character of the rarity we are now able, for the first time, to estimate with something like completeness. Boswell's nature and inner history cannot be fully understood from the works published by himself. It is only in his letters that the whole man is revealed. Professor

Tinker, by collecting together Boswell's correspondence and editing it with scholarly exactitude, has done a great service to English literature.[1] There is, in fact, only one fault to be found with this admirable book. Professor Tinker shows us more of Boswell than any previous editor, but he does not show us all that he might. Like the editors of Walpole's Letters and Pepys's Diary, while giving himself credit for rehabilitating the text of his author, he admits in the same breath that he has mutilated it. When will this silly and barbarous prudery come to an end?

Boswell's career was completely dominated by his innate characteristics. Where they came from it is impossible to guess. He was the strangest sport: the descendant of Scotch barons and country gentlemen, the son of a sharp lowland lawyer, was an artist, a spendthrift, a buffoon, with a passion for literature, and without any dignity whatever. So he was born, and so he remained; life taught him nothing—he had nothing to learn; his course was marked out, immutably, from the beginning. At the age of twenty-three he discovered Dr. Johnson. A year later he was writing to him, at Wittenberg, "from the tomb of Melancthon": "My paper rests upon the gravestone of that great and good man. . . . At this tomb, then, my ever dear and respected friend! I vow to thee an eternal attachment." The rest of Boswell's existence was the history of that vow's accomplishment. But his connection with Dr. Johnson was itself only the crowning instance of an overwhelming predisposition, which showed itself in a multitude of varied forms. There were other great men, for instance—there was Mr. Wilkes, and General Paoli, and Sir David Dalrymple. One of Professor Tinker's most delightful discoveries is a series of letters from the youthful Boswell to Jean-Jacques Rousseau, in which all the writer's most persistent qualities—his literary skill, his psychological perspicacity, his passion for personalities, and his amazing aptitude for self-revelation—are exquisitely displayed. "Dites-moi," he asked the misanthropic sentimentalist, "ne ferai-je bien de m'appliquer véritablement à la musique, jusques à un certain point? Dites-moi

[1] *Letters of James Boswell.* Collected and edited by Chauncy Brewster Tinker. 2 vols. (Oxford: Clarendon Press.)

quel doit être mon instrument. C'est tard je l'avoue. Mais n'aurai-je le plaisir de faire un progrès continuel, et ne serai-je capable d'adoucir ma vieillesse par les sons de ma lyre?" Rousseau was completely melted. The elder Pitt, however, was made of sterner stuff. When Boswell appeared before him in the costume of a Corsican chieftain, "Lord Chatham," we are told, "smiled, but received him very graciously in his Pompous manner"—and there the acquaintance ended; in spite of Boswell's modest suggestion that the Prime Minister should "honour me now and then with a letter. . . . To correspond with a Paoli and with a Chatham is enough to keep a young man ever ardent in the pursuit of virtuous fame."

Fame—though perhaps it was hardly virtuous—Boswell certainly attained; but his ardent pursuit of it followed the track of an extraordinary zigzag which could never have had anything in common with letters from Lord Chatham. His own letters to his friend Temple lay bare the whole unique peregrination, from start to finish. To confess is the desire of many; but it is within the power of few. A rare clarity of vision, a still rarer candour of expression—without these qualities it is vain for a man to seek to unburden his heart. Boswell possessed them in the highest degree; and, at the same time, he was untroubled by certain other qualities, which, admirable though they be in other connections, are fatal for this particular purpose. He had no pride, no shame, and no dignity. The result was that a multitude of inhibitions passed him by. Nevertheless he was by no means detached. His was not the method of the scientific observer, noting his introspections with a cold exactness—far from it; he was intimately fascinated by everything to do with himself—his thoughts, his feelings, his reactions; and yet he was able to give expression to them all with absolute ingenuousness, without a shade of self-consciousness, without a particle of reserve. Naturally enough the picture presented in such circumstances is full of absurdities, for no character which had suppressed its absurdities could possibly depict itself so. Boswell was *ex hypothesi* absurd: it was his absurdity that was the essential condition of his consummate art.

It was in the description of his love affairs that this truly marvellous capacity found its fullest scope. The succession of his passions, with all their details, their variations, their agitations, and their preposterousnesses, fill the letters to Temple (a quiet clergyman in the depths of Devonshire) with a constant effervescence of delight. One progresses with wonderful exhilaration from Miss W——t ("just such a young lady as I could wish for the partner of my soul") to Zelide ("upon my soul, Temple, I must have her"), and so to the Signora, and the Moffat woman ("can I do better than keep a dear infidel for my hours of Paphian bliss?"), and the Princess ("here every flower is united"), and the gardener's daughter, and Mrs. D., and Miss Bosville, and La Belle Irlandaise ("just sixteen, formed like a Grecian nymph, with the sweetest countenance, full of sensibility, accomplished, with a Dublin education"), and Mrs. Boswell ("I am fully sensible of my happiness in being married to so excellent a woman"), and Miss Silverton ("in the fly with me, an amiable creature who has been in France. I can unite little fondnesses with perfect conjugal love"), and Miss Bagnal ("*a Ranelagh girl*, but of excellent principles, in so much that she reads prayers to the servants in her father's family, every Sunday evening. 'Let me see such a woman,' cried I"), and Miss Milles ("*d'une certaine âge*, and with a fortune of £10,000"), and—but the catalogue is endless. These are the pages which record the sunny hours of Boswell's chequered day. Light and warmth sparkle from them; but, even in the noon of his happiness, there were sudden clouds. Hypochondria seized him; he would wake in the night "dreading annihilation, or being thrown into some horrible state of being." His conscience would not leave him alone; he was attacked by disgraceful illnesses; he felt "like a man ordered for ignominious execution"; he feared that his infidelities to Mrs. Boswell would not be excused hereafter. And then his vital spirits rushed to his rescue, and the shadow fled. Was he not the friend of Paoli? Indeed he was; and he was sitting in a library forty feet long, dressed in green and gold. The future was radiant. "My warm imagination looks forward with great complacency on the sobriety, the healthfulness, and the worth of my future life." As for his infidelities, were they so reprehensible after all? "Concubinage is almost universal. If it was *morally* wrong, why was it permitted to the pious men under the Old Testament? Why did our Saviour never say a word against it?"

As his life went on, however, the clouds grew thicker and more menacing, and the end was storm and darkness. The climax came with the death of his wife. Boswell found himself at the age of fifty alone in the world with embarrassed fortunes, a family of young children to bring up, and no sign that any of the "towering hopes" of his youth had been realized. Worse still, he had become by this time a confirmed drunkard. His self-reproaches were pitiable; his efforts at amendment never ceased; he took a vow of sobriety under "a venerable yew"; he swore a solemn oath that he would give up drinking altogether—that he would limit himself to four glasses of wine at dinner and a pint afterwards; but it was all in vain. His way of life grew more and more disorderly, humiliating, and miserable. If he had retired to Scotland, and lived economically on his estate, he might have retrieved his position; but that was what he could not do; he could not be out of London. His ambitions seemed to multiply with his misfortunes. He exchanged the Scotch bar for the English, and lost all his professional income at a blow. He had wild hopes of becoming a Member of Parliament, if only he toadied Lord Lonsdale sufficiently; and Lord Lonsdale promised much, asked him to his castle, made a butt of him, hid his wig, was gravely concerned, and finally threw him off after "expressing himself in the most degrading manner in presence of a low man from Carlisle and one of his menial servants." Consolations now were few indeed. It was something, no doubt, to be able to go to Court. "I was the *great man* at the late drawing-room in a suit of imperial blue lined with rose-coloured silk, and ornamented with rich gold-wrought buttons. What a motley scene is life!" And at Eton, where he was "carried to dine at the Fellows' table," it was pleasant enough to find that in spite of a Scotch education one could still make a creditable figure. "I had my classical quotations very ready." But these were fleeting gleams. "Your kindness to me," he burst out to Temple, in April, 1791, "fairly makes me shed tears. Alas, I fear that my constitutional melancholy, which returns in such dismal fits and is now aggravated by the loss of my valuable wife, must prevent me from any permanent felicity in this life. I snatch *gratifications;* but have no *comfort,* at least very little. . . . I get bad rest in the night, and then I brood over all my complaints—the *sickly mind* which I have had from my early years—the disappointment of my hopes of success in life—the irrevocable separation between me and that excellent woman who was my cousin, my friend, and my wife—the embarrassment of my affairs—the disadvantage to my children in having so wretched a father—nay, the want of *absolute certainty* of being happy after death, the *sure prospect* of which is *frightful.* No more of this."

The tragedy was closing; but it was only superficially a sordid one. Six weeks later the writer of these lines published, in two volumes quarto, the *Life of Dr. Johnson.* In reality, Boswell's spirit had never failed. With incredible persistence he had carried through the enormous task which he had set himself thirty years earlier. Everything else was gone. He was burnt down to the wick, but his work was there. It was the work of one whose appetite for life was insatiable—so insatiable that it proved in the end self-destructive. The same force which produced the *Life of Johnson* plunged its author into ruin and desperation. If Boswell had been capable of retiring to the country and economizing we should never have heard of him. It was Lord Lonsdale's butt who reached immortality.

EMIL LUDWIG

"CHARACTER IS FATE"—what a fitting motto for a Uniform Edition of *The Works of Emil Ludwig*. For character, to Herr Ludwig, is clearly and overwhelmingly the determining factor in every man's destiny—at least, since chance may affect external events, in every man's spiritual and intellectual destiny. There the modern biographer's first duty is to examine the consistency of a man's character *per se*, "the personality almost devoid of temporal coördinates, considering the volume, intensity, and resistance of its vital forces, the restless fluid of its emotional configurations, and the balance between its impulse towards action and its repression through precept. Whereas our fathers asked, 'How did the individual harmonize with his world?' our first question is, 'Does he harmonize with himself?' Questions of success and responsibility have been shifted from the environment back to the individual, so that the analysis which was formerly expended upon the milieu now seeks to penetrate within." How Herr Ludwig reached these interesting conclusions his own life may possibly show.

His family name was Cohn; his grandfather was an important iron and steel man of Upper Silesia and his father, Professor Hermann Ludwig Cohn, a celebrated eye-specialist of Breslau. His father dropped the last name for his children at their birth to spare them needless abuse in a country where anti-Semitism has always run high. Emil Ludwig, born in 1881, was intended for a legal career and, though not a very promising student at Breslau and Heidelberg, actually took his Doctorate of Jurisprudence. His thesis, on "Emotional Murder," suggests the psychology back of the sentences quoted above. For some time, stimulated by his father's contributions to public health, he studied social problems, but until the age of twenty-five he was uncongenially occupied in a coal business.

He had, however, become interested in the drama when still a boy of fifteen, and before he was thirty he had written a dozen plays in verse, six of which have been staged. The reader of Ludwig's biographies will not be astonished to learn that the themes of these early plays are Napoleon, Tristan and Isolde, the Borgias, and the like. By that time love, literary ambition, and an acquaintance with Gerhart Hauptmann had determined him, once for all, to be a writer; a multitude of motives had made him a Swiss citizen; and the encouragement of the poet Richard Dehmel (whom he depicts in *Genius and Character*) had confirmed him in the psychological study of great men's characters and in the particular biographical *genre* he has made his own.

In 1911 his mind was stimulated by a table conversation between his father and Prince Bismarck's personal physician and he at once set about dramatizing the Iron Chancellor's life. As later with Goethe and his other subjects, Herr Ludwig first examined carefully and with passionate ardor all the portraits, busts, letters—particularly the letters, which suggested a prose style—and came, as he says, by a purely optical sense to certain conclusions, which he set forth in a preliminary sketch. Later he read every word he could find to gain a truer and deeper idea of the man. He published a huge biography of Bismarck (1926) and a trilogy of plays on his career (1927). When all this scholarly and creative work was accomplished it was found to bear out exactly the author's original intuitive characterization. The same is true of *Goethe: The History of a Man* (1920), for which the study of one hundred and fifty volumes of Goethe's works only reenforced Herr Ludwig's first impression. He has pursued the same method in *Napoleon* (1924), *William Hohenzollern* (1925), *Genius and Character* (1926), *The Son of Man* (1928), *Lincoln* (1929), *Three Titans: Michelangelo, Rembrandt, Beethoven* (1930), *Schliemann of Troy* (1931), *Nine Etched from Life: Leaders of Europe* (1934) and a forthcoming study of Masaryk. More recently he has been able to place greater reliance on his intuitive insight by meeting personally his living subjects. He has written novels, a study of the causes of the War, a book of Mediterranean travel sketches, an interview with Mussolini, and his own reminiscences. In short, Herr Ludwig has turned all his experience and study into books. His journalistic work, which began when he was the London correspondent for the *Berliner Tageblatt* before the War and continued during the War when, as a pacifist and a neutral, he observed and wrote for the German press in various parts of Europe, has in later years appeared more and more to fuse with his writing of biography.

"What chiefly interests me," says Emil Ludwig, "is the interaction between genius and character." For him, as for his master Plutarch, "the most trivial habit will often suggest the interpretation for some major trait of character." To carry out the work entailed by this method he holds that the biographer "must have more than the knowledge of a period: he must be versed in the study of man, must be a psychologist and an analyst. He must be skilled, through both intuition and training, in interpreting a character by the symptoms of its behavior. . . . Yet a knowledge of genius is demanded also—and herein lies the most formidable difficulty of all. To understand and interpret a poet, one must have the creative gift; to discuss the man of the world, a taste for worldly living is necessary; the biography of a statesman demands political insight; an understanding of women is called into play when an erotic character is analyzed—in a word, when writing of genius one must draw upon resources in himself which are akin to its dominant characteristics."

Herr Ludwig has not been uniformly successful in matching his own resources to the requirements of his subjects, but he has used this method of analysis with great independence of other living biographers. He does not possess, or seek, the cool detachment of Strachey (who, himself, is not always impartial), and he does not mind admitting that he expects his portraits to serve as examples and warnings to youth. This "impure" biographical motive, however, grows logically out of his thoroughly modern assumption that "great men are not gods, that they have been gripped by the same all-too-human passions, repressions, and encumbrances as afflict every other mortal, and that they have fought through, regardless, to their goals." After all, he may not be so very far from André Maurois, who says, "A great biography must not have a moral aim, but it is good that we should hear from time to time the trumpet call of Destiny." This emphasis upon the individual's essential character results sometimes in rather exaggerated "close-ups," in contrast to the populous panoramas of Philip Guedalla. Herr Ludwig's tendency toward a Freudian reading of the human heart, as in the following study of Leonardo (*Genius and Character*), may be profitably compared with the method of Gamaliel Bradford. In this piece, too, is visible Herr Ludwig's practice of moving "from intuitive prepossession to evidential conviction," as well as his fondness for dramatic scenes and for epigrams. Leonardo was a genius and a titan, if there ever was one; and the spectacle of titans and geniuses wrestling with their Daemons is Emil Ludwig's favorite sport.

LEONARDO DA VINCI

Once I have learned how to die,
then I shall know how to live.

HIS LIFE was a dialogue with nature.

Often this dialogue may have been obscured by the silence of his eternal loneliness; at other times it was revealed in brief notes, in comparisons, deductions, observations, and notations. Frequently it attained expression in formal works —yet with a few exceptions these too remained fragmentary or soon lost their power of survival. Since he valued things purely as experiments, and since neither ambition nor jealousy nor the sheer feel of mastery could induce him to mirror himself in his works, nothing now is left but a few tables, a painted wall, a few dozen drawings, and the diaries with their 5,000 pages or so of notes.

These papers, the documents of an essayist, were soon as thoroughly enshrouded in legend as the works of a mystic. Mystery seemed latent in these reliques of a creative life—and the less tangibly his life was revealed, the more readily it took on the compensatory veil of mystery, as with the life of a prophet. Later generations told of his riding through the streets like a prince, on a white, gold-bridled horse, wrapped in flowing silks, and preceded by the laughter of beautiful boys, his pupils and minions: a symbol of the artist in the heyday of that era.

The truth is simpler and deeper. The life-long dialogue between himself and nature exacted of him a profound loneliness—for this sort of dialogue is not only a dialogue; it is also a monologue. In these countless musings of his note-books, which almost seem as though they had been washed up from alien shores and which whole centuries have labored to decipher, he admonishes himself repeatedly: "Remember . . . wrong! right! mistake! . . . That is a beautiful possibility, worth further investigation! . . . How then would you account for the presence of gravel on high mountains? . . . And do you have all the necessary anatomical data?" And in order that his dialogue with himself and nature might be made less accessible, he resorted to mirror writing.

For Leonardo was both a student of nature and a prophet—and this duality of his character produced marked contrasts which had an important effect upon his work. Without his scientific eye—his observation—he would never have become the greatest pathfinder of the new Occident. Without his mystical gaze—his vision—he could not have used his knowledge to make himself, we might say, the prehistoric discoverer of all that a later era worked out patiently and laboriously. For a thousand years, there has been no other prophetic temperament except Goethe so richly endowed with this intellectual duality, this pliant realism. Leonardo occupies the relatively easier position of groping prophetically into regions not yet explored. Goethe, likewise an observer and an essayist, but with the mania of the genuine collector, was better able to coördinate his discoveries. And although he too left very little finished work behind him, the thousands of pages of notes have rounded themselves off into a consistent interpretation, so that his results become more tangible. Goethe produced more, and carried more of his works through to completion. In many-sidedness Leonardo remains unmatched.

But as his work was never assembled or completed, his endowments were much greater than his results. He did plan to collect his notes into books, arranging them by subject, such as a treatise on water, on mechanics, on painting, and so forth. The whole was to be called: On the Things of Nature. But his curiosity drove him restlessly on from decade to decade; a roving and vigorous pioneer, he had none of Goethe's resignation, restraint, and punctiliousness. Thus the tangible results were few, everything remaining in the stage of theme and hypothesis. Like a sportive god, this genius took up the works of nature one by one, looked at them, and laid them down again—and thus Leonardo himself remained hardly more than a sport of nature, almost without predecessors, and wholly without successors.

He preferred to be known as an inventor—and he did maintain his interest in inventions throughout his entire life. As a young man he wanted to raise the baptistery at Florence and set it on a new base of marble. At thirty he offered his services to the Duke of Milan as an inventor, to construct for him pontoons and chariots, galleries and mortars. Then he built tanks, testudines with a double covering, dray-horses inside the shell and embrasures in the cope. At the same time he applied himself to the problem of canalizing the Ticino and connecting it with the lakes. At fifty he wanted to transform Florence into an ideal city, planned the canalization of today, and proposed streets with an upper and lower level connected by steps, the upper level for promenade, the lower for commercial traffic. He invented modern chimneys, self-closing doors, and roasting spits turned by currents of warm air.

Meanwhile he renewed an old plan for canalizing the Arno

from Pisa, to do away with the silt deposits in the river by the use of embankments. In his old age he laid out a network of canals in France for the Saône. Four hundred years later, the Ticino, the Arno, and the Saône are canalized very nearly as he had proposed.

In countless drawings he designed hydroplanes and the first parachute, diving bells and the submarine. "Why not describe my way of remaining under water? Because of the evil nature of men who would destroy their enemies on the bottom of the sea by boring through the hulls of ships and drowning the passengers. But what I disclose here cannot do damage: The mouth of the tube through which I breathe would reach above the water, sustained by cork or inflated skins." He tried to use steam as a means of propulsion, designed the first steam cannon, made powder, constructed a glass oven and a still. He built machines for sawing, spinning, shearing, washing, pottery-making. He constructed artesian wells, all sorts of mills, scales, the concave mirror, and the pendulum.

These were all inventions of a self-taught man who began at thirty teaching himself Latin and mathematics. For this reason he was the enemy of all the academic humanists of his day, who looked down upon him "because I am not educated,—I, an inventor!" And he felt scorn, most often a gentle scorn, for all sophists and philosophers. For an experience, an empirical experiment, always marked the starting point of Leonardo's dialogues with nature.

While planning the flying machine: "In order to learn how to fly, you must first understand the winds. And the winds are explained by studying the undulations of water." Instead of theorizing with the humanists over the problem "Is warmth a substance?" he drew his conclusions by comparing the weight of an object when at white heat with its weight when cold. He observed the accelerated motion of a falling body and found the law—which he was not looking for—two centuries before Newton. Employing engines of war to lift weights, he constructed the block-and-tackle, and was the first man since Archimedes to record the principles of the lever. In drawings which he made for the study of difficult problems in physics, he developed the law of the conservation of energy. When wandering over the Maritime Alps he discovered mussels on the mountain tops and founded the science of paleontology—then, he added what he knew of stratified rock, of fossils, and of tidal movements, all of which brought him back to astrological studies of an earlier period.

Like golden fish, laws leap out to him unbidden from the cascades of his experiments. Before Galileo he discovered the law of virtual velocity. He stated the principles of gyration and the vortex, and the law of communicating vessels. He was the founder of hydrostatics and of the entire science of hydraulics. He understood the undulatory motion of the sea, and applied its principles of transmission and reflection to sound and light; he measured sound-waves, explained the echo and the vibration of overtones four hundred years before Helmholtz and Herz. Before Goethe he inaugurated comparative anatomy in a book with red chalk drawings of bodies which he himself had dissected; he compared the tongue of the woodpecker and the jaw of a crocodile with the corresponding parts of the human body and indicated a common prototype. He explained the eye as a camera obscura, recognized the functions of the lens and of the retina and the mechanics of sight. All medieval piety and traditionalism had vanished. The first man of a new era, Leonardo had faith solely in experimentation. He, and not Bacon, was the founder of the experimental method.

Yet while these *human* eyes were seeing and recognizing everything that nature put before them, he also possessed the clairvoyance of the *prophet.* In the midst of matters totally different, he suddenly wrote down in large and solemn letters: "*Il sole non si muove.*" And there is a jotting elsewhere: "In your teachings you must show that the earth is a star, like the moon: in this way you will establish the world's splendor." Written fifty years before the book of Copernicus, and without explanation or proof.

Like Goethe, he observed and recorded everything that his

eye lighted upon: the chimes in Siena, the fountain of Rimini, the form of the carts in the Romagna. And again like Goethe, his diction and his thoughts mount suddenly to distant heights. Leaving the mathematical formula, the business of numbers and roots, he would soar gradually into the air of metaphor, like a hydroplane rising from the surface of the water. "Weight, by its own nature, perishes when it reaches the desired position. . . . Weight is material and force is spiritual. . . . If force yearns continually for flight and death, weight yearns for perpetuity. . . . Propulsion results from the death of motion, and motion from the death of force. . . . Force is born of restraint and dies of freedom—and the greater it is, the more rapidly it is consumed. . . . Whatever resists it, it expels with violence, wishing to destroy the very conditions of its existence, and in victory causing its own death."

From this high pantheistic outlook he then drops lightly back to the mechanics of the physical world which he had, we might say, begrudgingly abandoned. Again and again, however, the inspired accents of the prophet interrupt the concise conclusions of the investigator. He was the first to explain with exactness the function of the pupil—then suddenly, in the midst of his notes, he adds: "O great necessity! With the highest wisdom, compelling all effects to participate in their causes! Who would believe that such a fraction of a second could encompass the transformations of the universe? Thus human thought rises to the contemplation of the divine."

This scientific nature-worship betrays the dual aspect of his character. He angrily derided the necromancers, spiritists, and ghost-seers of his day. "Take no miracles on trust; always look for causes. . . . Those who avoid the absolute certainty of mathematics must live in confusion and will never be able to silence the endless clamor of the sophists." Words of scorn flare up at the mention of alchemy, the music of the spheres, and *perpetuum mobile*. He laughs at monks who live on long-dead saints. The deluge was for him a purely geological phenomenon.

But the same pages contain fantastic prophecies which he has heard, half-burlesqued and half-allegorical accounts of plagues, disasters, and crucifixions. He described at length a giant in Asia Minor—where Leonardo never traveled, by the way, despite the legend. One day he painted on his tablets imaginary azure-blue cliffs and valleys, grottoes and rocks; and the next, on Monte Rosa, he explains the blue color of the sky in a manner which was to delight old Goethe three hundred years afterwards. Goethe, who understood Leonardo profoundly, wrote of him (in a remote passage): "As an artist who perceived and apprehended nature immediately, thinking of the phenomenon itself and penetrating it, he always found the truth."

And suddenly, without any connection, there breaks forth from Leonardo's monologue the boldest sentence which ever mortal man has cast to the world: "I am discovering for mankind the first or perhaps the second reason of their existence."

Despite this constant interplay, he did not seem at all disturbed, as Goethe was, by this double life. On the contrary, it produced in him a state of equipoise, as his life, his portrait, and his art testify.

The vicissitudes of his era had some effect upon his career: he rose, fell, and recovered. But aside from this, his outward personal life was uneventful, and his inner life too was lived without irruptions. One single day of his many years is wrapped in secrecy, and it in turn conditions all his secrets. This is the day of his birth.

In a century of famous bastards, among the hills near Empoli, fate chose a certain young traveling Florentine as the man who was to make a peasant girl the mother of a genius. No one knows her name or her history. The young man, later a fashionable lawyer in Florence, married her off with her child to some unknown peasant. He was the father of nine more sons, legitimate and forgotten—and she perhaps bore several more children.

After his rightful father adopted him, she must have fallen almost completely out of touch with Leonardo, for not a single one of the many entries in his note-books indicates that he knew his mother. Also, he received nothing from his father—and in later years he entered into litigation with his brothers over the inheritance. Finally he provided for them in his will. All the details of his race are lost; but one thing survives, the name of the village. And so a maid brought this poor place immortality: Vinci resounds through the centuries because Leonardo was born there.

Until the age of thirty he roamed, unknown; like all the artists of his time, he was looking for a prince to whom he could offer his services and who would give him in return the protection of his house. Then he found Lodovico Sforza, the powerful Duke of Milan, called Il Moro. In a high-sounding document, Leonardo offered himself particularly as an expert in military engineering and an inventor of weapons. He also wrote that he could build houses and conduct water, that he knew how to model in marble, bronze or clay—and finally that he could paint and play the lute.

Yet the Duke first commissioned him to do an equestrian statue in honor of his brother. After this, with a few interruptions he kept Leonardo engaged for the next twenty years on all the things in which the Florentine—since he passed as a Florentine—had boasted his abilities.

When the King of France conquered the Duke and threw him into prison, Leonardo promptly transferred his allegiance to the victor, merely writing on the cover of one of his diaries the words: "The Duke has lost country, property, and freedom; he could not complete any of his plans." Alongside is a passage: "Rhodes has in the interior 5,000 houses." Someone had told him this on the same day.

For sale to any master who could pay the price, like every *condottiere* of the age, he now went over to the man of the hour, France's ally—for this was just after the turn of the century, when Caesar Borgia was at the height of his power. Leonardo became "general engineer for all fortifications." After Borgia's campaign the city of Florence, which was at war with Pisa, sent him into the field for the purpose of diverting the course of the Arno from Pisa towards Livorno. But corruption and stupidity defeated him, and he attempted unsuccessfully to live again in Milan, from whence he was recalled by Florence.

A niggardly republic, however, could not suffice for Leonardo; he needed some generous prince if he was to pursue his work unhampered. So at this moment fate sent him a more powerful patron whose wishes the Florentine councilors had to respect: for the next few years, until the beginning of his sixties, Leonardo was engaged in the service of the French king at Milan. Then political upheavals again deprived him of his haven. In the war between the pope and France, the son of Il Moro regained his father's duchy of Milan. Leonardo again took sides with the opposing party, and went to Rome, where Leo Medici, the friend of genius, had become pope. By his mechanical artifice, which he palmed off as alchemy, he enthralled the handsome decadent Giuliano, the pope's brother. But Raphael continually threatened to eclipse him.

Once again history took a turn in his favor. King Louis was succeeded in Paris by King Francis, the nephew of Giuliano. Being determined to despoil his ally Italy of everything transportable, he also took with him the old enchanter who might still produce almost any sort of mechanism. With a title and a good salary, he established Leonardo in a castle of the Touraine, and here, at Cloux, the aging man spent his last years in perfect freedom and without the slightest feeling of homesickness for his fatherland.

As he surveys the whole of life, he encompasses both belief and doubt, humility and pride, in the profound words: "Our life is subject to heaven, but heaven is subject to reason."

His life was uneventful in an age of great unrest, and clement at a time of pronounced inclemency. He was consistently successful in living the sort of existence which he preferred. For he was interested in the contemporary situation only in so far as it affected his shelter, food, and security; he felt no attachments of friendship or politics. Consequently he placed his ability at the service of one Maecenas after another, with the complete and naïve cynicism of his century. He had no desire to enter the combat; he wanted to be an observer. While engaged as a military engineer, his feelings were wholly pacifistic. He arraigned men for their warlike frenzy, but finally assembled all his impressions of the horror into a single work: "The Battle of the Standard." It is immaterial to him who conquers and who is defeated. And while drawing with punctilious fidelity the body of his patron's assassin as it swung on the gallows, he wrote no damning epitaph on the margin, but a list giving the colors of the hanged man's garments.

When in the pay of Sforza he designed the statue for a Sforza; and when Il Moro was defeated, he altered his plans for the same monument so that it might suit the commander who had defeated Il Moro. He left Milan at the time when his master of the last twenty years was about to fall and lose his realm. For after all, what did he owe the Duke! While the Duke's fate was in the balance and no one knew what would happen next, Leonardo was studying winds and waterspouts and investigating the nature of sea waves. "For kindly nature sees to it that you may find something to learn everywhere in the world."

Then in the service of Florence he depicted the severest defeat of Milan on the wall of the Hall of Council. Three times he transferred his allegiance to the victorious enemy. He knew how to use tact and flattery with rulers whose goodwill involved his own well-being. He appealed to the naïve taste of the young French king on his entrance into Rome by making a comical lion which took a few steps forward and then opened its breast with its paws, allowing the Bourbon lily to fall from its bosom. By this absurd invention, it seems, he won the king's favor and bettered his own position.

He advised young artists to remain polite when being censured. He, who scattered the profoundest bits of wisdom throughout his notebooks couched in succinct epigrams, outlines half a dozen letters to his master accusing his assistants of frivolity. Even in his sketch-books he takes precautions, and they do not stop at mirror writing. When writing against the eating of meat, he is afraid "to say more, since it is not permissible to speak the truth."

Yet in all walks of life he was borne up by his sense of dignity. "The master gives commands; the slave carries them into effect." That is the form in which his pride sanctions the essayistic nature of his work. He never gave his patron the proper title, but addressed him as Signore. With the intense pride of a man at peace with himself, this rebel wrote in the midst of a thousand revolutionary jottings: "I will let the crowned books stay, because they contain the highest truth."

Handsome and well-groomed, obviously careful to preserve a distinguished appearance, he loved the body and laid emphasis on the matter of dress. "Coarse people of bad habits and shallow judgments do not deserve so beautiful an instrument, such a complex anatomical equipment, as the human body. They should merely have a sack for taking in food and letting it out again, for they are nothing but an alimentary canal." For such fastidious reasons he disapproved of sculpture; he did not like to "be forced to stand, dusty and dirty, while the painter sits comfortably and quietly at his work, using beautiful colors and a brush as light as a feather. He can dress as well as he pleases; the room is filled with lovely paintings, and often there are musicians sitting about, and people to read aloud." Similarly he was fond of animals and would not eat them. He bought caged birds in the market and freed them immediately afterwards.

In youth he may have affected and exaggerated these natural traits. He may, when he had money, have ridden on horseback through the streets with friends and servants, to give the people a display and give himself the feel of splendor. But in the countless jottings to do with money and expenditures which keep turning up in his diaries—and most of these go back only to the beginning of his thirties—there is no mention of horses and luxury. Even the handwriting, which is precious and fantastic only in the oldest books, becomes plainer.

In his fifties he rescued from the vicissitudes of war his entire wealth, 600 gold florins, the savings of seventeen years, depositing it in the savings bank at Florence, drawing sums from time to time, paying debts and lending to friends. Everything definite which we know about his public and private life indicates that during the latter half of his career, the period in which all his intellectual and artistic achievements took place, he lived a quiet, comfortable, and ordered existence, much like a distinguished stranger, for "only by being alone can you belong completely to yourself."

But when it was to his advantage his public dealings were strained and undependable; he acted as a Bohemian towards everyone who commissioned him to do work. Neither a sense of duty nor a desire for fame could drive him to complete a work, so that he hardly ever abided by his contracts; and since none of his contemporaries understood him, and least of all his biographer Vasari, no one who gave Leonardo a commission was ever satisfied with him.

Churches and individuals with whom he contracted to finish a painting within a definite period of time would give him gold florins, lodging, and wine as advance payment; he would begin work, and then he would not like it, or he grew bored with it; he would go away, and they would complain about him or even bring action against him.

When the city of Florence gave him, in his fifties, an important commission "for a beautiful work" to decorate a wall in the Signory, the city fathers were cautious in dealing with this untrustworthy man: they bound him to an agreement whereby, if he had not finished by a definite date, he should refund his monthly payments and surrender the cartoon to the city. But when the citizens paid him his gold in copper coins, he began to grumble. He could no longer lay eyes on the gigantic picture, which he was endangering by new technical methods; he wanted to return to Milan; he took leave of absence. The gonfalonier threatened him with a fine if he did not return. The matter came to court—whereupon the King of France appeared *ex machina* and the wishes of His Majesty prevailed.

He often got into difficulties with Il Moro as well. The remarkable thing is that they were on good terms for so long. A ruler who had risen to power by force, who feared a similar violent end, who was continually harassed and was continually making demands; a philosopher who was always equable and observant, but who was an inveterate experimenter and never brought his work to completion. As the equestrian statue, the "great horse," continued to remain in the stage of trials and models, the Duke hired another artist. But when he did not paint the *camerini* of his castle, and finally failed to finish the "Last Supper" in Santa Maria delle Grazie, their relations became strained. Already, for some time past, the Duke had assigned him, instead of money, the income from certain city gates and water rents which he was to procure for himself as best he could. "The painter made somewhat of a row today, and on account of this he has left," the Duke writes, but the painter notes: "First the benefices, afterwards the work, then the ingratitude, and finally these unseemly scenes." Yet they became reconciled—just as the Weimar Duke much later was to quarrel and become reconciled with his factotum. The Duke restored him to favor, gave him money, and a vineyard besides.

He took what was given him, and asked for what he needed. But in his book there is the murmur of his monologue: "Oh, do not place a low value upon me, I am not poor. He is poor whose wants are many."

There was no place in this life for passion. Leonardo moved through the *Secolo appassionato* with the perfect composure of a philosopher. His genius and his beauty, his association with the nobles, and the universality of his achievements put him in touch with the interesting women of his country; but none of those humanistic feminine epistles in which the society of that time discussed matters of love mentions his name, and there is no love story connected with this most fascinating of all Renaissance artists. In keeping with his narcissus-like monologue and his reserve, and with the sweetness of the characters in his paintings, he might be expected to show a predilection for male youth—and as a matter of fact there are documents and anecdotes bearing on Leonardo's interest in young boys.

Few of the records of his earlier years are dependable; but we do have reliable evidence that he was tried for the corrupting of an unruly boy and was only partially acquitted. And when his diaries, amidst all their macrocosmic and microcosmic questionings and answers, sketch the arabesque of his life, we see emerging everywhere from his pages those blond heads which his drawings and paintings have immortalized. For the most part they are students—and what curly locks this one has, and what a loquacious fellow that other one must have been. Between mathematical calculations of the pendulum, along with drawings of sluices and basins, we can decipher how at Rome, instead of polishing his concave mirror for him, they ran off with the Swiss guardsmen of the pope, or on a bird hunt, or to a drinking bout. And then again, immediately adjoining: "Ask how skating is done in Flanders."

Generous, hospitable as an oriental, he gave the beautiful lads what he had, made them presents of his best pages, which they signed and sold. And when they stole from him, he stood for it, acting as though he had noticed nothing. But he devotes an entire page to a list of the things which a certain Giacomo pilfered from him and his friends, and to an account of what this boy had cost him in clothes, shoes, and belts. And along the edge, in all clarity, we read: "Thievish, deceitful, selfish, greedy. . . . How much does the boy cost me?"

As he and they grew older, most of them gradually drifted away. Only two—Andrea Salaino and Melzi—remained with him, as comrades, helpers, and friends.

And suddenly, in the later monologues he writes: "Intellectual passion drives away all lusts."

Leonardo's art flows from the sources of this sublime eroticism.

Since painting was by no means a monomania with him, or even a predominant interest, he could at some other period in the history of art have become a musician, even had he not constructed instruments of silver and excelled as a flute-player. The truth is that no other painters painted so musically as Correggio and Leonardo, the two most delicate eroticists of the south.

But there is still a closer path from scientist to painter: the path of observation. For his pure experimentation was no less pronouncedly visual than his painting. In this also he resembled Goethe, whose visual perceptions disturbed the equilibrium of his genius for twenty years and struggled to make of him a painter. Leonardo was always searching for pictures, precisely because he was searching for knowledge. Constantly, in his youth and in old age, he was seen with a sketch-book in his belt. When he began his work on anatomy by listing four ways of registering emotions through movement and expression, here the scientist was almost a painter. And when, according to the testimony of a contemporary, he followed odd-looking people halfway across the city in order to get their features accurately, here the painter is very nearly the scientist.

There is a passage in the monologues: "Giovannina, fantastic face, lives in Santa Catherina, in the hospital." To paint a character from the Bible, for an old man, a beggar, or a shepherd, he would go to the public squares and the drinking dens, where he would be most likely to meet such persons. And he would draw a type or an animal from observation a hundred times before turning to his picture to fix it there for all time. He is said to have brought home peasants from the market and got them drunk in order to draw them. At the same time he was looking for laws; while studying the facial traits, he recorded the transitions in the closing and opening of the eyelid, the wrinkling of the nose, the pouting of the lips, in laughing, sneezing, yawning, cramps, perspiration, weariness, hunger—always he looked for the cause behind the expression which he was painting.

While Michael Angelo, at times even under the same roof, was covering enormous walls with the colossi of his imagination, giving them their ultimate form and leaving them thus to glitter or pale through the centuries; and while Raphael's skillful eclectic fingers were at work to capture the absolute in beauty, Leonardo was the essayist, the relativist, a tester and a player. He declined to paint alfresco or in tempera, since he could not interrupt such work for "the subtlest reflections," as he called them.

For when he painted, he must be able to abandon the oil picture suddenly whenever he felt a change of mood and the desire to study some aspect of nature elsewhere. From a cloister near Florence, which had ordered a Madonna of him and had been waiting several months for its completion, an ecclesiastic writes: "He is applying himself passionately to geometry, but he can't say a good word for the brush." Once—by the report of a

Milanese, who saw him busy on the "Last Supper"—he painted the whole day, beginning at sunrise and standing on his scaffold without food or drink. Then again, he would not appear for days, or he would sit before the canvas for a couple of hours, silent and meditative, and then would leave again. Or he came into the church at midday after a ride on horseback, heated and excited, touched one of the figures with two strokes of his brush, and vanished.

Since he was a pure intellect, and only occasionally attempted to reduce his observations to pictures rather than to laws, he never wholly mastered his medium. As an inventor, his struggles with matter were victorious; as a painter he was continually in retreat. It is as though the technologist in him refused to govern the musical precincts of his art. To be sure, he was continually immersed in the problems of his material. For his "Battle of the Standard" at Florence he mixed the coarsest stucco as a ground, lit a coal fire beneath it in order to dry it out; the whole began to sweat, his work perished beneath his hands—but he promptly turned his back on it and left it.

By his experiments with the ground-colors, he ruined a Madonna for a gentleman of the Vatican. And when as the first step in a work for Leo Medici, he began preparing the varnish by an involved process of distilling oils and herbs, the merry pope said: "Alas, you will never finish. You are thinking of the end before you have begun!" Similarly, he left both the principal works of Milan in an unfinished state. Even in his own days the "Last Supper" had begun to vanish into the wall as the result of one of his obdurate experiments with the mixing of oils. The gigantic statue, which stood in clay for years in the courtyard of the Castello, was never cast because he insisted that four furnaces should first be constructed for smelting the bronze. New wars intervened; Il Moro at times lacked money and at times interest. And so nothing was left of this work, on which he had been engaged intermittently for sixteen years, but a dilapidated model which drunken marksmen later demolished with their arrows.

"Without sound theories," he wrote to himself, "one cannot manage well in the hazards of painting." As an artist, Leonardo the technologist was a victim of his technique; but it seems that he was a willing victim, for since he always had a vision of the completed whole he could readily interrupt the incomplete experiment. Even the few pictures from his hand which we call completed, he himself considered to have been left in an unfinished state. "The desire obstructed the work," said Petrarch.

And yet he loved this art more than all others; and after several pages of reasons why painting is supreme among the arts, he concludes with the proud exclamation: "We, in our art as painters, dare call ourselves the grandsons of God!"

A single opponent arose in this battleless life. While the era was replete with the artistic rivalry of the cities, the jealousies of the patrons, the intrigues of the schools, Leonardo in his private diaries never once criticized his competitors for fame. Without time or country as he was, the battles of the artists did not excite him any more strongly than the battles of Italy's duchies and republics, and these did not interest him at all. Through all sorts of factional broils, we see him living and working in peace, like a distinguished stranger.

Only one man, his great antipode, could have aroused him to emulation. And the Signory of the city in which they both were reared actually did call them into the lists together. It may have been more than an accident: it may have been the design of some Florentine senator to bring Michael Angelo and Leonardo together by having them paint the two walls of the great Council Hall. At least Leonardo took it in this way, even if we do mistrust a banal artists' legend connected with the statue of the "David." For here, and here only, in the "Battle of the Standard," this painter of shimmering mystery, this composer of secular rhapsodies, this sensualist in the grand manner, has plunged into the subject of motion—apparently to compete with the master of motion. He amassed an egregious tangle of fighting, tearing, shrieking men and beasts, enraged, ominous, and distorted to the point of madness.

Yet while the bathing soldiers on Michael Angelo's wall stretched their naked limbs, Leonardo clothed all his warriors.

This melting flesh which he painted elsewhere was not made for war—so he felt—but for pleasure alone. On the other wall the painter summoned all his art in the rhythm of the arms and legs; but Leonardo laid chief emphasis upon the expressions of the men's and horses' heads. Each an extreme of its type, the painter of bodies and the painter of souls placed their works opposite each other. Both works have been lost; yet after half a century there was enough of Leonardo's visible for Cellini to prize it as "the school of the entire world." And the drawings of the old soldier and the young soldier, their faces distorted with shouting, still stand like watchmen turned to stone before this sunken garden.

They could also be compared as sculptors, although in this instance too their principal works remained incomplete. Michael Angelo's tomb of the Medici has survived only in fragments, and Leonardo's tomb of Trivulzio only in sketches. Both found the same symbol of sovereignty: both had slaves in chains bowing at the feet of their heroes. These two masters, one of whom bore within him a tragic human world and the other a smiling realm of the gods, had this one melancholy thought in common.

For this realm is a landscape projected from within. And whatever visions he captured, whatever dreams he converted into art, whatever magic figures he drew, stemmed from that world. They seem to live in thinner air; midway between knowledge and desire, their passions are intellectual passions. "Art," he writes in his monologue, "creates the illusion of a divine beauty whose natural prototype has been destroyed by age or death."

And his realistic studies, the results of unceasing observation, though they were apparently intended merely as literal copies, carry us beyond accuracy. The counterplay of observation and clairvoyance which made Leonardo significant as an inventor, was of constant assistance to him in his art, where it has so pronounced an effect at decisive moments. For is not this transformation of a thing seen into an internal vision the very nature of art? Is there a better combination of endowments than an eye which can rest lovingly and understandingly upon the objects of nature, noting with greater and greater sharpness and silently recording the fluctuant connections between one detail and another—and a human heart, filled with an internal, ever-youthful melody, and veiling every clear perception with its own peculiar tonality? Given this—and the resultant record will be at once accurate and inventive, humble and independent. Even the most singular reflection of nature will, under such circumstances, reveal the stigma of the type, and yet in the copy of a flower done by an artist we can detect the evidences of a Divine intervention.

Leonardo drew a stone-cutter, a crow-bar, a dredging machine—and though these were without landscape, sky, or people, their wood and iron, their stone, wire, and plaster seem nothing less than living muscles, pulsing veins, and glowing flesh. The shadows play so musically along the cold and murderous edges of a cannon that no one who knows the madonnas of this master could fail to recognize the same hand here.

He would select the budding twig of an oak, or a forget-me-not, treating it in isolation as the Japanese artists of his day were doing unbeknown to him, and the result would be flooded with the same inward warmth and would envelop the observer in the same sweet redolence as the warmth and redolence of arms, breasts, and lips. The piece of a garment, laid sketchily across a thigh, a slight bit of material hardly amounting to more than a few folds, is so full of feeling that one might draw the face of the woman to whom this thigh is a part. Anatomical studies divided into squares and robbed of all illusion by the system of printed numerals in the corners, essays in proportion totally devoid of esthetic purpose, peer forth from the depths of the soul and live their own secret life independently and in defiance of their maker's will. None of Leonardo's great masterpieces brings us so close to an understanding of his processes as these studies whose unintended magic puts them beyond the sketches of every other master.

How each the Whole its substance gives, each in the other works and lives! Like heavenly forces rising and descending, their golden urns reciprocally lending. How these faces stream from the pages to make new harmonies with one another! There the elder Jacob, sketched for the "Last Supper," looks down, handsome in his fright, upon a castle drawn small in the corner, and seems of a sudden like a spirit, a great angel, who is calling upon the sleeping inhabitants of these towers to awaken. Alongside a hasty design of the "Last Supper," the mathematician had drawn circles in conflict with angles—and one cannot tell whether the mirror-writing on the bottom of the page applies to the magician at the table or the magic of the circle.

At times it is thought that this man lived by the laws of contrast, and that he would have failed had he not brought opposites together. In this way he put caricature next to beauty, not that a grotesque effect might result, but in order to make the marvelous still more unforgettable by emphasis. All these noses and mouths, hydrocephalic heads and hunched backs which he jumbles in among his lovely youths are products of his perception, but also of his vision; and since they did not originate in either mockery or madness they mean to us, as they did to him, merely the observance of peculiar accidents of nature.

Everything on this earth which has aged partakes in Leonardo's work of the nature of caricature, and scrutinizes critically the heaven of eternal youth which lives in his imagination. Thus he puts two profiles on a page, each a separate study, unrelated to the other—and the old man, with his seven hard lines as profile, seems to be saying to the charming youth: Do you know that I was once like you, and that some day you will be like me?

To get the answer, we have but to place the portrait of himself in old age alongside the superb version of earlier youth.

Nine paintings are now recognized as his own. All the others are doubtful; and since neither the Vienna picture nor the two in the Biblioteca Ambrosiana, neither the "Madonna Litta" nor the "Leda" are up to his level, we are willing to accept this verdict. Of the nine authentic pictures, the "Jerome," the "Annunciation," and the "Madonna Benois" are second-rate, and the "Adoration of the Kings" is hardly begun. There are left not more than five pictures which completely represent for us Leonardo as a painter: the "Virgin of the Rocks," the "Last Supper," "La Gioconda," "Saint Anne," and the "Saint John"—while we might also recognize among the authentic works of the master the brother-piece to the "Saint John": "Bacchus." All these five or six pictures were painted late in life: the "Virgin of the Rocks" and the "Last Supper" in his forties, "La Gioconda" and "Anne" after fifty, and "Bacchus" and "John" about sixty or later. Except for the "Last Supper" all of Leonardo's masterpieces are in the Louvre.

All these pictures are pervaded with the same melody. With the exception of the "John," each of his characters arises from the same landscape, this dream-landscape of greenish lakes and white waterfalls, of brush-covered islands and cliffs magically blue. These are nocturnes lighted by an unseen aurora. But his people are not native to these places; the veil-like garments of these delicate, placid creatures could not shield them from the tempests which lie sleeping in such grottoes. It is purely the symphony of the dream which binds man and landscape, man and man.

For they all resemble one another, much as though they were brothers and sisters. And then again they resemble the figures of the drawings, even when the drawings are not preparatory studies for the paintings. "A figure is not worth noting," he writes once in his monologues, "unless by some gesture it expresses the passion of the soul." This sign-language is utilized most powerfully in the "Last Supper," his one major group. Here a dramatic moment heightens the expression of thirteen men, although their agitation and the absence of women take from the work the flower-like repose which elsewhere is so profound an aspect of the Master. This compendium of emotional expressions is robbed of its full effect as much by Christ's reproof as by the partial demolition of his figure. It stands quite alone among Leonardo's works; even if we include the paintings by him which have perished, it could at the outside be classed only with the "Battle of the Standard." And the picture cannot readily be grasped as a whole, but must be viewed as a series of events.

That passion of the soul, which is the subject of his meditations and which figures in all his paintings, is a knowing passion. There is no suffering in Leonardo: he painted Christ as a Wise Man; and we can more readily understand why Leonardo left Him incompleted in the "Last Supper" if we look at a faded, obliterated drawing of the Thorn-crowned King in Venice. And there is no innocence in Leonardo: the "Virgin of the Rocks" is a fallen angel—and the other angel beside her looks out knowingly at the observer. Neither Saint Anne nor her daughter, nor the Christ child, nor even the John of the "Last Supper," to say nothing of the others, shows evidence of that high innocence which possessed the Umbrian painters and which even Raphael sometimes mastered.

Yet Leonardo's figures are not worldly like the saints of the Venetians. Rather, they live far removed from strong light; they live in the regions of the intellect. But they all understand love, and this is the passion of the soul which their creator demands of them.

The same kind of love stirs in both his men and his women. On a page of profile sketches of girls and boys, one cannot always be sure of the sex. The heads of John, Philip, and Matthew in the "Last Supper" could be the heads of girls, but the angel in the "Virgin of the Rocks" could very easily be a boy. Bacchus, and above all the John in Paris, are pure hermaphrodites. It is not until the men grow beards, as with the elder Jacob of the "Last Supper," not until a wealth of love-nights has compressed the mouths of his women deeper into the flesh of the cheeks, that the sexes are differentiated; but even then they retain in common an element of spontaneous sweetness which speaks through the browless, long-lashed, ever-knowing eyes, through these always lightly trembling lips.

And yet, in the midst of their sensuousness, these same figures have a super-sensual trait in common: it is the modicum of knowledge in their pleasure, the sadness of dreams fulfilled. It is the trait of a bewitching melancholy which sets Leonardo's creatures apart from all others, and raises them above all sensuous painting, even above the charming figures of Correggio. All of them remember their master's self-admonishment: "Decipimur votis et tempore fallimur et mos deridet curas."

He seldom painted men at their prime of life; they are either youthful or aging. The virile type is never prominent. But he did depict mature women, since they did not affect him erotically: in particular as the Gioconda, as Anne, and in the red chalk drawing of the duchess Isabella d'Este, who belongs among his immortals.

The Gioconda, on which he is said to have painted for four years, and the Isabella, which he may have drawn in an hour, are the two of his women most distinct from each other; and precisely because even these have some unescapable trait of kinship, we recognize the one man author to both. La Gioconda is more suggestive, and stranger—made more attractive by the landscape behind her hair, by the ironically sweet language of eyes turned almost full upon us, by the charm of lips inured to love, and by her calm assertion of experience.

Isabella, ten years younger, with more race and less personality, generally firmer, more seclusive and expectant, turns from us, despising the unknown observer at whom the other woman had smiled. With her averted glance, and her powerful but immobile features, she is less captivating. But this queenly neck, caught in a single line, this tumble of metallic hair which crowns her like a helmet, the clarity of her eyes and the boldness of her posture—in short, the entire freedom of her splendid figure, speaks less of the painter than of his era; and more thoroughly than the most famous pictures of women of that time, it preserves for subsequent centuries a type of high-strung womanhood firm in her grasp on life.

Between them, and perhaps beyond them, soars the figure of Saint Anne. Related to La Gioconda, superior to her though hardly older, she sums up in her mature smile all the spiritual adventure and love-enchantment that has ever been painted; and as she looks at her daughter and the angel, there seems to be more retrospection than hope in her contemplation of the generations. This painting, the "Gioconda," and the "John," which are now assembled on the walls of the same high room, ultimately contain all that the prophet sank into human picture.

In the "John" he seems for the last time to recapture the vivacity of his youth. With a mouth which might have belonged to La Gioconda's eldest son, with such eyes as might have tried to fascinate the mother, with breast and arms which seem more natural to a woman in evening dress than to a man, he dares to point upwards with his voluptuous finger, thus in the name of his Master promising Bacchic beatitude to those who have already enjoyed such, here below.

He was an old man when he painted this youth. He was then living in his old castle, attended by a servant and the oldest of his favorites. He was living like an enchanter. To be sure, he was called court painter to the King of France, who honored him in his letters as "*notre très chier et bien aimé Léonard*," collected all of Leonardo's work he could find, and even tried without success to remove to Paris the wall on which the "Last Supper" was painted.

Yet the master lived in seclusion. As weathered as the hundred-year-old Faust, he spied himself again in the mirror; and though he copied himself imperturbably, he wrote in his diary: "O Time, devourer of all things; envious old age, which destroys all! When Helen saw herself flaccid and wrinkled in the mirror, she wept and thought: How have I twice been the cause of plunder!"

Finally his right arm was lamed, and he devoted himself exclusively to invention. A Spanish cardinal found him in the midst of his dissections and compounds, retorts and machines—and when permitted to look through the manuscripts the cardinal wrote: "If all this were to see the light of day, how great our delight and our profit!" Now the old man, near the close of his career, tried to collect and order his material. He did bring together a few treatises, but it was too late: the constant experimentation of a lifetime could not at the last be hastily assembled into the systems which he had always despised. When one has been consistently a learner, one does not become a teacher in old age. It was too late, and it was also too early, for he was still constructing and planning unceasingly: now, in accordance with his earlier ideas, he wanted to build embankments for the river near him, drain the swampland, and reclaim areas now lying under water.

Then he felt that his strength was diminishing. He apportioned his property among his friends, dignifiedly put all his affairs in order, and in the spring when he felt that death was near, the dying prophet wrote in his monologue:

"Man, always festively awaiting the new spring and the new summer, complains that the longed-for things are slow in coming, and fails all the while to notice that he is longing for his own end. Yet precisely this wish is the true quintessence of the elements which feel themselves imprisoned in the body through the soul and wish constantly to return to their maker. But I would have you know: this same wish is also the true spirit of nature, and man is but a cosmos in miniature."

PHILIP GUEDALLA

Literature is a house of many mansions in the modern wing of which Philip Guedalla dwells honorably among the historians for having written some of the best biographies of our time. "Historians" is said under advisement, since Mr. Guedalla sees biography as only an annex of history, "a branch of history devoted to the reconstruction of personal careers," instead of as an independent department of literature. But the distinction is not worth the pain of disagreement, since all readers of biography today have this gifted author to thank for many hours of sheer delight.

Philip Guedalla, born in 1889, was educated at Rugby and at Oxford (Balliol), where, besides being for a term president of the Oxford Union Society, he published two pleasant volumes of prose and verse, *Ignes Fatui, A Book of Parodies* and *Metri Gratia* (1911) and took a First in Modern History and the degree of M.A., 1913. From the university he went directly to the Inner Temple, became a barrister (1913), and began practicing law. In 1914 he produced his first historical work, *The Partition of Europe, 1715-1815*. During the War he was a legal adviser to the Contracts Department, the War Office, and the Ministry of Munitions, and organized and acted as secretary to the Flax Control Board (1917-20). In 1920 appeared the first of his books of short biographical sketches, *Supers and Supermen;* in 1921, *The Industrial Future;* and in 1922, *The Second Empire*, the brilliant study in history and biography with which his fame as a writer began. Thenceforth, retiring from legal practice, he divided his energy between letters and politics, standing several times for Parliament. Two more series of portraits came in rapid order: *Masters and Men* (1923) and *A Gallery* (1924); then, after *A Council of Industry* and the Davis lecture, *Napoleon and Palestine* (1925), another group, *Independence Day* (published in America as *Fathers of the Revolution*, 1926), of which the following life of George III is the opening chapter. In 1926 he published also his second long biography, *Palmerston.* Then, after an amusing excursion in *Conquistador* (1927), came *Gladstone and Palmerston* (1928). Again, following another series of delightful portraits, this time of real and imaginary Victorian ladies, in *Bonnet and Shawl: An Album* (1928), came *The Duke* (*Wellington*, 1931). And once more, after a vacation trip in *Argentine Tango* (1932), a study in "parallel" biography, *The Queen and Mr. Gladstone* (1933), and *The Hundred Days* (1934).

The list of Mr. Guedalla's works is long, but few readers would have it shorter. For there is hardly a page that does not sparkle with wit, irony, satire, or humor. He is a natural sequel to Lytton Strachey. Somewhat too little disposed, at times, to attend to the *souls* of his subjects, he stands at the opposite end of the biographical scale from Gamaliel Bradford, who seems to take the soul and let the body go. Mr. Guedalla never neglects the physical aspects of his characters, who almost invariably appear in full-bodied participation in large events. There is even something of Cecil de Mille's cinematographic technique in this author's longer books. He has made himself the reconstructer, *par excellence*, of the crowded, dramatic scenes of the past. And while his habit of filling his panoramas with people and events contemporary with, but not related to, the main subject (as in the second paragraph of the piece that follows) has been frequently reproved, the common reader is usually thankful for the orientation they supply.

Mr. Guedalla shares certain qualities of imaginative endowment with André Maurois, certain historical predilections with Emil Ludwig, numerous expressive talents with Lytton Strachey. In racial antecedents, in literary brilliance, and in political ambitions he has been described as reminiscent of Disraeli, whom he has yet to make the hero of a book.

THE STEPFATHER OF THE UNITED STATES

PORTRAIT OF H.M. KING GEORGE III

It was a cold February night in 1820; and from the black meadows by Eton they could see lights moving in the Castle. From the park, where the trumpeters stood in the darkness, the dismal note of horns rose on the night mist; and the Yeomen of the Guard, all in black, loomed "like black giants" through the half light of a room all hung with black. In a room beyond, the King of England lay dead; and anxious heralds were forming up a long procession of solemn gentlemen by candle-light. The King was dead; and in the darkness at Windsor they were burying the poor mad old man who, for nearly twenty years, had been King Lear without Goneril, without Regan, without Cordelia. The long round of imaginary ceremonials, of unreal reviews passed with royal dignity, of illusory Parliaments opened with royal affability, was over at last; and this strange replica of one of Blake's long-bearded allegories was still. The conqueror, the captor of Napoleon; the father of the Arts and Sciences; the royal person of whom the most sonorous of his subjects observed, after a conversation in the library at the Queen's House in St. James's Park, "Sir, they may talk of the King as they will; but he is the finest gentleman I have ever seen"; the master of Lord Chatham, of Lord North, of Mr. Pitt; the pupil of Lord Bute; the sovereign of Garrick and Siddons and Sir Joshua and Mr. Wesley and Mr. Burke; all this and more lay in the silent room beyond the tall Yeomen in their black. For on that winter night in 1820 they were burying the Eighteenth Century.

I

It all seemed so far away. The sun shone in St. James's and Sir Robert Walpole was minister, when the Prince was born in a great house at the corner of the Square. Gin was the leading recreation and Captain Macheath the favourite character of the people of England; the sad, tinkling melodies of Miss Lockit and Miss Peachum were barely five years old, and the Italian singers had driven Handel into bankruptcy. Young Mr. Walpole was making the most of the Grand Tour, "very glad that I see Rome while it yet exists"; and little Mr. Pope was exasperating his contemporaries, whilst the outraged delicacy of Mr. Hogarth retorted in emphatic caricature. At Norfolk House the Princess of Wales lay beside a rather puny infant in the morning light. Anxious ladies scurried about the house; and her Frederick, unconscious of the impending tennis-ball, looked on with large, indifferent eyes. Someone rode off to the King with the news; and outside in the Square the tiny lake gleamed in the June sunshine of 1738.

With a kind provision for its soul's welfare and a sad feeling of its approaching end, they baptised the little creature before night. But it survived them all, survived the century, even survived itself. That hurried morning and that sudden baptism were the strange opening of George's eighty years. A bishop called the next day and gave him a string of royal names; the Poet Laureate, visited by his punctual Muse, improved the occasion in a smooth copy of heroic couplets, which contained a happy, though hardly an unexpected, allusion to Ascanius; and the infant in St. James's Square was fairly launched upon his long career of royalty.

The surroundings, it must be confessed, were not inspiring. A house in a London square without even a sentry at the door may be an apt school of simplicity. But for the other graces there was a sad dearth of instructors. The happy father, absorbed in the rather clumsy frolics to which the House of Hanover is lamentably apt in its deviations from propriety, was a rare visitor in the nursery; although he once took the child to a concert at the Foundling Hospital. Yet this dismal figure, whose heavy eyes stare aimlessly out of history, was strangely popular. Nothing endears their rulers to the people of England so much as the extremes of raffishness and respectability; and Frederick's claims upon the former count were singularly high. Alike by the scale of his debts and the range of his affections he stormed the popular heart. But possibly his absence from his son may be counted for a gain to George, since Frederick was unlikely to form the young mind; although he once composed an ode in French, and cherished an obscure ambition to become Chancellor of Cambridge University on the strength, perhaps, of a silver cup which he had offered to be rowed for in a boat race. But before the boy had turned thirteen, his father was removed. A fickle nation observed without discomposure that it was "only Fred"; and graduates of either University pursued him to the sky with dirges in all the learned languages. His royal grandfather was little beyond a distant vision of an alarming old gentleman with staring eyes and a large wig, who interrupted the child with boisterous noises at an investiture of the Garter and quite frightened out of his head the little speech which he had got by heart. Nothing remained for George to lean on but his mother. She was a patient lady, who had endured without complaint her introduction into a family which exhibited most of the filial imperfections

GEORGE III

From a colored print in the Harvard College Library

of the Atreidae without their more pleasing features; and there was that "quiet sense" which she had brought with her from Saxe-Gotha to St. James's Square.

Two Earls, two bishops, and two gentlemen of mathematical attainments were enlisted to perfect the young intelligence, but with uneven success. The bishops did their work *à merveille* and produced a sound young Churchman. The Earls imparted whatever of peculiar attainment is in Earls. But the two scholars were a lamentable failure; and in his education George hardly reached the modest standard of a squire's son at a country grammar-school. His ignorance even became noticeable to himself in later years; and his tastes, in an age of taste, were non-existent. To this meagre curriculum his mother made two contributions, a distaste for society and the third Earl of Bute. Perhaps the first was almost natural in her. The poor lady had small cause to love the world; and she taught her son to avoid the bright and crowded assemblies, where he might, perhaps, have learnt by candle-light many lessons upon the management of men. So he remained always queer and a little lonely.

But Lord Bute was a more considerable ingredient in George's education. This accomplished person drifts into English history in a shower of rain, which stopped a cricket match near Richmond and drove the Prince's father to the dismal expedient of whist in a tent. Bute made a fourth at the card-table. His manners pleased; he called at Kew; and when he came to Court, he was attached to Frederick's Household. The Fates propelled the dreadful tennis-ball; and his master died, as he had lived, with bad French on his lips. But Bute remained beside the widow; and when her son was training to be King of England, she turned often to the graceful Scotchman. He was a man of taste; he had a leg, collected drawings, and patronised the Society of Scottish Antiquaries. His proximity to the bereaved Princess invited scandal; but he had the sense to face it. He was no fool, but merely (both by race and by conviction) a Tory. Slow to convince, the Scotch are still slower to abandon a conviction which they have once reached by the painful processes of logic; and having absorbed with difficulty the royal doctrines of the Seventeenth

Century, they still adhered to the creed in 1745. Perhaps the Prince's training owed a tinge of absolutism to Bute's direction. The comforting logic with which Jacobite writers excused the errors of the Stuarts could be adapted without undue strain to the House of Hanover; and it is not surprising that a startled bishop once came upon the boy reading a Jesuit's vindication of King James II. Such studies were unlikely to incline him to resign the throne in favour of Charles Edward (since even Princes are human); but they might prove a useful repertory of ideas, should he incline to revive the glories of the royal Prerogative. This tendency owed something also to his mother's guidance. Reared in a German Court where royalty had its due weight, she was pardonably shocked by the British system which confined the Lord's anointed to making stiff bows at a Levée, whilst the nation was administered by unconsecrated Whigs. This feeling, with a mother's pride, insisted that her son should "be a King"; and there can be small doubt that Bute showed the way. What else he taught the Prince is tolerably obscure. A tepid interest in medals, which Mr. Walpole once urged Sir Horace Mann to buy for him in Tuscany, and a total ignorance of law (imbibed from early study of Chief Justice Blackstone's *Commentaries* in manuscript) appear to be the only traces.

So the boy grew up; whilst the young men hunted Sir Robert Walpole out of office, and Mr. Pitt propelled his cheering countrymen through the great round of victories. He was a trifle solitary, "shut up in a room," playing at Comet (but for diminutive stakes) with the family, or living among his mother's plants at Kew. These mild pursuits exasperated his virile grandfather. The hero of Dettingen learned with disgust of a royal visit to a tapestry factory. "Damn," he exclaimed, "dat tapestry—I shall have de Princes made women of." A repetition of the offence evoked reprisals: he had "oder dings to show dem dan needles and dreads," and promptly took off a small Princess to a military review in Hyde Park. He was irked by the rather Methodist virtues of his heir, who seemed "good for nothing but to read the Bible to his mother." But when he proposed to the Prince of Wales a marriage of the usual pattern with a princess from

Brunswick, the mild young man refused; and Mr. Walpole was in transports over his reluctance to be "*bewolfenbuttled*, a word which I do not pretend to understand, as it is not in Mr. Johnson's new *Dictionary*." George's prejudice was personal rather than patriotic; since it appeared that he had no objection to the daughter of a German prince, upon whose territory "some frow," as Mr. Walpole said, "may have emptied her pail and drowned his dominions." For he boldly made application for the portrait of a rival beauty, who resided in the more favoured region of Saxe-Gotha. Perhaps his mother, who valued her own position as "the Lady Dowager Prudence," discouraged the Brunswick match. Perhaps (who knows?) he had a will of his own. No one could say, since the world knew little of him. And how little he knew of the world! His travels, in the age of the Grand Tour, took him no further than Cheltenham, with one wild excursion (in delicious *incognito*) to the south of Scotland. His studies kindled little beyond a mild taste for agriculture; though he betrayed that faint inclination towards mechanics which often haunts those whose livelihood is not dependent upon their skill. He once designed a watch of tiny proportions, "rather less than a silver twopence"; but the execution was wisely left in other hands, his own mechanical achievements being almost entirely confined to turning upon a lathe, with which he was positively believed to have made a button. As a little boy he had walked through the town at night with his father

> To look at garters black and white
> On legs of female rabble.

But in spite of this initiation he never figured in the raffish world, where it was the lofty ambition of young gentlemen

> To run a horse, to make a match,
> To revel deep, to roar a catch;
> To knock a tottering watchman down,
> To sweat a woman of the town.

Indeed, he was scarcely seen in those more elegant quarters where Mr. Selwyn paraded his wit and the hackney-chairs lined up outside assemblies. One catches a glimpse of him at Miss Chudleigh's party for his birthday, when she opened the dance with the Duke of York and the court was illuminated with "a battlement of lamps." There were "pyramids and troughs of strawberries and cherries" for supper, which covered all the sideboards and even filled the chairs, although the party from the Spanish Embassy supped off fish for their conscience' sake; and the gamblers played upstairs in a long room full of bookcases, "with the finest Indian pictures on different colours and with Chinese chairs of the same colours." But he was a rare visitor; and the world knew little of him.

Yet there was so little to know. If not to be a bad man is to be a good man, George was a good man. Indeed, the private virtues consist so largely of abstention that, on the private side, his negative equipment suffices to render him quite blameless. He was a dutiful son, a faithful husband, and a devoted parent, "revered," in the pleasant terms applied to another squire, "by his family, honoured by his tenants, and awful to his domestics." But such innocuous epitaphs rarely suffice for kings. Public figures are judged by more exacting tests; and in the sphere of politics George owed his failure (for he failed) to those more positive qualities which he did not possess.

II

At twenty-two, this paragon of somewhat negative virtues became King of England. The season, in 1760, was singularly apt for his accession; and his subjects seemed to demand of him precisely what the mild young man could offer. Two revolutions and two elderly German kings had developed a new convention of the Constitution. The sovereign was no longer required to govern England. That anxious business had been transferred to a committee of his subjects, partly because, unlike the last two monarchs, they understood the English language, and partly because they were the political heirs of the men who had deposed James II and decapitated Charles I. This readjustment of responsibilities, which found a succession to the Protectorate of Oliver Cromwell in the virtual Premiership of Sir Robert Walpole and

Mr. Pitt, seemed to mark the end of effective monarchy in England. The Cabinet had replaced the throne; and the sovereign, at the death of George II, had become a costly (if not particularly decorative) dignitary with purely ceremonial functions. The Birthday, the Levée, the Drawing-room were his occasions; and he was expected to perform these exacting duties, moving with due solemnity through a respectful forest of white wands and gold sticks. He might even add a military touch from time to time with a review or so, or give a bright example of royal condescension with an occasional act of charity in the more benevolent modern taste. But his main, his foremost duty was to smile and, at the appropriate moment, to incline his head. The King, in a word, had dwindled into royalty.

George was designed by Providence to play this amiable part. His physical equipment was sufficient, and the mental strain was not severe. His deportment satisfied the exacting standards of his age. He sat his throne, "graceful and genteel"; he read quite distinctly little speeches composed by other people; and in the Circle he "walks about and speaks to everybody" instead of standing, as a courtier wrote with a graceful reminiscence of his predecessor, "in one place, with his eyes fixed royally on the ground, and dropping bits of German news." The prevalent refinement seemed to have refined the coarse art of kingship into a sort of minuet. It was almost a dancing-master's business; and the formal movements, the royal airs and graces, and the ritual acts were well within George's range.

But some unhappy prompting set him a larger task. The middle years of the Eighteenth Century witnessed in almost every part of Europe a queer, belated revival of monarchy. Its inspiration came, perhaps, from the splendid pageant of autocracy through which the *Grand Monarque* had walked at Versailles. The gilt, the marble, the long perspective of respectful courtiers had stirred the envy of half the kings in Europe; and their emulation gave a sharp tilt to the falling scale of royal authority. The Seventeenth Century had been an age of great ministers; but the succeeding generations saw the kings assert themselves once more. They built great palaces and enamelled the ceilings with vast, impending goddesses; they ruled solemn vistas through the formal verdure of state gardens, with "pyramidal yews, *treillages*, and square cradle walks, with windows clipped in them"; and, stranger still, they resumed the government of their astonished countries. All Prussia was a rapier in the steady hand of Frederick; Austrian policy followed the changing moods of the Empress; and far to the north a stout, jewelled lady controlled the slow advance of Russia. Even in Spain there was a brisk revival of authority; and the scared Portuguese were bullied into progress by Pombal, as the new, glaring streets of Lisbon rose slowly in the sunshine from the dust of the earthquake. So George was in the mode when he resolved to be a King.

This project was almost the sole fruit of his meagre education. He had learned no law from Blackstone; but Lord Bute and the Jacobite pamphlets taught him a stranger lesson. George learned that he should be a King: it was his tragedy that no one taught him how to be one. His furtive study of high Stuart doctrine impressed the slow mind; ill-equipped persons are frequently consoled for their inadequacy by a belief in their sacred mission. If King James had been right (and his early reading taught George to think so), the Lord's anointed must surely be something more than a graceful gesture in a gilt chair, or an obliging signature on official sheepskins. And if, under the Whig dispensation, the royal function had almost come to that, then the Whigs must be wrong. So George, in his effort to be a King, turned Tory. There was, indeed, a Tory pattern of kingship ready to hand. The conduct of an ideal Tory on the throne had been foretold by the strange fancy of Bolingbroke; and George stumbled hopefully into the steps prescribed by that agile person for his *Patriot King*.

Defeated parties are frequently unanimous upon the impropriety of party government. Minorities are always apt to be stern critics of popular folly; and Tory thought, in the first years of Whig domination, harped on the vice of faction. But its main obsession was still the sanctity of kingship; and Bolingbroke, when he reeled back defeated from the hopeless task of imparting ideas to the exiled Stuarts and resumed the less exacting functions of a Tory oracle, blended the two notions into a strange amalgam. His friends were out of place; but he refreshed them with an odd vision of office. A new sort of monarch was to "espouse no party . . . but govern like the common father of his people." This chimera "must begin to govern as soon as he begins to reign"; and to achieve his purpose he will "call into the administration such men as he can assure himself will serve on the same principles on which he intends to govern." Such men, since the Whigs were unlikely bedfellows for an autocrat, must clearly be Tories; and in this happy dream, the dejected friends of Bolingbroke would march back into office behind the triumphant banner of "the most popular man in his country and a patriot king at the head of a united people." The bright vision faded; and in the grey light Sir Robert Walpole was ruling England for the Whig families and the German king, whom they had brought from Hanover. Even when Mr. Pitt controlled the nation, he preferred to lean on a Whig duke. So George, who wished to be King above all parties, found party in the ascendant on his coming in.

This queer young man, whom no one knew, set out to transform the government of his country; and, to a strange degree, he was successful. The odds were remarkable. The King's resources were his slender personal equipment, the vague prestige of a new reign, his mother's guidance, and the friendship of a Scotch Earl. With singular courage (and courage never failed him) he gathered these slight forces for an attack on the Whig system. A more intelligent man, one feels, would have discarded the attempt as hopeless. But George's nerve was unimpeded by sagacity; and he succeeded. The Whig façade in 1760 was impressive; Whiggery was entrenched in Parliament behind the serried rows of Newcastle's placemen; and its chosen minister, Mr. Pitt, was conquering half the world. "Two victories every week" formed an inspiring diet for civilians; and a cheering town responded with huzzas and fireworks, whilst the distant boom of the Park guns answered the salvos from the Tower. The world observed Lord Bute at the King's elbow and made little jokes about Pitt-coal, Newcastle-coal or (hateful alternative) Scotch-coal. The

King alarmed opinion with an announcement that he gloried "in the name of Briton," which sounds to posterity a brave denial of his German origins; but for contemporaries it had the more sinister ring of an admission that Scotland was in his thoughts. There was a Scotch Earl on the back stairs; and the town was not averse to little stories about "the Signora-Madre." Then, on the full tide of victory, Mr. Pitt was adroitly parted from the Whigs. His Olympian air prepared the way. That eye, that hooked, commanding nose, which awed the House of Commons, were merely intolerable in council. For almost six years he had monopolised the control of war and foreign affairs; and British armies followed British fleets to victory in three continents. But infallible pontiffs are rarely popular with their colleagues. An issue (upon which he was plainly right) was raised in Cabinet. The oracle spoke; but the priests refused to listen. He was exasperated into resignation; and when the Whigs lost Mr. Pitt, they forfeited their sole claim to popular esteem. The oracle retired to Bath; and as the priests sat on in the temple, the outer courts were slowly emptying.

The King had made his breach in the walls of the Whig system, and the Scotch Earl became his minister. Whiggery trailed sadly into Opposition or assumed the new livery. The King, like all opponents of the party system, recruited a new party briskly. Its principles were obscure; but its advantages, since the King's Friends were grouped conveniently round the fountain of honour, were obvious. The opinions of the House of Commons were governed through its appetite for places; and Masters of the Buckhounds followed Admirals of the Red into the lobby, whilst Comptrollers of the Green Cloth, Rangers of St. James's Park, and Verdurers of Whichwood Forest abandoned their absorbing duties in order to support Government in the congenial company of Lords of the Bedchamber and Governors of the Isle of Wight. For nine years the King worked steadily to impose his system. Sometimes he seemed to reach the goal, and his proud mother cried: "Now my son *is* King of England." Sometimes the dark forces of Whiggery returned upon him in the dreary form of George Grenville or the blameless incarnation of Lord Rockingham. Once there was a queer resurrection of Mr. Pitt; but he was hastily reburied under the dignity of Lord Chatham, and the patient King went on. It was a strange struggle; and it was waged against an even stranger background.

England, in the ten years between the accession of George III and the ministry of Lord North, was an odd blend of hysteria and decorum. The poets scanned; the magazines abounded in formal eloquence; and taverns echoed with the sonorous antiphonies of Johnson. The great world solemnly pursued the grave inanities of the Eighteenth Century. It dressed its hair; it played at ombre; it sat sedately through interminable plays. Mr. Walpole, up to the knees in shavings, fortified his home with gingerbread breastworks and asked the town to view the battlements, or pelted Sir Horace with commissions to buy up half the brocadella in Florence for his hangings. But beyond this decorous scene something was stirring. An odd ferment seemed to threaten the trim dignity of the age. Excited gentlemen defied propriety in hell-fire clubs; and less select assemblies grew strangely violent. There had been queer frenzies earlier in the century, when Sacheverell drove through the roaring streets, and later when half the world ran mad on stock-jobbing. But the crowds (even Mr. Walpole called it "the century of crowds") seemed madder than ever in the new reign. At first they stood to watch the little Queen come in, then stared at a Coronation, and mobbed the streets between-whiles to huzza for Pitt and Martinico or the Havannah. But their pleasant tumult dropped sharply to a deeper note as the town was swept by an odd fever; and astonished Liberty beheld the strange apostolate of Mr. Wilkes.

This indecorous, cross-eyed figure became an emblem of popular disorder upon one of those points of law by which the passionate interest of Englishmen is sometimes engaged. His private tastes lay in a simpler direction and had inspired him with an ambition to represent his country in the matrimonially congenial atmosphere of Constantinople. Failing of this, he declined in disappointment upon popular journalism and abused the Court with gusto. Involved in a welter of duels and litigation, his name became an excuse for unlimited mobbing. The tumult deepened;

and for a few years the London streets were a vulgar replica of Rome in the crowded, angry days of the dying Republic, when Milo's *bravi* fought with Clodius. Bute was scared out of public life, or effaced himself to save his master; but the King persisted. It was apparently no part of the duty of a *Patriot King* to be popular; and he faced the mobs without flinching. For he had always courage. Then, gradually, the tide of disorder ebbed. The voice of authority became faintly audible above the sound of breaking glass; and when it came, it spoke in the King's name. The Whigs were quite subdued now; and England was governed by George himself through a peering, pouting minister with "the air of a blind trumpeter." It was the year 1770, and Lord North was waiting sedately in the wings.

III

Personal government depends for its success upon two factors, the person and the governed. When a rare conjunction unites administrative talent with a docile or a sympathetic people, the world is presented with the strange miracle of successful autocracy. But how rare such unions are. Capacity, infrequent among statesmen, is still less frequent among kings; and docility, west of the Vistula, has been extinct among subjects for almost three centuries. A national impulse rarely coincides with a monarch's wishes. The case, of course, is not unknown; the laborious versatility of Frederick might drive an obedient Prussia, and the universal competence of Napoleon found its true partner in the French energy released by a national revolution. But these are the rare triumphs of monarchy. More often, far more often, a distracted autocrat fumbles with his work; or a nation, disinclined to play its humble part, renders it impossible. If the ruler is unequal to his high position, autocracy fails. If his subjects withhold consent to his wide authority, it fails as gravely. The sole possibility of success for personal government lies in the combination of an adequate person with a consenting people; and its failures, for lack of that rare conjunction, are more numerous than its successes.

The King's experiment was sadly deficient in both elements. Viewed as a candidate for autocracy, George was singularly unimpressive; even Bolingbroke, one feels, would have been discouraged by the spectacle of his *Patriot King* in action. The patient, punctual creature minuting his correspondence with the hour of despatch; directing at "2 min. pt. 11 a.m." the march of some cavalry from Henley to Hounslow; consenting at "53 min. pt. 5 p.m." to the appointment of a Mr. Fountayne to the living of Worplesdon; complaining at "12 min. pt. 10 p.m." that if James Adam is appointed Surveyor-General to the Board of Works, he "shall certainly think it hard on Chambers, and shall in that case only think he must not be passed by"; insisting at "57 min. pt. 11 a.m." that the new prebendary of Durham must "continue to attend the young Chancellor"; this plodding figure, stooping over his green box in the candle-light and holding the papers close to his face before he traced the big G.R., seems so remote from the high dream of kingship. "The common father of his people . . ." and a light burning late in the Queen's House, where an angry man was writing little hints to the Common Council for unseating Mr. Alderman Wilkes. "The most popular man in his country . . ." noting gentlemen of the House of Commons to receive a frown at the Levée for an injudicious vote. "A patriot king at the head of a united people . . ." pelting a driven Minister with little punctual notes. How far they seem, those busy, irritable little figures, below that imagined monarch who was to sit enthroned above the clouds of party and bathed in the pure sunlight of autocracy. His teachers had urged him to be a King; and someone, it seemed, had taught him to be a passable Patronage Secretary. Clerks in his Treasury formed such habits; industrious merchants sought vainly to impart them to their sons; and his intellectual counterparts crouched on tall stools in counting-houses east of Temple Bar.

Yet he was not content to drug himself with the deadly narcotic of administrative detail. For he was King; and policy, as well as patronage, claimed the royal attention. Patronage was his forte, and it served well enough as a solvent of most domestic problems. He set about to govern England single-handed. Now, there was a House of Commons to be perpetually shielded from unwholesome influences, and George went in pursuit of political purity down unusual paths. The minor disorder of elections was cured with "gold pills"; and the tiresome scruples of elected persons yielded on most occasions to a gracious nod from the throne and a word behind Lord North's hand, followed after a becoming interval by a line in the *London Gazette* and a precious package from the Pay Office on quarter-day. The King, by this simple artifice, was his own First Minister and Chief Whip. His deputy sat dozing in the House of Commons, ran errands for his master, and stoutly maintained that the office of Prime Minister was unknown to the Constitution. The King had formed a party, led it, satisfied its simple needs, and maintained it in office. To that extent his experiment in personal government was verging towards success at home. The Whigs were helpless; since Parliament was for the King, and they professed to believe in government by Parliament. They roared in debate; they brought down votes "in flannels and blankets, till the floor of the House looked like the pool of Bethesda." But they were outvoted and retired to mutter in the deep libraries of country houses. Nothing seemed to remain in opposition except the City and the mob. But the Mansion House, strange temple of democracy, was a mere nest of preposterous Aldermen; and if the mob stirred, there were still the Guards.

George governed England with an odd blend of force and persuasion; and his subjects seemed curiously content to acquiesce. He had made peace; and great liberties are permitted to statesmen who make peace. He had unseated Mr. Pitt; but Mr. Pitt had made his name grotesque with a peerage. He challenged democracy; but democracy, in 1765, stood for little beyond the mob. Men had died for Hampden; but it would be fantastic to die for Mr. Wilkes. It almost seemed, at home, that it was possible to govern an empire with the arts of a Chief Whip. But one section of his people presented a queer, unyielding obstacle. Three thousand miles from the Levée, six weeks away from Lord North's significant smile, the Americans still persisted in their tedious debate. The ripe intelligence of Mr. Grenville had devised some taxes for them. Taxes, it seemed, were the common lot of victorious nations. So that imperial mind, which added the Isle of Man to the British Empire, sent stamps to Boston that inspired a strange repugnance. Mr. Grenville was frankly baffled. He had drawn the scheme (and he was at home in the schedule of a revenue Bill), because the neat device of stamps appealed irresistibly to that orderly mind. He had looked up the law (and he was a fair lawyer) and discovered the helpful precedent of the Channel Islands. Yet it was odd that mobs paraded in the clear American light and local orators abounded in deep-chested sentiments about liberty: perhaps the colour of the stamps was wrong. Then the grave leaders of the Whig groups faced the strange problem (and even Mr. Walpole began to notice that it was a "thorny point"). Mr. Grenville had thought of stamps; they thought of tea; few men in England thought of a larger issue. Then the Whigs subsided; and the King (with him, Lord North) resumed control of his bewildered empire. That he grasped the American issue is improbable. It was enough for that determined, angry man that the law of England had been defied on British territory. Wilkites in Southwark or Sons of Liberty in King Street, Boston, were the same to him; the troops must do their duty. Men who had ridden out the wild storm of the Middlesex election were not likely to parley with a mob; and at a distance of three thousand miles the solemn ratiocinations of a Boston town meeting were indistinguishable from the Brentford rabble. Even if he reflected, it was unlikely that the King would side with the colonists. Had he not learnt the sanctity of authority in a stiff Jacobite school? Passive obedience was the first duty of a loyal subject. Admirable in Great Britain, this virtue was yet more essential in America, since colonies (it was the lesson of his master Bolingbroke) were "like so many farms of the mother country." George was a farmer; and the strange claim of one of his farms to be consulted about its cultivation was clearly inadmissible.

The angry voices rose higher in the deepening tumult; and as the scattered shots rang out down the long road to Concord on a spring day in 1775, the argument drifted into civil war.

The King was firm. Indeed he had already fortified his resolution with the advice of the sagacious Gage. The conversation of military men upon political topics is a rare stimulant for civilians; and that warrior had persuaded his sovereign that the Americans "will be lyons whilst we are lambs; but, if we take the resolute part, they will undoubtedly prove very meek." In this hopeful mood he flogged the Boston Port Act through Parliament and hallooed Lord North to hunt the Opposition through the lobbies. He was still "well convinced they will soon submit," as Israel Putnam drove his sheep to Boston and Colonel Washington insisted warily that it was "a folly to attempt more than we can execute." The issue looked so simple in St. James's; and as the American tone hardened, the King could only ejaculate, "The dye is now cast, the colonies must either submit or triumph." But his mood was not one of blind repression. Like all Englishmen on the verge of a practical concession, he insisted firmly on his technical rights: "I do not wish to come to severer measures, but we must not retreat; by coolness and an unremitted pursuit of the measures that have been adopted I trust they will come to submit; I have no objection afterwards to their seeing that there is no inclination for the present to lay fresh taxes on them, but I am clear there must always be one tax to keep up the right, and as such I approve of the Tea Duty." So the student of Blackstone pressed his point of law, seeking little more than an admission which might cover his retreat. How many solicitors have been instructed to threaten proceedings in that confident tone. Unhappily he knew too little of men to measure the results of his threat. The lonely boy had become a lonely man; and his solitude was increased by the still lonelier elevation of a throne. He saw his fellow-creatures down the warped perspective of a king. But some instinct might have told him that Englishmen, in Boston or in Westminster Hall, willing enough to make all practical concessions, rarely give up a point of law. That, in essence, was his own attitude in the argument; and he lacked the wit to see that other men might feel the same. He knew so little of other men; and those incalculable creatures in America remained a mystery upon the far horizon of the world.

But when his challenge was accepted, when the expected lambs declined to play their part, he entered with gusto upon the detail of the war. Provisions for the army, the loan of infantry from Hanover, a purchase of recruits in Hesse-Cassel, sea strategy, dates of embarkation, biscuit and flour, the beating orders for enlisting Campbells, Gordons, and Macdonalds, plans of campaign, and news of privateers passed rapidly under the busy pen at Kew or the Queen's House. He watched the war like an eager parent, sailed the crowded troop-ships in imagination from Hamburgh to Sandy Hook, and followed his red-coats, as the winding line of bayonets vanished into the darkness of the great trees. Dimly he saw that personal government had met the fatal challenge of an unconsenting people. He seemed to feel that he was fighting for the throne of England; because if England thought with the unhappy rebels, "I should not esteem my situation in this country as a very dignified one, for the islands would soon cast off all obedience." It was (he saw the issue now) the decisive struggle of authority against all the dark forces which had ever opposed him, against the Whigs, against the mob, against the grinning mask of Wilkes and the sonorous tutorship of Chatham, against Mr. Burke and his heresies and the insidious logic of Dr. Franklin. George saw all his enemies gathered into the head of a single rebellion, and struck hard. The swelling strength of the Opposition alarmed Lord North; but the King's nerve was steady. "Whilst any ten men in the kingdom will stand by me, I will not give myself up into bondage. My dear Lord, I will rather risk my crown"—the sprawling hand wrote firmly on—"than do what I think personally disgraceful; and whilst I have no wish but for the good and prosperity of my country, it is impossible that the nation shall not stand by me; if they will not, they shall have another king, for I will never put my hand to what would make me miserable to the last hour of my life."

The French guns chimed in, as Versailles discovered a pleasing coincidence of romantic impulse with national interest; and for a moment he seemed almost to face the certainty of surrender in the revolted colonies. But "I will never consent that in any treaty that may be concluded a single word be mentioned concerning Canada, Nova Scotia, or the Floridas, which are colonies belonging to this country . . . for it is by them we are to keep a certain awe over the abandoned colonies." The issue had travelled far beyond taxation. In Europe it was now a war of existence with an ancient enemy; and in America it raised the vital problem of secession. That question was to haunt the continent for ninety years, and George stated it in terms which strangely anticipate the American echoes of a century later: "If Lord North can see with the same degree of enthusiasm I do the beauty, excellence, and perfection of the British constitution as by law established, and consider that, if any one branch of the empire is allowed to cast off its dependency, that the others will infallibly follow the example,"—how odd to find the thought of Lincoln in the mind of George III!—"that consequently, though an arduous struggle, that is worth going through any difficulty to preserve to latest posterity what the wisdom of our ancestors have carefully transmitted to us, he will not allow despondency to find a place in his breast, but resolve not merely out of duty to fill his post, but will resolve with vigour to meet every obstacle that may arise, he shall meet with most cordial support from me; but the times require vigour, or the state will be ruined." That cry, half strangled by the long, tortuous sentence, is not ignoble. The tenacious man, who stumbled into war in blind resentment of disorder, had a wider vision. The King could see the issue now; and, granted the fatal difference between autocracy and republic, he saw it almost with the eyes of 1861: "I own that, let any war be ever so successful, if persons will sit down and weigh the expenses, they will find, as in the last, that it has impoverished the state, enriched individuals, and perhaps raised the name only of the conquerors; but this is only weighing such events in the scale of a tradesman behind his counter; it is necessary for those in the station it has pleased Divine Providence to place me, to weigh whether expenses, though very great, are not sometimes necessary to prevent what might be more ruinous to a country than the loss of money. The present contest with America I cannot help seeing as the most serious in which any country was ever engaged; it contains such a train of consequences that they must be examined to feel its real weight. Whether the laying of a tax was deserving all the evils that have arisen from it, I should suppose no man could allege that without being more fit for Bedlam than a seat in the Senate; but step by step the demands of America have arisen; independence is their object; that certainly is one which every man not willing to sacrifice every object to a *momentary* and inglorious peace must concur with me in thinking that this country can never submit to: should America succeed in that, the West Indies must follow them . . . Ireland would soon follow the same plan and be a separate state; then this island would be reduced to itself, and soon would be a poor island indeed . . ."

The harassed man at Kew wrote on; and three thousand miles away the guns were booming in the summer sunshine of 1779. His courage held; he searched himself with "frequent and severe self-examination." When the news was good, he prepared to show America "that the parent's heart is still affectionate to the penitent child." When it was bad, he reflected that "in this world it is not right alone to view evils, but to consider whether they can be avoided, and what means are the most efficacious." In this sturdy temper he held on, defying the Opposition, heartening the pardonably despondent North. On a July day in 1781, he was still insisting that "this long contest will end as it ought, by the colonies returning to the mother country, and I confess I will never put my hand to any other conclusion of this business." But in those hot summer weeks a tired army was trailing about Virginia behind Cornwallis. At the fall of the year they stood behind a line of battered earthworks by the York River. The French lay off the coast; and in the sloping fields beyond the little town the parallels crept slowly nearer. There was a steady roll of musketry. Then the British guns fell silent; and the war was ended.

IV

Four years later, on a dark winter afternoon Miss Burney was mildly startled by a visitor. They were playing Christmas games after dinner in Mrs. Delany's little drawing-room at Windsor, when the door opened quietly. It closed again behind "a large man in deep mourning," whom no one except Miss Burney seemed to notice. He said nothing; but as that sharp little eye travelled down the black suit, it encountered, heavens! the glitter of a star. Then one of the young ladies turned round on him, stifled a scream, and called out, "The King!—Aunt, the King!" The little company backed uneasily into the corners of the room; and presently there was a loud royal whisper of "Is that Miss Burney?" Her sovereign bowed politely; and the talk ran upon the whooping-cough, which prevailed in the royal nursery, and James's Powders, which Princess Elizabeth found so beneficial. Then he rained little questions on her; how she came to write *Evelina,* how to publish, how to print without a word to her father. Urged by the royal *What!* she said with a simper that she had "thought it would look very well in print." The awkward questioning went on, until a rap at the door announced the Queen, and someone slid out for candles to light the ugly little lady in.

Another day the royal mind was easier. The children were off to Kew for a change of air, and James's miraculous powders had done their work; so the talk ran on books. Voltaire was "a monster—I own it fairly." Rousseau was thought of "with more favour, though by no means with approbation." And Shakespeare—"was there ever such stuff as great part of Shakespeare? Only one must not say so! But what think you?—What?—Is there not sad stuff?—What?—what?" Miss Burney temporised. But her sovereign enjoyed his little heresy and laughed. "Oh! I know it is not to be said! but it's true. Only it's Shakespeare, and nobody dare abuse him." So the arch monarch developed his wicked theme and shocked the bookish lady—"but," as the coy iconoclast confessed, "one should be stoned for saying so!"

The "fatal day" had come, bringing an end to the strange experiment of personal government. At home he dwindled by slow degrees into an almost constitutional monarch; and overseas Mr. Jay read with some surprise that when Mr. Adams made his bow as ambassador, the King had stifled all resentment in a graceful confession—"I will be very frank with you. I was the last to conform to the separation; but the separation having been made, and having become inevitable, I have always said, as I say now, that I would be the first to meet the friendship of the United States as an independent power."

This pleasant, ageing, stoutish man, with his odd, jerky questions and his staring eyes, slowly became a ceremonial monarch of the standard Hanoverian pattern; displaying, on the appropriate occasions, a becoming versatility of martial and civilian accomplishments; strolling in the evening light on the Terrace at Windsor, surrounded by a family that was a Court in itself; admiring Miss Burney in the famous lilac tabby which the Queen gave her; pressing the remedial virtues of barley-water upon an exhausted colonel after a hard day in the hunting field; trotting, gnawed by the incurable inquisitiveness of royalty, into half the shops in Windsor; taking, after a more than usually incompetent attempt on his life, "his accustomed doze" at the theatre; peering, smiling, bowing. This amiable, domestic, elderly person, with his little jokes and the quick, questioning *What?—what?* forms a queer postscript to the high adventure of the young, friendless King, who set out to govern England and lost America. It all seemed so far away now. Mr. Wilkes had faded, Mr. Pitt had died in that theatrical way of his; Lord North was still living somewhere, but he was quite blind now. The King lived on, before all else a father and a husband, the Georgian head of an oddly Victorian court.

But he had still, had always his courage. It had not failed him on "Black Wednesday," when at the height of the war the mob ran wild for "No Popery" and Lord George Gordon. The streets were alight with the disordered worship of this singular idol, whose evangelical quest for a form of Christianity uncorrupted by Popish additions finally led him, by the fatal logic of a Scotsman or a lunatic, into a clear air where it was uncontaminated even by a Saviour. London passed sleepless nights and crept about behind its shutters. But the King informed his Council that, if the Riot Act was to be read before the troops could fire into the crowds, one magistrate at least would do his duty and then could take command of his Guards in person. The same even temper bore him up when a mad woman thrust a knife at him one afternoon outside the garden door at St. James's. He steadied the crowd, went in to hold his Levée, and then drove down to Windsor to show himself to the Queen. Three royal persons and two ladies in waiting mingled their tears. But the careful King enquired, "Has she cut my waistcoat? Look! for I have had no time to examine." His courage barely failed beneath the slow, dreadful gathering of a darker cloud, which hung above him. That he saw its coming is almost certain. Little doubt is left by his choking exclamation, "I wish to God I may die, for I am going to be mad." Then, staring with pitiable eyes at the ebbing tide of reason, he faded into insanity.

Once he returned; and for ten years he presided over the state where he had reigned. The Whigs were out; but England was ruled by a minister again, and Mr. Pitt—there was a new Mr. Pitt now, whose "damned long ugly face" was almost as trying as Chatham's eye—sat in his father's seat. The *Patriot King* had declined into dogeship, although there was a faint flicker of the old authority, when the minister roused his sovereign's Churchmanship with some nonsense about equality for Irish Papists. He rode; he played piquet; he bathed in the loyal waves of Weymouth. There was a pleasant jingle of Light Dragoons on the little Esplanade, and his troopers lounged in their sunny Capua beside the Wessex sea—

> When we lay where Budmouth Beach is,
> O, the girls were fresh as peaches
> With their tall and tossing figures and their eyes of blue and brown!
> And our hearts would ache with longing
> As we paced from our sing-songing,
> With a smart *Clink! Clink!* up the Esplanade and down.

The bathing-women all wore "God save the King" on ample girdles round their waists; and as the royal person plunged, that pious invocation burst from the muffled fiddlers in a bathing-machine. He strolled again upon the Terrace at Windsor. But this time his airing was a martial exercise. For the French guns were speaking across Europe, and George called for the band to play, "Britons, strike home." So the old man (he was rising seventy now) confronted Buonaparte. He grasped, one feels, as little of the strange forces which opposed him as of the American tangle. He did little more than clench an English fist and shake it in the face of France.

But whilst he struggled to retain the last remains of sight, his watchful frigates kept the sea; his guns rang out where the Spanish hills dip to Trafalgar, and his red-coats stared at the cactus along the dusty roads of Portugal. Then, once again, a cloud swung over the sun and his sky darkened. The war went on; there was a steady thunder of guns in Europe, until at the last they stood smoking in the sodden fields by Waterloo. But the King sat muttering in a closed room at Windsor. He was far away in a pleasant world, where he gave interminable audiences to dead ministers. For hours, for days, for years he talked with them; and sometimes he made himself a little music on an old spinet, which had been silent since Queen Anne. Then he faded out of life; and on a winter night in 1820 Mr. Croker watched the mourners marshalling and heard the dismal note of horns from the Great Park.

GAMALIEL BRADFORD

The success that some men without genius win from long, continual, systematic, and indomitable effort in one spot on a single, well-defined task could not be better exemplified than by Gamaliel Bradford. He was born in Boston in 1863 of a well-to-do family and of strong New England literary and historical antecedents. He attended the public schools, fell very early in love with books, and enjoyed as a boy many rich intellectual contacts with the elder generation of scholars and philosophers of that "Athens of America." At fifteen, threatened by tuberculosis, he spent a year in Europe. The sojourn did not restore his health, but it stimulated a lifelong devotion to languages that opened up to him a familiar converse with the Greek and Latin classics and with the great minds of France, Germany, Spain, and other countries. When, at nineteen, in his first weeks at Harvard College, he was compelled by an illness that proved permanent to live at home in Wellesley Hills, he adopted letters as a profession. He also began recording in the utmost detail, by way of practice and memoranda, his daily reflections on books and his own private thoughts. Mr. Van Wyck Brooks has edited in a large volume (1933) about one-seventh of this immense *Journal*. In this and in Bradford's score of books is the story of his struggle through the next fifty years to win fame as a writer.

Books were the substance of his life and Bradford wanted, above all else, to be a poet and novelist. Failing there, he tried plays, the most unsuitable of all forms for a man so isolated; then novels again, and poems. With a sickly man's will to achieve, he apportioned his day's work according to a most productive routine. For years he groped for the right medium. In 1895 he published a book of essays called *Types of American Character* that now seems to foreshadow his true *métier*. But not until the immediate success of his first psychological biography, *Lee the American* (1912), when he was already fifty, was the subsequent course of his life work clearly set. Then, through twenty years, came that long series of portraits—*Confederate Portraits* (1914), *Union Portraits* (1916), *Portraits of Women* (1916), *A Naturalist of Souls* (1917), *Portraits of American Women* (1919), *American Portraits, 1875-1900* (1922), *Damaged Souls* (1923), *Bare Souls* (1924), *Wives* (1925), *As God Made Them* (1929), *Daughters of Eve* (1930), *The Quick and the Dead* (1931), *Saints and Sinners* (1932), *Biography and the Human Heart* (posthumous, 1932)—the one hundred and fifteen "psychographs," by which Gamaliel Bradford will be longest remembered. With these came three more full-length lives—*The Soul of Samuel Pepys* (1924), *Darwin* (1926), *D. L. Moody: A Worker in Souls* (1927)—also a play, two books of verse, and, right up to his death in 1932, a steady succession of articles and prefaces elaborating his special biographical aims.

What permanent artistic success he attained it is too soon to say. Insulated from the world as few men can be—though his wife and family and home made him an ideal environment—he had nothing whatever in common with contemporary movements or schools; and the loose talk in this country about his being an American Lytton Strachey was never more sharply denied than by himself. The two writers were not alike in aims, methods, temperaments, or capacities; and beyond saying that Bradford the plodder, who began earlier, discerned the weak points in the genius's work and admired to desperation the virtues, there is no comparison. Bradford produced no single outstanding book of psychographs. Yet the uniform standard of character analysis which he perfected and which he applied throughout the one hundred and fifteen portraits and the four longer studies may prove to have given, if not great literature, at least an extremely valuable instrument for biographers to come.

Bradford did not like the name "portrait" for his own studies. Though it had, he admitted, the excellent authority of his master Sainte-Beuve and others, and looked better on his books, it designated too strictly a face and figure seen only at one particular moment, rather than a picture of the sum of many particular moments. He preferred "psychograph," a term not coined by him but independently arrived at. For there is a basic difference between the two. "Biography," he said, "is bound to present an elaborate sequence of dates, events, and circumstances, of which some are vital to the analysis of the individual subject, but many are merely required to make the narrative complete." Psychography, being "the condensed, essential, artistic presentation of character, . . . swings clear from this chronological sequence altogether. . . . Out of the perpetual flux of actions and circumstances that constitutes a man's whole life, it seeks to extract what is essential, what is permanent and so vitally characteristic." It differs, on the other hand, from psychology in dealing primarily with individuals.

In analyzing character into its component elements, Bradford discerned certain universal qualities and forces—love, ambition, money, religion, etc.—by which every man and woman can be tested. His method was to master all the available printed evidence on his subject and then to walk round and round him, filling out, as it were, a set of personal questionnaires on each of these general qualities and on any others peculiar to that individual. In order quickly to orient his reader, Bradford invariably prefixed a brief chronology, while to support his deductions he always appended a bibliography and full reference notes. He finished in eight thousand words. This dry, schematic procedure, as Bradford feared, is apt in the long run to tire the reader. But the rigidity is somewhat softened by the author's profound interest in his "victim," by his shrewd and fresh perceptions, and by his clear, even, and flexible style.

"More and more," he confessed, "as I study the lives of men of prominence, or of any men, for that matter, do I feel the curiosity of studying their wives." With Mary Todd Lincoln (*Wives*), accordingly, Bradford is at the top of his bent. He himself considered *Bare Souls* to contain his best psychographs, because with Voltaire, Cowper, Gray, Horace Walpole, and the other great letter-writers he found unlimited evidence of their characters. The present study is valuable for just the opposite reason. Here was an exceptional dearth of material. This very handicap, added to the special challenge of the subject, brings out some of Gamaliel Bradford's finest workmanship.

THE WIFE OF ABRAHAM LINCOLN

CHRONOLOGY

Mary Todd Lincoln.
Born, Lexington, Kentucky, December 13, 1818.
Educated in Kentucky and lived there till 1839.
Married Lincoln, November 4, 1842.
Son Willie died, 1862.
Lincoln assassinated, April 14, 1865.
Son Tad died, 1871.
Died, July 16, 1882.

KINGS and princes are in the habit of selecting their wives, or having them selected, with a view to the exalted station they are destined to occupy. Presidents of the United States usually marry young, like other men, and do not arrive at the White House until they are old, and sometimes they bring with them partners not wholly adapted to such a conspicuous career. The complication in Lincoln's case is peculiar. A brilliant but uncouth and almost grotesque lawyer and politician from the backwoods, with no inherited social position or distinction, marries a showy, popular belle, who considers herself an aristocrat in the limited circle which is all she knows, and feels that she is condescending vastly in accepting the husband whose only asset is an extremely nebulous future. Then the husband shows an unexampled capacity for growth and development, intellectual and spiritual, if not social, and the wife, remaining to the end the narrow rural aristocrat she was in the beginning, is decidedly left behind. The strange destiny which made the man who was to save the future of American democracy a typical American and a typical democrat was hardly equal to making him also an ideal husband, at any rate an ideal husband for such a wife. Mrs. Lincoln married Lincoln with condescension and hope that he might rise to her level, or even above it. He did, and so far as to be altogether beyond her limited power of ascent. She made a useful helpmate for a practical, aggressive lawyer in Springfield, Illinois. As the wife of the great, dreaming, smiling, creating democratic statesman of the modern world, she was just a trifle over-parted.

The difficulty of getting at the actual Mrs. Lincoln is extraordinary and exasperating. The cloud of anecdote and hearsay and gossip which envelops Lincoln himself, hangs even more impenetrably about her, because we have not the solid substance of her own words, as to a considerable extent we have his. There are but a few of her letters in print, and those few are not very significant. Many people have written about her, but they contradict one another, and misrepresent, according to their own prejudices and the strange passion for exalting Lincoln by either elevating or debasing everybody about him. How unsatisfactory the materials are may be judged from the fact that the most illuminating document, on the whole, is the record of Mrs. Keckley, the colored seamstress at the White House. Mrs. Keckley was an intelligent observer, devoted to Mrs. Lincoln, and admitted to many intimate scenes and experiences. But I suppose few women would care to have their lives filtered to posterity through such a record. In short, I cannot ask my readers to give implicit belief to anything I say about Mrs. Lincoln, for I believe very little of it myself. Yet the difficulty of investigating her adds to the fascination. One sighs at times for such superb self-presentment as one gets in the letters of Sarah Butler or Harriet

Blaine. But there is a peculiar pleasure in finding little hints and threads of suggestion and following them out patiently, even when they seem to lead nowhere.

The bare indisputable facts in the life of Mary Todd Lincoln are few and simple. She was born of a good Kentucky family, in 1818, ten years after her husband. In 1839 she came to live with her sister, Mrs. Edwards, in Springfield. After a stormy courtship Lincoln married her in 1842. Her life then led her through Illinois law and politics to the White House, and the war, and the culmination of triumphant peace. All the triumph and hope were blasted by the assassination of her husband, and her remaining years, in spite of a brief sojourn in Europe, were darkened by sorrow and misfortune till a temperament, always impulsive and intense, was unbalanced to a point of oddity approaching and at times reaching actual derangement. She died in 1882.

In studying Mrs. Lincoln, one must admit that, while it is possible to get more or less reliable accounts of her external interests and activity, her inner life is almost hopelessly obscure. She had apparently a very good education, as educations went in Southern girls' schools in the middle of the nineteenth century. Mr. Rankin tells us that "while a resident of Springfield before and after her marriage, she impressed all who were acquainted with her with the excellent and accurate literary taste she had acquired by education and general reading, especially in history, poetry, and fiction." But this was in a country town in 1840, and it must be remembered here, as elsewhere, that we are dealing with Mr. Rankin's kindly after-dinner memory. Education of a sort Mrs. Lincoln certainly had, education superior to that of many about her, and at any rate far superior to her husband's. She had also a nimble gift of words, and wrote with ease when she wished. Her natural intelligence was unquestionably shrewd, quick, and keen. Within her limits she saw into the nature of things and the motives of men, and she had a notable faculty of making observations upon them, often with a turn of wit and sarcasm which did not add to her popularity. That she had a trace of the larger humorous attitude seems unlikely, and it is still more unlikely that she ever grasped or enjoyed that attitude in the subtle, pervading, dissolving form in which it was constantly manifest in her husband. The element of Touchstone, of Charles Lamb, the instinct of remoteness, of detachment, even in the midst of vast tragic passions, perhaps most precisely in the midst of such, of illuminating them with the strange glory of laughter, which was so haunting and so fascinating in Lincoln, evidently annoyed and perplexed her, as it has many other excellent people.

If she read, we should like to know a little more definitely what she read. Mr. Rankin enlarges on her familiarity with French, as a matter of both reading and speaking, and assures us that she read the latest French literature. I wonder if Sainte-Beuve was included in the list. I doubt it. Victor Hugo she did read, which perhaps is all one could expect. She read current novels, since Lincoln writes to a friend in regard to one, "I am not much of a reader of this sort of literature; but my wife got hold of the volume I took home, read it half through last night, and is greatly interested in it." She liked to read aloud; but what I should be glad to know is whether she was one of the two or three to whom Lincoln enjoyed reading aloud in quiet evenings; yet no one tells us. And in the middle of an agitated night he used to traverse the White House corridors to read the trifles of Tom Hood to his sleepy secretaries; but I do not hear that he read them to her.

Again, we have little light as to other amusements of an intellectual order. There is no sign of any considerable aesthetic interest. Lincoln liked music, of a rather rudimentary type, but it does not appear that she played it to him. She does not seem to have cared for natural objects. Her husband enjoyed the pet goats who played about the White House. They bored her. She liked to give away the flowers from the conservatory, but I do not read that she had a passion for them, any more than had Lincoln, who complained that he had "no taste natural or acquired for such things." One pleasure they shared, that of the theater, and in Washington they were able to indulge this till it culminated in the performance that was ruinous for both.

As to Mrs. Lincoln's religion, there is a good deal to be said on the practical side. She was generous and kindly, ready to help and to give. Stoddard's account of her hospital visitation during the war is very attractive. She made no display, sought no publicity whatever, but just went and gave and sympathized. In regard to the higher elements of spiritual life she was probably rather conventional, though she was a faithful member of the Episcopal, and then of the Presbyterian, Church, and Doctor Barton thinks that after her boy Willie's death she had some profounder religious experience. It may seem a trifling matter to note, but Mrs. Keckley's record of the ejaculation, "God, no!" as habitual seems to me singularly indicative of the woman.

I cannot think that there was much spiritual sympathy between her and her husband. We have, to be sure, Whitney's delightful sentence, "They were *en rapport* in all the higher objects of being." I do not believe that anybody was really "*en rapport*" with Lincoln in such matters, and I certainly do not believe his wife was. They both had, indeed, a superstitious turn of mind, and when the husband had dreams of horror and foreboding, the wife was ready to accept and interpret them. But, in Mr. Stephenson's admirable phrase, Mrs. Lincoln's soul "inhabited the obvious." The remote, gloomy, spiritual regions haunted by him, whether he was smiling or praying, were hardly likely to be visited by her. Thousands of pages have been written about Lincoln's religion; but he still smiles and remains impenetrable. He practiced with God the same superb, shrewd opportunism by which, as contrasted with the dogmatic idealism of Jefferson Davis, he saved the American Union. With him, if ever with anyone, it seems a case for remembering Lamb's remark, which Lincoln would have thoroughly enjoyed, that he was determined his children should "be brought up in their father's religion—if they can find out what it is." Yet it is curious that, after all, the practical, unmystical wife should have given us what is perhaps the very best summary on this point (italics mine): "Mr. Lincoln had no faith and no hope in the usual acceptation of those words. He never joined a church; but still, as I believe, he was a religious man by nature. . . . But it was *a kind of poetry in his nature*,

MRS. ABRAHAM LINCOLN

From a carte-de-visite photograph by Brady in the Harvard College Library

and he was never a technical Christian." Excellent example of the keen common sense of the woman who understands even where she is wholly unable to appreciate. And we come across this with Mrs. Lincoln at every turn.

II

In dealing with Mrs. Lincoln's external life we are on somewhat surer ground, though not much, for still the cloud of intangible gossip is likely to mislead us. Socially it is evident that she was ambitious and eager for success. On the whole, it cannot be said that she achieved it. Her appearance was by no means against her. Her face, in the photographs, is to me totally without charm. It is a positive, aggressive face, without a ray of sensitiveness in it. But, even in the heaviness of later years, she had a certain formal beauty and dignity, both of face and figure, and could bear herself well. It would seem that she dressed with taste, though at times too ostentatiously, and Lincoln objected to her extreme low necks. As regards this matter of clothes I cannot resist quoting one passage, both because it is one of the few touches of real self-revelation that we have from her own pen and because it is so thoroughly human. Three years after her husband's death she writes to Mrs. Keckley: "I am positively dying with a broken heart, and the probability is that I shall be living but a *very* short time. May we all meet in a better world, where *such grief* is unknown. Write me all about yourself. I should like you to have about four black widow's caps, just such as I had made in the fall in New York, sent to me. . . . The probability is that I shall need few more clothes; my rest, I am inclined to believe, *is near at hand*."

There are pleasant accounts of the Lincoln hospitality in Springfield. As to what happened in the White House observers differ. But it must be remembered that few hostesses have been subjected to such cruel criticism as Mrs. Lincoln had to meet. Those who watched her impartially, like W. H. Russell, Bancroft, and Laugel, report in the main favorably, though it is noticeable that they are inclined to speak of her as better than they expected. The truth is, her ardent and impulsive temper made her tactless and uncertain. People could not count upon her, and it is said that she changed her intimates and social advisers too frequently. The basis of her social zeal was rather an intense ambition than a broad human sympathy, and for the widest popularity and success the latter is indispensable. Then it must always be remembered that she had the strange, incalculable, most undomestic and unparlorable figure of Lincoln to carry with her, which would have been a terrible handicap to any woman. His dress was strange, his manners were strange, his talk was strange. And there was always that flood of homely stories, reeking with the unexpected. He would not lay himself out to be agreeable to his wife's callers. Not that he was untidy. This is always justly denied. But he was magnificently inappropriate, disconcerting. One must not think of him as Dominie Sampson, but rather as if one were to attempt to introduce Charles Lamb or Shelley into a complicated conventional social life. So, if the poor lady failed, it must be admitted that she had her difficulties.

In her housekeeping and domestic arrangements she seems to have been excellent. Her table is highly spoken of and she was an exact and careful manager as to neatness and punctuality. Here again her husband was far from being a help to her. He was quite indifferent to what he ate and it was impossible to make him systematic about meals or hours generally. The remote world in which he lived was but imperfectly accessible to the tinkle of the dinner bell.

As regards the most essential element of domestic tranquillity, money, he was unsystematic also. In his legal business he could not be kept to exact accounting, had no commercial or speculative instinct whatever. Also, he was largely generous and more anxious to win his client's cause than to get his money. But he was no spender, had few needs and no costly tastes, and above all he abhorred debt, though circumstances sometimes forced him into it. How simple his financial ideas were appears in his reported remark shortly before his election as President: "I have a cottage at Springfield and about eight thousand dollars in money. . . . I hope I shall be able to increase it to twenty thousand, and that is as much as any man ought to want." As a matter of fact, his estate was much larger than this at the time of his death.

Mrs. Lincoln no doubt did her best. In the early days she made her own dresses and she had always moments of violent economy. Her first remark to Mrs. Keckley was: "We are just from the West, and are poor. . . . If you will work cheap, you shall have plenty to do." But her tastes in the matter of outlay were far different from her husband's. She liked to give, and did give. She liked the pleasant things of life, especially the kind that cost money. We have her own written words—and it is such a comfort when we do have them—on this subject: "When I saw the large steamers at the New York landing ready for the European voyage, I felt in my heart inclined to sigh that poverty was my portion. I often laugh and tell Mr. Lincoln that I am determined my next husband shall be rich." Which of course was agreeable for him. But the most pitiable exhibition in regard to Mrs. Lincoln's finances is Mrs. Keckley's story of the debts incurred from real or imagined necessities of dress to keep up the presidential dignity. The maddening pressure of these debts doubled the wife's anxiety as to the chances of her husband's second election in 1864. It must not be supposed that Mrs. Keckley's record of conversations that took place is verbally exact, but it is surely close to reality in its general tone. She says to Mrs. Lincoln, "And Mr. Lincoln does not even suspect how much you owe?" And the answer is, " 'God, no!' This was a favorite expression of hers. 'And I would not have him suspect. If he knew that his wife was involved to the extent that she is, the knowledge would drive him mad. He is so sincere and straightforward himself, that he is shocked by the duplicity of others. He does not know a thing about my debts, and I value his happiness, not to speak of my own, too much to allow him to know anything. This is what troubles me so much. If he is re-elected, I can keep him in ignorance of my affairs; but if he is defeated, then the bills will be sent in and he will know all.' " Such are the domestic tragedies of money.

In her dealings with those about her in subordinate positions

Mrs. Lincoln's uncertain temper is said to have caused her a good deal of difficulty. Herndon declares very definitely that "on account of her peculiar nature she could not long retain a servant in her employ." But it is evident that she was much attached to Mrs. Keckley, who served her faithfully for a number of years. And the testimony of the White House secretary, Stoddard, is exceedingly friendly and favorable. She was considerate, he says, and did not burden you with unreasonable demands. Probably, like many people of quick temper, she regretted her outbursts and did her best to make amends for them.

It is with her children that Mrs. Lincoln is most attractive. Both she and Lincoln were devoted to them, he in his gentle, humorous, abstracted fashion, she with no doubt erratic but effusive and genuine demonstrations of tenderness. She was interested in their education, in their health, in their mental and moral development. But fate was as cruel to her in the maternal as in the conjugal relation, and she lived to bury three of her four sons. The eldest died in the early days in Springfield. The youngest, Tad, who was her chief consolation after her husband's death, so that she wrote, "Only my darling Taddie prevents my taking my life," was snatched away in 1871. But the death of Willie, in the midst of the at once anguished and triumphant days in the White House, was the bitterest blow of all. The mother was inconsolable, and her grief led her into strange and fantastic ecstasies of passion, till the crisis came in the scene so vividly related by Mrs. Keckley, when Lincoln took his wife by the arm and led her to the window. "With a stately, solemn gesture, he pointed to the lunatic asylum, 'Mother, do you see that large white building on the hill yonder? Try to control your grief or it will drive you mad, and we may have to send you there.' "

Yet, with the curious perversity of fortune which attended so much of Mrs. Lincoln's life, even her mother's sorrow, which would seem as if it ought to have won her public respect and doubtless did so, was turned by her inborn tactlessness into an element of unpopularity. The military band had been in the habit of playing in the square near the White House. But Mrs. Lincoln's reminiscent grief could not endure the music, and she insisted upon its being stopped for months, till the people became so indignant that Lincoln was forced to overrule her. Truly, one cannot but sympathize with Mrs. Keckley's exclamation, even if it is a little exaggerated: "I never in my life saw a more peculiarly constituted woman. Search the world over, and you will not find her counterpart." And she was married to a man as strange as herself, and as strangely different.

III

Now, having established Mrs. Lincoln's general character, as far as it is possible to do so, we come to the profoundly curious and interesting study of her relation with her husband, and this should begin with the history of their marriage.

In early life Lincoln seems to have had a susceptible imagination with regard to women, the more susceptible, perhaps, because he had so little to do with them. His profound affection in his twenties for Ann Rutledge, which has been embroidered by so many story-tellers, and her melancholy death, almost unhinged him for the time, and Herndon insists that he never really loved anyone afterward. But a varied list of feminine names appears. There is the robust Mary Owens, with whom his courtship seems mainly to have consisted in endeavors to persuade her that she would do better not to marry him. There is a more shadowy Sarah Rickard. And there is Matilda Edwards, sister-in-law of the lady with whom her own sister, Mary Todd, was also staying. But the substantial charms of Mary and her decided habit of getting what she wanted, in the end fixed the rather wandering lover, and in 1840 they were definitely engaged.

Here we strike one of the most debated points in Mrs. Lincoln's life, and in dealing with the course of this engagement we are at once confronted with the question of the veracity of Herndon. It seems to me that his essential tone and attitude must be regarded as satisfactory. He ventured a prophetic protest against the drift of a silly legendary atmosphere tending to envelop Lincoln as it enveloped Washington. Such a tendency evinces much more the timidity of the worshiper than the greatness of the idol, for if he is really great, nothing will make him more so than to prove that he was really human. At the same time, after the industrious researches of Miss Tarbell, it is difficult to accept in detail Herndon's account of the stormy progress of Lincoln's love-affair. According to Herndon, the day for the wedding was actually fixed, the supper was ordered, the bride arrayed, the parson present—and the bridegroom failed to appear, tormented by doubts and hesitations approaching mental derangement. The disturbance was so great that Lincoln's friends for a time feared suicide.

Without pronouncing positively on the more highly colored details of this narrative, we may regard the indisputable facts as curious enough. It is certain that the engagement was broken, certain that Lincoln a year later referred to the "fatal first of January, 1841," the day which, according to Herndon, was set for the wedding. Also, we have the remarkable series of letters to Speed, a near friend who was wooing and marrying at the same time, in which Lincoln uncovers his tormented soul, a soul clearly well versed in all the tortures of self-analysis, self-criticism, and self-reproach. Long before this crisis he had written to Mary Owens: "Whatever woman may cast her lot with mine, should anyone ever do so, it is my intention to do all in my power to make her happy and contented, and there is nothing I can imagine that would make me more unhappy than to fail in the effort." In March, 1842, he writes to Speed that, since the breaking of his engagement he "should have been entirely happy but for the never-absent idea that there is one still unhappy whom I have contributed to make so. That kills my soul. I cannot but reproach myself for even wishing to be happy while she is otherwise."

Then Speed is married and likes it, which impresses Lincoln, and somehow or other Mary regains her control, and on the 4th of November, 1842, the two are married very simply and quietly. In a letter of Lincoln's only recently published there is this admirable phrase, turned with a delicate significance which Lamb or Touchstone might have envied, "Nothing new here, except my marrying, which to me is a matter of profound wonder."

It is matter of profound wonder to most of us, and we endeavor, without much success, to find out how it happened. To begin with, what was Mary's motive, why did a woman so proud as she seek to retain a lover who appeared so obviously reluctant? Herndon's theory is fantastic. He asserts that Mary's pride was so bitterly wounded that she married Lincoln to make his life miserable, purely for revenge. Even put in more rational fashion, with the idea that she was a person who persisted relentlessly in getting what she had once wanted, the explanation is scanty. There is also the theory that Mary was ambitious and that she foresaw Lincoln's future, even preferring him in this regard to so promising a candidate as Douglas. Something there may be in this: she was a keen-sighted woman, and she is said to have prognosticated her husband's success from the start. But I think we must add that she loved him, felt instinctively the charm that so many men felt, the almost inexplicable charm which went with that strange, ungainly, physical make-up of which an early friend could say, "he was the *ungodliest* figure I ever saw."

In the same way I feel that probably something in her fascinated Lincoln. His conscience forced him, say some; her family forced him, say others. Both may have contributed. He was morbidly sensitive. He was indolent and in some ways easily led. Yet I have no doubt he loved her, and that quick, narrow, masterful spirit gained and kept a hold over his vaguer and more fluid one.

I imagine that the love on both sides persisted to the end. Herndon insists that there was no love at all. To Mr. Rankin the whole affair apparently seems a sweet idyl of uninterrupted bliss. It was probably just an average earthly marriage, with an increasing bond of association overcoming all sorts of wear and tear and pulling and hauling. Lincoln could never have been a comfortable husband for any wife. His casual ways, his irregular habits, his utter disregard of the conventions and small proprieties would have worn on a far more tranquil temper than Mary Todd's. And her temper was not tranquil at all; in fact, patience was the least of her distinguishing qualities. Her violent outbursts on small occasions are matter of record, and it is impossible to put aside altogether the scenes of furious, disgraceful public jealousy described by Badeau and confirmed by General Sherman. Lincoln took it all quietly, though it must have wrung his heart, patted her on the shoulder, called her his child-wife, and she was ashamed of herself—and did it again.

It was an every-day marriage, with some rather dark spots in it, but hardly so bad as has been represented. They loved their children and called each other "father" and "mother," in the old homely way, and their hearts grew more and more bound up in each other, and they just took life as it came. There is the cruel saying of La Rochefoucauld, "there are comfortable marriages, but no delicious ones," which simply means that life, as we go on with it, with all its trials, may at its best be comfortable, but can rarely be delicious. There is the other saying of the French comic writer, "in marriage, when love exists, familiarity kills it; when it does not exist, it gives it birth." Both have a certain significance in connection with the marriage of the Lincolns.

But what has afforded infinite entertainment to the inquiring biographer, and what I think must be equally entertaining to the judicious reader, is the violent contrast with which the same simple facts may be stated according to the prejudice of the person who states them. Take the two extremes, Herndon and Mr. Rankin: their analysis of Lincoln's married life cannot but be instructive as well as diverting.

First, there is Lincoln's absence from home. He left on every excuse, Herndon says. He lived in his office. Where other lawyers returned from their work to the comfortable fireside, he lingered in the country store or anywhere, rather than face the nagging that daily tormented him. All a mistake, says Mr. Rankin. He was a great deal from home, attending to more or less important business, and why? Because he had such a competent, careful, devoted wife that his presence at home was entirely unnecessary.

Take clothing. Mrs. Lincoln was always fussing about her husband's dress. Again, explains the unfailing Mr. Rankin, this was all a matter of health. He was threatened with consumption and her loving care in seeing that he was properly clothed may have saved his life. It was the same with food and regularity at meals. Innumerable stories are told of her sending arbitrarily at the most inconvenient times to insist upon his attendance, and even appearing herself, with some indulgence of shrewish tongue. Wrong, wrong, urges Mr. Rankin. She may have spoken quickly, but affectionate anxiety about his health was at the bottom of it all.

The best is the story of the ring. Herndon enlarges, with rather fiendish satisfaction, upon Lincoln's reluctance when even the *bona fide* wedding day arrived. Speed's little boy, says Herndon, seeing the bridegroom so finely dressed, inquired where he was going. "To hell, I suppose," was the gloomy answer. Oh, cries Mr. Rankin, cruel, cruel, even to imagine that he could have uttered such a word! There was the wedding ring. Did not Lincoln have engraved in it the tender sentiment, "Love is eternal"? Innocent Mr. Rankin! he apparently does not remember Jaques's remark to Orlando: "You are full of pretty answers. Have you not been acquainted with goldsmiths' wives and conned them out of rings?" I will not suggest that the sentiment may have emanated from Mary herself, though there have been such instances. But, alas! we know how many rings with similar mottoes are clasping unloved and loveless fingers all about the world. And always, to sum the whole, there is the cynical, cruel, profound, significant sentence of Dumas *fils:* "*Dans le mariage, quand l'amour existe, l'habitude le tue; quand il n'existe pas, il le fait naître.*"

IV

Having thus analyzed, with delightful inconclusiveness, the conjugal affection of the Lincolns, we may consider with equal inconclusiveness, the important question of Mrs. Lincoln's influence over her husband. It is clear that she was a person who naturally tended to dominate those about her. Could she dominate him? In little things he was no doubt yielding enough, to her and to others, as appears from his jocose remark that it was fortunate he was not a woman, since he never could say no. When it came to great matters, especially moral, he may not have bothered to say no, but he did what he thought right, without the slightest regard to the demands of others. Hear what Mrs. Lincoln says herself: "Mr. Lincoln was mild in his manners, but he was a terribly firm man when he set his foot down. None of us, no man or woman, could rule him after he had once fully made up his mind." Can you not read the outcome of many fruitless battles here? Mrs. Edwards gives a pretty picture of the wooer's absorbed attention during their courtship, how Mary talked and Lincoln listened. No doubt he listened all his life. Sometimes he heeded.

Mrs. Lincoln's chief wrestle was with her husband's social peculiarities. Here she was obviously in part successful and it cannot be questioned that her experience and knowledge of the world were of great benefit. As Newton puts it, she "taught him particularly that there was such a thing as society, which observed a man's boots as well as his principles." At the same time, from his boots to his hat, and through all the long six feet between, the man was thoroughly unconventional and nothing could make him otherwise. In the early married days in Springfield he would open the door himself in his shirt sleeves and assure august visitors that his wife would be down as soon as she could get her trotting harness on. Such things torment any well-constituted woman. Mary resented them. Yet she was sweetly contrite afterward. When a friend said to her, "Mary, if I had a husband with such a mind as yours has, I wouldn't care what he did," she answered, "It is foolish—it is a small thing to complain of." The oddities may have been toned down a little in Washington; but they were never got rid of. You could believe in the man, you could admire him, you could scold him; but you could not domesticate him.

On broader matters, less naturally within her sphere, even on the conduct of the war, Mrs. Lincoln evidently had her word. What wife would not? And sometimes it was the apt and poignant one. How characteristic is her retort to Stanton, who proposed to have her painted as she appeared at Fort Stevens, when she had come under fire: "That is very well, and I can assure you of one thing, Mr. Secretary, if I had had a few *ladies* with me, the rebels would not have been permitted to get away as they did." Large military policy was perhaps beyond her, but she gave her sharp, quick judgment of military commanders, bearing out, to some extent, her husband's admission that she had quicker insight into character than he. The words, as reported by Mrs. Keckley, can hardly be relied upon; but the general drift of them must be accurate. Of McClellan she said: "He is a humbug. . . . He talks so much and does so little. If I had the power, I would very soon take off his head and put some energetic man in his place." As to Grant, she is equally severe: "He is a butcher and is not fit to be the head of an army. . . . He has no management, no regard for life. . . . I could fight an army as well myself." How perfect is Lincoln's quiet answer to all this: "Well, mother, supposing that we give you command of the army. No doubt you would do much better than any general that has been tried."

With politics Mrs. Lincoln was of course more interested and more at home than in military details. She watched her husband's career from the time of her earliest acquaintance with him and followed every step of it with the intensest ardor. Lincoln's appreciation of this shows most charmingly in his remark, on first hearing the result of the presidential nomination in 1860, that there was "a little short woman at our house who is probably more interested in this dispatch than I am; and if you will excuse me, gentlemen, I will take it up and let her see it." [1] Abstract political principles may not have appealed to her much. Before the war her sympathies were more or less Southern, and this brought her criticism and added to the unpopularity which she was not able to overcome. But there can be no question about her entire loyalty to her husband's cause, which was in every sense her own. And whenever there was a personal point

[1] It is profitable to compare this remark, as thus reported by Lamon, with the refined, genteel version given by Mr. Rankin (*Personal Recollections of Abraham Lincoln*, page 190), "There is a lady, over yonder on Eighth Street, who is deeply interested in this news; I will carry it to her." Very likely neither version represents what Lincoln actually said; but the Rankin method is always the same.

to be decided, her judgment was always quick and sometimes sure. It is only just to say that I have not found one single case of her attempting to exert influence for the benefit of her friends or family, no soliciting of offices or commissions where they were not deserved. But she did interfere when her husband's, and her own, interests seemed to be involved. It was she who prevented Lincoln from accepting the governorship of Oregon in 1849, from political foresight, say Lamon and Mr. Rankin, because she did not want to go off into the woods, say Nicolay and Hay. And in other cases she exerted a pressure which was strong and perhaps effective.

As in army matters, so in politics, it was the human side which interested her, and she criticized Seward and Chase just as savagely as she criticized Grant. Also, she was much inclined to work on human agents where it was possible. Russell complains that she was accessible to flattery and filled her parlors with "men who would not be received in any respectable private house in New York." Her own explanation of this proceeding, in the dialogue with Mrs. Keckley, bearing on the election of 1864, is profoundly interesting: "In a political canvass it is policy to cultivate every element of strength. These men have influence, and we require influence to re-elect Mr. Lincoln. I will be clever to them until after the election, and then, if we remain at the White House, I will drop every one of them, and let them know very plainly that I only made tools of them. They are an unprincipled set, and I don't mind a little double-dealing with them." When Mrs. Keckley inquires if Mr. Lincoln knows, the answer is: "God, no! he would never sanction such a proceeding, so I keep him in the dark and will not tell him till all is over." Somehow in all these political concerns Mrs. Lincoln reminds one at times of Mr. Strachey's Victoria. There is the same dignified, yet dumpy figure, the same round, hard, positive, dominating face. And one cannot but think of the remark of an Englishman to Mrs. Fields, which Mr. Strachey would enjoy. "We call her 'Her *Un*gracious Majesty.' "

It is clear enough that back of Mrs. Lincoln's political interest and indeed back of all her life there was a tremendous driving force of ambition. There is much debate whether she had more ambition or he. They were different in this, as in everything. His ambition was vague, dreamy, fitful, mystical. Hers was narrower, more concrete, but it never rested, and went straight at its ends. How much we are to believe of the apparently well-authenticated stories of her aiming at the White House almost from girlhood, is a question. Any girl may aim at the White House, I suppose. No doubt a good many do who never get there. Perhaps the most impressive anecdote on the subject is Lamon's account of his first talk with her, in 1847. "Yes," she said, of her husband, "he is a great favorite everywhere. He is to be President of the United States some day; if I had not thought so, I never would have married him, for you can see he is not pretty. But look at him! Doesn't he look as if he would make a magnificent President?" That a woman should speak thus in her first interview with a stranger is extraordinarily suggestive, if you can believe it. And Lamon's emphatic insistence upon her use of the word "magnificent" makes the story somewhat more credible.

At any rate, she got to the White House and reigned there through four of the greatest years in the history of the country. I wish I had a little more authority for the seemingly sane and not unfavorable account of her White House career given by Mr. Willis Steell, the immense effort for popularity and social success and supremacy, ending in satiety and disappointment: "The 'court' she set up had turned into a mock bubble, shining in iridescent colors only in her imagination; created from sordid materials, and wholly empty." Then the triumphant election of 1864 set the crown upon it all, if crown there was. In April, 1865, the war was over. On the afternoon of the 14th Mr. and Mrs. Lincoln drove out alone together and Lincoln seemed singularly happy, so much so that Mary's ill-divining soul presaged the woe to come. He talked to her of well-earned rest, of peaceful plans and projects for the future. In the evening they went to Ford's Theater. And still his mind was rather on the coming dreamy years than on the play. We will go to Europe, he said to her, go to the Holy Land, go to the city I have always wanted to see, Jerusalem– While he was busy with such thought, the pistol of Wilkes Booth shattered the world of Mary Todd Lincoln into diminutive fragments, which no man ever again could piece together.

V

As this portrait is mainly made up of questions that cannot be answered, we might as well conclude with the most unanswerable of all: would Lincoln's career have been different, for better or worse, if he had married a different wife? Here again a variety of speculations present themselves, each urged with partisan eagerness. It would perhaps be possible to work out some such theory as Mr. Van Wyck Brooks cleverly applied to the case of Mark Twain—that is, that the constant conventionalizing pressure of a prosaic wife chilled and deadened, to some extent, the quick burst of spontaneous genius; but we should always have to remember that Mark was passionately devoted to Livy from beginning to end. There is, on the whole, a singular unanimity of biographers in the view that Mrs. Lincoln was helpful to her husband; but there is an astonishing difference as to the way she helped. Herndon, always critical, admits the helpfulness, in fact emphasizes it. Lincoln, he says, was naturally indolent, contented, stay-at-home (though elsewhere he calls him ambitious). If home had been delightful, he would have enjoyed it and would not have been so eager to make a mark in the world. Mary made home hideous, and by so doing made her husband great. Mr. Rankin does his best to involve this cynical explanation in the rosy mist of his amiable memory, and goes to the other extreme. According to him Mary was a sort of protecting angel, who advised, cautioned, impelled, always at the right time. "Without Mary Todd for his wife, Abraham Lincoln would never have been President. Without Abraham Lincoln for her husband, Mary Todd would, probably, never have been a President's wife." This beatific solution may be correct; but if it is so, I find it difficult to explain the fact that, though Nicolay and Hay were intimately present in the White House, in all the ten volumes of their *History* Mrs. Lincoln gets only a few lines here and there, and in the close daily record of Hay's *Diary* her name is hardly mentioned.

Surely a guardian, ministering angel would deserve and receive a little more than this. For myself, I find Mr. Stephenson's moderate statement very satisfying: "She had certain qualities that her husband lacked. . . . She had that intuition for the main chance which shallow people confound with practical judgment. Her soul inhabited the obvious." Lincoln's natural danger was the world of dreams and going astray in it, said Mr. Stephenson: "That this never occurred may be fairly credited, or at least very plausibly credited, to the firm-willed, the utterly matter-of-fact little person he had married."

The problem of Lincoln's melancholy brings the question of his life with Mary to a point: that haunting, brooding sadness, which rarely left him, though he shot the dark cloud through with constant fantastic sallies of laughter, that sadness which Herndon expressed with such extraordinary power when he said that "melancholy dripped from him as he walked," and which Lincoln himself described as so terrible that "if what I feel were equally distributed to the whole human family, there would not be one cheerful face on the earth." Did Mary cause this grief or did she alleviate it? Herndon by no means affirms the former, but he evidently thinks that the misery of home surroundings much augmented a constitutional tendency. Then along comes Mr. Rankin, from whom a mellow optimism is constantly dripping, and assures us that, on the contrary, so far from causing the melancholy, Mary was the one who could cure it. When the spells grew acute, "she . . . was the only one who had the skill and tact to shorten their duration. . . . I revere her memory for this most gracious service." Again Mr. Rankin may be correct; but when I think of that concise, hard, unsympathetic face, I wonder.

Among the varied possibilities connected with Lincoln's other early loves, the suggestion of melancholy brings up most of all the image of Ann Rutledge. It has even been suggested that the melancholy had its origin in the loss of her of whom he said, the thought of "the snows and rains falling upon her grave filled him with indescribable grief." If he had married Ann, would it all have been different? We know so little of her that we cannot conjecture further than that a devoted, self-forgetful passion such as he hardly felt for Mary Todd might have changed his world. As for the substantial, hearty Mary Owens, it is not likely that his experience with her would have been very different from his experience with the other Mary.

And then one thinks of a woman of real genius, of large capacity, of sweet human comprehension, a woman like Theodosia Burr or Sarah Butler. With a wife like this would Lincoln have done, perhaps not greater things, but done them with an ampler serenity and spiritual peace?

I doubt it. Lincoln was not in any way a woman's man, in spite of the early loves. Mary Owens thought him "deficient in those little links which make up the chain of woman's happiness." Lincoln himself, much later, wrote, in his dry way, "The truth is, I have never corresponded much with ladies; and hence I postpone writing letters to them, as a business I do not understand." He may have been a master of men; for dealing with women he was at once too self-contained and too sincere. I am sure the words of the *Imitation* would have pleased him: "Be not a friend to any one woman in particular, but commend all good women in general to God."

More than that, he lived in a solitude which neither man nor woman ever perfectly penetrated. No doubt we all live in such a solitude. The difference is that nine hundred and ninety-nine out of a thousand rarely think of it. Lincoln thought of it all the time. He ruled over millions of men and women who loved him; yet he was enormously alone, because he felt himself to be so. In this one point there is a curious resemblance between him and the greatest of all his contemporaries, a man who differed from him in so many other respects, Robert E. Lee. Lee was lonely as Lincoln was. Yet Lee had a most exquisite, devoted, sympathizing wife and children whose affection was constant and complete. The loneliness, with him, as with Lincoln, was that isolation of the human soul which the yearning of the deepest love merely accentuates. Lincoln's own words to Speed convey it with clarifying intensity, "I have no doubt it is the peculiar misfortune of both you and me to dream dreams of Elysium far exceeding all that anything earthly can realize." When there was such an ideal as this to compete with, neither the perfection of wit, nor of beauty, nor of sacrifice, would have been any more satisfying than poor Mary Todd.

ANDRÉ MAUROIS

"A beautiful portrait is at once a portrait resembling its subject and an artistic transference of reality." This characteristic utterance of M. André Maurois may be set with another, quoting Bacon: "'Art is essentially man added to nature'; that is, facts ordered by the human mind." From the kernel of truth expressed in these sentences has sprung the modern conception of biography as a work of art, of which M. Maurois is both the clearest exponent and the happiest practitioner. As a Frenchman, he is heir to that nation's great classical tradition of clarity, form, and restraint; as a modern intellectual—through events as fortunate for us as for him—he fell in congenially with the new scientific and literary ideals of certain Anglo-Saxon contemporaries, especially the Bloomsbury Group; as an artist, he combines with a racial romanticism the acutest gifts of perception and expression and a remarkable creative imagination.

André Maurois (Émile Herzog) was born in 1885 in the small manufacturing town of Elbeuf, a dozen miles above Rouen on the Seine, where his family owned and operated textile mills. At the Lycée of Rouen he mastered English, distinguished himself for his French prose, and came under the direct influence of the philosopher "Alain," to whom he pays the high homage of saying, "À Chartier, professeur de philosophie, je dois tout." After his formal education he married and returned to the Elbeuf mills, writing in spare hours. But he was freed from this distasteful work by the War, in which his knowledge of languages soon made him valuable as a liaison officer to a Scottish regiment and later at the British G.H.Q. There in the officers' mess he noted, with eyes and ears and pencil, the refreshing manifestations of the Anglo-Saxon mind. Toward the end of the War, having composed these jottings into a small narrative, he showed it to a fellow officer, through whom it finally reached the hands of a young Paris publisher who was rash enough to print it. *Les Silences du Colonel Bramble* (1918) has gone into well over a hundred editions. It was followed by a companion volume, *Les Discours du Docteur O'Grady* (1920), and an experimental novel, *Ni Ange ni Bête* (1919), based on the life of Shelley which, after being reënforced and entirely recast as *Ariel, ou la Vie de Shelley* (1923), was at once taken up enthusiastically in Europe and America and established its author in the first rank of modern biographers. The success was repeated in *Disraëli* (1927). But the "biographie romancée" found also plenty of detractors. These were chiefly skeptics reluctant to accept as authentic a life that read like a novel, that dissociated the man from his works, and that lacked the reassurance of footnotes and bibliography. M. Maurois, who has of course used secondary as well as primary sources, was publicly attacked as a plagiarist. But the author's answer was conclusive. Most of his critics have been silenced by his full defense of his working methods, by his evidence of exhaustive research, and especially by the life of *Byron* (2 vols., 1930), in which he uses the same vivid narrative method but illustrates more generously from his subject's writings and supplies full and detailed documentation at the end. His study, *Edouard VII et Son Temps* (1933), is an excellent sequel to *Disraëli*. M. Maurois has produced also short biographies (*Meïpe, ou la Délivrance*, 1926; *Dickens*, 1927; *Voltaire*, 1933); novels (the autobiographical *Bernard Quesnay*, 1926; *Climats*, 1928; *Le Peseur d'Âmes*, 1931); critical works (*Études Anglaises*, 1927; *Aspects de la Biographie*, 1929); fantasies, articles, reviews, and many miscellaneous pieces. Nearly all his books are translated into English. He has made successful lecture-visits to England and America and even taught for a term at Princeton; and he retains a very high place in the contemporary letters of his own country.

Whoever would understand M. Maurois's biographical aims and methods, and to a great extent those of the whole modern school, should read his Cambridge University lectures, *Aspects of Biography*, and should contrast his three main biographies (of Shelley, Disraeli, and Byron) with the corresponding Victorian works. But in a smaller scope the reader may see the same principles applied in the following selection from *Meïpe*, translated as *Mape: The World of Illusion*. To M. Maurois, biography is not only an art and a science, but a personal means of expression as well, the subject chosen "in order to respond to a secret need in [the author's] own nature." Thus after purging himself of certain feelings in his lives of Shelley and Disraeli, M. Maurois wished to study, "in a third manifestation, the reconciliation of an incurable romanticism of youth with the perfect serenity of a purified philosophy [of old age]." For this somewhat homeopathic treatment no character seemed more fitting than Goethe, who "begins his life with Werther, that is, in the full tide of romantic enthusiasm, and towards the end of it attains an equilibrium." Hence "The Sorrows of the Young Werther," in which the creator of an illusory world is finally reconciled to the actual one.

But the fact that the author sees himself in the character and that the character is real and historical need not prevent the resulting study from being a work of art. For the character has been selected partly because his career has a natural symmetry of its own. Like the painter in oils, then, the biographer eschews the photograph, which tells everything without color, shading, or "values," and by a skillful selection of details, by the use, not of invention, but of a re-creative imagination, and above all by a singularly limpid style (in the original), he paints his portrait of the individual as he sees him. The details in this portrait of Goethe are all veracious and most of them may be found in G. H. Lewes's full-length biography. The picture, like Goethe's own far freer adaptation of life in *Werthers Leiden,* must be accredited to the artist who made it.

THE SORROWS OF THE YOUNG WERTHER[1]

He is said to have been so given over to Love that, as soon as he met a woman he liked, he tried to win her favours. If he failed, he painted her portrait, and thus extinguished his desire.—LIFE OF FRA FILIPPO LIPPI.

STRASBOURG

THE FRANKFURT coach stopped at the Geist; a German student set down his luggage, astonished the inn-keeper by refusing dinner, and rushed wildly off to the Cathedral. The vergers, as they watched him climb the tower, looked at each other with some misgiving.

The gabled roofs surged in waves against the hard, pure lines of the Castle of the Rohans. The plains of Alsace sparkled under the midday sun, dotted with villages, forests, and vineyards. At this very hour, in every one of those villages, girls and women would be dreaming. As he looked at this virgin canvas on which his desire had begun to sketch out so many and so various delights, he felt all the vague delightful charm of amorous expectancy. He came again many times. The platform at the top overhung the adjacent parts of the building so that he could imagine himself surrounded by the open sky. At first he felt giddy. Long illnesses in his childhood had left him morbidly sensitive and afraid of empty space, noise, and the dark. But he wanted to cure himself of these weaknesses.

Gradually the vast plain, a chart upon which his heart had written nothing, became enriched with names and recollections.

[1] From *Mape: The World of Illusion* by André Maurois. Copyright D. Appleton-Century Company, Inc. Used by permission of the publishers.

Alsace had become "my beloved Alsace." He could now distinguish Saverne, where Weyland had taken him; Drusenheim, whence a lovely meadow path leads to Sesenheim. There in a rustic parsonage, surrounded by gardens and embowered in jasmine, lived the charming Frédérique Brion. In the far distance, beyond the hills and castle towers, dark clouds were gathering. The student's thoughts turned to the little moving human figures who were hurrying about the narrow streets three hundred feet below. How much he would have liked to enter into those lives, remote as they seemed from one another and yet united by all manner of mysterious bonds; to lift up the roofs of the houses, to be present unseen at all those secret and surprising actions through which alone we can understand our fellows. On the previous evening, at the Marionette Theatre, he had seen a performance of the legend of Doctor Faust.

As he looked up and watched the clouds sail past the spire he felt as though it had suddenly taken flight and was carrying him away. "Supposing the Devil offered me power, possessions, women in return for the bond of Faust; should I sign?" After a short but honest examination of his conscience, he said to himself, "I would not sign it to be master of the world; but for knowledge—yes. Ah, you are too inquisitive, my fine friend."

Rain began to fall and he made his way down the narrow twisting stairway. "One might write a Faust. There are a good many already. . . . But Spiess, and poor old Widmann—that is second-rate stuff. Their Faust is a vulgar rascal who is damned by his own baseness. The devil was cheated: he would have got him anyhow. . . . Mine? Mine would be a greater character—a kind of Prometheus. Defeated by the gods if you like, but at least because he tried to snatch their secret from them."

Below, in the Cathedral, a dark velvety light poured through the stained windows. A few kneeling women were praying in the gloom. The organs were murmuring vaguely as though under the touch of gentle fingers. Goethe looked long at the vaulting of the roof. When he saw a beautiful tree, he often had the sensation of losing himself in its growth and penetrating its perfect scheme. His thought rose like sap, spread into the branches, and expanded into leaves, flowers, and fruits. The immense converging arches of the nave recalled the same manifold and splendid design.

"Here, as in the works of Nature, everything has its purpose, everything is proportioned to the whole. . . . Oh, to write books that should be like cathedrals! If only you could express what you feel! If you could only put on to paper the fire that runs through your veins! . . ."

As soon as he withdrew into himself like this he came upon a whole world of his own. He had just discovered Shakespeare, and he admired him as a man does who takes the measure of a rival. Why not be the German Shakespeare? He had the power; he knew it. But how could he lay hold on it? What form should he impose upon this living force? He longed to see his emotion, a prisoner at last, rigid like those mighty vaultings. Perhaps the architect himself had once hesitated and despaired in the presence of the dream-cathedrals that had preceded the Cathedral.

There were plenty of subjects. The story of Sir Götz . . . Faust . . . idylls of the German countryside, in the manner of a modern Theocritus. A Mahomet perhaps, or a Prometheus. Any hero would do through whom he could fling a challenge to the world. He would model his heroes from himself, but on gigantic scale, and then breathe his own life into them. A Caesar perhaps? His span of life would not be long enough for so many projects. "A bird-like nature full of vain excitement," his master Herder had said of him. But to fill these wonderful empty frames he needed ideas and feelings: he had to live and live a thousand lives. "Not the being," he said to himself again and again, "but the becoming everything."

"Being nothing? Not even the husband of the charming Frédérique? No, not even that." He pictured to himself Frédérique's grief. Had he really the right to leave her, when his entire behaviour had let her believe that he would marry her, when Pastor Brion had welcomed him as a son? "The right? Are there any rights in love? After all, the adventure was as pleasant for her as for me. Had not Frédérique understood all along that the son of Councillor Goethe of Frankfurt would not marry a pretty country girl? Would my father ever have consented?

Would she have been happy in a world so different from her own?"

"Sophisms! If you must be false, at least be frank. The son of Councillor Goethe is of no greater importance than the daughter of the Pastor. My mother was poorer than Frédérique. And as for the world so different from her own, was she not delightful this winter when she danced on the waxed floors of the great drawing-rooms of Strasbourg?"

"You are right, but what am I to do? I cannot . . . no, I cannot . . . I should be in bondage if I did. The first duty is to develop all that one has, all that one can become. I shall always be Goethe. When I use my name I mean all it stands for. My qualities and my faults—all are good, all are part of my nature. I was right to love Frédérique because I felt so at the time. If one day I feel I must go away from her to recover myself, I shall still be Goethe when I go and all will be as it should."

At this moment he imagined Frédérique in tears by the roadside and himself riding away, his head bent, not daring to look back. "What a scene for a *Faust*," he thought.

II

A parchment with a red seal turned the student into a lawyer. The deserted Frédérique wept, Doctor Goethe's horse trotted towards Frankfurt. Skating and philosophy proved effectual remedies against some tolerably sharp attacks of remorse. In the spring a course at the Imperial Chamber at Wetzlar seemed to Councillor Goethe an indispensable adjunct to his son's legal studies.

For a century the Holy Empire had been sinking into the sands of oblivion, and only three mutilated arches of the vast edifice which had for so long sheltered the land of Germany could still be observed: the Aulic Council at Vienna, the Diet at Ratisbon, and the Imperial Chamber at Wetzlar. This latter, the supreme tribunal for all the kings, dukes, archdukes, palatines, bishops, and margraves who had divided the authority of the Emperor between them, should have been maintained by contributions from the various States; but, as often happens in the case of collective institutions, each of the participants, in order to make sure that he should not be the only one to pay, had fallen into the habit of paying nothing. The customary financial expedients were under discussion: some proposed a special stamp, others a lottery or a tax upon the Jews. In the meantime, as some means of subsistence had to be found, the judges obtained their salaries from the litigants.

The principal sovereigns of Germany maintained legations in attendance on this grandiose and sordid shadow of a great judicial institution, and thus created an agreeable and leisured little circle in this provincial town. When Goethe arrived at the Kronprinz Inn he found a noisy table of young attachés and secretaries. He was at once invited to join it, and from the moment of his first conversation realized that he was in familiar spiritual surroundings.

Europe was going through one of its crises of intellectual unrest. For nine years its kings had lived in peace; within their States worn-out constitutions had managed to preserve enough vigour to make revolutions seem impossible. The contrast between the ardour of youth and the stagnation of society gave birth to a feeling of impatience and disgust, a melancholy peculiar to periods of transition and peace, which was then called, as it always will be, the malady of the age. The young attachés at Wetzlar were afflicted like all their contemporaries. They were great readers: they sought for emotional inspiration in Rousseau and Herder; and when in doubt, and while they were waiting to find it, they drank a great deal of wine.

They were delighted with Doctor Goethe, who was one of their own kind and yet their superior. He, like them, repeated at the turn of each phrase: "Nature . . . respect Nature . . . live in Nature." For Nature was the key-word of that time, as Reason had been for the preceding generation, and as Liberty, then Sincerity, then Violence and then Justice were later to become. But for Goethe Nature was much more than a word. He lived in her, became part of her and accepted her with a kind of gay abandonment. While his new friends, diplomats and literary amateurs, shut themselves up in their offices in order at least to make a pretence of work, Goethe, boldly displaying his contempt of the Imperial Court and his own determination to learn public law out of Homer and Pindar only, set out every morning with a book under his arm into the lovely country that surrounded Wetzlar. The spring was exquisite. The trees in the fields and meadows looked like great white and pink bouquets. Lying among the tall grasses, near the bank of a stream, Goethe lost himself in the contemplation of all the myriad little plants and insects, and the blue sky. After the tortures of Strasbourg, the doubts and the remorse of Frankfurt, came a strange serenity, and an amazing activity of mind.

He opened his Homer, and the modern, human aspect of the story delighted him. Those young girls at the fountain were Nausicaa and her companions. The green peas and roast meat which a woman was preparing in yonder great inn kitchen was the banquet of the suitors and the kitchen of Penelope. Men do not change; heroes are not statues of white marble; their skin is hairy and cracked, their hands swollen and restless. Like the divine Ulysses we sail upon the open sea, in a little vessel suspended above an abyss, and in the hands of the mighty Gods. A fearful yet a beautiful thought when one is lying on one's back among soft grasses, gazing at the vault of heaven.

In the evening, at the Kronprinz Inn, the great delight now of the Round Table was to listen to Doctor Goethe relating his discoveries of the day. A verse of Pindar, or a rustic church that he had drawn as well as he could; some lovely lime trees in a village square, children, or a beautiful farm girl. He had the gift of charging his stories with an almost naïve enthusiasm which made the most trifling things interesting. As soon as he came in, the movement of life seemed to grow quicker. Among the young men who listened to him, some had talent, but none had genius. "Ah, Goethe," said one of them to him, "how can one help loving you?"

All Wetzlar soon sought his acquaintance. Two of the secretaries, although unmarried, lived on the outskirts of the Round Table. One of them, young Jerusalem, of the Brunswick Legation, was a very handsome youth with soft, melancholy blue eyes.

He kept himself at a distance, people said, because of an unhappy passion for the wife of one of his colleagues. He came once or twice to see Goethe, who was interested in his pessimism. But Jerusalem was too reserved to allow of the establishment of a real friendship.

The other hermit was Kestner of the Hanover Legation. When his comrades spoke of him they always called him the "Fiancé." He was, in fact, understood to be engaged to a girl in the town. He was extremely serious-minded, and his chief, who had a great respect for him, left him, in spite of his youth, a great deal of responsibility. It was for this reason that he had not time to come and dine at the Kronprinz. At the outset, the praises which the choicer spirits bestowed on the new arrival had put Kestner against him. But one day, when he was taking a walk in the country with a friend, they came upon Goethe under the trees. The conversation at once became deep and earnest, and after two or three meetings, Kestner, too, made up his mind, with the solemn deliberation that was characteristic of him, that he had undoubtedly met a very remarkable man.

Admired by his circle, free from all worldly or academic restraint, enraptured by the beauty of that springtime, Goethe was completely happy. Sometimes a transitory feeling clouded his enthusiasm as a light ripple stirs the calm surface of a lake. . . . Frédérique? No, it was not her recollection that passed across the steady glow of his thought. Once more it was like an uneasy expectation. He looked down upon Wetzlar as in days gone by he had looked down upon Alsace from the Cathedral.

"Shall I one day feel a delightful shiver as I open one of those doors? . . . Shall I be unable to read a stanza without my thoughts flying to a beloved face? . . . When I leave a lady, in the evening by moonlight, shall I already find the night too long and the morning too far off? Yes, all this is coming; I feel it. . . . And yet, Frédérique . . ."

He noted down a recollection. "When I was a little boy I happened to plant a cherry tree, and I loved to watch it grow. The spring frosts destroyed the buds and I had to wait another year before I could see ripe cherries on my tree. Then the birds ate them, then the caterpillars, and then a greedy neighbour. . . . And yet if I ever have another garden I shall plant another cherry tree."

Thus Doctor Goethe took his walks beneath the blossoming trees, afire with his new passion. He knew all about it, except the name of his beloved.

III

When the fine weather came the young men of the Legations used to organize dances in the country. A village inn was appointed as rendezvous. Some came on horseback, others brought their partners from Wetzlar in carriages. When Goethe was invited for the first time to one of these little fêtes it was agreed that he should go with two of the girls to fetch Fräulein Charlotte Buff, whom everyone called Lotte.

She was the daughter of old Herr Buff, the steward of the Teutonic Order, and she lived in the house of the Order, a pleasant white mansion. Goethe got out of the carriage, crossed quite an imposing courtyard, and, as he saw no one, went into the house. A young girl was standing in the middle of a group of children to whom she was handing out bread-and-butter. She was a blonde with blue eyes and a slightly turned-up nose; her features were not regular and a severe critic might perhaps have thought her scarcely pretty. But she busied herself with the children with so much charm and simplicity, she seemed so joyous, so unaffected, the whole scene was so happy a picture of one of those Germanic idylls that haunted Goethe's mind, that he was delighted with it.

A man pursues all his life among the race of women the type which, for some mysterious reason, is the only one that can arouse his feelings. In Goethe's eyes the bread-and-butter and the children formed part of this typical picture. It was a rustic grace, a delicate touch in homely matters that moved him. Frédérique of Strasbourg had already figured as a Muse of the countryside. Nausicaa, a king's daughter washing her linen, had perhaps given birth, in his mind, to this race of pure and homely maidens. In any case Charlotte Buff's slices of bread-and-butter seemed to him a perfect theme for a domestic symphony.

The girl's conversation during the journey, her childlike pleasure, the good-humoured determination which she showed in amusing her friends with little games during a storm, finished her conquest of the Doctor. In the completeness of his delight he realized beyond all question that he had found the woman with whom he had been in love for a fortnight.

Lotte herself was also well aware that she had found favour. It must be admitted that she was pleased. Goethe was handsome and agreeable; for a month past all Lotte's friends had talked of nothing but this marvellous intellect. She was a coquette, and a dangerous one, as only virtuous women can be.

Later in the evening Kestner, who had been, as he always was, kept later than the others by his work (he was a meticulous person—he made a rough copy of every letter and never sent off the despatches to Hanover without having read everything before signing it), rode out to join the little party, and from his attitude and that of the young girl, Goethe understood that Lotte Buff was the famous fiancée. This discovery took him aback, but he controlled himself, and without any sign of discomposure went on dancing, and amusing and entertaining the company. They did not break up till dawn. Goethe escorted his three companions back through the misty woods and the fields refreshed by the storm. Charlotte and he were the only ones who did not fall asleep.

"Please, please," said she, "do not trouble about me."

"As long as I see those eyes of yours still open," he answered, looking at her, "I cannot shut mine."

From that moment they did not speak another word.

When Goethe moved he lightly brushed the young girl's warm knees, and this imperceptible contact gave him one of the keenest pleasures he had ever known. The beauty of the morning light, the slightly ludicrous slumbers of their companions, the astonishing happiness that they shared made them feel like confederates in some delightful plot.

"I am in love with her," thought Goethe. "I am sure of that.

But how is it possible? At this moment at Sesenheim . . . Ah, well . . . one love fades and another blooms. This is Nature's way. . . . But she is engaged to Kestner, to the good and loyal Kestner. What can I hope for? Need I hope? It will be enough to see her, watch her living among the children, in her house, talk to her and listen to her laughter. What will come of all this? Who knows, and why try to foresee the end of anything? One should live like a running brook."

When the carriage at last stopped at the Teutonic House, which was still sleeping in the grey morning light, he felt quite dazed with happiness.

IV

On the following day he came to ask after Nausicaa and made the acquaintance of Alcinoüs. Old Herr Buff had lost his wife a year before; he had eleven children over whom Lotte reigned with benevolent despotism. Goethe, at his very first visit, as might have been expected, immediately won the hearts of the old gentleman and his children. He told some excellent stories and invented some new games. In everything that he said or did there was something youthful and captivating that was quite irresistible.

When he took his departure all the little company begged him to come back soon. A smile from Lotte confirmed the children's invitation. Goethe reappeared on the following day. He had no business to keep him away; he found no happiness except in Lotte's company, and he was not the man to deny himself a happiness that was within his reach. He came in the morning and in the evening, and in a few days he was an established visitor to the house.

Charlotte's life was indeed delightful to watch. Goethe found once more in her what he had so much loved in Frédérique: an activity practical in its purpose but poetic, too, from a certain delicate ease in the performance. She worked from morning till night. She washed the small children, dressed them, played with them, while at the same time superintending the studies of the older ones with a great deal of good sense and modesty. She took Goethe out to pick fruit in the orchard and occupied him in shelling peas or stringing beans. When it grew dark the whole family assembled in the drawing-room and at the request of Charlotte, who did not like leaving a friend without useful employment, Goethe tuned the harpsichord. Lotte was not sentimental. She was sensitive, but she was too much occupied to have the leisure or the wish to make play with her feelings. Her conversations with Goethe were instructive and serious. He talked about his life, his religious beliefs, and sometimes, too, about Homer and Shakespeare. She was intelligent enough to appreciate the rare qualities of the companion who was becoming a part of her daily life. She was conscious of emotion and perhaps love in all he said, and she was pleased without being disturbed. She knew that her own heart was untouched and that she remained Kestner's faithful and immaculate fiancée.

On his part the Fiancé was a little melancholy. His devotion to his diplomatic duties kept him away from her nearly all day. When he reached Lotte's house he saw Goethe sitting on the terrace at the girl's feet, holding a skein of wool, or found them in a corner of the garden choosing flowers for a bouquet. They welcomed him warmly and at once carried on with him the conversation that they had begun, so that his arrival never gave rise to an embarrassed silence. Nevertheless Kestner guessed that Goethe was not very pleased to see him. He would himself have sooner been alone with Charlotte, and Goethe, on the strength of his standing invitation, was in no hurry to take his leave. As they were both men of education and breeding, they did not in any way betray these somewhat painful feelings, but both of them were on their guard. Kestner was all the more alarmed because he was extremely modest. He greatly admired his rival; he thought him handsome and clever. What was worse, Goethe was unoccupied, and one who is always at hand to unburden the restless and unsatisfied souls of those eternal hermits of the home gains great power over them.

The Fiancé would have been more reassured if he had been able to read the more intimate thoughts of his rival. From the very first day the latter had understood that Lotte would not fall in love with him. A woman of her character does not give up a

Kestner for a Goethe. He was sure she liked him, and that was a good deal. Besides, what could he have asked for? To marry her? That would certainly ensure his happiness. But that was a happiness that did not tempt him. No, he was satisfied as he was. To sit at Charlotte's feet, watch her play with her young brothers, wait for a smile when he had done her a service or said something that she liked, receive a little tap, light as a caress, when he had ventured too direct a compliment—in this monotonous and narrow life he found an infinite contentment.

The spring was warm and they passed the days in the garden. All the incidents of this tranquil, pure affection figured in Goethe's journal like little scenes out of an idyll. He began to create. Not indeed his mighty edifice, not the Cathedral, but charming little Greek temples in a lovely countryside. What was to come of all this? He would not think about it. He began to accept his actions more and more as natural phenomena.

The evenings grew ever more delightful. When Kestner arrived the three friends went and sat together on the terrace and talked very late into the night. Sometimes they went for a walk by moonlight in the meadows and orchards. They had achieved that quality of perfect confidence which gives so much charm to conversation. No subject seemed absurd, and they had for one another that affection and mutual regard which alone make possible a true simplicity of intercourse.

For the most part it was Goethe who talked; Kestner and Lotte delighted in the amazing brilliance of his intellect. He described his Frankfurt friends, Fräulein von Klettenberg, Doctor Merck, strange creature of evil eye and insinuating talk, who looked for cures in books on mysticism. He told them how he had read the alchemists in his company and populated the universe with sylphs, Undines, and salamanders. For a long while he had been devoted to the pietists. They seemed to him more sensitive than others to personal religion, less attached to empty practices. Then he had grown tired of them. "They are people of commonplace intelligence who imagine there is nothing outside religion because they are ignorant of all the rest. They are intolerant; they want to mould other people's noses to the shape of their own."

Goethe himself believed that the truth could not lie in the idea of a God external to man. "It must be so very inconvenient to believe in the perpetual presence of God at one's side. I think I should feel as if I had the Great Elector always at my elbow. I believe in the presence of God within me."

Religion, next to love, is women's favourite topic. Lotte followed their conversation with the liveliest interest.

After having escorted their friend home, Goethe and Kestner would often go on wandering about for a long while in the deserted streets of Wetzlar. The edges of the shadows were sharply cut by the moonlight. About two in the morning, Goethe would sit on the top of a wall and declaim the wildest poetry. Sometimes they heard a noise of footsteps, and after a moment saw young Jerusalem pass by, walking bv himself with measured steps and bent head.

"Ah," said Goethe, "the Lover!"

And he burst out laughing.

V

Spring gave way to summer and affection to desire. Lotte was too kind and Goethe too young. Sometimes as they were walking along the narrow paths of the garden their bodies brushed against each other for one instant; sometimes as they were disentangling a skein of wool or picking a flower their hands met. The recollection of such moments kept Goethe awake for entire nights. He found it very difficult to wait for the morning, when he could see Charlotte once more. He recaptured even to their slightest shades the powerful and exquisite emotions that he had experienced with Frédérique, and this return of the seasons in his heart put him out of humour.

"When love comes back it destroys its own quality, which is the expression of the Eternal, the Infinite." Since this, too, was to repeat itself, human life was a mortally monotonous performance.

With the heavy August days, which cut short their little common tasks and left him long hours to spend at Charlotte's feet,

Goethe became more enterprising. One day he kissed her. Unimpeachable fiancée as she was, she told Kestner.

It was a difficult position for the grave and tender secretary. An unguarded remark, a reflection on the unconscious coquetry of Lotte and all would have been lost. But Kestner, no doubt because he was deeply in love with her, had the secret of a gift which, in a lover, is called delicacy. He contented himself by assuring Charlotte of his confidence in her and, as she asked him to do, left it to her to bring Goethe back to the ways of propriety. In the evening she asked the Doctor to stay after Kestner had gone, and told him that he must not make any mistake about her feelings: that she was and always had been in love with her betrothed and that she would never fall in love with any other man. Kestner watched Goethe come up with him, his head bent and looking rather sad, and he at once felt incomparably happy, kind, and sympathetic.

The three friends then became united in an odd and charming conspiracy. Following the example of Goethe, who concealed nothing, Kestner and Charlotte fell into the habit of revealing their feelings with the greatest freedom. Of an evening on the terrace Goethe's love for Lotte was the subject of long and delightful conversations. They talked of it as of a natural phenomenon, at once dangerous and interesting. Goethe's birthday was the same as Kestner's. They exchanged presents. Kestner's to Goethe was a little pocket Homer; Lotte's was the pink ribbon she had worn in her bosom on the day of their first meeting. Kestner had thought of sacrificing himself. He did not tell the others, but he noted down his misgivings in his private diary. Goethe was younger, handsomer, and more brilliant than he was. Perhaps he would make Lotte happier. But Lotte herself had reassured him: she had said she liked him best, and that Goethe with all his striking qualities was hardly made for a husband. And then no doubt Kestner's courage would have failed him, for he was deeply smitten.

Goethe, himself, under a gay and natural exterior, was suffering. Lotte's firm decision and her quite definite choice wounded his self-respect. The continual temptation of their life in common increased his desires. He had attacks of violent passion during which, in the presence of the indulgent and sympathetic Kestner, he seized Charlotte's hands and wept and he kissed them.

But in the worst moments of despair he knew that underneath this layer of genuine sadness there lay dormant a deep serenity in which he could one day find refuge. Just as a man out in a storm knows that the sun is bright above the clouds and possesses some means of reaching that untroubled space, so Goethe in his torment knew that he would soon escape his sorrow and would perhaps find something like a bitter and gloomy pleasure in describing it.

The evenings became shorter and cooler. The September roses began to fall. Goethe's satanic friend, the brilliant Merck, came to Wetzlar; he met Charlotte and found her charming, but he did not tell Goethe so. With a grimace of indifference he counselled flight to other loves. The Doctor, somewhat out of humour, thought that the time had come to tear himself away from a vain delight that was nearing its exhaustion. The man still found the same pleasure in living in Charlotte's shadow, in feeling the rustle of her dress against him in the darkness, in winning from her infinitesimal and precious proofs of her affection, snatched from the silent watchfulness of Kestner; the artist was satiated with these monotonous emotions. He had increased his spiritual resources by his stay in the place; he had made a collection of beautiful landscapes saturated in romance; the vein was worked out, the harvest gathered, and he must go.

"Must I really go? My soul is turning like the weather-vane on the top of a steeple. The world is so beautiful, and he is fortunate who can take pleasure in it without thinking overmuch. I am often annoyed because I cannot do this, and preach myself sermons on the art of enjoying the present."

But the world was calling him, the world with its infinite promises. "Not to be anything, but to become everything," that must be his aim. He had his work to do, his cathedral to build. What would it be like? That was still a mystery, hidden in the mists of the future. Yet it was to this dim prospect that he was going to sacrifice joys that would be secure. He forced himself to settle the day of his departure, and thenceforward, sure in his determination, he could plunge into the pleasing frenzy of his passion.

He had arranged to meet his friends in the garden after dinner, and he was waiting for them under the chestnut trees on the terrace. They would come, full of friendliness and gaiety; they would treat this evening just like any other. But this was the last evening. The Master of Events, Doctor Goethe, had decided it; nothing could alter his decree. Departure was painful, but it was not unpleasant to find oneself so inflexible.

He had inherited from his mother such a lively horror of scenes that he could not endure the idea of formal farewells. He wanted to pass this last evening with his friends in a serene and sad enjoyment. He felt in advance the pathos of this conversation, in which two of the participants, in their ignorance of the true position, were unconsciously to wound the third, who, because he alone was aware of it, would be the only one to be hurt.

He had indulged himself for some time with the agreeable torment of these reflections when he heard the footsteps of Charlotte and Kestner on the sandy path. He ran to meet them and rapturously kissed Lotte's hand. They walked to a dark leafy arbour at the end of the avenue and sat down. The garden was so lovely under the pale moonlight that they stayed a long while in silence. Then Charlotte said:

"I never walk in the moonlight without thinking of death. . . . I believe we shall be born again. . . . But shall we meet again, Goethe? . . . Shall we recognize each other? . . . What do you think? . . ."

"What are you saying, Charlotte?" he asked, completely overcome. "We shall meet again. In this life or the next we shall meet again."

"Do the friends that we have lost," she went on, "know anything about us? Do they feel all that is in our minds when we think of them? The image of my mother is always before my eyes when I am sitting quietly in the evening among her children, among our children, when they cluster round as they did round her."

She talked thus for a long time in a voice as soft and tender as the night itself. Goethe wondered if this unwonted melancholy were due to some strange presentiment. For himself, he felt his eyes fill with tears, and the emotion that he had wished to avoid was gaining possession of him. In spite of Kestner's presence, he took Charlotte's hand. It was the last day. What did it matter?

"We must go in," she said gently: "it is time."

She attempted to withdraw her hand, but he held it forcibly.

"Let us agree," said Kestner gaily, "let us agree that the first of us who dies shall give the two survivors some information about the other world."

"We shall meet again," said Goethe: "under whatever form it may be, we shall meet again. Good-bye, Charlotte. Good-bye, Kestner; we shall see each other again."

"Tomorrow, I think," said she, smiling. She got up and went with her fiancé towards the house. Goethe saw her white dress still gleaming for a few seconds in the shadow of the lime trees, and then everything disappeared.

After Kestner had gone, the Doctor wandered alone for a while in the lane from which the front of the house was visible. He saw a window lit up: it was Lotte's room. A little later the window grew dark. Charlotte slept. She knew nothing. The novelist was satisfied.

The next day when Kestner came home he found a letter from Goethe.

"He is gone, Kestner. When you receive this letter, he will have gone. Give Lotte the enclosed note. I had made up my mind, but your conversation yesterday has shattered me. I cannot say anything at the moment. If I had stayed with you an instant longer I could not have held out. Now I am alone and tomorrow I go. Oh, my poor head!

"Lotte, I hope I shall indeed come back, but God knows when. Lotte, what were the feelings of my heart when you were talking, knowing that I was seeing you for the last time? . . . He is gone. What spirit made you choose such a subject? . . . I am now alone and I can weep. I shall see you again, but 'tomorrow' never comes. Tell my young ruffians he has gone. . . . I cannot go on."

Kestner took the letter to Lotte early in the afternoon. All the children of the house echoed sadly, "Doctor Goethe has gone."

Lotte was sad, and while she was reading the letter the tears came into her eyes. "It was better for him to go," she said.

Kestner and she could talk of nothing else. Visitors came; they were amazed at Goethe's precipitate departure and found fault with his want of courtesy. Kestner defended him with much warmth.

VI

While his friends, much affected, read and re-read his letters, pitied him and pictured to themselves with feelings of anxious sympathy what his solitude would be like, Goethe was walking quickly down the lovely valley of the Lahn. He was going to Coblenz, where Merck was to meet him at the house of Frau de la Roche.

In the distance a hazy chain of mountains, above him the white summits of the rocks, at his feet, in the depths of a gloomy gorge, a river flowing under a curved roof of willows—all this composed a pleasantly melancholy landscape.

The pride of having broken the enchantment of Wetzlar tempered the melancholy of his still lively recollection. At times when he thought over the adventure he had just lived through, he said to himself, "Could not an elegy be made out of it? . . . or perhaps an idyll?" Or again he would ask himself if he were not better fitted to draw and paint landscapes like the one he was then passing through. "Come," said he, "I will throw my fine pocket-knife into the river. If I see it fall into the water, I will become a painter; if the willows hide it from my sight as it drops, I will give up the idea for ever."

He did not see the knife plunge into the stream, but caught sight of the splash, and the oracle seemed ambiguous. He postponed his decision. He walked as far as Ems, then went down the

Rhine in a boat and arrived at Frau de la Roche's house. He received the most delightful welcome. Councillor de la Roche was a man of the world, a great reader of Voltaire, a sceptic and a cynic. His wife was accordingly a woman of feeling. She had published a novel, she was interested in literary men and had turned her house, in spite of her husband and perhaps in protest, into a meeting-place for the Apostles of the Heart.

Goethe was more particularly interested in the dark eyes of Maxmiliane de la Roche, a beautiful girl of sixteen, intelligent and precocious. He took long walks with her in the country, talked about God and the Devil, Nature and the Heart, Rousseau and Goldsmith, and indeed spread himself superbly just as if Lotte had never existed. And the recollection of Lotte even gave a zest to this new friendship. "It is a very pleasant sensation," he noted, "to listen to the first accents of a dawning affection murmuring in one's heart before the echo of the last sigh of an extinct affection is altogether lost in the void. Thus when we turn our eyes from the setting sun we like to see the moon rising on the opposite horizon."

But he had soon to return to Frankfurt.

A return to the paternal house, after a reverse, brings a double feeling of relief and of discouragement. The bird has tried to fly away but has had to fold his wings once more. While he keeps to the nest he pines for the free air for which his wings had not proved strong enough. The child escapes from the difficulties of a hard and hostile world; he is absorbed once more in the familiar round, which is naturally less opposed than any other to the habits he has formed. There he discovers again the monotony of sensations grown too familiar, the affectionate slavery of the family.

His travels have been teaching him a sense of proportion, and he is surprised to find his own people still engaged upon their old foolish disputes. Goethe once more heard at home the very phrases that had so exasperated his childhood. His sister Cornelia complained of her father, his mother complained of Cornelia, and Councillor Goethe, whose temper was not accommodating, wished to send back to the study of lawyers' files a son whose head was full of half-created characters and who had no notion of the world of reality.

Goethe had a positive dread of melancholy, and realizing that it was mastering him, decided that his only chance of salvation lay in at once undertaking an important literary work. He was still thinking of a Faust, perhaps of a Prometheus, and perhaps, too, of a Caesar. But after having sketched out several plans, written a few verses, crossed them out and torn them up, he recognized that he was doing no good. Between them and his work came the image of Lotte.

His lips retained the savour of the only kiss that he had ever had from her, his hands the touch of her firm soft hand, and his ears the sound of that vivid, lively voice of hers. Now that he was far away from her, he found out that she was everything to him. As soon as he sat down at the table his mind went off into sad and fruitless reveries. He tried, as one always does, to reconstruct the past as he would like it to have been. If Lotte had not been engaged. . . . If Kestner had been less estimable and less kind. . . . If he himself had been less conscientious. . . . If he had had the courage to stay . . . or the courage to disappear altogether and force his mind to destroy the images that tormented him. He had hung above his bed a silhouette of Lotte cut in black paper by a gipsy artist, and he looked at this picture with a sort of frenzied devotion. Every evening before he went to bed he kissed it and said, "Good-night, Lotte." When he wanted a pin he took one of those that fastened the portrait to the wall and said, "Lotte, will you let me take one of your pins?" As evening fell he would often sit down and carry on long conversations in an undertone with his lost friend. These acts, which were natural and spontaneous on the first occasion, had in a few days become empty and melancholy rites, but he found in their accomplishment a certain relief to his distress of mind. He looked upon the commonplace, even absurd silhouette as a kind of altar.

He wrote to Kestner nearly every day and gave him affectionate messages for Charlotte. When speaking of his love he still kept up the half-jesting, half-tragic tone that he had assumed at

Wetzlar, because it was the only one that made it possible for him to express the feelings that troubled him without offending Kestner.

"We have spoken," he wrote, "of what may possibly take place beyond the clouds. I do not know; but what I do know is that the Lord our God must be a very cold-blooded person to leave you Lotte."

Another time: "So Lotte has not dreamed about me? I take this very ill, and I insist on her dreaming about me this very night and telling you nothing about it."

Sometimes he gave way to spitefulness and pride. "I shall not write again until I can tell Lotte that I am loved, and deeply loved, by another."

After a few attempts he was forced to realize that it would be impossible for him to get to work again on the subjects that had interested him in the past until he had rid his mind of this obsession. The only task of which he felt capable was to write about Lotte, to write a work of which Lotte should be the heroine.

But though he had considerable material—his diary, his recollections, even his feelings, which were still vivid—he was faced with great difficulties. The subject was very thin: a young man arrives in a town, he falls in love with a woman who is not free and draws back before the difficulties of the situation. Would this make a book? And why did the hero go away? His female readers would not like this at all. If he had been truly in love he would have stayed. In the adventure as it really happened Goethe had gone away because the call of his art, the will to create, had been stronger than his love. The more he thought about it the more commonplace and inadequate the subject seemed, the more incapable he felt of working it out, the more his weariness and disgust with all literary labours increased.

In the middle of November Kestner made known to him a surprising piece of news. Young Jerusalem, the handsome, melancholy youth who took so many walks in the moonlight wearing a blue frock-coat and yellow waistcoat, and who had been called in jest "The Lover," had lately shot himself.

"Unhappy Jerusalem!" Goethe wrote in reply. "Your news

was shocking and quite unexpected. . . . The people who know not joy because their hearts have been hardened by vanity and the worship of illusions are responsible for this and for all our misfortunes. For them there is no forgiveness, my friends! Poor young fellow! When I came back from a walk and met him in the moonlight, I said, 'He is in love,' and Lotte will remember that I laughed. I spoke with him very little. When I left I brought away with me one of his books, which I shall preserve, with his memory, as long as I live."

Events in another's life always aroused sincere emotion in Goethe when they represented possible and unrealized fragments of his own existence. He studied Jerusalem's story with an almost morbid curiosity. He was quite aware that if he himself had been slightly different, if certain elements had been lacking in the composition of his intellect, he might have gone the same way. But he was especially interested in it because his first thought had been, when he heard the news: "Here is my *dénouement*." Yes, the hero of his unlucky idyll might, indeed he ought to, commit suicide. Death, and death only, supplied the element of tragic grandeur that had been lacking in his adventure.

He asked Kestner to send him a complete account of all that he could learn about the affair, and Kestner did so, not without ability.

VII

The memories of Wetzlar and the account of Jerusalem's death certainly provided Goethe with the beginning and the end of a notable book. It would be a work of the truest and most vivid passion. The part played by the imagination would be, as was always Goethe's aim, reduced to a minimum. He had confidence in himself and he liked his subject. And yet he could not get to work and was still absorbed in his dreams.

He had always needed, before he could start writing, a brief illumination in which, as in a flash of lightning, he had a sudden view of the work as a whole without having time to distinguish the details. But this time he could get no such view of it. His love affair with Lotte and the death of his friend were two episodes taken from two different series of Destiny's successions and did not fit in together.

There was nothing in the characters of the people in the diary that suggested the drama of the *dénouement*. Kestner's kindness and freedom from jealousy, Lotte's wholesome simplicity and lightness of heart, Goethe's unassailable happiness and curiosity—such qualities made the hero's suicide improbable. He tried in vain to picture to himself what the scene between Frau Herd and Jerusalem could have been like, and Jerusalem's final reflections. He must remodel the characters and weave another chain of events. But events are strangely linked together. As soon as one is touched the whole edifice is shaken. It seems that the truth must be one, and that if it is touched up a little, even with the most delicate and careful strokes, the mind is torn between an infinity of possibilities.

Once more Goethe was unable to find peace. A fantastic population of plans and projects ranged over his weary brain. Sometimes he thought he could distinguish shadowy and lovely forms, but they vanished forthwith. Like a pregnant woman who cannot find relief, he sought in vain for a position in which he could be at rest. The hour of his delivery seemed far off.

He travelled to Wetzlar to get details of the drama. He saw the house in which the young man had killed himself, the pistols, armchair, and bed. He spent a few hours with Charlotte. The happiness of the engaged pair seemed complete. The very recollection of their evenings of old seemed to have passed out of their calm and well-ordered life. Goethe felt very unhappy and very lonely. His love revived. As he sat upon the sofa in the Teutonic House looking at the cool and peaceful Lotte, who continued to manage the household with her graceful competence, he said to himself, "Jerusalem was right. Even I myself could perhaps . . ." But Goethe remained Goethe and he returned quietly to Frankfurt.

The house seemed more melancholy than ever. The time of Kestner's marriage drew near. In the evening, alone in his room, "in his barren bed," Goethe pictured Charlotte in the nuptial chamber, in a blue striped dressing-jacket, her hair arranged for the night, chaste and charming. Desire and jealousy kept him painfully awake. In order to live, a man needs to look forward to some shining point, the goal of his journey. But what was there left for him to hope for? He saw himself condemned to live, as a humble lawyer or official, in this town whose commonplace middle-class would always dislike him for his intellectual gifts. His mind, which he knew to be capable of creation, would be worn out in drawing up reports or stupid statements for the courts. He thought, without modesty, but not without reason, "I shall live here like a giant chained by dwarfs."

He saw himself buried alive. All the companions of his youth left him one after another. His sister Cornelia was going to be married. His friend Merck was soon leaving for Berlin. Charlotte and her husband would in their turn go away from Wetzlar. "And I am alone. If I do not marry or hang myself, you may say that I like life very much"; thus he wrote to Kestner, and a little later: "I am wandering in waterless deserts."

He came to think that the cause of suicides must often be the need felt by a man leading a monotonous and melancholy life to astonish himself and, one might almost say, to divert his mind by an unusual action. "The love of life," he thought, "depends on the interest we take in the regular alternation of day and of night, of the seasons, and in the pleasure that these alternations offer us. When this interest comes to an end, life is simply a tedious burden. An Englishman hanged himself so as not to be forced to dress and undress every day. I heard a gardener exclaim wearily: 'Must I always be looking at those gloomy clouds passing from west to east?' These are symptoms of a disgust with life which, in thoughtful people, is commoner than is believed. As for myself, if I think about the matter coldly, what has life still to give me? Another Frédérique whom I shall desert? Another Lotte who will forget me? The foolish career of a lawyer at Frankfurt? Truly it would be a natural and courageous act to renounce such splendid prospects of one's own free will.

"And yet when we think of the various ways of suicide, we recognize that to diminish the number of the living is so contrary to human nature that in order to achieve the result man has recourse to mechanical aids. Though Ajax transfixes himself with his sword, it is the weight of his body that renders him this last service; when we turn a pistol on ourselves, it is the backward movement of the trigger that really kills us. The only authentic suicide is that of the Emperor Otho, who himself drove a dagger into his heart."

For several evenings when he went to bed he laid a dagger beside him. Before he put out the light he tried to drive the point into his chest. But he did not succeed in inflicting even the slightest of wounds. The body betrayed the spirit. "Ah, well," he thought, "at the bottom of my heart I must want to live."

When he looked into his heart sincerely, trying to rid himself of commonplaces, those insubstantial phantoms that hover above genuine thought, and sought for the reasons which, in spite of everything, made him wish to live, he discovered first of all his pleasure, which for him was perennial, in the marvellous spectacle of the world, that god-sent curiosity of his; then the sad sweet certainty of the approaching birth of a fresh affection; and lastly the more obscure but irresistible instinct to watch over the work that was, he felt, forming within him with an implacable deliberation.

"Don't worry," he wrote to his friends at Wetzlar. "I am almost as happy as two people who are in love, like you. I have in me as much hope as lovers have."

When the time of Charlotte's marriage drew near he asked the favour of being allowed to buy the wedding-ring. He found something of a strange pleasure in irritating this sore. Determined to portray his own sad state, he insisted that it should be hopeless. Goethe was his own model and he posed to perfection.

On the morning of the marriage, Kestner, the perfect friend, wrote him an affectionate letter. As Goethe had requested, the bride's nosegay was sent to him; he put it in his hat for his Sunday walk. He decided to take down the silhouette of Lotte on Good Friday, make a grave in the garden, and solemnly bury it. When the day came, the ceremony seemed to him a little ridiculous and he gave up the idea. The black-and-white silhouette now watched over untroubled slumbers. The Kestners had left for Hanover. Knowing nothing of their life in this new world, Goethe could not imagine it. In his case pain as well as love needed images to make it last. Had he not already let go the favourable moment for recording such fragile feelings as these?

VIII

He was still in correspondence with the charming Maximiliane de la Roche, whose black eyes had so helped him to console himself after Wetzlar. One day he learnt that she was going to marry a wholesale grocer of Frankfurt, Peter Anton Brentano, a widower with five children, and fifteen years older than herself. "Admirable!" wrote Goethe to Kestner, "dear Max de la Roche is going to marry a prominent shopkeeper!" Doubtless the sceptical Herr de la Roche had considered a large fortune and a numerous family preferable to a youthful heart.

Goethe expressed great pity for poor Max, who, for a gloomy house in Frankfurt, was going to abandon one of the most delightful places in the world and exchange her mother's cultivated and charming circle for the society of opulent tradesmen. Still he was overjoyed to think that so charming a creature was to be within reach.

As soon as he heard of her arrival at Frankfurt, he rushed to the house, used all his powers of conquest to captivate the widower's five children, and naturally succeeded in a quarter of an hour in making himself indispensable for ever. When Goethe wished to be agreeable, no one could resist him. Brentano was flattered by the presence in his house of the Burgomaster's grandson who was said to be a bright youth, so he gave Goethe a warm welcome.

Goethe immediately recovered his ardour and flung himself into a passionate friendship with his customary impetuosity. Soon his sole purpose in life was to keep Max company, to console her for the smell of cheese and for her husband's manners, to distract her mind by taking her for walks and reading to her. Once more all work was given up. And why should he write? Is there anything that is worth the smile, the sweet expression of contentment and gratitude, that for one fleeting instant flashes on a lovely face?

Max was not a little unhappy among the jars of oil and the barrels of herrings. She did not like Frankfurt. She tried to love her husband, but it was a difficult undertaking. Goethe became her confidant. Less practical than Charlotte Buff, she did not employ him to peel vegetables nor to pick fruit, but she spent the days with him playing duets for violoncello and piano and reading the latest French novels.

They often went out skating together. Goethe borrowed his mother's red velvet mantle and threw it round his shoulders like a cape. He skated perfectly, and as he glided along with sovereign ease, the wind behind him swelling out his royal train, he looked like a young god. Such at least was the opinion of his mother, the Councillor's wife, and of pretty Frau Brentano, for whose benefit the performance was given.

"Everything is going very well for me," he wrote. "The three last weeks have been nothing but pleasure, and we are now just as contented and happy as it is possible to be. I say we, for since January 15th there is not a single occupation in which I have been alone; and fate, that I have so often cursed, I am now well ready to flatter and call kindly and wise, for since my sister went away this is the only gift that could be called a compensation.

"Max is still the same angel whose simple and delightful qualities appeal to every heart, and my feelings for her are the joy of my existence."

But, alas! perfect pleasure cannot last and Brentano was soon to upset this unduly agreeable situation. At the outset he had found this young fellow who took his wife for walks extremely convenient; his own time was entirely taken up by the wares of his business and no one could take his place. On several occasions he had chosen Goethe to arbitrate between his wife and himself. It seemed to him that on certain questions the good sense of all the males of the species must be in agreement. Unfortunately Goethe was an artist and, in so far, a traitor to his sex. A husband always becomes, as the comic poets have remarked, most agreeably attached to any right-thinking man, one who, in other words, is of his own way of thinking; but a lover who undermines marital authority must be deservedly odious.

Brentano, noticing that his wife was not settling down at Frankfurt, that she criticized the mode of life of an ancient and respectable family, always talked about music, literature, and other unhealthy subjects, concluded, not without reason, that some evil counsellor must be making suggestions contrary to conjugal good order, and that the enemy was Goethe.

As soon as he had come to this conclusion, he treated Goethe with such insulting coldness that the latter's position in the house became extremely difficult. If he retaliated furiously, as he would have liked to do, he would sentence himself to exile; to endure the affronts in silence was to invite their multiplication. Soon Max herself, who was tired by disputes that spoilt all her pleasure, begged him to be careful and come less often. "I ask you for my own peace and quiet," she said to him. "Things cannot go on like this, they positively cannot."

He fell to walking up and down the room with long strides, repeating between his teeth, "It cannot go on like this." Max, who noticed his violent condition, tried to calm him. "I beg you," she said to him, "I beg you to control yourself. Your intellect, your knowledge, your talents promise you every happiness; be a man. Why must it be I? I who belong to someone else, I and no other?"

He went home, having promised that he would not come back again, but he was in a state of despair, distraught and talking to himself. So he was always to come upon the pitiful laws of society on the path of happiness. He could only find peace of mind, joy, and self-forgetfulness in the constant and affectionate society of a woman, and to obtain the right to this happiness he had either to surrender his liberty or condemn the woman he loved to become "guilty." Never had the conflict between the desires of the individual and the rules of society appeared to him so intolerable. Charlotte . . . ? Charlotte was after all in love with Kestner. But Max could not love her oil merchant and did not even pretend to love him. And he had to give way. "Your talents, your knowledge will bring you happiness." How ludicrous! Knowledge is grey and the tree of life is green. Besides, knowledge also is limited by human imperfection. What do the greatest scientists really know? Nothing about the true nature of things. What is man? His strength fails him just when he needs it most. In his joy, as in his sorrow, is he not limited, always confronted by the melancholy feeling of his own littleness just when he is hoping to lose himself in the infinite?

Quite suddenly, without knowing how the transformation had been worked, he felt once more at peace, master of himself, soaring far above these melancholy thoughts, as if they had belonged to another. "Why, of course," he thought, "that is how Jerusalem must have argued with himself; and no doubt it happened after a scene like the one I have just had with Max."

Thereupon he suddenly saw, with amazing lucidity, how his last unhappy adventure could be worked into the account of Jerusalem's death. Max and her husband, Charlotte and Kestner, Goethe and Jerusalem, seemed to melt, dissolve, and disappear, while their constituent elements, moving with incredible rapidity over the vast plains of the mind, combined harmoniously and in due proportions. The artist was awake at last, and Goethe was completely happy.

Then three new characters were born: Werther, Charlotte, and Albert. Werther was Goethe if he had not been an artist. Albert was a slightly meaner Kestner, endowed with Brentano's jealousy and with Goethe's own intellectual powers. Charlotte was Lotte, but brought up by Frau de la Roche, and a reader of Rousseau and Klopstock.

On the following day he shut himself up to work, and in four weeks the book was written.

IX

When Goethe had finished *The Sorrows of the Young Werther* he felt as free and happy as after a general confession. Dreams, doubts, remorse, desires—all had found their eternal and inevitable place. The Cathedral was built. The last of his workmen-thoughts had already left the yard, and in the silence that had fallen on the place the Architect waited for the earliest worshippers. His past life was no longer in him, but before his eyes. It was beautiful, and as he contemplated it from the outside with a triumphant lassitude he thought vaguely of the new life that he now had the right to begin.

The book was not to be on sale until the Leipzig Fair, but the author could not wait so long before sending it to Charlotte at least. He often tried to imagine when and how she would read it. Perhaps she would begin *Werther* one evening, in bed, her firm breasts outlined under the delicate linen; or perhaps sitting in an armchair opposite Kestner, who would be a little jealous and try to find out without being observed what his wife was feeling. She would know for the first time what Goethe's love had been. She would doubtless blush when she came to the passionate scenes at the end, to the furious kisses which he had never given her and which, by an almost magical art, he could now force her to receive. . . . And dear Max Brentano? She, too, would doubtless fall to dreaming.

As soon as he had received the first volumes from the printer, he packed up two copies, one for Charlotte and one for Kestner, and wrote to Lotte: "You will realize when you read this book how dear it is to me; and this copy above all I value as much as if it were the only one in the world. It is for you, Lotte. I have kissed it a hundred times, and I kept it shut up so that no one might touch it. Oh, Lotte, I want each of you to read it by yourselves and separately. You by yourself and Kestner by himself, and then I want each of you to write me a line. Lotte—good-bye, Lotte."

Kestner and his wife smiled and hastened to obey. They each took one of the little volumes and opened it with affectionate eagerness.

Charlotte was a little uneasy. She knew Goethe's ardent nature, his refusal to restrain the violence of his feelings, to accept the useful conventions of the world. In real life, the fear of committing himself, of missing opportunities, had nearly always in the end confined this torrent of lava to a channel. But what would Goethe be like when let loose?

As soon as she had read the first pages she realized that her husband would be severely tried. The scene at the ball, so natural in her recollection, had here, she knew not how, taken on a passionate sensuality. "To hold the most charming of creatures in my arms! Fly with her like the storm! See everything about one pass and fade! To feel! . . . It was then I vowed that a woman I loved should waltz with none but me though I died for it! You will understand me."

Charlotte sat pensive. To be quite frank with herself, she had understood from the first day that Goethe loved her in this way. It was an idea that had slipped into the recesses of her consciousness; she had kept it carefully shut up there and had long since succeeded in forgetting this discreet and disturbing presence. Yet the recollection was there, for as she read the burning sentences, Charlotte felt the sweet uneasy impression of a reminiscence.

When she came to the passage: "What fire runs through all my veins when my finger happens to touch hers, when our feet come together under the table. I start away as from a flame, but a secret force draws me back once more. I am seized with giddiness and my senses are in a whirl. Ah! her innocence, the purity of her soul prevent her from realizing how the slightest familiarities put me to the torture. When she puts her hand on mine, as she talks to me . . ." Charlotte put the book down and reflected for some time. Had she not, in moments like those of which she had just read the description, nearly always guessed Gothe's agitation, and found it not at all displeasing? Even now to read the account of it made her, she had to admit, surprisingly happy. She reproached herself for her coquetry. She looked at her husband sitting opposite her. He was rapidly turning over the pages of the little volume with a gloomy and worried expression.

After a short interval he raised his eyes in his turn and asked her what she was thinking about. He seemed angry and ill at ease. "It is a disgraceful act," he said warmly. "Goethe describes people who at the outset are like ourselves and then he changes them in some way into false and romantic characters. . . . What sort of creature is this sentimental Lotte who weeps unceasingly over Werther's hand? . . . Did you ever say, 'Oh, Klopstock!' and look up at the sky, especially to a young man whom you had only just met? I find it difficult to picture you in such a part. . . . Ah! I can now see clearly that Goethe has never understood what gives you your charm. It is I alone, Charlotte, I alone who understand that. What is so attractive in you is just your perfect simplicity that is never out of place, that joyous and natural self-possession of yours that banishes all evil thoughts. But he has even spoilt his own portrait. The real Goethe behaved much better than Werther. There was something fine and generous about our relations during those four months which he has not been able to express. . . . As for myself, whom he has described as so destitute of sensibility, I whose heart 'does not beat sympathetically at the reading of a favourite book,' am I so cold as all that? Oh, I know very well that if I had had to lose you, Lotte, it is I who would have been Werther."

At this instant husband and wife drew near to each other, and there followed a little scene of conjugal affection which would not, perhaps, have been exactly in accordance with the author's wishes. They finished the book together, side by side and hand in hand. At the end of it Kestner, at any rate, was in a state of acute anger. The transformation of their innocent simple story into a tragic adventure seemed to him really abominable. He was indeed a monster—this two-headed individual who was both Goethe and Jerusalem. And no doubt Kestner did not fail to notice that the account of the last interview between Werther and his beloved was taken entirely from the letter that he had himself written to Goethe about the death of Jerusalem. But when he was confronted with a heroine whose name was Lotte, and who at the beginning of the book had been described with all Lotte's characteristics, he was as hurt as if some coarse-minded painter had taken the face and person of his wife for the subject of an obscene picture.

Charlotte herself was more moved than displeased, but she could imagine and sympathize with her husband's feelings, and in order to soothe him she said she thought he was right. Besides, she shared his apprehensions. What would be said about them in their own circle? All their friends in Wetzlar and even in Hanover could not fail to recognize them. How would it be possible to explain which parts of the book faithfully presented them and which were alien additions? How could they escape all the malicious and quite natural gossip? If they had been less sensitive they would have realized that society is, in general, profoundly indifferent and forgetful, and what seemed now so very important would be quite forgotten in six months. But Wisdom and Pain seldom keep house together. They felt that their happy retired life had been wrecked by their friend's indiscretion.

X

On the following day Kestner wrote to Goethe in terms of severe displeasure. "It is true that you have interwoven some alien elements into each character and that you have blended several persons into one. Well and good. But if in these processes of interweaving and blending you had consulted your heart, the real people whose characteristics you have borrowed would not have been prostituted in this way. You wished to draw from nature in order to give verisimilitude to your picture, and you have brought together so many contradictory elements that you have failed in your purpose. The real Lotte would indeed be a poor creature if she were like your Lotte. And Lotte's husband—you called him your friend, and God knows whether he was so—is in like case.

"What a wretched object Albert is! If he had to be commonplace, was it necessary to make him such an utter idiot for you to be able to dominate him so haughtily and say: 'See what a fine fellow I am'?"

Goethe had for several days waited very impatiently for Kestner's and Lotte's opinions. He hoped for two long and enthusiastic letters, a list of passages that had more especially struck them, some quotations perhaps, a reminder of incidents that he had forgotten or missed out. He broke the seal with a cheerful sense of curiosity and was dumbfounded to come upon this bitter criticism. Was it possible that an intelligent man could so little understand the nature of a book? Why should he want Werther to be Goethe? "No doubt there are elements of Werther in me. But I was suddenly rescued from all that by something that is called Will. Take this away from Goethe and Werther will be left. Take away his imagination and we shall find Albert. Why does he say that Albert is a wretched creature? Why should I have made Albert commonplace? The beauty of my subject is that though Albert and Werther are opposed to each other, they fight on equal terms. Besides, what makes Kestner think that he is Albert? Does he believe that I am incapable of discovering a reasonable being in myself?"

The more he thought it over, the more he re-read Kestner's letter, the less he understood it and the more astonished he was. Yet it was distressing to him to think that he was giving his friends pain. He tried for a long time to find a means of pacifying them. But what was he to do? Not publish his novel? He had not the courage for that sacrifice.

"I must write at once and unburden my soul to you, my dear angry friends. The thing is done, the book is out; forgive me if you can. I will not listen to anything until events have proved how exaggerated are your fears, until you come to see in the book itself the harmless mingling of fact and fiction that it contains. . . . And now, my dears, when you feel anger rising within you, think, only think, that your old friend Goethe is always, always, and now more than ever, yours."

The publication of the book involved the Kestners, as they had anticipated, in requests for explanations and expressions of sympathy. Lotte's brother, Hans Buff, sent them the impression of the Teutonic House. There, at least, everyone knew Goethe, and young Werther's sufferings had had an uproarious success.

"By the way," wrote Hans, "have you read *Werther?* What do you think of it? The situation here is singular. There are only two copies in the whole town, and as everyone wants to read the book, everyone steals them as best he can. Yesterday evening, Papa, Caroline, Lele, Wilhelm, and I were all of us reading a single copy whose cover we had torn off. Each page passed through five hands. . . . Poor Werther! We laughed a great deal when we read it. Did he laugh too when he wrote it?"

Kestner had to assure his officious friends who sent their condolences, that his home life was happy, that his wife had always loved him, that Goethe had never thought of committing suicide, and that a novel was only a novel. Finally, Charlotte induced him to write Goethe a letter granting him absolution.

But there was little question of forgiveness. The young author was completely carried away. All Germany was now shedding tears over Werther's fate. The young men wore his blue frock-coat and yellow waistcoat and his brown-topped boots. The young women copied Charlotte's dresses, and above all the white dress with pink bows that she had worn at her first meeting with her friend. In every garden romantic hearts raised little monuments to Werther's memory. Climbing plants twined themselves about Wertherian urns. Songs and poems were written about Werther. The French themselves, so often contemptuous, welcomed this disciple of Rousseau with enthusiasm. Europe had not been so roused by a work of the imagination since *La Nouvelle Héloïse*.

Goethe answered in a tone which was scarcely that of a penitent. "O ye of little faith! If you could feel the thousandth part of what Werther stands for in a thousand hearts you would not even stop to think of the sacrifice that you have made for him. I would not, to save my own life, see Werther suppressed. Kestner, believe me, believe in me; your fears and your uneasiness will vanish away like the phantoms of a night. If you are generous, and if you do not worry me, I will send you letters, tears, sighs over Werther; and if you have faith, believe me, all will go well and gossip does not matter. Lotte, good-bye. Kestner, love me and do not bother me any more."

After this date his correspondence with the Kestners became extremely desultory.

Thenceforward, embalmed and enshrined in his sentences, they had lost for him the greater part of their reality. Once a year, over a long period, he wrote them letters which began "My

Dear Children," to ask for news of a continually increasing family. Then the excellent Kestner died.

In 1816 Frau Sekretärin Kestner, a widow of fifty-nine, plain but pleasantly good-humoured, came to visit His Excellency the Minister of State von Goethe at Weimar. She hoped that the great man might be useful to her sons August and Theodore, especially to Theodore, who wished to devote himself to the study of natural science.

She found a cultivated but worn-out old gentleman in whose features she looked in vain for the face of the wild youth of Wetzlar, whom no one could help loving. Conversation was difficult. Goethe, who did not know what to say, showed her prints and dried plants. Each of them read in the other's eyes astonishment and disillusion.

The Minister finally offered the old lady his own box at the theatre, excusing himself for not being able to join her there later. She thought, as she went out, "If I had met him by accident and without knowing his name, he would have made no impression on me."

The truth is that Doctor Goethe had long been dead; dead too was Fräulein Lotte Buff, who had so loved dancing and walks by moonlight. Of all the characters in this story one only was still alive, and that was the unhappy Werther.

PAUL DE KRUIF

Paul de Kruif came to the writing of his first book not as a man of letters but as a rugged-minded bacteriologist whom various experiences and opportunities had driven from the study of microbes to the study of men. He was born in 1890 in Zeeland, Michigan, descending from sturdy and prosperous Dutchmen who had settled in that region forty years before. After an ordinary public schooling, he went to the University of Michigan, graduating, B.S., in 1912, but remaining in the department of bacteriology to take his Ph.D. and become, at twenty-six, Assistant Professor. On America's entrance into the War, he left his classroom for France, where, as captain in the U. S. Sanitary Corps, he made the first prophylactic injections of gas gangrene serum into the wounded of the Fifth Division. After the Armistice he worked at the Institut Pasteur and in other laboratories, then came back to New York as an associate in the Division of Pathology at the Rockefeller Institute. Three years later, having won wide recognition among bacteriologists and medical men for his scientific writings and research, he paused to deliver a slashing attack (*Our Medicine Men,* 1922) on certain aspects of his profession. It was the beginning of his literary career.

By this time Mr. de Kruif became eager to know more of the human side of scientific work, to find out who really had stamped out some great scourge, or bred the best corn, or made a great discovery which civilization now takes for granted. With abounding energy and thoroughness he sought out all the available facts about the unknown, or little known, benefactors of mankind, and in 1926 published *Microbe Hunters,* the story of fourteen pioneers of bacteriology in their fight against disease. *Hunger Fighters* (1928), in the same vein, tells of a few forgotten men who struggled with nature to maintain and increase the North American food supply. *Seven Iron Men* (1929) relates the lives of the family of pioneer iron-seekers in Minnesota whose labors led to the creation of the steel industry in America. *Men Against Death* (1932), a sequel to the second book, portrays the microbe hunters of a more recent date. Mr. de Kruif, who writes especially for the Curtis publications, has lately contributed to *The Saturday Evening Post* studies of Charles F. Kettering and other living inventors. He furnished Sinclair Lewis with most of the scientific material that went into the very successful novel, *Arrowsmith* (1925), and the chapter on Dr. Walter Reed in *Microbe Hunters* has been made the basis of the recent drama, *Yellow Jack, A History* (1933), by Sidney Howard. These praiseworthy collaborations are only another evidence of the force and timeliness of Mr. de Kruif's writings.

The story of Antony van Leeuwenhoek (1632-1723), "First of the Microbe Hunters," is characteristic of all the work of this exuberant author. As Mr. H. L. Mencken has said, Mr. de Kruif "knows how to give the quest of the scientific all the thrills and gaudiness of a fight with broadswords." He has the American gift of showmanship. With an honest enthusiasm that overrides restraint, with no attempt, apparently, at punctilious English, frequently even without much penetration into the psychological reactions of his subject, he manages to make the plain reader grasp the problems and consequences of the scientist's career. To the physically and mentally robust de Kruif, fired with a democratic zeal to broadcast his biographies, no other mode would be possible. His explosive, dramatic, colloquial style—a composite, it has been called, of Emil Ludwig and Sinclair Lewis—irritates many readers, but it has unquestionably conveyed his message to an innumerable public.

LEEUWENHOEK

FIRST OF THE MICROBE HUNTERS

TWO HUNDRED and fifty years ago an obscure man named Leeuwenhoek looked for the first time into a mysterious new world peopled with a thousand different kinds of tiny beings, some ferocious and deadly, others friendly and useful, many of them more important to mankind than any continent or archipelago.

Leeuwenhoek, unsung and scarce remembered, is now almost as unknown as his strange little animals and plants were at the time he discovered them. This is the story of Leeuwenhoek, the first of the microbe hunters. It is the tale of the bold and persistent and curious explorers and fighters of death who came after him. It is the plain history of their tireless peerings into this new fantastic world. They have tried to chart it, these microbe hunters and death fighters. So trying they have groped and fumbled and made mistakes and roused vain hopes. Some of them who were too bold have died—done to death by the immensely small assassins they were studying—and these have passed to an obscure small glory.

Today it is respectable to be a man of science. Those who go by the name of scientist form an important element of the population, their laboratories are in every city, their achievements are on the front pages of the newspapers, often before they are fully achieved. Almost any young university student can go in for research and by and by become a comfortable science professor at a tidy little salary in a cozy college. But take yourself back to Leeuwenhoek's day, two hundred and fifty years ago, and imagine yourself just through high school, getting ready to choose a career, wanting to know—

You have lately recovered from an attack of mumps; you ask your father what is the cause of mumps and he tells you a mumpish evil spirit has got into you. His theory may not impress you much, but you decide to make believe you believe him and not to wonder any more about what is mumps—because if you publicly don't believe him you are in for a beating and may even be turned out of the house. Your father is Authority.

That was the world three hundred years ago, when Leeuwenhoek was born. It had hardly begun to shake itself free from superstitions, it was barely beginning to blush for its ignorance. It was a world where science (which only means trying to find truth by careful observation and clear thinking) was just learning to toddle on vague and wobbly legs. It was a world where Servetus was burned to death for daring to cut up and examine the body of a dead man, where Galileo was shut up for life for daring to prove that the earth moved around the sun.

Antony Leeuwenhoek was born in 1632 amid the blue windmills and low streets and high canals of Delft, in Holland. His family were burghers of an intensely respectable kind and I say intensely respectable because they were basket-makers and brewers, and brewers are respectable and highly honored in Holland. Leeuwenhoek's father died early and his mother sent him to school to learn to be a government official, but he left school at

ANTONY VAN LEEUWENHOEK

From an engraving in the Harvard College Library made from the original painting by Verkolje

sixteen to be an apprentice in a dry-goods store in Amsterdam. That was his university. Think of a present-day scientist getting his training for experiment among bolts of gingham, listening to the tinkle of the bell on the cash drawer, being polite to an eternal succession of Dutch housewives who shopped with a penny-pinching dreadful exhaustiveness—but that was Leeuwenhoek's university, for six years!

At the age of twenty-one he left the dry-goods store, went back to Delft, married, set up a dry-goods store of his own there. For twenty years after that very little is known about him, except that he had two wives (in succession) and several children most of whom died, but there is no doubt that during this time he was appointed janitor of the city hall of Delft, and that he developed a most idiotic love for grinding lenses. He had heard that if you very carefully ground very little lenses out of clear glass, you would see things look much bigger than they appeared to the naked eye. . . . Little is known about him from twenty to forty, but there is no doubt that he passed in those days for an ignorant man. The only language he knew was Dutch—that was an obscure language despised by the cultured world as a tongue of fishermen and shop-keepers and diggers of ditches. Educated men talked Latin in those days, but Leeuwenhoek could not so much as read it and his only literature was the Dutch Bible. Just the same, you will see that his ignorance was a great help to him, for, cut off from all of the learned nonsense of his time, he had to trust to his own eyes, his own thoughts, his own judgment. And that was easy for him because there never was a more mulish man than this Antony Leeuwenhoek!

It would be great fun to look through a lens and see things bigger than your naked eye showed them to you! But *buy* lenses? Not Leeuwenhoek! There never was a more suspicious man. Buy lenses? He would make them himself! During these twenty years of his obscurity he went to spectacle-makers and got the rudiments of lens-grinding. He visited alchemists and apothecaries and put his nose into their secret ways of getting metals from ores, he began fumblingly to learn the craft of the gold- and silversmiths. He was a most pernickety man and was not satisfied with grinding lenses as good as those of the best lens-grinder in Holland, they had to be better than the best, and then he still fussed over them for long hours. Next he mounted these lenses in little oblongs of copper or silver or gold, which he had extracted himself, over hot fires, among strange smells and fumes. Today searchers pay seventy-five dollars for a fine shining microscope, turn the screws, peer through it, make discoveries—without knowing anything about how it is built. But Leeuwenhoek—

Of course his neighbors thought he was a bit cracked but Leeuwenhoek went on burning and blistering his hands. Working forgetful of his family and regardless of his friends, he bent solitary to subtle tasks in still nights. The good neighbors sniggered, while that man found a way to make a tiny lens, less than one-eighth of an inch across, so symmetrical, so perfect, that it showed little things to him with a fantastic clear enormousness. Yes, he was a very uncultured man, but he alone of all men in Holland knew how to make those lenses, and he said of those neighbors: "We must forgive them, seeing that they know no better."

Now this self-satisfied dry-goods dealer began to turn his lenses onto everything he could get hold of. He looked through them at the muscle fibers of a whale and the scales of his own skin. He went to the butcher shop and begged or bought ox-eyes and was amazed at how prettily the crystalline lens of the eye of the ox is put together. He peered for hours at the build of the hairs of a sheep, of a beaver, of an elk, that were transformed from their fineness into great rough logs under his bit of glass. He delicately dissected the head of a fly; he stuck its brain on the fine needle of his microscope—how he admired the clear details of the marvelous big brain of that fly! He examined the cross-sections of the wood of a dozen different trees and squinted at the seeds of plants. He grunted "Impossible!" when he first spied the outlandish large perfection of the sting of a flea and the legs of a louse. That man Leeuwenhoek was like a puppy who sniffs—with a totally impolite disregard of discrimination—at every object of the world around him!

II

There never was a less sure man than Leeuwenhoek. He looked at this bee's sting or that louse's leg again and again and again. He left his specimens sticking on the point of his strange microscope for months—in order to look at other things he made more microscopes till he had hundreds of them!—then he came back to those first specimens to correct his first mistakes. He never set down a word about anything he peeped at, he never made a drawing until hundreds of peeps showed him that, under given conditions, he would always see exactly the same thing. And then he was not sure! He said:

"People who look for the first time through a microscope say now I see this and then I see that—and even a skilled observer can be fooled. On these observations I have spent more time than many will believe, but I have done them with joy, and I have taken no notice of those who have said why take so much trouble and what good is it?—but I do not write for such people but only for the philosophical!" He worked for twenty years that way, without an audience.

But at this time, in the middle of the seventeenth century, great things were astir in the world. Here and there in France and England and Italy rare men were thumbing their noses at almost everything that passed for knowledge. "We will no longer take Aristotle's say-so, nor the Pope's say-so," said these rebels. "We will trust only the perpetually repeated observations of our own eyes and the careful weighings of our scales; we will listen to the answers experiments give us and no other answers!" So in England a few of these revolutionists started a society called The Invisible College; it had to be invisible because that man Cromwell might have hung them for plotters and heretics if he had heard of the strange questions they were trying to settle. What experiments those solemn searchers made! Put a spider in a circle made of the powder of a unicorn's horn and that spider can't crawl out—so said the wisdom of that day. But these Invisible Collegians? One of them brought what was supposed to be powdered unicorn's horn and another came carrying a little spider in a bottle. The college crowded around under the light of high candles. Silence, then the hushed experiment, and here is their report of it:

"A circle was made with the powder of unicorn's horn and a spider set in the middle of it, but it immediately ran out."

Crude, you exclaim. Of course! But remember that one of the members of this college was Robert Boyle, founder of the science of chemistry, and another was Isaac Newton. Such was the Invisible College, and presently, when Charles II came to the throne, it rose from its depths as a sort of blind-pig scientific society to the dignity of the name of the Royal Society of England. And they were Antony Leeuwenhoek's first audience! There was one man in Delft who did not laugh at Antony Leeuwenhoek, and that was Regnier de Graaf, whom the Lords and Gentlemen of the Royal Society had made a corresponding member because he had written them of interesting things he had found in the human ovary. Already Leeuwenhoek was rather surly and suspected everybody, but he let de Graaf peep through those magic eyes of his, those little lenses whose equal did not exist in Europe or England or the whole world for that matter. What de Graaf saw through those miscroscopes made him ashamed of his own fame and he hurried to write to the Royal Society:

"Get Antony Leeuwenhoek to write you telling of his discoveries."

And Leeuwenhoek answered the request of the Royal Society with all the confidence of an ignorant man who fails to realize the profound wisdom of the philosophers he addresses. It was a long letter, it rambled over every subject under the sun, it was written with a comical artlessness in the conversational Dutch that was the only language he knew. The title of that letter was: "A Specimen of some Observations made by a Microscope contrived by Mr. Leeuwenhoek, concerning Mould upon the Skin, Flesh, etc.; the Sting of a Bee, etc." The Royal Society was amazed, the sophisticated and learned gentlemen were amused—but principally the Royal Society was astounded by the marvelous things Leeuwenhoek told them he could see through his new lenses. The Secretary of the Royal Society thanked Leeuwenhoek and told him he hoped his first communication would be followed by others. It was, by hundreds of others over a period of fifty years. They were talkative letters full of salty remarks about his ignorant neighbors, of exposures of charlatans and of skilled explodings of superstitions, of chatter about his personal health—but sandwiched between paragraphs and pages of this homely stuff, in almost every letter, those Lords and Gentlemen of the Royal Society had the honor of reading immortal and gloriously accurate descriptions of the discoveries made by the magic eye of that janitor and shopkeeper. What discoveries!

When you look back at them, many of the fundamental discoveries of science seem so simple, too absurdly simple. How was it men groped and fumbled for so many thousands of years without seeing things that lay right under their noses? So with microbes. Now all the world has seen them cavorting on movie screens, many people of little learning have peeped at them swimming about under lenses of microscopes, the greenest medical student is able to show you the germs of I don't know how many diseases—what was so hard about seeing microbes for the first time?

But let us drop our sneers to remember that when Leeuwenhoek was born there were no microscopes but only crude hand-lenses that would hardly make a ten-cent piece look as large as a quarter. Through these—without his incessant grinding of his own marvelous lenses—that Dutchman might have looked till he grew old without discovering any creature smaller than a cheese-mite. You have read that he made better and better lenses with the fanatical persistence of a lunatic; that he examined everything, the most intimate things and the most shocking things, with the silly curiosity of a puppy. Yes, and all this squinting at bee-stings and mustache hairs and what-not were needful to prepare him for that sudden day when he looked through his toy of a gold-mounted lens at a fraction of a small drop of clear rain-water to discover—

What he saw that day starts this history. Leeuwenhoek was a maniac observer, and who but such a strange man would have thought to turn his lens on clear, pure water, just come down from the sky? What could there be in water but just—water? You can imagine his daughter Maria—she was nineteen and she took such care of her slightly insane father!—watching him take a little tube of glass, heat it red-hot in a flame, draw it out to the thinness of a hair. . . . Maria was devoted to her father—let any of those stupid neighbors dare to snigger at him!—but what in the world was he up to now, with that hair-fine glass pipe?

You can see her watch that absent-minded wide-eyed man break the tube into little pieces, go out into the garden to bend over an earthen pot kept there to measure the fall of the rain. He bends over that pot. He goes back into his study. He sticks the little glass pipe onto the needle of his microscope. . . .

What can that dear silly father be up to?

He squints through his lens. He mutters guttural words under his breath. . . .

Then suddenly the excited voice of Leeuwenhoek: "Come here! Hurry! There are little animals in this rain-water. . . . They swim! They play around! They are a thousand times smaller than any creatures we can see with our eyes alone. . . . Look! See what I have discovered!"

Leeuwenhoek's day of days had come. Alexander had gone to India and discovered huge elephants that no Greek had ever seen before—but those elephants were as commonplace to Hindus as horses were to Alexander. Caesar had gone to England and come upon savages that opened his eyes with wonder—but these Britons were as ordinary to each other as Roman centurions were to Caesar. Balboa? What were his proud feelings as he looked for the first time at the Pacific? Just the same that Ocean was as ordinary to a Central American Indian as the Mediterranean was to Balboa. But Leeuwenhoek? This janitor of Delft had stolen upon and peeped into a fantastic sub-visible world of little things, creatures that had lived, had bred, had battled, had died, completely hidden from and unknown to all men from the beginning of time. Beasts these were of a kind that ravaged and annihilated whole races of men ten million times larger than they were themselves. Beings these were, more terrible than fire-spitting dragons or hydra-headed monsters. They were silent assassins that murdered babes in warm cradles and kings in sheltered places. It was this invisible, insignificant, but implacable—and sometimes friendly—world that Leeuwenhoek had looked into for the first time of all men of all countries.

This was Leeuwenhoek's day of days. . . .

III

That man was so unashamed of his admirations and his surprises at a nature full of startling events and impossible things. How I wish I could take myself back, could bring you back, to that innocent time when men were just beginning to disbelieve in miracles and only starting to find still more miraculous facts. How marvelous it would be to step into that simple Dutchman's shoes, to be inside his brain and body, to feel his excitement—it is almost nausea!—at his first peep at those cavorting "wretched beasties."

That was what he called them, and, as I have told you, this Leeuwenhoek was an unsure man. Those animals were too tremendously small to be true, they were too strange to be true. So he looked again, till his hands were cramped with holding his microscope and his eyes full of that smarting water that comes from too-long looking. But he was right! Here they were again, not one kind of little creature, but here was another, larger than the first, "moving about very nimbly because they were furnished with divers incredibly thin feet." Wait! Here is a third kind—and a fourth, so tiny I can't make out his shape. But he is alive! He goes about, dashing over great distances in this world of his water-drop in the little tube. . . . What nimble creatures!

"They stop, they stand still as 'twere upon a point, and then turn themselves round with that swiftness, as we see a top turn round, the circumference they make being no bigger than that of a fine grain of sand." So wrote Leeuwenhoek.

For all this seemingly impractical sniffing about, Leeuwenhoek was a hard-headed man. He hardly ever spun theories, he was a fiend for measuring things. Only how could you make a measuring stick for anything so small as these little beasts? He wrinkled his low forehead: "How large really is this last and smallest of the little beasts?" He poked about in the cob-webbed corners of his memory among the thousand other things he had studied with you can't imagine what thoroughness; he made calculations: "This last kind of animal is a thousand times smaller than the eye of a large louse!" That was an accurate man. For we know now that the eye of one full-grown louse is no larger nor smaller than the eyes of ten thousand of his brother and sister lice.

But where did these outlandish little inhabitants of the rain-water come from? Had they come down from the sky? Had they crawled invisibly over the side of the pot from the ground? Or had they been created out of nothing by a God full of whims? Leeuwenhoek believed in God as piously as any Seventeenth Century Dutchman. He always referred to God as the Maker of the Great All. He not only believed in God but he admired him intensely—what a Being to know how to fashion bees' wings so prettily! But then Leeuwenhoek was a materialist too. His good sense told him that life comes from life. His simple belief told him that God had invented all living things in six days, and, having set the machinery going, sat back to reward good observers and punish guessers and bluffers. He stopped speculating about improbable gentle rains of little animals from heaven. Certainly God couldn't brew those animals in the rain-water pot out of nothing! But wait . . . Maybe? Well, there was only one way to find out where they came from. "I will experiment!" he muttered.

He washed out a wine glass very clean, he dried it, he held it under the spout of his eaves-trough, he took a wee drop in one of his hair-fine tubes. Under his lens it went. . . . Yes! They were there, a few of those beasts, swimming about. . . . "They are present even in very fresh rain-water!" But then, that really proved nothing, they might live in the eaves-trough and be washed down by the water. . . .

Then he took a big porcelain dish, "glazed blue within," he washed it clean, out into the rain he went with it and put it on top of a big box so that the falling raindrops would splash no mud into the dish. The first water he threw out to clean it still more thoroughly. Then intently he collected the next bit in one of his slender pipes, into his study he went with it. . . .

"I have proved it! This water has not a single little creature in it! They do not come down from the sky!"

But he kept that water; hour after hour, day after day he squinted at it—and on the fourth day he saw those wee beasts beginning to appear in the water along with bits of dust and little flecks of thread and lint. That was a man from Missouri! Imagine a world of men who would submit all of their cocksure judgments to the ordeal of the common-sense experiments of a Leeuwenhoek!

Did he write to the Royal Society to tell them of this entirely unsuspected world of life he had discovered? Not yet! He was a slow man. He turned his lens onto all kinds of water, water kept in the close air of his study, water in a pot kept on the high roof of his house, water from the not-too-clean canals of Delft and water from the deep cold well in his garden. Everywhere he found those beasts. He gaped at their enormous littleness, he found many thousands of them did not equal a grain of sand in bigness, he compared them to a cheese mite and they were to this filthy little creature as a bee is to a horse. He was never tired with watching them "swim about among one another gently like a swarm of mosquitoes in the air. . . ."

Of course this man was a groper. He was a groper and a stumbler as all men are gropers, devoid of prescience, and stumblers, finding what they never set out to find. His new beasties were marvelous but they were not enough for him, he was always poking into everything, trying to see more closely, trying to find reasons. Why is the sharp taste of pepper? That was what he asked himself one day, and he guessed: "There must be little points on the particles of pepper and these points jab the tongue when you eat pepper. . . ."

But are there such little points?

He fussed with dry pepper. He sneezed. He sweat, but he couldn't get the grains of pepper small enough to put under his lens. So, to soften it, he put it to soak for several weeks in water. Then with fine needles he pried the almost invisible specks of the pepper apart, and sucked them up in a little drop of water into one of his hair-fine glass tubes. He looked—

Here was something to make even this determined man scatter-brained. He forgot about possible small sharp points on the pepper. With the interest of an intent little boy he watched the antics of "an incredible number of little animals, of various sorts, which move very prettily, which tumble about and sidewise, this way and that!"

So it was Leeuwenhoek stumbled on a magnificent way to grow his new little animals.

And now to write all this to the great men off there in London! Artlessly he described his own astonishment to them. Long page after page in a superbly neat handwriting with little common words he told them that you could put a million of these little animals into a coarse grain of sand and that one drop of his pepper-water, where they grew and multiplied so well, held more than two-million seven-hundred-thousand of them. . . .

This letter was translated into English. It was read before the learned skeptics—who no longer believed in the magic virtues of unicorns' horns—and it bowled the learned body over! What! The Dutchman said he had discovered beasts so small that you could put as many of them into one little drop of water as there were people in his native country? Nonsense! The cheese mite was absolutely and without doubt the smallest creature God had created.

But a few of the members did not scoff. This Leeuwenhoek was a confoundedly accurate man: everything he had ever written to them they had found to be true. . . . So a letter went back to the scientific janitor, begging him to write them in detail the way he had made his microscope, and his method of observing.

That upset Leeuwenhoek. It didn't matter that these stupid oafs of Delft laughed at him—but the Royal Society? He had thought *they* were philosophers! Should he write them details, or should he from now on keep everything he did to himself? "Great God," you can imagine him muttering, "these ways I have of uncovering mysterious things, how I have worked and sweat to learn to do them, what jeering from how many fools haven't I endured to perfect my microscopes and my ways of looking! . . ."

But creators must have audiences. He knew that these doubters of the Royal Society should have sweat just as hard to disprove the existence of his little animals as he himself had toiled to discover them. He was hurt, but—creators must have an audience. So he replied to them in a long letter assuring them he never told anything too big. He explained his calculations (and modern microbe hunters with all of their apparatus make only slightly more accurate ones!), he wrote these calculations out, divisions, multiplications, additions, until his letter looked like a child's exercise in arithmetic. He finished by saying that many people of Delft had seen—with applause!—these strange new animals under his lens. He would send them affidavits from prominent citizens of Delft—two men of God, one notary public, and eight other persons worthy to be believed. But he wouldn't tell them how he made his microscopes.

That was a suspicious man! He held his little machines up for people to look through, but let them so much as touch the microscope to help themselves to see better and he might order them out of his house. . . . He was like a child anxious and proud to show a large red apple to his playmates but loth to let them touch it for fear they might take a bite out of it.

So the Royal Society commissioned Robert Hooke and Nehemiah Grew to build the very best microscopes, and brew pepper-water from the finest quality of black pepper. And, on the 15th of November, 1677, Hooke came carrying his microscope to the meeting—agog—for Antony Leeuwenhoek had not lied. Here they were, those enchanted beasts! The members rose from their seats and crowded round the microscope. They peered, they exclaimed: this man must be a wizard observer! That was a proud day for Leeuwenhoek. And a little later the Royal Society made him a Fellow, sending him a gorgeous diploma of membership in a silver case with the coat of arms of the society on the cover. "I will serve you faithfully during the rest of my life," he wrote them. And he was as good as his word, for he mailed them those conversational mixtures of gossip and science till he died at the age of ninety. But send them a microscope? Very sorry, but that was impossible to do, while he lived. The Royal Society went so far as to dispatch Doctor Molyneux to make a report on this janitor-discoverer of the invisible. Molyneux offered Leeuwenhoek a fine price for one of his microscopes—surely he could spare one?—for there were hundreds of them in cabinets that lined his study. But no! Was there anything the gentleman of the Royal Society would like to see? Here were some most curious little unborn oysters in a bottle, here were divers very nimble little animals, and that Dutchman held up his lenses for the Englishman to peep through, watching all the while out of the corner of his eye to see that the undoubtedly most honest visitor didn't touch anything—or filch anything. . . .

"But your instruments are marvelous!" cried Molyneux. "A thousand times more clear they show things than any lens we have in England!"

"How I wish, Sir," said Leeuwenhoek, "that I could show you my best lens, with my special way of observing, but I keep that only for myself and do not show it to anyone—not even to my own family."

IV

Those little animals were everywhere! He told the Royal Society of finding swarms of those sub-visible beings in his mouth —of all places: "Although I am now fifty years old," he wrote, "I have uncommonly well-preserved teeth, because it is my custom every morning to rub my teeth very hard with salt, and after cleaning my large teeth with a quill, to rub them vigorously with a cloth. . . ." But there still were little bits of white stuff between his teeth, when he looked at them with a magnifying mirror. . . .

What was this white stuff made of?

From his teeth he scraped a bit of this stuff, mixed it with pure rain-water, stuck it in a little tube on to the needle of his microscope, closed the door of his study—

What was this that rose from the gray dimness of his lens into clear distinctness as he brought the tube into the focus? Here was an unbelievably tiny creature, leaping about in the water of the tube "like the fish called a pike." There was a second kind that swam forward a little way, then whirled about suddenly, then tumbled over itself in pretty somersaults. There were some beings that moved sluggishly and looked like wee bent sticks, nothing more, but that Dutchman squinted at them till his eyes were red-rimmed—and they moved, they were alive, no doubt of it! There was a menagerie in his mouth! There were creatures shaped like flexible rods that went to and fro with the stately carriage of bishops in procession, there were spirals that whirled through the water like violently animated cork-screws. . . .

Everybody he could get hold of—as well as himself—was an experimental animal for that curious man. Tired from his long peering at the little beasts in his own mouth, he went for a walk under the tall trees that dropped their yellow leaves on the brown mirrors of the canals; it was hard work, this play of his, he must rest! But he met an old man, a most interesting old man: "I was talking to this old man," wrote Leeuwenhoek to the Royal Society, "an old man who led a very sober life, who never used brandy nor tobacco and very seldom wine, and my eye chanced to fall on his teeth which were badly grown over and that made me ask him when he had last cleaned his mouth. I got for answer that he had never cleaned his teeth in his whole life. . . ."

Away went all thought of his aching eyes. What a zoo of wee animals must be in this old fellow's mouth. He dragged the dirty but virtuous victim of his curiosity into his study—of course there were millions of wee beasties in that mouth, but what he wanted particularly to tell the Royal Society was this: that this old man's mouth was host to a new kind of creature, that slid along among the others, bending its body in graceful bows like a snake—the water in the narrow tube seemed to be alive with those little fellows!

You may wonder that Leeuwenhoek nowhere in any of those hundreds of letters makes any mention of the harm these mysterious new little animals might do to men. He had come upon them in drinking water, spied upon them in the mouth; as the years went by he discovered them in the intestines of frogs and horses, and even in his own discharges; in swarms he found them on those rare occasions when, as he says, "he was troubled with a looseness." But not for a moment did he guess that his trouble was caused by those little beasts, and from his unimaginativeness and his carefulness not to jump to conclusions modern microbe hunters—if they only had time to study his writings—could learn a great deal. For, during the last fifty years, literally thousands of microbes have been described as the authors of hundreds of diseases, when, in the majority of cases those germs have only been chance residents in the body at the time it became diseased. Leeuwenhoek was cautious about calling anything the *cause* of anything else. He had a sound instinct about the infinite complicatedness of everything—that told him the danger of trying to pick out one cause from the tangled maze of causes which control life. . . .

The years went by. He tended his little dry-goods store, he saw to it the city hall of Delft was properly swept out, he grew more and more crusty and suspicious, he looked longer and longer hours through his hundreds of microscopes, he made a hundred amazing discoveries. In the tail of a little fish stuck head first into a glass tube he saw for the first time of all men the capillary blood vessels through which blood goes from the arteries to the veins—so he completed the Englishman Harvey's discovery of the circulation of the blood. The most sacred and improper and romantic things in life were only material for the probing, tireless eyes of his lenses. Leeuwenhoek discovered the human sperm, and the cold-blooded science of his searching would have been shocking, if he had not been such a completely innocent man! The years went by and all Europe knew about him. Peter the Great of Russia came to pay his respects to him, and the Queen of England journeyed to Delft only to look at the wonders to be seen through the lenses of his microscopes. He exploded countless superstitions for the Royal Society, and aside from Isaac Newton and Robert Boyle he was the most famous of their members. But did these honors turn his head? They couldn't turn his head because he had from the first a sufficiently high opinion of himself! His arrogance was limitless—but it was equaled by his humility when he thought of that misty unknown that he knew surrounded himself and all men. He admired the Dutch God but his real god was truth:

"My determination is not to remain stubbornly with my ideas but I'll leave them and go over to others as soon as I am shown plausible reasons which I can grasp. This is the more true since I have no other purpose than to place truth before my eyes so far as it is in my power to embrace it; and to use the little talent I have received to draw the world away from its old heathenish superstitions and to go over to the truth and to stick to it."

He was an amazingly healthy man, and at the age of eighty his hand hardly trembled as he held up his microscope for visitors to peep at his little animals or to exclaim at the unborn oysters. But he was fond of drinking in the evenings—as what Dutchman is not?—and his only ill seems to have been a certain seediness in the morning after such wassail. He detested physicians—how could they know about the ills of the body when they didn't know one thousandth of what he did about the build of the body? So Leeuwenhoek had his own theories—and sufficiently foolish they were—about the cause of this seediness. He knew that his blood was full of little globules—he had been the first of all men to see them. He knew those globules had to go through very tiny capillaries to get from his arteries to his veins—hadn't he been the man to discover those wee vessels in a fish tail? Well, after those hilarious nights of his, his blood got too thick to run properly from the arteries to the veins! So he would thin it! So he wrote to the Royal Society:

"When I have supped too heavily of an evening, I drink in the morning a large number of cups of coffee, and that as hot as I can drink it, so that the sweat breaks out on me, and if by so doing I can't restore my body, a whole apothecary's shop couldn't do much, and that is the only thing I have done for years when I have felt a fever."

That hot coffee drinking led him to another curious fact about the little animals. Everything he did led him to pry up some new fact of nature, for he lived wrapped in those tiny dramas that went on under his lenses just as a child listens open-mouthed with saucer eyes to the myths of Mother Goose. . . . He never tired of reading the same story of nature, there were always new angles to be found in it, the pages of his book of nature were thumbed and dog-eared by his insatiable interest. Years after his discovery of the microbes in his mouth one morning in the midst of his sweating from his vast curative coffee drinkings he looked once more at the stuff between his teeth–

What was this? There was not a single little animal to be found. Or there were no living animals rather, for he thought he could make out the bodies of myriads of dead ones–and maybe one or two that moved feebly, as if they were sick. "Blessed Saints!" he growled: "I hope some great Lord of the Royal Society doesn't try to find those creatures in his mouth, and fail, and then deny my observations. . . ."

But look here! He had been drinking coffee, so hot it had blistered his lips, almost. He had looked for the little animals in the white stuff from between his front teeth. It was just after the coffee he had looked there– Well?

With the help of a magnifying mirror he went at his back teeth. Presto! "With great surprise I saw an incredibly large number of little animals, and in such an unbelievable quantity of the aforementioned stuff, that it is not to be conceived of by those who have not seen it with their own eyes." Then he made delicate experiment in tubes, heating the water with its tiny population to a temperature a little warmer than that of a hot bath. In a moment the creatures stopped their agile runnings to and fro. He cooled the water. They did not come back to life–so! It was that hot coffee that had killed the beasties in his front teeth!

With what delight he watched them once more! But he was

bothered, he was troubled, for he couldn't make out the heads or tails of any of his little animals. After wiggling forward in one direction they stopped, they reversed themselves and swam backward just as swiftly without having turned around. But they *must* have heads and tails! They must have livers and brains and blood vessels as well! His thoughts floated back to his work of forty years before, when he had found that under his powerful lenses fleas and cheese mites, so crude and simple to the naked eye, had become as complicated and as perfect as human beings. But try as he would, with the best lenses he had, and those little animals in his mouth were just plain sticks of spheres or corkscrews. So he contented himself by calculating, for the Royal Society, what the diameter of the invisible blood vessels of his microbes must be—but mind you, he never for a moment hinted that he had seen such blood vessels; it only amused him to stagger his patrons by speculations of their unthinkable smallness.

If Antony Leeuwenhoek failed to see the germs that cause human disease, if he had too little imagination to predict the rôle of assassin for his wretched creatures, he did show that sub-visible beasts could devour and kill living beings much larger than they were themselves. He was fussing with mussels, shellfish that he dredged up out of the canals of Delft. He found thousands of them unborn inside their mothers. He tried to make these young ones develop outside their mothers in a glass of canal water. "I wonder," he muttered, "why our canals are not choked with mussels, when the mothers have each one so many young ones inside them!" Day after day he poked about in his glass of water with its slimy mass of embryos, he turned his lens on to them to see if they were growing—but what was this? Astounded he watched the fishy stuff disappear from between their shells—it was being gobbled up by thousands of tiny microbes that were attacking the mussels greedily. . . .

"Life lives on life—it is cruel, but it is God's will," he pondered. "And it is for our good, of course, because if there weren't little animals to eat up the young mussels, our canals would be choked by those shellfish, for each mother has more than a thousand young ones at a time!" So Antony Leeuwenhoek accepted everything and praised everything, and in this he was a child of his time, for in his century searchers had not yet, like Pasteur who came after them, begun to challenge God, to shake their fists at the meaningless cruelties of nature toward mankind, her children. . . .

He passed eighty, and his teeth came loose as they had to even in his strong body; he didn't complain at the inexorable arrival of the winter of his life, but he jerked out that old tooth and turned his lens onto the little creatures he found within that hollow root—why shouldn't he study them once more? There might be some little detail he had missed those hundred other times! Friends came to him at eighty-five and told him to take it easy and leave his studies. He wrinkled his brow and opened wide his still bright eyes: "The fruits that ripen in autumn last the longest!" he told them—he called eighty-five the autumn of his life!

Leeuwenhoek was a showman. He was very pleased to hear the ohs and ahs of people—they must be philosophical people and lovers of science, mind you!—whom he let peep into his subvisible world or to whom he wrote his disjointed marvelous letters of description. But he was no teacher. "I've never taught one," he wrote to the famous philosopher Leibniz, "because if I taught one, I'd have to teach others. . . . I would give myself over to a slavery, whereas I want to stay a free man."

"But the art of grinding fine lenses and making observations of these new creatures will disappear from the earth, if you don't teach young men," answered Leibniz.

"The professors and students of the University of Leyden were long ago dazzled by my discoveries, they hired three lens-grinders to come to teach the students, but what came of it?" wrote that independent Dutchman.

"Nothing, so far as I can judge, for almost all of the courses they teach there are for the purpose of getting money through knowledge or for gaining the respect of the world by showing people how learned you are, and these things have nothing to do with discovering the things that are buried from our eyes. I am convinced that of a thousand people not one is capable of carrying out such studies, because endless time is needed and much money is spilled and because a man has always to be busy with his thoughts if anything is to be accomplished. . . ."

That was the first of the microbe hunters. In 1723, when he was ninety-one years old and on his deathbed, he sent for his friend Hoogvliet. He could not lift his hand. His once glowing eyes were rheumy and their lids were beginning to stick fast with the cement of death. He mumbled:

"Hoogvliet, my friend, be so good as to have those two letters on the table translated into Latin. . . . Send them to London to the Royal Society. . . ."

So he kept his promise made fifty years before, and Hoogvliet wrote, along with those last letters: "I send you, learned sirs, this last gift of my dying friend, hoping that his final word will be agreeable to you."

So he passed, this first of the microbe hunters. You will read of Spallanzani, who was much more brilliant, of Pasteur who had a thousand times his imagination, of Robert Koch who did much more immediate apparent good in lifting the torments that microbes bring to men—these and all the others have much more fame today. But not one of them has been so completely honest, so appallingly accurate as this Dutch janitor, and all of them could take lessons from his splendid common sense.

R. F. DIBBLE

Roy Floyd Dibble (1887-1929) could scarcely be called an "average American," although his beginnings and his background were those commonly recommended to future Presidents. Until his maturity he lived and worked on a farm near Lake Erie in the most westerly corner of New York State, Chautauqua County. But a creative instinct which set him composing amid his domestic routine a long adolescent sonnet-sequence impelled him, at twenty-one, to seek a higher education. He took his A.B. at Clark University in 1912. After a year of school-teaching, he began his connection with Columbia University which was doubtless the richest experience of his life. Graduate student (1914), University Fellow (1915), Instructor in English (1916), he rose steadily; then—it is his friend and colleague, Mark Van Doren, who tells us in *The Dictionary of American Biography*—with a surgical operation came the sudden news that he had but three more years to live. This sentence "dulled his ambition" for a time and "confirmed him in a 'quietism' inspired by Thoreau's *Walden*"; yet he did not die. Gradually aroused by radical reactions to the War, he summoned energy to write a thesis and take the degree of Ph.D in 1921. With this exacting work off his hands, he found himself caught up into a strong sympathy with the new biographies of Lytton Strachey, and set out to fashion an American book that would compare not too unworthily with *Eminent Victorians*, though it could not hope to match its success. *Strenuous Americans* (1923), dedicated with frank admiration "To the Greatest Living Biographer," won Dibble enough repute to persuade him to resign his post at Columbia and give himself entirely to writing. He published two long biographies, *John L. Sullivan: An Intimate Narrative* (1925) and *Mohammed* (1926); then failing to publish a life of Luther, he returned to teaching in 1927 as Associate Professor of English at Hunter College, where he was serving when disease, aggravated by the economic depression, ended his career in 1929. "Aunt Mary Emerson" is one of a number of uncollected short biographies contributed to the *Nation*, the *Century*, and other magazines, and intended for a second series.

The imitators of Lytton Strachey have been the target of some very heavy attacks, many of them just, most of them somewhat exaggerated. R. F. Dibble did not attempt to ride to success on the Stracheyan tide by a sensational play to the gallery, as many of the imitators did. But he was one of the first in this country to see that nineteenth century Americans, as well as Englishmen, needed a fresh revaluation. Like Strachey, he found his richest field in the careers of robust and active "extroverts" unlike himself: Jesse James, Brigham Young, James J. Hill, P. T. Barnum, Frances E. Willard, Mark Hanna, "Aunt Mary" Emerson.

In his obituary on Lytton Strachey in *The London Mercury*, February 1932, Mr. J. C. Squire regrets that though his books will be read, "his influence was not good, because his imitators lack his taste and skill." Especially true is this in America, he says, where there is a plethora of "books by authors who think they are doing something when they call Emerson 'Ralph' and Longfellow 'Harry'; books in which 'imaginative reconstruction' runs to seed." It almost looks as though the English critic were aiming his sarcasm at the author of "Aunt Mary Emerson." For was not Dibble admittedly inspired by *Eminent Victorians*, and does he not call Emerson quite openly "Ralph"? One may even hear Stracheyan echoes in the close-knit paradoxes of the opening and in the dramatized death scene at the end. Certainly, too, Dibble writes with some irreverence and detachment. Yet, imitation or not, it is a lively and authentic biography revealing a mellowness which did not come to Strachey until the last years of his life.

As for his method, Dibble explains in the preface to *Strenuous Americans:* "I have tried, so to speak, to view each one as though he were seated on some height; then I have paced round and round that height, in order to study him from every angle. At times I have stepped back for a considerable distance, at other times I have approached within arm's length, so that my viewpoint might be neither too distant nor too near. . . . In tracing their lives, I have strenuously endeavored to maintain a precise exposition, a scrupulous interpretation, a controlled but generous enthusiasm, and a cool-headed but warm-hearted detachment."

AUNT MARY EMERSON

PERHAPS the essential fact about Transcendentalism is that its germinal principle, nonconformity, soon became as conventional and stereotyped as Calvinism itself. Creedlessness became a creed, idiosyncrasy became normal, the gospel of individualism damned itself by becoming a Gospel, and the glorious duty of following whim degenerated into a codified regimen as stiff as the Thirty-nine Articles. The self-sustaining Thoreau sustained himself by obtaining generous snacks from his mother's larder; masculine Margaret Fuller became Mrs. Ossoli; Hawthorne ceased milking cows at Brook Farm to accept a political appointment; Emerson preached against preachers; and Fruitlands, the crowning absurdity of the period, perished because its lofty-minded founders failed to raise enough fruit to sustain themselves. But Transcendentalism, intrinsically unoriginal and unimportant in itself, accomplished what far more revolutionary movements have not always done: it fathered a brood of enormously, everlastingly interesting children. Kings, empires, and presidents might come and go, but the flaming devotees of Newness talked forever on and on—and how resourceful and stimulating that marvelous conversation was!

The minutest facts concerning most of them have been dug up and exhibited in countless books, pamphlets, and piously accurate dissertations, yet one austere and formidable figure in the movement has never received her due. Here and there, in the febrile journals which everyone of importance, and even of no importance, seems to have kept in that day, are to be found stray references to Mary Moody Emerson; but no one except her worshiping nephew has written at any length about her, and his sketch, composed shortly after her death, is—what else could it be?—fragmentary and elusive. And yet, if one may judge by the comments of her intimate associates, Aunt Mary was even more electric, more volcanic, and more unaccountable than Margaret Fuller herself. She can be defined only in the language of paradox: she was a female Diogenes, a philosophical saint, a devout skeptic, a Calvinistic rebel who revolted against everything and everybody, including herself. Thoreau called her the "wittiest and most vivacious woman" whom he knew; and years after she was food for those all-devouring worms that haunted her macabre imagination throughout her tempestuous life, Emerson continued to cherish her "monitory" diaries and her "moral inspirations." He wrote: "All the men and women whose talents challenge my admiration from time to time lack this depth of source, and are therefore comparatively shallow." Emerson, one reflects, was not invariably guiltless of hyperbole as well as of family pride, and it may be that he had momentarily forgotten, let us say, Plato,

Shakespeare, Goethe, and Carlyle; yet had any one of those worthies been privileged to be inmates of the Emersonian household for some years, as Aunt Mary was, one wonders whether such a sentence would have been written of him.

For Aunt Mary, with her scrawny angular form, her peaked face, her long sharp-pointed pug-nose, and her "eye that went through and through you like a needle," acted the part of fairy godmother to Ralph Waldo from his earliest years. Born in 1775, she lost her parents when she was but a baby, and was adopted by an aunt and uncle who were so hard up that one of the child's chief duties was to watch out for the deputy sheriff who, it was feared, might thunder in at any moment to arrest the uncle for debt. When her brother William, Ralph's father, died in 1811, Aunt Mary came to live with the widow and her children. The family was very poor, and once, when Ralph paid a few pennies for the loan of a novel from a circulating library, his aunt grimly reminded him that he ought to be ashamed of himself—"How insipid is fiction to a mind touched with immortal views!" she once burst out—but the lad got some revenge by plaguing her with quotations from *Don Juan*.

Her influence upon the boy's plastic mind can never be accurately known; it is possible, and even probable, that without it he might, like his forefathers, have been just another Reverend Emerson all his life. She constantly scourged and prodded him to essay higher things. "Scorn trifles, lift your aims; do what you are afraid to do," she primly admonished him over and over again. She advised him not to go to the Cambridge Divinity School because, she said, it lacked reverence. It was tainted, she firmly believed, with the aridities of German scholasticism; and the lowliest things in nature, "Mr. Horse, Mrs. Cow, and Miss Sparrow," aye, even "the whole of Calvinism," were better than it. When he earned the unbelievable sum of about two thousand dollars from teaching, she became much worried over his genius, which her acute perception had already detected; "hard fare for the belly" would be much better for him, she snorted, and she ceaselessly chided him for not *daring* more. In his ministerial days he corresponded regularly with his "Abbess of a humble Vale," seeking her "high counsels" to illumine him "upon the dark sayings and sphinx riddles of life"; and she in turn sent him multitudes of what he accurately called "moral scrawls and Sibylline scraps." Certainly no one but Emerson could have got any meaning from some of her outpourings. "How little can we recapitulate without vomiting at mortal conditions," is the opening statement in one of her paragraphs; and she doubtless strengthened his moral fiber by such a pronouncement as this: "Illimitable prospects can best apply euphrasy to the understanding." When Emerson's young mind was nourished upon such pap as this, who can wonder at the enigmas and obfuscations in his works? And yet . . . Aunt Mary unquestionably was, as he said, "always new, subtle, frolicsome, musical, unpredictable." When she realized that her amiable nephew had swallowed her metaphysical bait—hook, line, and sinker—she apparently became a little worried. She once wrangled with him about his "high, airy speculations" and refused to see him for a time; and once again, when he sent her his agonized questionings about the "miracle of life and the idea of God," she replied by asking him concerning the condition of his knee.

Indeed, despite her crotchety ways, her thorny mannerisms, and her incomprehensible style, she was "endowed with the fatal gift of penetration" into other people's weaknesses and vagaries. "She disgusted everybody because she knew them too well," wrote Emerson; and that seems to have been the central truth about her. This curious lady, who wrote prayers teeming with "prophetic and apocalyptic ejaculations," who believed implicitly in angels and archangels, who used her thimble less for sewing than for impressing seals upon the wax of her letters, and who deliberately chose bonnets that did not conform to contemporary tastes, sometimes manifested a hard-headed earthiness that utterly confounded her moonstruck associates. "I knew I was not destined to please," she wrote. "To live to give pain rather than pleasure (the latter so delicious) seems the spider-like necessity of my being on earth." In brief, it was her job both to inflate and ballast the flighty balloon of Transcendentalism. Nothing deterred her; she was, as Emerson remarked, "embarrassed by no

Moses or Paul, no Angelo or Shakespeare." He compared the impact of her terrific personality to the ponderous influence of Dr. Johnson; like him, she "impresses her company, as she does, not only by the point of the remark, but also when the point fails, because she made it." The most devastating thing about her was that one could never be quite sure whether she was thoroughly sincere or was merely amusing herself at the expense of her auditors; her most scorching discourses might be conceived in a spirit of levity, whereas her lightest remark might be loaded with dynamite. Thus, while she naturally hankered to get into "good society," her bewildering oddities so teased and exasperated people that she was perpetually debarred; for she was too proud and crabbed to conform.

In one respect she did conform: she kept a diary into which, "night after day, year after year," she poured her dark and incommunicable emotions. In reading these cabalistic sentences, filled with gnarled and knotty solecisms and inexplorable deviations into mysticism, one is reminded of Emily Brontë, of Sir Thomas Browne, of Thoreau, and of many more. Occasionally she is perfectly clear: "Rose before light every morn; visited from necessity once, and again for books; read Butler's *Analogy;* commented on the Scriptures; read in a little book,—Cicero's *Letters,*—a few; touched Shakespeare,—washed, carded, cleaned house, and baked." She can on occasion describe her mystic moments with crystal clarity: "Alive with God is enough,—'tis rapture . . . in dead of night, nearer morning, when the eastern stars glow or appear to glow with more indescribable lustre, a lustre which penetrates the spirit with wonder and curiosity. . . ." In her youth she had promised God that "to be a blot on this fair world, at His command, would be acceptable." She felt so assured of her own direct intercommunication with the Almighty, in fact, that she paid, says Emerson, a superciliously "polite and courtly homage to the name and dignity of Jesus" which patently showed her "organic dislike to any interference, any mediation between her and the Author of her being." She seems indeed to have had what amounted to a secure sense of private ownership of the Almighty. "Reading from my manuscripts to her," wrote Thoreau, "and using the word 'god' in perchance a merely heathenish sense, she inquired hastily in a tone of dignified anxiety, 'Is that god spelt with a little g?' " And he dryly adds, "Fortunately it was." This surely might be Thoreau himself speaking, though it was written ten years before his birth: "The evening is fine, but I dare not enjoy it. The moon and stars reproach me, because I had to do with mean fools." But then . . . there comes a change. "O Time. Thou loiterer. Thou, whose might has laid low the vastest and crushed the worm, restest on thy hoary throne, with like potency over thy agitations and thy graves. When will thy routines give way to higher and lasting institutions? When thy trophies and thy name and all its wizard forms be lost in the Genius of Eternity? In Eternity, no deceitful promises, no fantastic illusions, no riddles concealed by thy shrouds, none of thy Arachnean webs, which decoy and destroy. Hasten to finish thy motley work, on which frightful Gorgons are at play, spite of holy ghosts. 'Tis already moth-eaten and its shuttles quaver, as the beams of the loom are shaken." Small wonder that Emerson, constantly poring over her diary, was irresistibly reminded of Dante's *Inferno*. Perhaps that passage may at least suggest why, when she was offered marriage "by a man of talents, education, and good social position," she refused him. A woman who wrote like that would scarcely feel inclined to hitch her star to a matrimonial wagon.

Not that she despised men; they were much more endurable than women. When young people intrigued her interest, she would go to any lengths to win their confidence; and, having gained it, she made the most of the brief intimacy, for she realized only too well that they would soon tire of her queer impish grotesqueries; but if they proved to be dull—to her mind dullness was the one unpardonable sin—she was disgusted and got rid of them by asking them to run on some senseless errand. She habitually referred to the head of the family with whom she happened to be sojourning as the "clown," but she preferred even him to the lady of the house. One of the very few women whom she really admired she called "Whale-hearted." She once had a felon on her thumb and therefore decided to employ a nurse—a veritable Sairey Gamp, who immediately climbed into bed and began to snore so loud that Aunt Mary woke her "to forbid her making such a shocking noise"; and in the end she hustled the offender out of the house before morning, after having "passed the worst night she remembered." When a woman chanced to speak in mixed company, Aunt Mary would place a heavy hand on her shoulder and utter this admonishment: "Be still. I want to hear the men talk." If she heard any lady excessively praised, she would interrupt with the caustic query, "Is it a colored woman of whom you were speaking?" Once when a Mrs. Brown had waxed ecstatic over the Italian patriots, Aunt Mary broke in: "Mrs. Brown, how's your cat?" Observing Mrs. Thoreau wearing pink ribbons one day, she closed her eyes while the two chatted for a time; then she said, "Mrs. Thoreau, I don't know whether you have observed that my eyes are shut."

"Yes, madam, I have observed it."

"Perhaps you would like to know the reason?"

"Yes, I should."

"I don't like to see a person of your age guilty of such levity in dress."

Aunt Mary was assuredly guileless in that respect; her attire was far from gaudy. As old age drew on, she thoughtfully prepared for the end by making her own shroud; but the years continued to pass, she was still very much alive, and, thrifty and frugal as her Puritan ancestors, she finally wore it as a nightdress and a day-gown, and she sometimes rode about on horseback with a flaming scarlet shawl thrown over the ominous white. She wore one out, then made another—and another. Her eccentricities increased with age. In her peripatetic trips all over New England to find "boarding-houses" within the reach of her scrimped income, she encountered some families who were likable—and some who were not. Meeting one day a couple who looked vaguely familiar, she courtesied frigidly; then, recognizing them as a pair whom she had once dwelt with but had almost forgotten, she approached and unburdened herself thus: "I didn't know who you were, or should never have bowed to you." Perhaps the reason for her aversion was that the pair had children—for Aunt Mary loathed babies of every description. "Give us peace in our boarders," she once wrote, in words that were meant to be a prayer for the nation's welfare; when the error in spelling was pointed out, she laconically commented that "it would do as it was." Hating to throw away anything useful, she treasured her precious chest of medicines; and when she had a surplus of drugs on hand, she would mix a drop of laudanum with various pills, a little antimony and quinine, and then swallow the concoction to save it. On rare occasions she would drink tea, but she immediately made haste to sip some coffee to get rid of the tea-taste. Noticing an idle horse hitched to a chaise one day, she sought out the owner and asked him to let her take a ride to Dr. Ripley's while the man himself was making his purchases. When he mildly protested, she curtly informed him that she "was his own townswoman, born within a mile of him"; she then climbed into the gig, and the dumfounded fellow actually told her not to hurry but to take her time. Yet her own comment on her foibles should be noted: "My oddities were never designed—effect of an uncalculating constitution at first, then through isolation. . . . It is so universal with all classes to avoid me that I blame nobody."

She doubtless met all the notables who foregathered in Concord with Emerson, with Margaret Fuller, with Alcott and the others, but exasperatingly little information on this point has been recorded. Did she ever argue with Margaret on the position of woman?—what would one not give for a report of an encounter between these two dialectical giantesses! She certainly met Alcott —that half-crazy, half-inspired visionary who fervently believed in preëxistence, phrenology, and vegetarianism, and who founded the first kindergarten in America—for she wrote him a letter in which she deliberately parodied his spasmodic oratorical style: "While the form dazzled,—while the speaker inspired confidence, —the foundation of the—the—superstructure, gilded and golden— was in depths of—I will tell you plainly what, when I am furnished more with terms as well as principles,—after I have seen the account of your present instruction." Years later, however, she made amends. One night, in Emerson's house, for the first time in his life Alcott became utterly speechless when confronted with the scathing paradoxes of Henry James the elder; then of a sudden Aunt Mary bounced up and completely squelched James, as successfully as he had quieted Alcott, by her fiery pronouncements against his "dangerous Antinomian views concerning the moral law." Nevertheless she did not depend on the Concord savants for her intellectual stimulus; she read avidly all the time—Plato, Plotinus, Marcus Antoninus, Edward Young, Cousin, Jonathan Edwards, Goethe, and Madame de Staël were her constant companions. For years she conned *Paradise Lost* in a book without title-page or covers, and it was not until she bought a new copy—for someone told her that she really ought to know Milton—that she discovered she had been reading him all these years. She even gloated over the icy wit of Talleyrand, though she once closed his glittering pages with the sigh, "I fear he was not organized for a Future State."

Extreme old age drew on, bringing recurrent thoughts of death and worms—where was the serene sense of divine immanence, where were those youthful raptures now? "Could I have those hours in which in fresh youth I said, To obey God is joy, though there were no hereafter, I should rejoice, though returning to dust." For years she made up her bed like a coffin, and she was elated to note that a church steeple across the way cast a shadow shaped like a coffin before her window. But death still dragged, and the worms still loitered. "I have given up, the last year or two, the hope of dying. . . . Tedious indisposition:—hoped, as it took a new form, it would open the cool, sweet grave. . . . Ill health and nerves. O dear worms,—how they will at some sure time take down this tedious tabernacle, most valuable companions, instructors in the science of mind, by gnawing away the meshes which have chained it. A very Beatrice in showing the Paradise." Even death on the gallows would be preferable to life: "If one could choose, and without crime be gibbeted,—were it not altogether better than the long drooping away by age without mentality or devotion? The vulture and the crow would *caw caw*, and, unconscious of any deformity in the mutilated body, would relish their meal, make no grimace of affected sympathy, nor suffer any real compassion." And yet, as late as 1855, Thoreau wrote that she was "the youngest person in Concord, though about eighty. . . . She says they called her old when she was young, and she has never grown any older." Her friends—such is the high privilege of friendship!—were wont to say to her in all sincerity, "I wish you joy of the worms." And when the beatific worms triumphed in her eighty-ninth year, the event had something of cosmic comedy about it, and those same friends dared not look at each other during the funeral "lest they should forget the serious proprieties of the hour."

ROLLO WALTER BROWN

It is no slight achievement for a writer amid the chaotic standards of post-war America to have stood firmly and unsentimentally for the high principles of dignity, good taste, and honest workmanship in life and art. Yet this is one of the distinctions of Rollo Walter Brown, both as teacher, lecturer, and writer.

Born in the town of Crooksville, Ohio, in 1880, he was educated at Ohio Northern University, Litt.B., 1903, A.M., 1904, and at Harvard University, A.M., 1905. He was married, and after serving a year's apprenticeship as Instructor, held the post of Professor of Rhetoric and Composition at Wabash College from 1905 to 1920, then a similar position at Carleton College, 1920-23. He did his last formal teaching as Lecturer in English at Harvard in 1923-24. Meanwhile, he had written (with another) *The Art of Writing English* (1913) and edited a useful anthology, *The Writer's Art, by Those Who Have Practiced It* (1921). He had also investigated thoroughly the methods of teaching in French schools and set forth his findings in a book, *How the French Boy Learns to Write* (1915), which remains today one of the most suggestive manuals for teachers of English. So much, and more, he did for his first profession.

Confident that he could employ his talent to greater advantage elsewhere than in the classroom, Mr. Brown resigned his post and wrote a series of influential magazine articles which he collected in *The Creative Spirit, An Inquiry into American Life* (1925). In the next year he published his first biography, *Dean Briggs*, an illuminating, full-length portrait of a beloved educator whose personal influence has gone far beyond Harvard and Radcliffe Colleges to affect Americans of several generations. *Lonely Americans* (1929), from which the life of George Bellows is taken, supplies varied illustrations of the author's idea of the integral man at work. "It isolates one anywhere to think beyond a certain point," quotes Mr. Brown for his text. In a youthful nation where the democratic spirit has too often had a leveling effect on culture this isolation has never been popular. *Lonely Americans* singles out eight individuals, or "individualists"—C. W. Eliot, Whistler, Edward MacDowell, C. E. Norton, Raphael Pumpelly, Emily Dickinson, Lincoln—who have extended the reach of education, art, music, literature, science, and politics at the cost of living intellectually alone. Mr. Brown has recently published a tetralogy of novels depicting, through imaginary individuals drawn from actual life, the struggle of the creative spirit for expression in an unsympathetic environment.

The short biography of George Bellows (1882-1925) is characteristic of the author's work. Structurally, it illustrates Mr. Brown's aim to produce a study that is at once a character analysis and a narrative. Some writers make the analysis without helping the reader to move forward chronologically (Gamaliel Bradford, for instance), merely walk round the character. Mr. Brown tries to keep walking round him as he moves forward through his life. In substance, the piece is sympathetic without idolatry, realistic without irony, graphic without a play to the gallery. Nothing would be easier than to throw sensational lights and shadows upon the life of this painter who himself saw life in dramatic terms. Mr. Brown, in sincere and readable prose, makes us see the steady, purposeful artist as the public and even his friends rarely saw him.

AN ADVENTURER OUT OF THE WEST

GEORGE BELLOWS's short life was a joyous, unaccompanied pursuit. He looked about on the face of the earth and said: "Not so bad—as raw material. I wonder what it would all mean if you could get it straightened out so you could see it. And I wonder what it could be made to look like to anybody else." Before the bright terrestrial flash should pass he meant to explore as far as possible. There was not much to guide one. Why not inform oneself and act as one's own guide? Why not? He had all the capacities of a "lone wolf."

In trying to understand what he was about, his family, his friends, and the public were always a step or two behind; in trying to anticipate the direction of his next move, they were always wrong. His mother early dreamed that her slender, light-haired son would become a bishop. Every Sunday morning he was hauled to church in the high-wheeled surrey in the hope that his pushing young spirit would be impressed with the solemnity of mortal existence. Charley, a boy indentured by the family, had been so tremendously impressed that he decided to become an undertaker. In the back yard, in Columbus, Ohio, he fenced off a miniature cemetery and began with great enthusiasm to conduct funerals and inter remains. But George Bellows was interested only aesthetically: he made the designs for the tombstones that Charley erected. And as for the bishopric, the nearest he ever came to it was singing in a church choir—which is not necessarily a close approach. His father saw, evidently, that the bishopric was too far a reach. He proposed that his son become a banker. It would afford him an infinite peace in his last years to see this exploring son intrenched in an occupation of such solid respectability. But George said: "I don't want to be a banker. I'm going to Ohio State. I believe I can 'make' the baseball team."

In college he was a sprawling young barbarian very much concerned with finding something to do. When he reported for baseball and the coaches and fans said, "He looks like an outfielder," he replied: "Oh, no; I'm a shortstop." And, despite the fact that shortstops are usually not six feet two inches tall, he went daily with a team-mate and practiced throwing to first base from every position on his side of the infield until he was accepted generally as the greatest shortstop that had ever played on an Ohio State team. He played basket-ball too, and he sang in the glee club. Still there was energy left. So when his fellows had played or sung until they were exhausted and begged for sleep, he devised ingenious means of keeping them awake. But still there was energy left. So he made cartoons of his professors.

The newspapers were full of comment on this boisterous, good-natured athlete. Fellow collegians and fellow townsmen said he was good enough for the big leagues. "Of course you will go into professional baseball." But he amazed them by replying: "Hu-uh! I'm going to be an artist."

"Whew!" was all they could say; and they said that under their breath.

It had never occurred to him that there might be any doubt about his qualifications as an artist. He had begun the fundamentals early. In the rigid Methodist days of his childhood he had been permitted two activities on Sunday—reading and drawing. Since his mother always delighted in reading to him, he could draw undisturbed while he listened! That meant that he drew all the time on Sunday afternoons. This experience—and he always thought it had much to do in determining his career—enabled him to draw better than any of his fellow pupils in school. He was known as "the artist." In college he illustrated undergraduate publications. Professor "Joey" Taylor, sympathetic confessor for all brave spirits at Ohio State, encouraged him to believe that his ability was important. But in New York he encountered people who were not so sure. He came from way out in Columbus, Ohio, did he not, or some other unheard-of place? What did anybody know about art out there?

He met one teacher, however, who immediately supported his confidence in himself—Robert Henri. Henri had come from the Middle West himself, and he liked this stalwart chap with the intent face and the healthy will. A pupil who was always gay, always full of deviltry, yet always serious about the business of painting, was not to be found in the New York School of Art every day. From every word his original-minded teacher uttered, from every movement he made, from every criticism he offered, Bellows learned with white-hot mind. Henri never criticized anyone else so severely. He knew Bellows could stand what would crush others. But he also encouraged him. "You will succeed," he assured him; "some degree of success is certain. The quality of your success will depend upon the personal development you make." So, after all, maybe he might paint just as good a picture as anybody!

His fellow students looked upon him with inquiring, amused eyes. He was so little acquainted with the life of New York that the only social organization he knew when he arrived was the Y.M.C.A. It maintained a swimming-pool and a basket-ball floor, and he knew how to use both. In appearance nothing marked him as a devotee of the aesthetic. He was self-conscious in the presence of so many artistic strangers; he sprawled—there was so much of him that it was difficult to be graceful except when standing up; and he laughed with such untrammeled heartiness that everyone turned and stared at him whenever anything set him going. But how much did he care? Perhaps, if he only knew the truth, they were all just as raw as he was. Maybe they didn't

GEORGE BELLOWS

From a photograph by Nicholas Haz. Reprinted through the courtesy of Coward-McCann, Inc.

know half as much about painting! Certainly they didn't know one-tenth as much about it as he meant to know some day.

No one could deny that he was interesting. His fellow students soon became busy in trying to make him out. His clumsy externals could not prevent them from seeing his essential good nature, his essential dignity of spirit, and his sound emotional and intellectual power. They liked especially his glowing vigor. When the school had its first dance of the year he took a very beautiful Scandinavian girl—from Minnesota. His friends stood in wonder at the magnificence of this light-haired couple. "Wouldn't they make a prize-winning bride and groom?" everyone asked. But when the whisperings came to Bellows he exclaimed: "Oh, no! You are absolutely wrong! I'm going to marry that dark-haired girl from Upper Montclair!"

This girl from Upper Montclair, Miss Emma Louise Story, out of sheer pity for an overgrown boy who was spending his long Christmas vacation away from home, invited him to come to her father's house for a meal. "The steak," she assured her mother, "must be the biggest one you can find; for I never saw such an eater as he is." But George was so nervous he could not handle the silverware, much less eat. His embarrassment was increased, too, by the young lady's father. He did not care much for male artists. He had known one, a man who could paint a feather so perfectly that you couldn't tell it from the real thing; but, apart from being able to do that, he did not count for much. This feeling against artists was accentuated, too, when George Bellows began to appear on the landscape with a degree of regularity. But George was ready to contest with the father as well as with the hesitant daughter. What does a little matter of waiting around for six years amount to?

All the while he was painting, painting with unequaled persistence. "No time to waste! No time to waste!" One day John W. Alexander went home from his duties as a juror in the National Academy's annual exhibit and said to his wife: "There's a picture over there, by a young fellow named Bellows, from out West somewhere—'Forty-Two Kids' he calls it—that you must see. There's genius in it." Others saw it and were startled. "But," some of them asked, "is it an artistic subject? Do such things as boys in swimming lend themselves to artistic treatment?" "Why not?" Bellows asked in reply, and went on painting. He painted the river front, the prize-ring, the crowd in the steaming street, the city cliff-dwellers, the circus, the stevedores on the docks. All the things possessing everyday dignity and significance but long treated with disdain, all the unglorified struggle of his kind, cried to him for expression. The uncomprehending dismissed it as wild art, decadent art, drab art! They declared that Billy Sunday had broken into the aesthetic world. Those who were more sympathetic said: "Now we are getting him. He believes in painting the red-blooded American life. He is the painter with the punch!"

So he was hailed as the artist who made things anybody would understand; so, too, was he as completely misunderstood as ever. For if he was the painter of the vigorous, the physically dramatic, he was to be even more the painter of the subtle and the intimate. If he could produce "Sharkey's," he could also produce "Spring, Gramercy Park"; "Blue Snow, the Battery"; "Crehaven"; "Aunt Fanny"; "Portrait of My Mother"; "Emma in Purple Dress"; "Anne in White"; "Lady Jean"; "Portrait of Katherine Rosen"; "Eleanor, Jean, and Anna."

His diversity had kept the public guessing, yet he did not find enough in the entire range of painting to keep his own mind busy. It is not so easy to paint in New York in the dead of winter. Inasmuch as he liked black and white and enjoyed working on stone, he took up lithography. "But what are you doing that for?" his admirers asked. "Who cares anything about lithography in these days? If you want to work in black and white you ought to etch."

"But I can't etch," he insisted, "and I can make lithographs."

"But don't you wish to sell your work?" dealers protested. "There is no demand for lithographs."

"Then," he replied with characteristic braggadocio, "we'll put lithographs on the map!"

And he did. The first prints attracted favorable attention. One of his intimates counseled him: "You had better slip one or two proofs of each stone away and keep them awhile. The price might go up; you might make some money." He took the advice and he and his wife had much amusement over the fund they were going to develop for the college education of Anne and Jean. They never dreamed that the day would come when some of these prints would sell for a thousand or twelve hundred dollars apiece.

In lithography he found just the right opportunity to round out his record of America's emotional life. The stone served perfectly for many brief chapters that did not readily admit of treatment in color: "Village Prayer-Meeting"; "Initiation in the Frat"; "Benediction in Georgia"; "The Shower-Bath"; "Dance in a Mad-House"; "Old Billiard-Player"; "The Law Is Too Slow"; "Billy Sunday"; "Sixteen East Gay Street"; "Dempsey and Firpo"; "Business Men's Class, Y.M.C.A."; "Electrocution." In lithography, too, he could laugh as much as he liked. His "Reducing," the representation of a meek-looking husband calmly asleep in bed, and his very stout wife flat on her back on the floor doing some very energetic exercises, will be amusing as long as there are fat women of social importance in the world. A very stout woman, one day after Bellows had become somewhat the vogue among those who interest themselves in art socially, entered a museum and asked what there was new to be seen. She was told that yonder was a new lithograph by George Bellows. "Oh, how lovely!" she exclaimed, bringing her lorgnette to bear upon it as she moved nearer. "What is it, a shell?" When she saw, she was scandalized, and turned away with disgust that could be expressed only in a violent crescendo of "Pooh! Pooh!! Pooh!!!"

"Now we have him at last," the public said, after his lithographs had become current. "He gives us life just as he sees it. He has ability—great ability perhaps—but he lacks the imagination to make anything wholly new from simple elements. He cannot express himself in the symbolic." Then he produced "Edith Cavell," and later "Allan Donn Puts to Sea"; "The Return to Life"; "Amour"; "Punchinello in the House of Death"; and "The Crucifixion." In truth, he began to reveal so much interest in such subjects that some of his contemporaries were disturbed.

Joseph Pennell, known for his ability in combat as well as for his ability as an artist, on one occasion at the National Arts Club enlarged upon the dangers of painting when one has not the object before one at the time. "George Bellows," he went on to say, "would have made a better painting of Edith Cavell if he had been on the spot and seen with his own eyes. He was not there, certainly." When he had finished, Bellows was asked to discuss the point. In proceeding he said: "No, I was not present at the execution of Edith Cavell. I had just as good a chance to get a ticket as Leonardo had to get one for the Last Supper!"

II

When a man of such capacity to go his own way emerges from surroundings where he might little be expected to appear, he soon becomes a legend. Everybody wants to know about him. Few had learned about the personal George Bellows. He had not been seen much either in high places or in Bohemia; he had been too busy. But when people did see him, unless they came to know him intimately, they were as much mystified as ever. He did not conform to their notions of a great artist. He was only one of those typical Americans whom Americans are always talking about but rarely see. When they do see one, they have difficulty in believing their own eyes; he seems too good to be true.

Most of those magnified American qualities whose names have been outworn, but whose essences have not, he possessed. For instance, he was full of the American's gusto. He was unafraid to like things. Wherever he went everything was interesting and moving. Life was full of emotions to which he would give organized expression, architectonic integrity. The spectacle of New York—the Hudson, the East Side, the Battery, the parks—filled him with such enthusiasm that he confessed great difficulty in stopping long enough to paint what he saw. Columbus, Ohio, was just as interesting; people back there were bully, even if he did sometimes laugh in their faces. The spectacle that men make for themselves was fascinating, too. When he went to the theater—and he went often—he laughed with such unrestrained and honest joy that he heartened not only the audience but the actors. "Can't you see anything interesting?" he asked somewhat impatiently. The soporific "pure art" that the disillusioned and the burnt-out produce in an effort to "escape" something or other did not concern him. His times were overwhelming in their possibilities. He had fun in finding what seemed most significant, and he had greater, agonizing fun in struggling to expression. When one of his most brilliant portraits had been placed on exhibition with a note in the catalogue implying that it had been painted as a commission, he corrected the error by writing: "Painted for fun." He liked the world. He liked his friends. He liked himself pretty well, thank you, and his own work. And he liked good work done by others. No one ever joined the procession of honor with more enthusiasm than he did when he discovered genius in the work of somebody else.

American, too, was his zeal as a crusader. He was always fighting for causes. "I am a patriot for beauty. I would enlist in an army to make the world more beautiful. I would go to war for an ideal—far more easily than I could for a country." *The Masses*, a journal which Bellows had hoped might do something for the people to whom it was addressed, slowly deteriorated, and he drew up a complete program for its rejuvenation—and supported his contentions vigorously. Convinced that the jury system employed by the National Academy for selecting pictures for the annual exhibit was unfair to the young variants who did work of marked individuality, he waged war—a long and hot war—against the majority system of selection. "The iconoclasts among us, and I count myself one," had many changes to propose that would give the unlabeled man a better chance to have his work seen. And he was interested in international good will. Despite the fact that from the beginning to the end of his life he never left his own shores to visit another country, he dreamed of universal friendship. Especially did he wish to have his own country and France understand each other. One of the great enthusiasms of his life was the promotion of an American exhibition for the Luxembourg at the time of the World War.

There were, too, less agreeable matters that called for the crusader. The editor of an art journal undertook to have artists pay for his news notes about them and for the space that he proposed to devote to reproductions of their work. George Bellows wrote to the editor that he had always supposed news notes and reproductions were published because they were of public interest, and not because they were paid for as advertising. He would not lend himself to any such graft. The editor attempted to justify himself by saying that since every artist would buy space, there would be in the end a right comparative representation. Bellows asked what was going to happen to the good artist who chanced not to have money with which to buy news about himself, and proceeded to wage the most extensive war possible upon the editor and his practices. There was always something to fight for—or against!

He had the crusader's faith, too. Things might be bad enough—he sometimes declared that conditions were "rotten"—but they could be made better. "It is not because America has great wealth, great opportunities," he said, "and what is blandly termed 'great educational facilities' that she has any claim to the attention of the world's culture. It must some day be because of the fact that, among the vast sum of her population, there appears now and then a man who can create things of wonder and beauty." To this end something might be done. He did not, he protested, expect Mayor Hylan to proclaim a holiday when Glackens produced such a masterpiece as his "Portrait of Walter Hampden." Yet why should not an artist's neighbors in general be led to see their own need of art with such burning clearness that they would be moved to provide the artist with a normal, legitimate, economic support? "A great artist," he was accustomed to say, "can exist in a country which buys bad art; his situation is more difficult in a country which buys none." Nor need the public fear to buy the work of American artists. When the citizens of our own country free themselves from traditional prejudices and are able to exercise their own sense of delight, their own judgment, they will see how distinguished much American painting is. "It is not necessarily ridiculous to have faith. It is, however, very important to have it. Among some of our artists some time the great genius of America will arise. Some of him is probably here now. Look!"

American also was his feeling that he was just as good as the other fellow—at least. He never felt inferior; in fact, he liked the center of the stage. He was a brother to a certain manner of American soldier, who boasts before a battle that he will do thus and so, and then makes good his boast. He was not awed by sophistication; he could always match it with homely wisdom. He would pit himself against the most skillful, the most argumentative, and enjoy the experience. From the Catskills he wrote: "I have called it a summer, taken stock, showed the work to everybody, and am ready to pack up, go to New York, and start arguing with Pennell." And his feeling of equality or better he maintained in the presence of the most experienced, most "authoritative" art critics. Instead of waging a defensive war, as Whistler so often did, or suffering unspeakable agony, as Edward MacDowell did when assailed by the unintelligent, Bellows smoked the matter over a little, took his sturdy pen in hand, invited the critic to draw and paint awhile in order to discover how much he did not know, and told him to go to hell. "So that's that. I've got to paint."

In keeping with the great American legend, too, he was a family man. He gave the best of himself—his ability, his good humor, his boyish fun, his profound affection—to his kin. His father, an "Amen Methodist," was fifty-five years old when George was born. He was unapproachable on many matters close to a boy's heart. Yet George loved him while he stood in awe of him. "By charging less than he was worth," he once wrote of his father, an architect and builder, "and by investing in worthy causes, his fortune remained reasonably easy to calculate. He planned for me to become president of a bank. He had, however, the greatest respect for Michael Angelo, holding him second to no man with the exception of Moses. His main feeling seemed to be sorrow for the hard life I would be forced to lead as an artist in this generation. In this, owing greatly to his own support, he guessed wrong."

With his father it was not easy to be whimsical. But he could be with his mother. With her he could play the clown and the tease as much as he liked. He never ceased to chide her about his poor bringing-up, to make pseudo-sacrilegious remarks about the things she held sacred, to enlarge upon her son's financial plight, or to be shocked by the great range of vices that her Methodism permitted.

"*Dear Ma:*
'The melancholy days are come,
The saddest of the year,'
When the sluice gates of the pocketbook
Are opened from the rear."

Or:

"And what is the name of the new pastor?
"And does he Chew?"
"Now, now, now, don't be angry. Don't you remember Dr. Smith?
"Have you been flinching from Dominoes or dominoing from Flinch?
"Answer yes or no."

And who ever had such a wife and such daughters? Emma, whom he had won after six years of the most studious persistence! With all of his uproarious nonsense, he could never be wholly nonsensical about Emma. He loved her too passionately, too profoundly. And there were "the kids—Anne the slim and Jean the bean." He romped with them; he devised and wore the most astounding costumes to startle and delight them; he gave them the liberty of the studio while he worked; he wrote them letters in verse—good enough to be published; he dreamed of them; and he painted them in the best pictures he ever made.

And when the lean years were over and he seemed to have a long stretch of full ones ahead, he began to express his affection for his kin in new ways. To Aunt Fanny—the Aunt Fanny of the portrait, and the Eleanor of the "Eleanor, Jean and Anna"—he always felt especially attracted. She had helped to look after him when he was very small, and had kept him immaculately combed up and clean; and she had experienced the great romance of refusing twice to marry the man who loved her, and then accepting him the third time! But her possessions were few and her pride great. So when he once invited her to come to the Catskills for a visit, and received no reply, he suspected the reason. In the course of a shrewdly tactful letter, he wrote:

"I am aware, my dear Aunt Fanny, that you have not been blessed with the best of luck. I have. Therefore, I think it would be a nice idea to try and strike something like a mean proportion.

"I have what I think is a well-grounded belief that both you and your daughter Laura would welcome a vacation from the same scene—if you are anything like me. I must change around a bit.

"Further than this, I want to feel that you are not needing to worry about the future. As the chances are that it would not be a very available plan to leave you something in my will, I think I will leave you something right away. My mother is going to do exactly what I am proposing for myself, and between us you are to have a regular income of a thousand a year, which added to what income you have of your own, should make the days comfortable."

Then, after a description of his country place, and the information that the round-trip tickets and money for incidentals were on the way, he added the clinching postscript that he had chosen his picture of her to represent him in "the great exhibition in the Luxembourg, Paris."

He met the requirements of the national legend, finally, by combining a homely exterior with an essential refinement. He was tall, he was ungainly in some of his movements, and early he became bald. In addition, he was a believer in the informal. As a result, he looked much of the time like a plumber. Always he was making something at his work-bench on the mezzanine floor of his studio. He must have at hand every conceivable kind of nail and screw and bolt. For these he went to a neighboring hardware-store, where the salesmen liked him so much that they proudly kept the newspaper reproductions of pictures made by this customer who knew the names and sizes of nails as if he might be a person of solid character. In the country he plunged into every kind of manual labor. When his new house was ready for the roof he went to work on it. "Why don't you hire a man to do it?" his wife protested. "Can't ask anybody else to do what I'm afraid to do myself." But sitting on an unroofed house in the summer sun is not the easiest of chores. His untoughened body became so sore that he could scarcely proceed. But he stuffed a pillow into his overalls and worked valiantly, painfully on, until he had driven the last nail in the last shingle.

In general, strangers gained the impression that he was uncouth. When he was not sprawling, he was rocking. He brought from the Middle West the rocking-chair state of mind. So, whenever there was nothing else to do, he rocked—energetically, obliviously. Sometimes one of his intimates, who confessed that he loved the man more than a brother, would command: "You stop that rocking!" He would stop for a time. But as soon as the conversation or the meditation became absorbing again he fell into his rolling, swaying pace.

Yet in all matters of the spirit he was one of the most sensitive of men. He could not endure any music short of the best; he refused to listen to it even when played by Emma! He read not only great books, but books which require unusual refinement of intellect and feeling in the reader. Plays, too, must have quality. And his friends had to come up to the same requirements as his plays and books and music. When someone criticized him for having only friends of intellectual or artistic brilliance, he retorted: "What do you suppose I have friends for—to be bored by them?" His handwriting was that of a crude country boy, and he did not always spell according to the dictionary; yet he possessed a startling sense of fitness in words, a feeling for the rhythmical power in a sentence, and a perfect intuition for the total effect that a paragraph or a letter would produce.

III

Now a man with such an array of traditional American qualities would excite wonder—if not skepticism—wherever he chanced to appear. But the wonder was almost inexpressibly great when he chanced to appear in the world of art. Questioned concerning the peculiar artistic circumstances in which he arose, he replied jovially: "I arose surrounded by Methodists and Republicans!" And what he humorously implied was literally true: almost everything surrounding his early life, viewed in the obvious manner, was non-artistic.

Yet it is just because his individuality came from such an environment that he was able to make his greatest contribution to art. The tendency of art when it is wholly in the hands of organizations devoted to its perpetuation is to become ascetic, overrefined, "arty." American art schools for some decades have been filled, in the main, with young ladies who develop a technique for doing nothing in particular with great skill. If art is not to become drivel, there must constantly be injected into it some of the life of the soil, something that corresponds to the uncultivated health of a robust body. It requires a cross-fertilization of sanity from "the provinces." Somebody must occasionally give to it a strain of life comparable to what Abraham Lincoln gave to politics. It was this fresh life, this instinctive feeling for a healthy relation, that Bellows brought to art. He was unalterably a lone wolf. If somebody who professed to be very wise said in patronizing fashion, "Now that is the way artists do that," Bellows was certain to reply: "Well, hold on! Let's take a look. I don't know whether it is or not!" Not that he had any closed system of his own! "He was the readiest man in the world to have you prove that you were right," said the person who was the greatest single influence in his life as a painter; "but you had to prove it. He always brought himself to his work." This habit of bringing himself to his work was what led many to call him a revolutionist. "If I am," he said, "I don't know it. First of all, I am a painter, and a painter gets hold of life—gets hold of something real, of many real things. That makes him think, and if he thinks out loud he is called a revolutionist. I guess that is about the size of the matter." The reasonable thing to do, he contended, was to "watch all good art and accept none as a standard for yourself. Think with all the world and work alone."

Many, in attempting to evaluate his contribution, have compared him with Kipling, with Jack London, with Whitman. In each comparison there is a certain soundness. But he had more warmth, more fluidity, than Kipling; and he was more comprehensive in his sympathies, more healthy in his vigor, than Jack London. The parallel with Whitman is closest. Both were impatient with outworn forms and outworn subjects; both felt the energy of American life and were able to express it; both believed in the sacredness of the individual and hesitated not to take pride in themselves; and both believed that the artist should celebrate all life, whether "beautiful" or not, that reveals significance.

But Bellows was a more complete person than Whitman, a more representative person. Whitman was, with all of his democracy, an exotic democrat. He was an exotic American. He was not himself representative; he only wrote about representative things. He was, moreover, in his sympathies a remote pagan, and George Bellows was close and warm and reverential. Bellows might easily have painted something comparable to "The City Dead House," "By the Bivouac's Fitful Flame," "O Captain, My Captain," or "With Husky Haughty Lips, O Sea," but if Whitman had tried for a lifetime, he never would have written anything having the emotional tone of "Aunt Fanny," "Emma and Her Children," or "Lady Jean."

But any attempt to compare Bellows with somebody else must always be for convenience of discussion merely. The comparisons always turn out to be contrasts. He was made in his own proportions of vigor, understanding, dramatic power, humor, intimacy; and he had his own methods of supplanting the malarial sentimentality of American art with a robust sentiment.

IV

Nothing in anybody's effort to "place" him in the world of art, nothing in the solid fame that yearly became more solid, ever lured him away from the great pursuit. He meant to attain a perfection that Columbus, Ohio, and New York City had little dreamed about. He wanted to learn just because he wanted to learn. He was ready, too, to learn from anybody—from the ancient masters, from the most youthful of his artistic contemporaries, from the philosopher, from the fool. If he discovered some day that he was securing an effect as Tintoretto had secured it, he must write to his friends about the whole matter with boyish delight. If a new exhibition, a new school, or a new process was announced, he had to look into it at once to see if there were not something to learn. Such a possibility he approached with sublime expectancy. After he had gone through a new exhibition with alertness, he would say, "Nothing here I have not already learned"; or, "I mean to work until I can finish a canvas as perfectly as that myself." He was enthusiastic over the appearance of Jay Hambidge's *Dynamic Symmetry*, and later made frequent acknowledgment of his indebtedness to the volume. He was just as enthusiastic over new possibilities in color. If he applied himself to his painting until he grew stale and was unable to make progress, he did not try to sink into a restful stupor, but went to Brentano's, bought an armload of good solid reading, and buried himself from the world until he felt restored. "Can't paint if I don't feed my mind!"

By the time he had carried on his pursuit until he was forty, he had become the enriched person that must go into the making of a great artist. He was a philosopher, wise in his own increasing humility. "Try it in every possible way," he once told some art students. "Be deliberate—and spontaneous. Be thoughtful and painstaking. Be abandoned and impulsive. Learn your own possibilities. There is no impetus I have not followed, no method of technique I am unwilling to try. There is nothing I do not want to know that has to do with life or art." He was no longer—if he ever had been—a good-natured barbarian who had hit upon good painting and good lithography, but a man who had some coherent notions of the ways of men and artists. "Art isn't made in Bohemia, neither is it not made in Bohemia. It is wherever life exists and expresses dignity, humor, humanity, kindness, order." He quoted with approbation the words of Robert Henri: "To hold the spirit of greatness is in my mind what the world was created for—and art is great as it translates and embodies that spirit."

More and more he became impatient of mere formalities. "The Independent show this year is a hummer," he wrote in a letter. "The only stalling was on this damned dance which none of us want to go to. *And will not!*" What he wanted was a day that would give him a chance to work his head off, sometimes on a new canvas, often enough on one that he had kept about for months or years. In 1920 he wrote to a friend: "Have three fine portraits of Anne, Jean, and Emma, with no heads on any." Three years later the satisfying head was still not on Emma. After repeated attempts at it, he had her sit for him again one morning in the country. "Can't do it! Give it up! Go on!" he cried. But before she got away he called: "Come back here! Let me try just once more!" And in an hour the head that has been so widely praised for just the right reflective attitude was completed.

When he had worked himself to exhaustion he would call up one of his friends: "Hello! Is this Frans Hals?"

"Why, yes, Michael Angelo!"

"Well, how about a game of pool?" Or, if possible, baseball or tennis; he was not enough of a loafer to master pool.

Then dinner and music, or the theater, or some hours over a new lithograph, if he chanced to be in the city. Sometimes he worked on his lithographs till two in the morning, up on the mezzanine floor of his studio. That was the life!

There was ever a little crusading to do, too. Less than a year before the brief, agonizing days in the hospital that brought all to an end, the editor of a journal cut shamefully an illustration that Bellows had made under contract. "Result," he wrote, "the most awful botch imaginable. Emma has ordered me to war. I have gone. After two letters, very well done, not a glimmer of guilt from the editor. So I have started a legal attack—I expect to lose money, but I hope to line up the art world and get some kind of protection against the arbitrary changing of artists' work."

But nothing could permanently ruffle him. He was still the boisterous adventurer. The night before he was stricken with appendicitis—and he was only forty-two—Robert Henri had a number of friends in for the evening. They were the group that Bellows called "The Society of Perfect Wives and Husbands." As usual, he was much in the center of the stage. He found some old clothes and made himself up as Queen Victoria. Either because his friends were in special need of amusement or because he was in very high spirits, he never seemed such a perfect clown. The evening lasted until one or two o'clock. When the guests departed they descended from the studio—on the third floor—together. In the quiet that followed, the host stood by the window looking reflectively out. Below in the street there was a burst of laughter—genuine, honest, infectious laughter. It was George Bellows moving off into the night.

HAROLD NICOLSON

Harold George Nicolson came by birth and tradition to diplomacy, by marriage and taste to writing. Born at Tehran, Persia, in 1887, where his father, the late Sir Arthur Nicolson, 1st Baron Carnock, was British *chargé d'affaires*, he lived at Constantinople, Budapest, and Tangier before beginning his education in England. From Wellington College he went to Balliol, Oxford (M.A.), then entered the Foreign Office and the Diplomatic Service, in which he was alternately engaged, in various capitals, from 1909 to 1929. He was the Balkan expert of the British Delegation at the Peace Conference, 1919, and Counsellor of the British Embassy at Berlin, 1927. It is at the latter place that he came to know President Hindenburg and obtained the material for the following short biography. Resigning from the Diplomatic Service in 1929 to devote himself to writing, he joined the editorial staff of the London *Evening Standard*. He is a Fellow of the Royal Society of Literature, an Honorary Doctor of the University of Athens, and a Companion of St. Michael and St. George. He has stood for Parliament. In 1913 he married Victoria Sackville-West, the well-known novelist and poet. Together they visited and lectured in America in 1934.

Mr. Nicolson's main literary concern has been with biography, particularly the newer developments of this art, to which, as one of Lytton Strachey's compeers, he has made important contributions. First came his four authoritative and entertaining lives of poets: *Verlaine* (1921), *Tennyson* (1923), *Byron, The Last Journey* (1924), and the English Men of Letters Series *Swinburne* (1925). In 1926 he published *Some People*, a singular and delightful composite of biography, autobiography, and fiction. In it he sketches the characters of nine persons whom he knew at different times in his life in such a way as to reveal his own development. In 1927 he produced a little book, *The Development of English Biography*, which, though not the first manual of the subject, is the most concise and up-to-date. Mr. Nicolson is somewhat pessimistic about the future of "pure" biography and even predicts its disintegration. But he has done "that ungentle art" a service in separating its province from the conflicting claims of history, fiction, and science. In 1929 appeared Mr. Nicolson's *Portrait of a Diplomatist*, a life of Lord Carnock, his father, who was a prominent figure in pre-war European affairs. This was followed by *Peacemaking*,

1919 (1933), the author's personal recollections of the Peace Conference with a summary of its achievements and failures. As the third part of this political trilogy of the last half century, *Lord Curzon, The Last Phase, 1919-25* (1934) describes the author's chief as he knew him and studied his life work. *People and Things* (1931) and *Public Faces* (1932) are light and amusing excursions along the fringe of biography.

While Mr. Nicolson believes in the strict definition of "pure" biography, he admits (in an interesting article in *The Saturday Review of Literature*, May 26, 1934) that he has yet to practice it. But his *Byron*, with its "stream of consciousness" passages and its concentration on a single phase of the subject's career, is a valuable essay in modern technique. Mr. Nicolson stresses the importance of the choice of subject: "Never write a biography about anyone whom you personally dislike or from whose mental and topical atmosphere you are sundered either by prejudice or lack of knowledge." Yet, being an accomplished Stracheyan, he writes, as M. Maurois says, with "a mixture of irony and tenderness; but the tenderness is rather grim."

The late President of the Reich was clearly a man about whom Mr. Nicolson possessed adequate factual and personal knowledge and toward whom he was able to take both a sympathetic and a critical attitude. The combination of the intimate with the historical is what renders this portrait (from *The Yale Review*, Summer 1931) so successful. The reader cannot fail to notice that despite the death of Hindenburg and the growth of his legend in a Germany vastly altered since this piece was written, the characterization remains true.

HINDENBURG

THE UGLIEST of all legislative buildings is the Reichstag in Berlin. Born of the conquests and unifications of 1871, it endeavors to express both the arrogance of victory and the granite qualities which rendered victory so rapid and so complete. Cyclopean, and withal *bürgerlich*, is the base on which reposes this enlivened greenhouse, and the Nibelungen spirit, which simmers as a kettle in every German soul, is propitiated by green statues of Germania and of teutonic knights, perilously perched.

Other buildings in Germany, and indeed many of its railway stations, combine such massiveness with these glyptic effects. The Reichstag is unique in adding a third element, and in importing the barbaric elegance of the France of Napoleon the Third. For it was more than a passing recollection of the Avenue de l'Opéra which raised that pediment, or gilded the framing of that glass. "Graecia capta ferum victorem cepit." Only unfortunately Prussia hit, not upon the age of Pericles, but upon the age of Baron Haussmann.

The Reichstag, within, is equally gallic in appearance. Those helmeted ladies sculptured in varnished wood, those eagles so reminiscent in their strut and poise of the rooster of France, those garlands and those lozenges, are all due to the siege of Paris, but in the air of Brandenburg their elegance has suffered a sea change. It may be for this reason that on festive occasions the excellent Doctor Löbe, President of the Reichstag, decorates that wealth of heavy sculpture with pots of azaleas and bright swags of laurel tied in pink; and that behind his massive presidential chair are draped the republican colors of black, and red, and gold.

It was against such a setting that I first saw Hindenburg. His face had, of course, been long familiar to me from endless photographs, engravings, caricatures, and busts. I imagined a man as square about the shoulders, as rigidly opposite, as the King of Spades. Always when I thought of Hindenburg I regarded him as a purely token emblem, stylized and formidable as a figure in a pack of cards. And was I wrong? No—I was far less in error than I have sometimes supposed.

The occasion to which I refer was the tenth anniversary of the foundation of the republic. A commemorative ceremony was to be held in the Reichstag building, and we of the diplomatic body were summoned to attend. Being of a modest disposition and disliking acutely the pressure of diplomatic thighs, I took my seat in the back of the box, facing away from President Löbe's tribune, and commanding a direct view of the centre of the dress circle, where, upon an armchair covered with the republican colors, Hindenburg was about to sit.

The seats around him had been reserved for his personal staff, and the whole enclosure had been draped and carpeted so as to resemble a tent upon a field. The entrance towards the gangway was closed by curtains.

The soft clatter of conversation—that sound of water falling continuously into a tin bath—rose up from the body of the Reichstag towards us, mingling with the smell of chrysanthemums, stale cigars, ink, carbon paper, and those other odors so significant of the Legislative Assembly of the German *Reich.* Herr Löbe, a tiny figure at that distance and amid such immensity of panelling, took his seat beside his bell and his water-bottle. There was a momentary pause, a sudden word of command to some unseen guard of honor, and the curtains at the back of the tent were flung open and held in position by two officers in field-gray uniform. And then slowly, uncertainly, emerged a huge figure draped in a gigantic black frock coat, holding in his gloved hand an immense top hat—and as he advanced those who formed his staff seemed suddenly to shrink in size. The Assembly as a man rose in silence to greet him. I leant in the darkness of the diplomatic box taking my first clear glance at Hindenburg. As always, in such cases, he seemed different from what I had presupposed.

It was his shape, in the first place. So long had I based my image of him upon the contours of the King of Spades that it was unfamiliar to observe that he was in fact constructed in three dimensions. Hindenburg was not only a tall straight man: he was also round. The huge flowing panels of his frock coat emphasized a rotundity which, although not excessive for a man of his race and physique, was yet startling in the King of Spades.

Other differences then imposed themselves upon my analysis. The Hindenburg of the pictures wears invariably a dominant and sturdy look. He frowns. Was this bewildered octogenarian, this vast veteran who seemed to totter in his chair, indeed the victor of Tannenberg, the conqueror of the Masurian Lakes, the idol and the terror of half the world? No, it was not. It was merely dear old Papa Hindenburg. And the strange thing about it is that he had been Papa Hindenburg all along. No man has ever had a legend so fantastically thrust upon him.

Returning from this ceremony I doffed my uniform. I was changing flats at the time, and in the interval of flitting had secured a room high up in the Adlon Hotel. The window looked across a courtyard down into the President's garden. And as I dressed I looked out upon the anthracite being loaded in the hotel courtyard and beyond to the trees and promenades of the presidential garden. I then had my second glimpse of Hindenburg. There he was stumping round his garden still arrayed in his frock coat and his top hat. Straight he was, unbent and enormous —but there was something about his gait suggestive of the caution of age. He did not creep along the path, he did not limp, his knees were neither bent nor quavering. In fact he strode. And yet, even in his stride, there was something faintly tentative and hesitant. It was the walk of a magnificent "gym" instructor, who refused to admit, even to himself, that he was eighty-one.

Thereafter I had several successive visions of the teutonic hero. Inspecting *Reichswehr*, opening an exhibition, or merely driving out with his son along the scrubby alleys of the Tiergarten. These successive visions left upon me the impression only of a scarcely animate idol, of a wholly impersonal organism christened "Hindenburg" and preserved as some racial totem or as the weakening medicine man of a tribe. And then I met him face to face.

He gave a luncheon party to which I was invited. It was not a large party, nor can I say that it was the most festive meal which I have ever attended. The servants were dressed in rich but quiet liveries, the food was excellent, the wine superb, and the table was gay with pink roses in little porcelain jars. My earlier conceptions of Hindenburg were, during this luncheon, succeeded by a more personal representation. He sat there, shy, silent, enormous. An immense placidity of countenance above the pink roses. An impression of courteous boredom, of dutiful weariness, of heavy hospitality. He raised his glass to the Ambassador opposite him, he bowed to the lady on his right and to the lady on his left, taking some roses from the vase in front of him with clumsy fat-fingered hands. The roses dripped, and he wiped them carefully. There was something old-fashioned, provincial, almost ungainly about his gesture. With slow and almost somnolent courtesy he bade us farewell.

This impression again is overlaid with a third. The Maharajah of Patiala came to Berlin and was received by the President. I accompanied the Maharajah as interpreter. His Highness wore an immense turban of great magnificence, and against his elegantly curled whiskers twinkled two diamond earrings of great price. We were ushered by aides-de-camp into the President's sitting room. He bowed formally, and with slow deliberation conducted the Maharajah to a hard pink settee. I took a little armchair beside them. A long pause followed during which the sound of distant trams came to us grating round the corner by the Kaiserhof.

With an immense effort the President pulled himself together and began to repeat his lesson. "Your Highness," he said, "is, I understand, the leader of the Sikhs?" I translated, and the Maharajah indicated that the President was not incorrect in this surmise. "And the Sikhs," continued Hindenburg, "are the bravest of all Indian races?" The Maharajah bowed slightly at this compliment, and added that a reputation for great courage had also been gained by the Gurkhas. "Tapfer," I translated, "sind auch die Gurken." "Die *wass?*" boomed the President in startled surprise. "Die Gurken–" I repeated, explaining that they were an Indian tribe. At this the vast bulk of the President began to heave and rumble. His shoulders shook. A flush of color rose to his face. And to my astonishment his eyes wrinkled into little slits of merriment such as I have never seen out of Ireland. He laughed and laughed. He slapped me heavily on the knee. He rolled with laughter, and his little eyes shone with merriment and friendliness. For the word "Gurken," it will be remembered, signifies in German those little cucumbers which they delight to pickle. It was with some difficulty that I explained to the Maharajah what had provoked the presidential guffaws. He smiled politely and bowed so that his earrings twinkled gaily against his beard. And the ice was broken. Thereafter they spoke of shooting and the President became animated and gay. From that day onwards he always chuckled when he saw me. And the final impression thus left is one of an immense and genial child.

How comes it that this big octogenarian should personify the hopes and ambitions of seventy million people? Let me examine for a moment that strange herd phenomenon which has become the worship of Hindenburg.

After the war Hindenburg wrote his memoirs. They are not

very well written, and they contain passages of such naïveté that one is forced to smile. But there is one passage which does not make me smile. It is the man himself. This passage runs as follows:

"The decisive factor in my life and actions was not a desire for any applause from the world. It was rather my own convictions, a sense of duty, and my own conscience which have guided me throughout my life."

Many other men might have written this sentence. But when Hindenburg writes it, one knows that it is as true as the sun rising above the downs. It is so blazingly true that it dazzles the eyes. It must be very pleasant when one is eighty to be able to write a sentence like that and to feel that it is confirmed by every second of every minute of every hour of every day of eighty long years. Let me examine the curious and limpid life of Paul von Hindenburg.

For Hindenburg, as his English biographer—and incidentally the best of all his biographers—has written, "possesses a genius for sincerity." And there are few nobler types of genius.

He was born, on October 2, 1847, of an old "Junker" family of no great distinction. The expression "Junker" is difficult to render in English. "Small landed gentry" is the nearest we can get, and even then it is not very near. His grandfather had served in the Napoleonic wars, and young Hindenburg was sixteen when he died. At the family farm at Neudeck—it was little more than a large farmhouse—the young Hindenburg spent his first childhood and his earliest holidays. His old grandfather would tell him stories of the battles of Jena and Leipzig, and the gardener, even more aged, had actually served as a stripling under Frederick the Great. The great military tradition of Prussia—the suffering, the efficiency, the cold ordeals—was in this way imbibed by Hindenburg before he could walk.

His father, Robert von Hindenburg, was also an officer. They all were. It was impossible to conceive of a Hindenburg in any other terms. "It was not," wrote Hindenburg, "a matter of decision for me to become a soldier: I became a soldier as a matter of course."

Apart from those holidays at Neudeck, he followed the garrison life of his father. His earliest memories were attuned to the call of the bugle. The family moved with their regiment from Posen (where Paul was born—it is now Polish) to Cologne, from Glogau to Kottbus. Always the sound of the bugle in the mornings. For a time they were at a little garrison town called Pinne. They had a house with a large garden, and through the garden ran a stream which Hindenburg remembered. One always remembers the water of childhood. And sixty years later Hindenburg, the victor of Tannenberg, passed through Pinne. He spent the night in the house of his memories. He was immensely impressed by this coincidence. It was not a coincidence. What, in fact, was more natural than he should stop at Pinne? But to him it was miraculous. Simple-minded people are always overwhelmed by apparent coincidences.

The military discipline which he saw around him was reflected in the discipline of his home. His father, and even his mother treated him as a recruit. He was never allowed to ask questions. Three things alone were taught him: God, the Fatherland, and the King. Nothing else mattered.

At the age of eleven he was sent to the cadet school at Wahlstatt in Silesia. It was a brutal school. The boys were encouraged to believe only in physical prowess—all intellectual energy was sharply discouraged. "Since my days as a cadet," wrote Hindenburg, "I have never read a book that did not deal with military affairs." It might have been better for his country if he had.

At the age of eighteen, in the year 1865, he was given a commission in the Guard Regiment then quartered at Danzig. In a few months, war was declared by Prussia upon Austria. Hindenburg followed his regiment to the front. At the battle of Königgrätz he was struck by a bullet in the head. He recovered and led his platoon to the assault of a battery. He was decorated for this feat of courage. And the helmet, with a round hole in it, he preserves to this day. He shows it to his friends with a chuckle of pride.

After the seven weeks' war with Austria, Hindenburg went with his regiment to Hannover. For three years he trained recruits. And then in 1870 came the Franco-Prussian War. He received the Iron Cross at Gravelotte. From a distant hill (for his regiment was part of the reserve) he watched the battle of Sedan. He was part of the army which besieged Paris. And he was present, in the Hall of Mirrors, at Versailles when the German empire was proclaimed. And after all these excitements followed forty years of regimental duty.

He married. He had one son and two daughters. He passed from rank to rank. Lieutenant, Captain, Major, Colonel, General. In 1881 he was garrisoned at Königsberg in East Prussia. He studied the military geography of the frontier between Germany and Russia. It was known that few men had shot duck so frequently in the Masurian marshes. He knew every inch of the ground. And it was this hobby which brought him, almost forty years later, immortal fame.

In 1905 Hindenburg, in the ordinary course of events, became a General. In 1911 he retired from the army. In 1914 came the European War.

If in July, 1914, you had asked a German if he had heard of General von Hindenburg he would probably have answered that he had never heard of him. His name figured in the Army List and was known to a few colonels. To the great public this retired soldier of nearly seventy was completely unknown. Within nine weeks he was an almost mythical figure from the Vistula to the Rhine. Let me explain how this old officer became so famous.

In August, 1914, Germany was threatened on two fronts. There were the French and English in the West and the Russians in the East. The General Staff were not very afraid of the Russians, and their whole plan was to allow the Russians to do what they liked, and to throw the full weight of the German army against Paris. Unfortunately, the Russians advanced faster and further than was expected. The experts knew that it would not matter very much even if they reached the outskirts of Berlin. Public opinion, however, was not so well-informed. The people felt that it was alarming to have the Russians in East Prussia and that something must be done. The High Command decided, against their better judgment, that the Russians must be stopped at once. They were told that an old dugout was living at Hannover who knew all about the Eastern front.

At 3 P.M. on August 22, 1914, von Hindenburg received a telegram from the Emperor, asking if he were ready for immediate service. He replied, "Am ready," and hurried into his dressing room to put on his uniform. He was told that General Ludendorff had been appointed his Chief of Staff, that he was coming to Hannover by special train arriving the next afternoon, that Hindenburg must board that train, and that Ludendorff would explain everything on the journey. He did. Four days later began the battle of Tannenberg. The Russians were surrounded and lost 350,000 men. The German losses were only 37,000. The Russian menace had been crushed. And from that moment, Hindenburg became the idol of his country.

As a matter of fact, he himself knew very little about it. The victory of Tannenberg, one of the greatest victories in history, had been prepared by von Prittwitz, elaborated by General Hoffmann, improved by Ludendorff, and was carried out by General von François. But Hindenburg, as Commander of the Eighth Army, as the man who signed the telegrams, got all the credit. Germany was so hysterically relieved that it forgot all about the battle of the Marne. It suited the German government to boom the victories in the East in order to conceal the fact that in the West their whole plan had miscarried. The victory of Tannenberg was followed by the two astounding but less important victories at the Masurian Lakes.

Within a few weeks Hindenburg emerged as the hero of Germany. His portrait was in every home. A battleship was christened with his name. He was invincible, majestic, infallible. Huge wooden statues of Hindenburg, impenetrable and vast, were erected in the larger towns. Millions flocked to pay them homage. He became Commander-in-Chief. Ludendorff remained his right-hand man. The Hindenburg legend grew to the proportions of an epic. And Paul von Hindenburg was immensely embarrassed by all this adulation.

Without desiring such eminence, Hindenburg became the dominant figure in Germany. Everybody, even the politicians, looked to him. Hindenburg understood nothing about politics and disliked them. Ludendorff also understood nothing about politics but liked them very much indeed. It was under his influence that decisions were made. They were bad decisions. They included such things as the unrestricted submarine warfare, the annexationist programme, the Treaty of Brest-Litovsk, and the dismissal of Kühlmann. Herr von Kühlmann had had the courage in 1918 to state that the war could not be won by military means alone. He was right. Ludendorff *knew* he was right. But Ludendorff had him flung from office and replaced by a nominee of his own. Germany thereby lost the chance of an honorable peace. But of all these things Hindenburg knew nothing. He merely initialled the telegrams which Ludendorff had drafted.

And then, in the autumn of 1918, came the crash. Ludendorff escaped to Sweden disguised in civilian clothes, huge tinted spectacles, and a passport in the name of Herr Lindström. Hindenburg remained. Puzzled but anxious he watched the defeat and disintegration of the German army. Puzzled and distraught he learnt that a republic had been proclaimed in Berlin. He advised the Emperor, whom he loved, to fly to Holland. He did not join him. He remained behind with what was left of the army. And when the republic was established he offered it his services. It was his duty. He remained on as Commander-in-Chief until the Treaty of Versailles was signed. And then he returned to his little flat in Hannover—an old unhappy man. He remained in retirement for six further years, refusing to raise a hand against the republic, which, however much it might conflict with the Wahlstatt traditions, was yet the accepted government of his country. He remained there—honored, aged, and unimportant, visited on occasions by his old comrades, and surrounded by his family and the absurd pictures of the Madonna which he had for years been collecting.

Then in 1925 came another and even more unexpected summons. President Ebert, the first republican statesman of Germany, died suddenly. None of the political parties could agree on his successor. The first election was a fiasco, and the nation was menaced by a renewal of disturbance. The friends of Hindenburg urged him to stand for the presidency. He refused, claiming, and with justice, that he was now too old. They urged him that it was his duty to resume his own legend. The old war horse was fired by the use of this watchword. He agreed. He polled nearly fifteen million votes. And there he remains today [1931] in his presidential palace, an almost mythical figure, the emblem of the sacred continuity of German tradition.

It is in this symbolic character of a racial deity that resides the immense strength of Hindenburg and his legend. His presence has given dignity and balance to the German republic. His very longevity invests him with an almost theocratic prestige. In the vast solidity of their President the German people recognize the embodiment of their triumphs and their sufferings, for those childish eyes have seen the greatest victories and the greatest defeats of the German armies: they have gazed on the men who fought at Jena, at Sedan, at Tannenberg, and at the Marne; they have witnessed that proud day in the Galerie des Glaces, and they have clouded to that bitter morning, almost half a century later, when the last of the German Emperors took train for Holland; and back in the remote past they have looked up with equal integrity and confidence to an old gardener who mumbled stories of Frederick the Great.

The German people have nearly every quality, but they lack self-confidence. Being romantic by nature, they love to create mythological figures to personify their own virtues. Hindenburg is one of those figures. He is not intelligent, and, in fact, his mental processes are as simple as those of a child. He is not interested in politics, and his actions as President have been taken invariably on the advice of others. But his very solidity of structure and outlook, the astounding *permanence* of his very presence, act as a tonic upon the neurotic diffidence of his countrymen, as his sublime sense of duty and of service responds to all that is finest in the German character.

J. G. LOCKHART

John Gilbert Lockhart was born in 1891 with the highest family precedent for becoming a biographer and man of letters. A Scotsman by birth, he is a great-nephew of John Gibson Lockhart, who, as one of the famous "Scotch Reviewers" of *Blackwood's* and the *Quarterly*, painfully tried the souls of the Romantic poets more than a century ago, who married the eldest daughter of Sir Walter Scott, and who wrote the colossal Life which helped to repay the dead novelist's creditors and is recognized as the most valuable documentary biography since Boswell's *Johnson*. He is also a cousin of Bram Stoker, author of *Dracula*.

Educated at Marlborough College and at Trinity College, Oxford, Mr. Lockhart served during the War in India, Egypt, and Palestine. He was for some years director of Philip Allan and Company and is now director of Geoffrey Bles, Ltd., both London publishing firms. His literary works include half a dozen books relating little-known mysteries and adventures of the sea, an account of a journey to Russia, two outspoken biographical volumes, *The Feet of the Young Men* and *Pulpits and Personalities* (under the pseudonym of "The Janitor"), *The Peacemakers*, and a convincing life of Cecil Rhodes. He is now engaged, by request of the family, on a life of the late Lord Halifax.

The Peacemakers (1814-1815), published in England in 1932 and in America in 1934, took its starting-point from the plausible analogies between the peace achieved by the Congress of Vienna and that expected of the Treaty of Versailles a hundred years later. "There is an astonishing contrast," writes Mr. Lockhart, "between the treatment of France in 1814 and 1815 and that of Germany in 1919. When full allowance has been made for the difference in circumstances, two points appear: the extraordinary skill with which Talleyrand maneuvered his country back from outlawry into international fellowship, and the resolution with which Castlereagh opposed a punitive peace. In 1919 Germany had no Talleyrand, Britain no Castlereagh; the conquered were not even permitted to state their case, but had to accept the decision of the victors. We find a second contrast between the voice of France in 1814 and in 1919, between Talleyrand, who with all his faults had a European mind, and Clemenceau, who with all his virtues was a French provincial." Then as the book progressed, some of the parallels faded, the contrasts became "trivial and even meaningless," while the figures of the diplomats themselves only gained in salience. "The study of the political man," Mr. Lockhart concludes, "retains its fascination. It takes us to the center of the problem, older than Aristotle, of the perfect government. It cannot give us flawless analogies, but it can repeatedly suggest answers to the questions which we are asking ourselves today. It is, above all, an absorbing study in personality."

The focal point of this short life of Talleyrand is, naturally, the Congress and the momentous public events through which that statesman moved so influentially. Yet the portrait is at once rounded and familiar. In method, it resembles somewhat the "psychographs" of Gamaliel Bradford, with their analysis of the character under several heads—money, love, religion. In style it is more like the critical narratives of Strachey, even to the closing paragraph of imaginary death-bed memories. But the honest and skillful workmanship comes from Mr. Lockhart's thorough comprehension of the subject and his mastery of the biographic art.

TALLEYRAND

A PEACEMAKER

THERE is a point in the career of most political climbers when they cease to be unedifying and begin to become shining examples, when they discard the shifts and questionable devices that were incidental to the ascent, and appear as patriots, with a past which they earnestly hope will be forgotten and a set of principles which very soon seem inseparable from their equipment. It may be true that very few politicians are heroes to the contemporary biographer. People, however, have short memories; they have, where the dead are concerned, a large bump of veneration; and fortunately the biographer seldom approaches his task until his subject is dead, when the career may be viewed as a whole and in due proportion, when the earlier misdeeds sink into the insignificance of peccadilloes and all the emphasis can be laid on the later statesmanship.

But while some politicians, like William Pitt the elder, succeed in creating the desired illusion of a life devoted from the very beginning to the public weal, others have been less fortunate. Although Charles Maurice de Talleyrand-Périgord performed notable services for his country during his last twenty-five years, and died in an effluvium of sanctity, his enemies refused him an amnesty while he lived and an oblivion when he was dead. They pursued him to the end with the most scurrilous libels—some of them the more scurrilous for their truth—and embellished his career with legends so unflattering as to border on the diabolical.

Yet embellishment was hardly necessary. The plain facts were sufficient. The life of Talleyrand, gloss it as you may, stands out as the supreme example of the ungodly man who flourished in spite, not only of his ungodliness, but of the fact that all the world was aware of it.

Born in 1754, he came of one of the most ancient families in France. Tradition would have sent him into the army, but a careless nurse, who let him fall from a chest of drawers, to the permanent injury of his foot, was responsible for his entering the Church. He was trained at St. Sulpice and ordained by parental wish in 1778, a witty and philosophical young priest, with a social advantage that opened for him the doors of the salons, and a reputation for freethinking which drew on him the suspicions of the Court. The world began to be entertained, though hardly to be improved, by this young man with his epigrams, his gaiety, his gambling, and his successful pursuit of women. Even if we reject as legendary an early affair with a poulterer's daughter, his liaisons were too numerous and notorious to escape attention, or to admit of his early promotion, even in the lax world of his day. "I was thinking, madame," he told the Comtesse du Barry, "that in Paris it is much easier to obtain women than a fat abbacy." So at least Talleyrand found it. Authority, which might have overlooked a few youthful scrapes in a young abbé of promise, found it difficult to ignore his affairs with ladies of such prominence as the Comtesse de Flahaut. It was at once Talleyrand's good taste and his misfortune to sin in the best company, to find his mistresses among those who were at the top of their profession and whose attachments were consequently public events. The queen was shocked, authority was displeased, but Talleyrand went on in his light-hearted way. "He dresses like a fop, thinks like a deist, and preaches like an angel," was the report of one of his critics.

In 1782 he was Agent-General of the Clergy; in 1785, through the good offices of the Comtesse de Brionne, he nearly obtained a cardinal's hat; and in 1789 he actually became Bishop of Autun. Those were disturbing days, when the monarchy was dying of quack remedies, when ministers succeeded each other in a monotonous sequence of failure, and when anyone with ideas was sure of a hearing. Talleyrand, who never lacked ideas, began to be regarded as a person of importance. Less than a month before the fall of the Bastille he even paid a midnight call on the king's brother, the Comte d'Artois, and suggested that he and his friends should be entrusted with the task of government; a modest offer which was politely declined. Whereupon Talleyrand, disappointed in his ambition to be a second Richelieu, openly declared for the Third Estate.

In the new turmoil which was transforming "the absolute monarchy tempered by lampoons" into a republic ruled by the guillotine, he further scandalised the faithful, and ultimately earned a papal excommunication, first by attaching himself to the Left of the Assembly, and next by leading the so-called "constitutional" clergy. In 1791 he abandoned an unequal struggle between the prejudices and the privileges of his position and resigned his see. He had entered the Church with reluctance, and in obedience to his parents' wishes; but he had never loved his orders and, indeed, had shown them scant respect by his way of life. Now, when bishops were at a discount, he gradually and unostentatiously unpriested himself, with no ill-feeling towards the Church, but with an iron determination that for the future he would be his own master; so that even Napoleon, who dallied with the idea of having him made a cardinal, was to accept him as a permanent layman.

A man who had had a seminarist training, yet held the right views, was a valuable recruit to the new men who were trying, with an empty treasury and a passively resisting monarch, to govern France. Talleyrand was adopted by Mirabeau and Delessart, and sent on a mission to London, which proved so successful that he secured an appointment as unofficial adviser to Chauvelin the ambassador. But since Chauvelin's indiscretions were likely to demand an unlimited supply of scapegoats, Talleyrand soon returned to Paris, where he found the Revolution in full career, the monarchy tumbling, the prisons full, and the Commune marching to power. Paris had ceased to be a safe place for the disciple of Montesquieu—or for any man who detested disorder as heartily as did Talleyrand—and, after swallowing all his principles and seeing most of his old associates murdered, he resolved to return to London. But in what capacity should he go? If he went with a passport, he went as a citizen; if without, he became an *émigré;* and he had the wit to foresee that, even when the Terror was past, the *émigré* would be unforgiven. He lingered, with increasing discomfort, through the September massacres, secured at last the coveted passport and the pretence of a mission, and fled without a backward glance.

In England he tried for a while to play the part of a semi-official representative of France, but opinion was hardening against the Jacobins. Chauvelin and the events of the summer had antagonised the ruling classes, and, in Paris, indifference to the activities of the ex-bishop was changing into hostility. Talleyrand found himself a man without a country and almost without a party. Lord Lansdowne might ask him to dinner, and Canning might visit him in his house in Kensington Square; but he had lost most of his money, the *émigrés* would have nothing to do with a revolutionary, and the Revolutionary Government at length proscribed him as an *émigré*. Hard is the fate of the Kerensky in exile! Still, Talleyrand, a royalist to London and a republican to Paris, continued to intrigue with anyone who was ready to intrigue with him, keeping a foot in either camp and his head very firmly on his shoulders, until at last even the long-suffering English lost patience and forbade him the country.

Since Europe, it seemed, was averse from harbouring an ex-bishop and a suspected Jacobin, he sailed for the United States, one of the strangest emigrants that ever left the Old World. Landing in Philadelphia, he quickly ingratiated himself with leading Americans, to the fury of the French minister, who could not prevent him from dining with Alexander Hamilton, and only just prevented President Washington from granting him an audience. The minister suspected plots, because Talleyrand and plots were already inseparable terms; but actually the exile was too busy trying to make money to trouble himself with the politics of his hosts, though not too busy to follow with the closest attention the course of events across the Atlantic. He would return, somehow, some day, when his name could be erased from the list of the proscribed. Meanwhile, since it was a nuisance to be poor, he would get rich as quickly as he could. He speculated and dabbled in real estate, without much profit, for his capital was small. He went into the backwoods and consorted with trappers. He seized on the idea of seeking his fortune in India, but at the last moment his chosen companion exhibited signs of homicidal mania, and Talleyrand prudently allowed him to sail for the East alone. But he was getting desperate. Time was slipping by and he was still an exile in a country too new for his sophisticated taste. He missed the company and the good things of civilisation. "I found thirty-two religions in the United States," he said, "but only one dish." His homesickness grew on him. "If I stay here another year," he wrote to Madame de Staël, "I shall die."

But it was Robespierre who died. After the 9th Thermidor the Terror lifted in France and voices were raised on behalf of some of the less compromised exiles. Talleyrand's most active intercessor was Madame de Staël, whom he afterwards treated with flagrant ingratitude. Des Renaudes, an ex-abbé and a staunch supporter, pointed out that Talleyrand had left France on a mission from which he had never been recalled. His friends worked hard; his enemies counter-worked viciously, but with less success; and on the 13th Fructidor the Convention repealed the decree against "Talleyrand-Périgord, ex-Bishop of Autun," struck his name from the roll of *émigrés*, and gave him permission to return.

We may assume that Talleyrand, like our Charles II, thereupon resolved never to go on his travels again. If, in the perilous days of the future, he was ever in danger of being tempted out of this resolution, his American exile was an excellent mnemonic. He might fall from favour, but he would not again make the mistake of fleeing from the country.

Once in Paris, with more help from Madame de Staël, Talleyrand made good his footing, obtaining from the Directory the portfolio of Foreign Relations; but he had less confidence in his new colleagues than he had in a young artillery officer who was winning victories in Italy. He courted Bonaparte with delicate compliments, welcomed him from Egypt, assisted in the *coup d'état* of the 18th Brumaire, and thenceforth attached himself as firmly to the fortunes of the First Consul as he was capable of attaching himself to any fortunes not his own. When Napoleon became Emperor of the French, Talleyrand put on gold lace and became Grand Chamberlain; and while the other figures of the revolutionary years faded into obscurity beside the growing genius of Napoleon, Talleyrand continued to shine. For ten years he helped his master to direct the foreign policy of France, and if in serving his country he did not forget to serve himself, the brilliance of his diplomacy was admitted even by those who had best cause to hate him. The association had begun with high promise. It seemed that Machiavelli had found his prince. The dynamic efficiency of the Consulate contrasted happily with the muddle and improvisations of the early years of the Republic. Abroad and at home everything suddenly began to work, and the Government, which had been labouring like some large, disorganised machine, fell into a new and easy rhythm. But this was not to last.

It is a paradox of Talleyrand's career that while he genuinely desired peace, these years of his glory were devoted almost entirely to war. He found that military success, which in the struggling days of the Directory had proved so admirable a lubricant to foreign policy, had started his country on a career of conquest which he was quite unable to check. He did not want war; he preferred to gain his ends by diplomacy. He did not want hegemony; he aimed at a balance of power. Rank, primacy, preponderance—to him they were but the reefs on which the Empire must ultimately suffer shipwreck.

"True primacy . . ." he had written as early as 1792, "is to be master of one's own house and never to be ridiculous enough to try to be master in other people's. We have heard, rather late, no doubt, that for States, as for individuals, true prosperity consists, not in acquiring or invading the domains of others, but in making the best of one's own." Such amiable sentiments might proceed from the lips of any statesman, in any age, to tickle the ears of any international gathering; and they mean, as a rule, exactly nothing. But with Talleyrand they were the confession of a faith which he held and practised as consistently as his own interests and the will of his masters allowed. England must be placated, Austria, at all costs, must be maintained, France must consolidate herself within her borders, must seek peace and ensue it. All of which, though sound sense, scarcely commended itself to Napoleon. When Talleyrand made a peace, the emperor turned it into an armistice; when Talleyrand had dissolved one coalition, the emperor straightway provoked another. To Talleyrand's mind they were like two children, one of whom laboriously built houses of cards which the other straightway demolished.

The friction between the two men grew. The years were bringing disillusionment to Talleyrand. In 1796 he had pictured an association in which Napoleon would win such battles as were necessary and preserve under his spectacular leadership the unity of the nation, while his minister, less ostentatiously, would form and control policy. It was an ideal partnership—on paper; but Napoleon wanted not partners, but subordinates, and Talleyrand soon found himself carrying out policies which he had not devised and of which he profoundly disapproved. He could not even flatter himself that he was an effective brake on the wheel; for the brake, when applied, no longer gripped.

He chafed and fretted, and tried to console himself with the huge fortune which he was amassing—from the Portuguese, from the German princes, from almost anyone, men said, who wanted anything and could pay Talleyrand's price. He gambled wildly, gave sumptuous entertainments, coined bitter epigrams about his master, and faced the hard truth that, having realised all that he had dreamed of in his years of exile, his very success had risen up to taunt him with his impotence. Napoleon, meanwhile, watched him closely. He disliked and mistrusted this lame little aristocrat whose name he consistently mispronounced; he resented the gibes which the talebearers were so ready to carry to his ears; but he found him too useful and too dangerous to dispense with his services.

In the end it was Talleyrand who resigned. He went in 1807, on the plea of ill-health. He remained Grand Chamberlain, received the empty dignity of Vice-Grand Elector, and continued to interview ambassadors, to give advice to his late master, and to make things exceedingly difficult for his successor. In 1808, Napoleon, possibly with the idea of keeping him out of mischief, forced on him the humiliating task of entertaining the captive Spanish princes at Valençay. Talleyrand accepted the duty and performed it with his customary magnificence, while secretly resenting the transformation of the Grand Chamberlain into a gaoler. He no longer served Napoleon; on the contrary, he began quite deliberately to betray him. He was in close touch with the Russian and Austrian ambassadors; he gave them advice and titbits of advance information; and at Erfurt, whither he accompanied the emperor, he established a personal understanding with the Tsar. "The French people are civilised," he told Alexander; "their sovereign is not. The sovereign of Russia is civilised; his people are not. It therefore behoves the sovereign of Russia to be the ally of the French people." Such flattery was exquisitely attuned to Alexander's vanity. He was delighted to be told that he alone could save Europe and civilisation. From whom and how? From Napoleon, said Talleyrand, and by resisting Napoleon. It is most encouraging to have your private convictions confirmed so authoritatively.

Unconscious of the treachery that was afoot, Napoleon plunged into his Spanish campaign. At Astorga he learnt the truth. Austria was preparing war, and the dagger that was about to stab him in the back was in the hand of—Talleyrand.

He returned to Paris in a fury to confront the traitor in full council. "You're a thief, a coward, a man without faith," he raged at him; "you don't believe in God. All your life you've failed in your duty; you've betrayed everybody; you hold nothing sacred; you would sell your own father! . . . Now, because you think things are going badly with me in Spain, you have the impudence to go about saying you've always condemned my conduct towards that country, while all the time it was you who first put the idea into my head, you who have persistently egged me on. If you got your deserts I'd smash you like a bit of glass. But I won't take the trouble; I've too much contempt for you."

Talleyrand listened to this tirade with the courteous, impassive interest which he knew so well how to assume and which once led Marshal Lannes to remark, "If someone kicked Talleyrand's backside while he was talking to you, his face would not move a muscle." The emperor fumed, the ministers twittered with delight, and Talleyrand, limping out of the Tuileries, was heard to murmur reflectively, "What a pity such a great man should have been so badly brought up!" This last sneer was typical of a series of epigrams that slowly poisoned the personal relations of the two men. It galled Napoleon that one of his ministers should regard him as a *parvenu*, and should not even trouble to conceal his sentiments.

Everyone expected this outbreak to be the prelude to some stern reprisal, to disgrace, exile, even imprisonment. But Napoleon merely contented himself with appointing a new Grand Chamberlain. Talleyrand remained in Paris; he continued to give occasional advice; he had the freedom of the inner circle without the responsibilities of office; he did not even interrupt his correspondence with Napoleon's enemies, but drew a handsome salary from Alexander, to whom he gave early and priceless information of the impending invasion of Russia.

All through 1812 he watched the clouds bank up against the Empire. "This is the beginning of the end," he remarked, when news of the Russian disasters reached Paris, and characteristically he began to lay his plans. What was to happen next? A regency under Marie-Louise? A new dynasty? The Orleanists? The Bourbons? The last idea prevailed. It promised France a monarch, and Talleyrand was at heart a monarchist; it offered a principle, that of legitimacy, and Talleyrand held that every policy should be founded on a principle or on something that sounded like a principle. So he became a king-maker, and because he knew exactly what he wanted at a moment when hardly anyone else did, he persuaded Alexander to adopt his proposal. The Bourbons returned, and Louis XVIII, partly in gratitude and partly out of good sense, appointed Talleyrand his representative in making peace. After all that had passed, the treaty of May 30th, 1814, gave France much better terms than she had any business to expect, or than some of her enemies had reasonably hoped to wring from her. After disturbing the peace of Europe for twenty-two years she returned to the frontiers of 1792. When we remember that the Allies had learnt their peacemaking in the school of Napoleon, we must admire their moderation. But we must also recognise the adroitness with which Talleyrand exploited their mutual jealousies to the advantage of France.

After Paris, Vienna. Once more, in a tone that vibrated through the chancelleries, Talleyrand was the voice of France. In the previous chapter we have described the success with which he brought his country back into the comity of nations, flung the Allies into discord, worked to prevent the destruction of Saxony and the elimination of the Bourbons from Naples, and finally kept his embassy in being for many months after his Government had disappeared.

It was the greatest work of his life. At last, we might suppose, he would win the gratitude and respect of his countrymen. But he won nothing of the kind. The returned *noblesse*, who had swarmed into the high offices, detested him because he was not an *émigré;* the survivors of the Empire hated him for his betrayal of Napoleon; even Louis, who owed him his kingdom, found it hard to conquer his prejudice against an ex-bishop with a wife. "Yesterday, after Mass," gibed a malicious newspaper, "the Bishop of Autun had the honour of presenting his wife to the son of St. Louis." It was not the kind of jest that Louis enjoyed.

While Talleyrand was at Vienna, the king wrote to him in the friendliest terms—"*Mon cher cousin*"—gave him all his confidence, and received in return as much of Talleyrand's as he was in the habit of giving to anybody. But Louis' native shrewdness warned him that Talleyrand was too expensive a luxury for the Bourbons to indulge for long: too many people hated him too much. When Talleyrand, after the dissolution of the Congress, posted from Vienna to Mons to give an account of his stewardship, the king tried to avoid him. His carriage and Talleyrand's met at the gate. The minister made his bow. The king smiled and said: "Well, Prince de Bénévent, you're leaving us? The waters will do you good; let us hear from you." Such was the Bourbon welcome to the French plenipotentiary at Vienna.

It must have been a few days later that Talleyrand, conquering his resentment and the king's elusiveness, at last sat down to a meal in the royal presence. Matters of high importance were awaiting discussion, but scarcely a word was spoken until the Duc de Duras, rising suddenly but respectfully, said, "I regret to tell Your Majesty that the butter is rancid." In theory the *ancien régime* may have been admirable; in practice a diplomatist of the Republic and the Empire must sometimes have found it very tiresome.

After Waterloo, fresh terms were imposed on France. Talleyrand was again to be the negotiator, but by this time he had no illusions left. He was to be used and then discarded; he was to do the work and carry the odium of an unfavourable peace. But Louis had mistaken his man. Talleyrand preferred to resign, giving as his pretext the humiliating conditions which were being forced upon his country. Napoleon, in his remote island, could at least console himself with one fulfilled prophecy.

For fifteen years, Talleyrand lived in retirement, almost in disgrace. He never ceased to expect his recall to power; meanwhile, like other exiled politicians, he composed his memoirs, a magnificent piece of special pleading. The royalists could not leave him alone. They recalled that old business of the murder of the Duc d'Enghien and, ignoring that the evidence of Talleyrand's complicity rested upon a forged document, forgetting his famous comment—"It is worse than a crime, it is a blunder"—sought quite unjustly to fix the guilt on him. In 1827 an aristocratic street bully even assaulted the old cripple—he was now seventy-three—in the Church of St. Denis and felled him to the ground.

Talleyrand waited. He saw Louis die. He saw the new king, Charles X, stumble from one pious folly to another. He saw the barricades in the streets again and heard the long, nearly forgotten snarl of the Paris mob. Then legitimacy disappeared across the Channel, and Louis Philippe, finding himself by the merest accident King of the French, sent for the greatest of living French statesmen. For the July monarchy was suspect abroad; the more so as the explosion at Paris had its reverberations in Belgium, Italy, and Poland, and men were asking if the peace treaties were to be torn up, and if this were not a revolution within the meaning of the Holy Alliance. Once more France had fallen outside the comity of nations; once more Talleyrand was the man to bring her back into it. In a changing world he had all the comfort of a familiar landmark to the statesmen of Europe.

Talleyrand saw that the vital point was London, where the Duke of Wellington was still ruling as Prime Minister. The Duke and he knew each other; they had common memories of the Congress of Vienna, in particular of a tedious visit to Frederick Augustus of Saxony that was interrupted by the news from Elba. Two men could scarcely have been less alike, yet they had a mutual regard.

Talleyrand was now seventy-six, but he did not hesitate; he went to London as French ambassador.

His embassy was an unqualified success. He allayed the apprehensions of those who feared that history was about to repeat itself and Jacobinism to be born again from the revolution of 1830. On the contrary, he insisted it was all a most respectable business, rather like our own affair of 1688, the arrival at last of the Liberal monarchy, the deathblow to reaction, to imperialism, to republicanism, to everything, in fact, that the Englishmen of 1830 had been brought up to dislike. Belgium, meanwhile, had risen in revolt against Holland and had established her independence. Her affairs were settled at a big international conference in London, in which Talleyrand, by working in close conjunction with the British Government, secured a reasonable solution for Belgium and a guaranteed northern frontier for France. He, therefore, had his share in the writing on that "scrap of paper" which, eighty-four years later, was to bring France an ally in her hour of need.

It was the old man's penultimate and perhaps most spectacular phase. The French Embassy, where his niece the Duchesse de Dino presided as hostess, gave the smartest parties in London;

CHARLES MAURICE DE TALLEYRAND-PÉRIGORD
From a sketch made in London in 1834 by Carl Vogel von Vogelstein

the fashionable folk, whose parents had looked down their noses at the needy adventurer of the 'nineties, angled for invitations to ambassadorial balls and receptions; and Talleyrand's epigrams were noted, repeated, and written down as the latest bulletins from the headquarters of wit.

In 1834, Talleyrand had reached his eightieth year. The Duke was out and the Whigs were in. Parliament had been reformed, and the conduct of foreign affairs was in the hands of Lord Palmerston, who had insular prejudices and a rooted distrust of the French ambassador. It was a new England, in which bishops were rabbled, and mobs were loose, and machinery was broken up, and men talked the language of 1789. The old ambassador was ill, tired, and profoundly depressed. He resigned, and withdrew to spend his remaining years at his country home in Valençay.

Only once again, in 1838, did he emerge from his retirement. One of his former colleagues, an inconspicuous diplomat named Reinhard, had lately died, and his funeral panegyric was to be declaimed at the Academy of Moral Science. Talleyrand let it be known that he would like to deliver the eulogium, an intimation upon which the secretary, greatly wondering, hastened to act. The day arrived. The hall was crowded with the *élite* of Paris; and Talleyrand, deaf to the remonstrances of his friends and physicians, made his last public appearance, a frail little dandy, with powdered curls and a limp. He had an amazing triumph. His nominal theme was the career of a painstaking but colourless public servant. His real subject—apart from the brief but necessary panegyric—was the career of Charles Maurice de Talleyrand-Périgord. It was his apologia, the sum of the diplomatic philosophy which he had always held, but had not always followed. He ended with a picture of the perfect Foreign Minister, leaving his audience to make the necessary identification.

"The combination of qualities," he declared, "necessary for a Minister of Foreign Affairs is rare. He ought, indeed, to be gifted with a kind of instinct which prevents him, before any discussion, from ever compromising himself. He needs the faculty of appearing open while remaining impenetrable; of being reserved, with an outward show of frankness; of showing skill even in the choice of his recreations. His conversation must be simple, varied, original, always natural, and sometimes ingenuous; in a word, he must never cease for one moment in the twenty-four hours to be a Foreign Minister.

"Yet all these qualities, rare as they are, would be insufficient if good faith did not give them a guarantee of which they nearly always stand in need. I must state here, in order to destroy a widespread prejudice, that diplomacy is not a science of cunning and duplicity. If good faith is necessary anywhere, it is necessary above all in political transactions, for it is that which makes them solid and durable. Cunning has been confounded with reserve. Good faith never authorises cunning, but it admits of reserve; and reserve has this peculiar quality, it increases confidence.

"Dominated by honour, the interests of his royal master, and love of liberty, based on order and the rights of the community, a Foreign Minister who knows his duty is placed in the finest position to which a noble mind may aspire."

The audience recovered from the shock and broke into enthusiastic applause. The orator bowed and withdrew. The curtain was down, the stage was empty, the play was over. Ten weeks later Talleyrand was dead.

To reach any tolerable conception of so baffling a character, we must penetrate behind the public career into the private life; for of the three forces which act most powerfully on a man, money—or the career—is one, women are another, and religion, perhaps, is the third.

Of Talleyrand's relations with women a volume might be written, as unedifying and as monotonous as such volumes generally are, when the hero is one of the most accomplished rakes of his day and most of his victims are complaisant from habit. His marriage was a more perplexing business.

It is strange how often the men who are most skilful and successful in public affairs are the biggest domestic blunderers. Talleyrand's marriage with Madame Grand is an example of how a really clever man can make a fool of himself. We may well ask what can have led him to so unsuitable and embarrassing a match, which was to prejudice, not once but many times, his public career. The lady arrived in Paris with a past which she scarcely troubled to conceal. She came from the East, the daughter of a small French official in Chandernagore. While in India, she met and married George Grand, a young Englishman in the service of the East India Company. He took her to Calcutta, where her fair complexion and deep blue eyes under black brows made an immediate impression. George was dull and came from Wandsworth, and among the members of Council was Sir Philip Francis, the enemy of Hastings, the reputed author of *The Letters of Junius*, and a very handsome adventurer. There was an affair and a scandal, which led to the escape of Francis, under incriminating circumstances, down a bamboo ladder, a challenge to a duel, a lawsuit, and an end to the conjugal felicity of the Grands. They separated. Mrs. Grand drifted back to Chandernagore, and on to England and to France. In 1782 she was in Paris, living expensively and dangerously on a succession of wealthy men. During the Terror she emigrated to London, and thence to New York, returning to France in 1797. In a few weeks, gossip was linking her name with that of Talleyrand. When she was imprisoned as an undesirable character, his influence procured her release, and the liaison developed into an institution. But the Republic was becoming respectable, and the first Consul, in one of those domestic moods to which he was liable, and under pressure from Josephine, suddenly decreed that his Foreign Minister and Madame Grand must either marry or part. Talleyrand seems to have accepted this decision with equanimity, though afterwards he took his revenge on the empress. Madame Grand was nearly forty and becoming fat, but she still retained the good looks which had vanquished the heart of Philip Francis. The poor lady, if rumour spoke the truth, had little else to commend her. Her stupidity has probably been exaggerated: obviously, if she had been as witless as the tittle-tattle of Paris made out, she could not have risen so high in her profession. Talleyrand himself, in explaining his marriage, was wont to encourage this legend of her folly. "A clever woman," he said, "often compromises her husband; a silly one only compromises herself." "Sire," he told Napoleon, "I married her because she was the greatest fool I could find." Paris rang with stories of her *gaucheries*, but sometimes in her blundering talk a touch of shrewdness—and even of shrewishness—made people wonder if she was such a fool as she seemed. "I hope," said Napoleon rather pompously, when the bride paid her first visit to the Tuileries, "the good conduct of Citoyenne Talleyrand will cause the levity of Madame Grand to be forgotten." "On that point," the lady demurely answered, "I cannot do better than follow the example of Citoyenne Bonaparte." The retort was apt, but very unwise. Napoleon turned from her in a temper and never forgave her. He insulted her whenever he saw her, and, when his affronts failed to keep her away from Court, he formally forbade her to appear there.

The marriage itself was surrounded with a zareba of difficulties, prickly enough to daunt the ordinary lover. To set the seal of respectability on the Republic, Napoleon was arranging a reconciliation with Rome, and it was unfortunate that, at the very moment when the negotiations with the Papacy were in progress, the French Foreign Minister should be an ex-bishop who was contemplating matrimony with an ex-prostitute. Pius VII, with the papal respect for a *fait accompli*, was quite ready to allow the ex-Bishop of Autun to be secularised; but a search through the archives of eighteen centuries failed to disclose a satisfactory precedent for a married ex-prelate. The arguments passed backwards and forwards. The Pope stood firm. Napoleon began to be angry. The fact that Madame Grand had been the wife of Mr. Grand and that no ecclesiastical tribunal had ever annulled the marriage does not seem to have troubled anyone at first: perhaps a marriage east of Suez was thought to be no great matter; but the arrival of a papal brief which Napoleon was able, with the slightest of justification, to twist to his purpose coincided with the Peace of Amiens and the appearance in Paris, not only of Sir Philip Francis and Sir Elijah Impey, late Chief Justice of Bengal, but of Mr. Grand himself. Here were some inconvenient ghosts from a buried past. There was a whiff of blackmail, and George vanished from history as Councillor to the Regency at the Cape of Good Hope, a remote and lucrative appointment which the Minister for Foreign Affairs to the Republic of Batavia was inspired to put at his disposal.

So the course of true love at last ran smooth. The marriage was celebrated at the Mairie of the 10th Arrondissement of Paris, and later, if we may believe Pasquier, at Epinay by the local curé. The Pope was as scandalised and indignant as he dared to be, Napoleon, who had made the match, began at once to abuse it, and Madame de Talleyrand opened a *salon* at the Hôtel Galliflet, while her husband became wittier and more inscrutable than ever.

The union continued as irregularly as it had begun. Reluctant to forsake her old profession, Madame Grand's indiscretions were more serious in her new position, since Talleyrand's enemies could always attack him through her, and with the deadliest of weapons, that of ridicule. She lost all her looks and grew mountainously fat; her face coarsened, her complexion became red; and people who had never known Madame Grand were at a loss to account for Madame de Talleyrand. But she continued to babble at parties, for she was insatiably social and had a passion for small talk which effectually destroyed any other sort of conversation. In fact, she presented the comical and almost pathetic figure of the worst kind of Anglo-Indian lady, translated, as though by some grim practical joke, from Calcutta to the Tuileries; the heroine of a Plain Tale from the Hills, three-quarters of a century before her time and five thousand miles out of place.

With the return of the Bourbons and the subsequent strait-lacing of society, Madame de Talleyrand became an intolerable incubus. She had long ceased to be a wife; now she could not even play at being a hostess. Talleyrand's niece by marriage, afterwards the Duchess de Dino, replaced her in the second capacity and, if the scandalmongers spoke the truth, in the first as well. Madame Grand went into a gloomy and dignified retirement, surrounded by memories and white mice and all the paraphernalia of a *salon* without the people. She died in 1835. "This simplifies my position very much," was her husband's comment.

When we have discounted the wealth and beauty of the bride, the puzzle still remains: Why did Talleyrand, with his unsurpassed ingenuity, allow himself to be jockeyed by Napoleon into marrying her? We can only reach the odd conclusion that he wanted her for his wife. The levity with which he approached the married state is in contrast with the pertinacity of his long struggle to overrule the papal objections. How, again, did he tolerate for fifteen years a wife who did him nothing but harm and gave him ample excuse for a divorce? This last question is easier to answer. Women were a necessity to him, and one more or less was a small matter. He was not a grudging husband; he could not afford to be; when the infidelities of either party were so persistent and notorious there was little to be said. Besides, he had had trouble enough to arrange the marriage; he would have more trouble to arrange a divorce. His wife might go her own way, as indeed she did, and he would go his. He would console himself as he pleased, careless of the voice of scandal, and regarding his wife rather as a lumbering piece of furniture which he had chosen in a moment of bad taste. So long as she did not attempt to interfere with his affairs, and conducted her own with reasonable discretion, and was not too outrageously extravagant in her expenditure, he would tolerate her. As he did.

As strange as Talleyrand's marriage was his relationship with the Church. As a youth he had taken orders because he was unable to enter the army, his parents insisting that there was no other possible vocation for a crippled aristocrat. He was a sceptic at a time when a little freethinking was not unfashionable among the higher clergy of France. He welcomed the Revolution when it offered him an escape from his orders, but regretted it when it attempted to substitute a fantastic philosophy for the Catholic Faith. He was excommunicated, he was anathema to the believers, yet he never lost his respect for organised Christianity, or bore any grudge against the Church which he had nearly ruined. Having won his freedom, he was quite ready to make friends; and as a token of his forgiving nature he played a part at least as great as Napoleon's in establishing the concordat of 1801, by which the Gallican Church lost its old independence and the papal see became in effect the residuary legatee of the Revolution. The Church, on her side, was not so easily placated. Apart from the unfortunate business of his marriage, an admission of past errors was clearly demanded; and, while Talleyrand was agreeable to a recantation, its terms must not be such as to compromise him in the future. So he passed into retirement in a state of armed neutrality with the Church. He continued to profess the greatest respect for the Christian religion, he read books of devotion, he went to Mass on days of obligation; but the pious ladies who watched over his declining days were not satisfied, and a small army of monseigneurs and abbés vowed they would have him properly reconciled to Mother Church before he died.

That magnificent trophy, the soul of Talleyrand, fell at last to the spiritual weapons of the Abbé Dupanloup, confessor to Talleyrand's favourite great-niece Pauline. A little conspiracy, to which the old man was a willing victim, brought the abbé to a dinner-party. Talleyrand was charming. He recalled memories of St. Sulpice and the old masters of his seminary days. He praised the Church of France. He deplored the attacks on religion. The abbé went home in his host's carriage, enchanted and full of hope. The negotiations had begun.

Talleyrand approached his reconciliation with the Church in the spirit of a monarch negotiating his last treaty. He was conscious of a growing weakness, of the nearness of death; he must sign the treaty before he died, but, if he signed it before he was actually *in extremis*, he would have lost his diplomatic battle with time and the Church of Rome. A protocol was prepared. He disputed it clause by clause and phrase by phrase, with the learning of the seminarist and the skill of the minister plenipotentiary. The demands of the Church were formidable enough. The penitent must repudiate the schismatic Church he had helped to set up, the intruding bishops whom he had consecrated, the scandal of a marriage which was no marriage. The length and keenness of the negotiations are themselves an answer to the suggestion that this was the deathbed conversion of an old man who had nearly lost his wits. Never, on the contrary, was Talleyrand more alert to make and take a point than in these last pourparlers. The contest swayed to and fro. One day the sick man would be better and his resistance would stiffen; on the next he would be worse and prepared for a compromise. The intermediaries hurried from the penitent's bedside to the palace of the archbishop and back again. The pious ladies wrung their hands over each fresh contumacy. Talleyrand, we may presume, enjoyed himself as much as a dying man may. "I have almost exceeded my duty," groaned Monseigneur de Quélen, as yet another concession was drawn from him.

At last a formula was reached to which Talleyrand was ready to subscribe. Only his signature was needed, but this he continued to withhold. A treaty unsigned was no treaty at all, and it was possible—just possible—that the doctors were wrong and that he was going to recover.

But the doctors were right. Talleyrand was at last dying. The Duchesse de Dino implored him to sign and be at peace. He agreed. But when? He would sign the next day between five and six in the morning.

That night the suspense was almost unbearable. All Paris, it seemed, was hanging on the obstinacy of a dying man; and quite half Paris believed he would die without signing. Talleyrand lay in his big bed with green curtains. He was livid, gasping, in great pain, and by the light of a solitary candle the women watched him, with the precious paper in their hands. At dawn the witnesses arrived; and at six o'clock, without the least hesitation, Talleyrand quietly took the paper and signed his name in full. He died at half-past three in the afternoon, flattered by a farewell visit from the king and fortified by the rites of the Church.

What are we to think of a man who was utterly venal and had made a vast fortune by selling information to his country's enemies; who, in an age of libertines, excelled most of his contemporaries in licence; who betrayed in turn the Church, the Monarchy, the Republic, and the Empire; who lacked loyalty, decency, gratitude, and truth; who was so wanting in humanity that he could walk over the field of Austerlitz on the morrow of the battle and view its 15,000 corpses with complete composure; whose egoism was as shameless as his greed, and whose death was scarcely more edifying than his life?

All this is true, and yet only half the truth. Such considerations as these do not really touch Talleyrand. Now and then, in every other generation or so, the true man of politics appears. He is a Chatham, a Talleyrand, a Disraeli. We may frame against him an indictment which will satisfy our sense of morality and consistency, yet in doing so we are appealing to an inapplicable code. Such a man rises in obedience to a law which we may not explain, an instinct of which he alone is conscious. He only knows, like Bishop Blougram,

> There's power in me and will to dominate,
> Which I must exercise, they hurt me else.

A force, mysterious and irresistible, is drawing him upwards as a plant is drawn through the soil to the sunshine and the rain of the upper air. With such a man patriotism is nothing, morality is nothing, service is nothing. He is factious, inconsistent, unscrupulous, opportunist. He must obey the instinct that rules him; he must push on, blindly, callously, recklessly, to the heights that beckon him. Such a man, then, is most dangerous when he is climbing, for he knows no law but that of his ascent, and heeds no impulse but that one overmastering force within him. His service begins when the dizzy heights have been scaled. Then, and for just so long as he can keep his footing on the summit, there is no conflict between his interests and those of his people. He is the nation; their aims have become one; he can no longer serve himself without serving his country. We must picture Talleyrand as such a man. Ruthless in self-advancement, once he had won his position he tried to serve France. If he took bribes, he usually took them, as Bacon took them, to reward his judgment and not to alter it. If he betrayed his masters, he betrayed them when, in his opinion, they had ceased to further the policies in which he believed. "I have never deserted a party," he declared with some justification, "before it deserted me." His own convictions remained, at the end, very much what they had been at the beginning. He was an aristocrat, yet too much of a realist not to grasp that terms must be made with democracy, and too able a man to have any charity for incompetence, even when sanctified by sixteen quarterings. Probably he really wanted an aristocratic government, with a democratic façade, something which Louis

XVI could not, and Charles X would not, give France. Had he been an Englishman, he would have been a Whig; as a Frenchman he accepted each *régime* in turn and tried to mould it to his ideas.

He was not a profound or original thinker. He seldom evolved a policy out of his own brain; but he was amazingly quick to seize the ideas of others, to modify them a little, and to trick them out as his own. In the department of Foreign Affairs he was probably unequalled in his generation. He had the European mind, which rejects grandiose schemes of conquest and regards war as a confession of diplomatic failure. The Duke of Wellington—no mean judge of men—was not indulging in idle flattery when he told the House of Lords that he had always found Prince Talleyrand "as loyal and honourable towards foreign Powers as he was steadfast and enlightened with regard to the interests of his own country." But in government Talleyrand was not so effective. He could work for a master, but he could never have ruled a Cabinet or dominated, for more than a few passing hours, an Assembly. It may be that he despised his fellows too comprehensively and that they mistrusted him too deeply; or that he could not always leave an epigram unsaid to save himself an enemy; or that the habit of intrigue was too strong, and that he neglected the truer arts of statesmanship; or that he never surrendered his detachment to become one with the people he served.

At least he had the courage and temperament of the true political adventurer. He accepted rebuffs without flinching. He never despaired. When his mind was made up he acted with little regard for the consequences. He never apologised and seldom explained. And his wit and charm were such that he could pass lightly over ground in which duller men would have been bogged.

He had the qualities of his defects. If he had small love and smaller respect for his contemporaries, his malice towards them passed in the flash of an epigram. He would crush them without ill-will, a capacity rare among politicians, and be thwarted by them without a grudge in a forbearance still rarer. It was part of the game to give and take hard knocks, and be friendly with the enemy of yesterday. Perhaps he really hated only one man—Napoleon—the man who had used him without illusions, given him honours, paid his debts, and publicly and deservedly disgraced him. We may believe, however, that Talleyrand's animosity was not merely that of the man whom Napoleon abused more openly and contemptuously than any other, but that it was, in truth, the child of his own disappointment. He hated Napoleon because he might have done so much more—for Talleyrand and for France; he could ignore the insults; he could never forgive the neglected opportunities. When the news of Napoleon's death was brought to him, the old hatred flared up in one last gibe. "It is not an event," he said scornfully, "it is merely a piece of news."

What memories must have crowded round him on that May night when he lay on the big bed behind the green curtains! Of St. Sulpice and the fresh voices of the seminarists, the low, pattered Latin of the priests, the sunshine of the cloister, and the hush and candlelight of the sanctuary; of a young sub-deacon at the solemn crowning of Louis XVI at Reims; of the turmoil of Paris in the dawn of revolution, the cries of the mob and the disputes of the constitution-mongers; of Mirabeau, who taught him more, and Robespierre who alarmed him more, than he ever admitted; of the fog and cold and heartsick waiting of his years in London; of the long line of the American coast as it thrust above the western horizon; of Alexander Hamilton, whose portrait still hung in his bedroom; of firelit nights in the backwoods, when he dreamed of France and lost opportunities; of a young general who won astounding victories and was not afraid to speak of his destiny; of that second coronation when, no longer Talleyrand the sub-deacon, but Talleyrand the Grand Chamberlain, he had seen the young general become Emperor of the French; of the glory and doom of the Empire; of the festive wranglings at Vienna, when he had pitted his wits against Castlereagh who was so ignorant, and the Duke of Wellington with his long nose and his horse sense, and Hardenberg who never quite heard what was said, and Metternich with his eye for a pretty woman, and Alexander with his appetite for flattery; of the pompous follies of the Restoration; of Paris in the pedestrian 'twenties, and London in the stormy 'thirties, and then Valençay, the plaudits of the Academy, the arguments of the priests. And so back to the whispers of the waiting women, while the candle flickered as uncertainly as the little vital flame that burned within him.

A strange business, this life, of which so much was made; strange, interesting, yet curiously empty. You worked and fought and made love and lied and intrigued, and, in the end, what was there to show for all your years of fretful endeavour? Perhaps the old priests at the seminary were right after all, and nothing that happened outside a man mattered very much. Perhaps it all amounted to just this: "I have planted trees," he muttered, "I have built a house, and I have done many other foolish things."

GILBERT SELDES

A more active American writer than Gilbert Vivian Seldes would be hard to find. Born at Alliance, New Jersey, in 1893, he attended the Central High School at Philadelphia, then went up to Harvard, where, after distinguishing himself on the staff of *The Harvard Monthly*, in the Dramatic Club, and as a member of Phi Beta Kappa, he graduated, A.B., 1914, just in time to test his literary talents as war correspondent for *The Philadelphia Evening Ledger* on the British front. He later served in the U. S. Army as a sergeant. In 1918 he became political correspondent in Washington for *L'Écho de Paris;* next, associate editor of *Collier's*, 1919; and then associate, later managing and dramatic, editor of *The Dial*, and contributing editor to *The New Republic*. In 1929 he became dramatic critic for *The New York Evening Graphic*, and since 1931 he has been a columnist for *The New York Evening Journal*.

But Mr. Seldes has been scarcely more active as journalist than as dramatist and critic. Two of his plays have been produced, and his adaptation of Aristophanes' *Lysistrata* was the New York theatrical sensation of 1930. His books, *The United States and the War* (1917), *The Seven Lively Arts* (1924), *The Stammering Century* (1928), *The Wings of the Eagle*, one of three novels (1929), *The Movies and the Talkies* (1929), and *The Future of Drinking* (1930), indicate the still wider range of his interests.

"Hammerstein the Extravagant," which was printed in *Harper's Monthly Magazine* in July 1932, is less the work of a professed biographer than a by-product of a thoughtful critic's familiar converse with the arts of the stage. Mr. Seldes apologizes for its incompleteness, since–as we might say of every biography, short or long–"the legends and even the facts of Hammerstein's career were carefully selected," but adds that none of his statements having been disputed, it is "probably correct." It is an engaging narrative and analysis of that flamboyant impresario's life and character which, though not at all novel in treatment, stands a favorable comparison with the work of more practiced biographers. It owes little, visibly, to the technical examples of the modern school and at most can be said to emulate that group only in its underscoring, from a normal point of view, of Hammerstein's eccentric lavishness. It proceeds in the traditional manner from an orientation of the man under this head to a connected story of his career and then to a series of reflections on his prodigious flair for publicity. But it leaves, in the end, a likeness one does not soon forget.

HAMMERSTEIN THE EXTRAVAGANT

At the beginning of his great pamphlet on Napoleon III, Karl Marx quotes Hegel's remark that "upon the stage of universal history all great events and personalities reappear in one fashion or another," and then Marx adds that "on the first occasion, they appear as tragedy; on the second, as farce." One reason is, of course, that the first appearance of a personality is original, the second is imitative. Napoleon I was the first Napoleon; Napoleon III was the hundredth, or perhaps the hundred-thousandth, who fancied himself Napoleon. By some force of character or circumstance a man impresses or imposes himself upon a generation as the great soldier, the typical poet, the masterful lover, the lavish spender, and these individuals become powerful influences because they set the pattern to which the lives of thousands of other people are cut. The pattern becomes sanctified, like a toga for statues of statesmen. Political parties are still happy if they can suggest that the career of their candidate runs from the towpath to the White House, although the towpath has long ceased to exist and the very idea that to be poor is to be righteous is looked on with suspicion. Political parties, of course, lag behind the average intelligence, but even the average man is profoundly affected by these original living statues. Men wear beards and collect paintings and smoke cigars and recite limericks because generals and financiers and presidents have done these things. Because of the fame of Diamond Jim Brady, rich men still come to the nightclubs in New York and buy champagne for dancing girls as he did; they may never have heard of Brady, but he has become part of a mythology, a demigod more real than living men. Because of Geraldine Farrar and Lillian Russell, thousands of girls study singing and dancing and spend depressing days in the waiting rooms of booking agents. A varied, energetic character like Theodore Roosevelt creates half a dozen pictures in the common mind; he does more because images must be destroyed, as well as created. What Roosevelt destroyed was the picture of the Harvard dude and the tenderfoot and the tennis-playing "sissy" as a figure of fun.

Oscar Hammerstein was one of these profoundly influential originals. Because he existed, it is natural for Roxy to turn from the presentations of a movie cathedral, take charge of a theater in Radio City, and threaten to dominate grand opera in America; and dozens of other men who manage concerts or own a few theaters see themselves in the light of Hammerstein's extraordinary career. The influence passes beyond the operatic field in which Hammerstein made his mark because the general lines of his life conform to the myth of the immigrant boy who rose to fame and fortune; in those lines he may have been influenced by some shadowy forerunner, or by the vast myth which brought millions of Europeans to America. And where he deviates from the myth by the force of his own character, by the special form of his activities, he creates a new myth for the succeeding generation.

If one couldn't be born an Adams and be a diplomat, a scholar, and a President of the United States, one could still be typically an American of the last fifty years by being what Oscar Hammerstein was. He was an immigrant, an inventor, a developer of real estate, an inspired master of vaudeville, and a devoted lover of music who revolutionized the production of grand opera in America. He said once, "My life has been one of romance," but this was perhaps the only under-statement he ever made. His life was one of wild extravagance, as an ideal American life should be; his thought—what there was of it—his speech, which was fluent, and his actions, which were magnificent, were all excessive in tone; what others did by units, he did by the half-dozen; what others suffered occasionally, he suffered continually. He built eleven theaters, ran several opera companies and, having a passion for litigation, was once involved in forty separate, but simultaneous, lawsuits. His versatility (which we also like to think of as being typically American) is deceptive; there was no lack of constancy in him. He was a musician before he became a cigar maker, and he remained a cigar maker long after he became an impresario; his inventive genius and his passion for grand opera were the two bounding lines of his career. But he was not a "split personality." He made money out of inventions which put an end to the sweatshop and the tenement workroom in the cigar industry; and he made money out of grand opera which shocked the Metropolitan out of its fusty lethargy. It was natural to him to make and lose fortunes and, while he considered grand opera "after religion the most elevating influence in modern society," he saw no reason why it should be the special property of those who were willing to enjoy it merely as a costly form of social exhibitionism. Yet with all his success he remained a homely figure; his German-Jewish accent stuck to him all his life (although he once made an effort to please the English by talking like a Piccadilly nut); his stocky form could always be seen in the lobby of the opera house with the special properties which became dear to the cartoonist and the impersonator—the high shiny topper, the cigar, and the goatee, and the large flat gold watch which lay in his hand as curtain time approached; the more people joked about these, the more he emphasized them, until he seemed to be impersonating himself, like many a Western senator.

He was born in Berlin in 1847, and in his later life he used to reproach his father for brutality. What he objected to was the method of education; knowledge was pumped into him, so that by sixteen Oscar knew chemistry, French, and English in addition to his native tongue, and played the piano, the flute, and the violin. The musical education was of prime importance, and when the boy skipped violin practice in order to go skating, his father whipped him. He ran away, sold his violin, and with the proceeds went first to Hamburg, then to Dover, and finally worked his way to New York in the winter of 1865. His first job (at two dollars a week) was cigar making, a tedious, dirty, and diseaseful process at the time. Within a few years he made the first of his many inventions, applying machinery to this work; he found a new way of stripping tobacco and a way of applying air suction

OSCAR HAMMERSTEIN

From a crayon sketch by Aspell in the Theatre Collection, Harvard College Library

to making cigars. Out of his first invention he made six thousand dollars, and the American Tobacco Company, which bought it, began its march to fortune. These, and a few other of his inventions, made the process of cigar making so much swifter and cleaner that the foul sweatshop disappeared under economic pressure. In a few years Hammerstein was the first expert on the tobacco trade and editor of its journal. He continued to invent long after he had gone into other fields and took out a total of over one hundred patents, including a process for making barrels and an automatic window shade. To the end of his life he preferred to make his own cigars on a little machine which he kept in the bare little room on top of the Victoria Theater where he lived.

Five years after he landed in America he was part owner of two theaters and impresario of one. He had attended the old German theaters in downtown New York even when he had barely money enough to live on. His first investment when money began to be easy was in the Thalia Theater; then he became affiliated with the Germania and wrote for it three one-act comedies, including the music for one of them, and in 1870 he took control of the Stadt Theater. We see at once that his artistic and his practical interests were not at war. He financed theaters because he liked the theater; he wrote for the theater because he was financing it. Although he went into real estate, he had too much intelligence, or too much integrity, to consider the theater as real estate. Each of his interests ministered to the other. For his first setting he went far uptown into Harlem.

At the beginning of the 1880's the houses on 125th Street were still wooden shacks; above that street not more than two hundred houses existed on all the West Side. Hammerstein saw an opportunity. Characteristically, he built not two or three, but a dozen apartment houses and about thirty private dwellings. One of the apartments on Seventh Avenue ran from 136th to 137th, and there was some complaint because Hammerstein put a statue of Kaiser Wilhelm, after whom the block was named, on the cornice. There was, however, no population. By a peculiar logic, the builder decided that what Harlem needed was a theater to attract people, even if there were no people there to support a theater. So he built the Harlem Opera House. Modjeska and Joseph Jefferson were so hesitant about going that far uptown (and so correctly informed about the theater's prospects) that he had to guarantee them ninety per cent of the gross receipts. Hammerstein lost enormously; to recoup he engaged the popular Theodore Thomas orchestra at two thousand dollars a week; it played to a gross of seven hundred dollars. In desperation because no one would play in the house at New Year's (when bookings elsewhere were profitable), he engaged Kellar, the magician, and a troop of lions. Six patrons appeared in the orchestra on New Year's Eve; confronted by the lions, they moved to the balcony. So at the beginning vaudeville failed to finance the arts.

"Having lost so much money," said Hammerstein, "I reached the somewhat curious conclusion that what Harlem needed was not one theater, but two theaters." This time he was right. He built the Columbus Theater on the East Side, and its immediate profits financed the Harlem long enough to establish that house as well. The first period of Hammerstein's spectacular operations was beginning. He was done with real estate; in the next ten years he built and operated seven theaters.

His imagination was always grandiose. Because Koster and Bial were making a success of a small vaudeville house, Hammerstein felt sure that he would make three times as much if he rolled three music halls into one. The result was the Olympia. For a single admission of fifty cents the patron could hear, at the opening performance, Yvette Guilbert in one auditorium, Fay Templeton in another, and a concert in the smallest of the three. Hammerstein's analysis of public psychology was totally wrong. After the opening, when he could afford only one headliner and filled the halls with midgets and flying ballets, the crowds would not admit that the star alone was "worth the price of admission." They felt that something unworthy was being foisted upon them. Hammerstein lost $2,000 a week. To recoup himself, he produced "La Poupée" with Anna Held and lost $3,000 a day. When the mortgage was foreclosed he had lost $1,000,000. For years he crossed the street rather than pass in front of the theater and he cherished a childish hate against the life insurance company which had held the mortgage. It was not like him, for usually he laughed off his losses. (His instinct for real estate was good; the building stands to this day and is occupied by three vaudeville and picture houses.)

The Olympia was, in a sense, given over to the art of the music hall; the Victoria definitely was not. Good vaudevillians came and went, but the Victoria thrived on another type of headliner. Hammerstein picked them from the newspapers, the heroes of adventure and the heroines of scandal. By the time the Victoria reached its height and was earning a quarter of a million dollars a year, Hammerstein had lost interest in it; the control was in the hands of his son, William, but the policy remained the same. It may be summed up in the well-attested episode concerning an untalented performer engaged because she had been involved in a scandalous shooting. When she asked on Saturday night whether she was hired for a second week, Oscar or William answered, "Not unless you shoot a second man."

II

He was already approaching the central purpose of his life, and in 1906 he gathered his moneys and his powers and began the four years of war which rocked the dismally smug Metropolitan, brought the modern opera repertory to America, made Mary Garden famous, and ended in a spectacular defeat which Hammerstein, more spectacular than ever, turned into a triumph for himself. He opened the Manhattan house conventionally enough with "Aïda," as if to show that he could do the Metropolitan repertory as well as anyone. But before he was done Hammerstein had produced "Thaïs," "Louise," "Le Jongleur de Notre-Dame," "Hérodiade," "Pelléas et Mélisande," and "Elektra." He had brought over a style of operatic singing and acting which the Metropolitan had totally neglected—the style of the French; he had Mary Garden and Lina Cavalieri not only as stars on the stage, but as blazing personalities in the news. While Mary Garden was rehearsing "Salomé," Hammerstein announced that, in order to spare her energies, he had put his new star, Lina Cavalieri, into "Thaïs." Miss Garden announced to the press that if he did she would scratch out his eyes. Madame Cavalieri was equally temperamental. Miss Garden complained that her impresario treated her like a chorus girl; he replied that "Miss Mary Garden, the distinguished song bird, is a loafer." Under this artful pretense of a row between temperamental operatic stars Hammerstein was preparing the great sensation of Mary Garden's "Salomé." The timid Heinrich Conried, whom Hammerstein had brought over from Germany years before as stage manager, was then directing the Metropolitan and ventured a single performance of "Salomé," choosing it, of all things, for a benefit. "This specimen from the pathological museum of Messrs. Wilde and Strauss" was not exactly well received and, although Conried half-heartedly announced further performances, the directors refused to allow them. Hammerstein knew that the spearhead of offense was the dance of Salomé, and he took the spearhead into his bosom. Olive Fremstadt had sung the rôle at the Metropolitan, but had discreetly retired to let a ballerina do the dance of the seven veils. When the time came for Mary Garden to withdraw, she went forward and did the dance herself. The shock of surprise, multiplied by the intense interest which Hammerstein had concentrated on Mary Garden's personality, distracted from the moral shock while it left the impropriety of the proceedings a livelier topic of controversy than ever.

Hammerstein had opened the opera with an advance sale of only thirty thousand dollars; when he announced his second season, his advance sale was ten times as great. In his first year he made a profit of one hundred thousand dollars, and each of the next two years nearly three times as much; and all the time he thought he was creating a rival to the Metropolitan, which had been losing money for years, and was hardly aware of the fact that he was establishing an Opéra Comique to stand beside the official opera, as it does in France. The repertory was fresher, the acting more realistic, the singing less florid—except for Tetrazzini, Hammerstein never had any vocalist in the great Italian tradition, never found or developed a second Caruso. The directors of the Metropolitan also were unaware of Hammerstein's actual accomplishment; they did not see that the new style might exist side by side with their own. After badgering Conried for allowing Hammerstein to engage a single good star "when Conried had all the money in the world" and after ruefully considering their losses (most of them were also involved in the ghastly failure of The New Theater), they decided that Hammerstein must go. They bought him out. For a million and a half dollars Oscar Hammerstein agreed not to produce grand opera in New York for ten years, and would forfeit a quarter of a million if he did. The Metropolitan celebrated; Hammerstein went to bed. He was given to these psychological illnesses. He had lost the one thing he cared for most in the world, and so for four days he played sick. On the fifth he decided to build an opera house in London and rose from his bed alert with interest and health.

The London venture drove home the lesson first announced at the Manhattan, and it was characteristic of Hammerstein that, although he boasted of everything else he had done, he never took pride in his greatest achievement, which was not defeating the Metropolitan, but re-creating it. The directors of the Metropolitan were equally dull of perception. They thought they had driven Hammerstein out; in reality they had taken him and all he stood for into their hearts. The Metropolitan never succeeded in making grand opera as interesting, as exciting, and as popular as Hammerstein had made it; but after 1910, with Gatti-Casazza in the place of Conried, the Metropolitan extended its repertory to take in the modern French, became more hospitable to mild innovations, and no longer went to sleep with "Norma" and "Il Trovatore," to waken with "Tannhäuser" and go to sleep again with "La Traviata." The resurrection of the Metropolitan was Hammerstein's greatest work, and neither he nor the Metropolitan ever took much pleasure in it.

Against the slow-moving English background Hammerstein's pace seems more "typically American" even than it had in New York; the measure of his audacity is best taken in contrast with the timidity of the English. The whole conception was audacious.

Sir Thomas Beecham, installing himself in the old Covent Garden Theater, had lost half a million dollars in a vain effort to make the English like grand opera. (Sir Thomas's father, the manufacturer of the famous pills, supplied the only note of hustle to this enterprise because, unofficially, the advertising slogan of the pills was applied to the opera: "Worth a guinea a box.") Hammerstein's whole plan of campaign was to startle the public into consciousness of his enterprise; he was preparing, as he always did, to present something both sound and brilliant, but he did not rely on these qualities to make the English aware of him. Fresh from New York, where he had only to tip his hat at a strange angle in order to get a front-page story, Hammerstein found the indifference of the London press unaccountable and mortifying. He broke down all resistance; affably, but with determination, he sent announcements of his plans—they were thrown into the wastebasket. He began building a new opera house in Kingsway—the choice of site was a challenge, since merely not to be at Covent Garden was against all the traditions. When the director of Covent Garden went to the newspapers, asserting that he owned exclusive rights to all the operas Hammerstein could produce, he opened the way. Hammerstein's reply was that every brick in his new building was a British brick. Wireless was fresh and new, and he put a wireless station on the roof so that one could order seats from midocean and—double advertisement—from New York. For some strange reason it pleased him to draw the water used in the building from an artesian well under its foundations, and this also made its way into the press. Slowly Hammerstein became a personage; he irritated, but he did not offend, society; by the time the opera house was ready to open, every newspaper in London had a reporter assigned to cover Hammerstein. He repaid them by inserting three- and four-column advertisements and for his climax took an entire page in the London *Times*. It still seems miraculous that the *Times* accepted the advertisement.

He was always willing to shock if he did not have to abandon his own principles of good business and good opera. He did not like the system of selling programs and gave his free and, a much more perilous enterprise, he attempted a democratic opera which depended altogether for success on the patronage of the aristocracy. He said, quite correctly, that all previous opera houses had been built for the comfort of the rich; the poor might hear, but they could not see. In his new house the sight lines were correct for every seat. At the same time he handed over the actual seating arrangements to a committee which assigned the boxes so that "members of different social sets would not be placed in embarrassing proximity." Thus reassured, no less than thirteen duchesses attended the première.

They experienced more of Hammerstein's calculated audacities. One of the decorative motifs on the façade was a mask of Oscar, and it appears that only the persuasion of the architect had eliminated his silk hat and cigar. On the stage within he presented "Quo Vadis," with a burning of Rome, which must have been rather like a Coney Island sideshow, but which struck the London critics, accustomed to dim and dreary productions lagging far behind the Continental standard, as "the real thing." As for singers, Hammerstein had so bedazzled his audience that they, the most loyal of all people to stage favorites, hardly noticed that, with the exception of Maurice Renaud, all the principals were strangers. Further impertinence, he brought not well-known American stars, but unknown ones—Orville Harold and Felice Lyne. Harold had been in a vaudeville team at the Victoria, and Hammerstein sent him abroad for two years to study. Felice Lyne came from Kansas City and had never been heard of before Hammerstein made her the sensation of the year. Even when he was giving the Londoners a familiar work, he managed to startle them; into "Les Cloches de Corneville" he interpolated three songs of his own composition which were sung in English.

He said when he came to London that producing opera gave him pleasure and that, although "he was infallible" with opera, he was not "looking to make money." He was right on both counts. He got his pleasure; as a symbol of his delight in England he took to a monocle, tea, and what he assumed was an English accent. As in America, he was a favorite subject for impersonators in the music halls. He was famous, but the season was not a success. He played to houses sometimes of a hundred people, and even the production of a native opera by Lord Howard de Walden failed to bring in the crowds. At the end of the second season a syndicate was formed to finance a third. On the final night Hammerstein insisted upon telling the London public what he thought of its refusal to come to his house and grew so insulting that the syndicate disbanded. On arriving in New York Hammerstein said, "I'd rather be dead than alive in London."

From that point his career is disorganized, fruitless, and sad. He had grandiose schemes—a chain of twenty opera houses from Philadelphia to New Orleans to San Francisco, with identical buildings, identical dressing rooms, stage, and scenery, so that he could move whole productions rapidly from one to the other. Only one house was actually built—the one in Philadelphia. There was not much push behind it, and the project was involved in litigation. Oscar's heart was still in New York. He went to the directors of the Metropolitan and, promising to hold loyally to his agreement, begged permission to cultivate the field they contemptuously neglected, opera in English. It was an innocuous proposal, but the Metropolitan had had its experience with Hammerstein; there was no telling what he might do even in this despised medium. The directors refused. Hammerstein promptly began to build a new opera house on Lexington Avenue, announcing that opera could succeed only at theater prices—a three-dollar top. Instantly an organization never heard of before or since announced opera at two dollars. Hammerstein accused the Metropolitan of instigating this attack; he wrote endless letters to the press; he cried out for justice; his publicity was becoming hysterical. He announced that he would produce operas in French, German, and Italian, as well as in English, and the Metropolitan got an injunction against him. Hammerstein, as usual, fell ill, recovered to quarrel with his family, tried to sell the profitable Victoria to finance himself, and sent a lawyer to Congress to invoke the Anti-Trust Law against the Metropolitan. He was coming to the breaking point.

The actual opening of the Lexington on August 1, 1914, was pathetic. Between one act of "Aïda" and one act of "Faust," he showed a hastily created war film, "The Last Volunteer." At the end of three months he closed the house and, still fighting for his illusion, gave as his reason that the public was getting tired of the movies. Thereafter he built no more, and the zest of producing had left him. He lived on for five years, drifting out of public notice, wearying himself with lawsuits and illnesses. He had always suffered from temporary fits of melancholia which lasted a day or two, usually at some lull in his work, and then disappeared the moment something interested him. Now they became frequent and prolonged. His energy left him, and his heavy body wasted away. In his last months his wife carried him in her arms to move him from room to room, pathetically followed by a little dog to which Oscar had been devoted. He knew he was dying and did not want to die; he had always refused to have flowers in his rooms, asking, "Why should I care to have anything around me that is dying?" He died in 1919.

III

Hammerstein is the only impresario mentioned in the portion of Mark Sullivan's *Our Times* which covers the Rooseveltian era, and with good reason. Except for Roosevelt himself, who had the inestimable advantage of being President of the United States, Hammerstein appeared more often in the newspapers than anyone else, more often than Vernon Castle or James Hazen Hyde or Thomas W. Lawson or the Nature Fakers or Andrew Carnegie or John McCormack or Harry Thaw or William Travers Jerome or Hugo Münsterberg or Alexander Dowie. Hammerstein was such good publicity that he could even communicate to his associates the secret of instantly capturing the public mind. It is a familiar story that Mary Garden bet the publisher of a conservative newspaper that she would appear in his columns for thirty-one consecutive days and, having achieved thirty, disclosed the wager in order to win it. Barnum is the only other business manager of musical enterprises who became a national figure, but Hammerstein never needed a museum. Belasco is the only other figure in the arts of the theater and he lived into the day of intensive publicity.

Hammerstein made his way into the papers because he naturally *was* news, not because he deliberately *made* news. That is his prime distinction and it is an important one. We live in an era of "build-ups." It is almost impossible to penetrate through the layers of publicity to reach the actual character of public men in business or political life. The negativism of the methods of Ivy Lee are as bewildering as the flaring stunt publicity of the late Harry Reichenbach. Mr. Lee's skill re-creates a figure of the elder Rockefeller, correcting the "bad publicity" of the early years of Standard Oil, and creates his shadowy successors by eliminating their persons from the news. The publicity of the Republican Party labors vainly to humanize President Hoover, who fights doggedly against the process, obviously embarrassed and a little ashamed to think that the President of the United States, in a time of unparalleled crisis, must receive boy heroes from Colorado and be photographed with a fish. Publicity builds up painters and senators and gadget manufacturers by the process of inflation. It is a series of promises having no relation to the character of the man or to his work.

It seems to me that Hammerstein, essentially incorruptible, would have looked with contempt upon these balloons. It was not that he minded appearing greater than he was (it is hard to imagine anyone speaking better of him than he spoke of himself), but what he gave to the press again and again was the accomplished fact, and even when he was most picturesque and spectacular he was himself—a man interested in his work. I have mentioned his victory over the press in London; except for a few trivial items, every element in it came out of the building of the house or the presentation of the operas; a few humorous grace notes of temperament were added, as when he asked for police protection because an infuriated tenor had challenged him to a duel.

He appreciated temperament in others. "In handling prima donnas," he said, "there is no precedent; each is a law unto herself. The women stars are bad enough; the men are often worse."

So he stood by while Tetrazzini dropped a dagger three times to the floor, because if it stuck each time she knew she would sing well. Emma Trentini refused to go on unless Hammerstein handed her a quarter of a dollar just before her entrance—and she kept the quarters, to Hammerstein's delight. But his greatest satisfaction came in the fulfillment of the contract with Regina Pinkert which provided that she was to receive a thousand dollars in gold before each performance. It was Hammerstein's enormous pleasure to jingle a bag of twenty-dollar gold pieces as he solemnly paid the salary. The oddity of others never offended him, provided they were those of genuine talent.

The same solidity underlies his American publicity. One of his earliest "stunts" was to write an opera in forty-eight hours on a bet. It sounds like the invention of a press agent, but it came from his leaving the theater at the première of Gustave Kerker's "Venus" before the end of the performance because he did not like the score. When Kerker accused him of not knowing anything about music, Hammerstein replied, "I could write a better opera than that in forty-eight hours." The bet was made. To prevent Hammerstein from palming off any opera he might have written, the subject was dictated—the theft of the Kohinoor, followed by the arrest of everybody in the street (for plenty of chorus work) and a crowd at the Old Bailey when the diamond is recovered. Hammerstein went to work in a hotel room. Kerker engaged three organ grinders to play outside the window. Hammerstein threw furniture and all the movable objects at them and called a foul. The noise in the streets brought in the newspapers, which were presently getting out extras to report progress. Legitimate so far, the publicity proved itself over again when the opera he composed, "The Kohinoor," ran for four months in New York. When he went to Paris to recruit stars he enchanted the French press by nailing to his door a sign conveying the simple truth: "French not spoken here." When he engaged the vast auditorium of the Châtelet for his auditions the French put it down to American extravagance, but it happened to be the best place for hearing voices. When he learned that the Sultan of Sulu was out of funds he sent him a cable offering him twenty-five hundred dollars a week to appear in a music hall; this is regular stunt publicity, only a little more legitimate in Hammerstein's case because he probably saw no reason why the Sultan should not accept.

But the major publicity—when he worked in grand opera—always rose out of the opera and always concentrated attention on the opera. He seldom bothered to deny rumors whether they were favorable to him or not. The story that he heard, or heard of, Tetrazzini's great success in San Francisco and then spirited her out of the country so that she might make a triumphant appearance in London and then be brought here as a new star was not true. But of course it did Hammerstein no harm to let it run because it was "typical" of him, as people said. He did often discover stars in odd places. Mme. Gerville-Réache was discovered by him in a café in Paris. But Tetrazzini had already made her reputation and was beginning to dwindle after a South American tour in which she had become careless of her voice, when she was heard in San Francisco. It was one of the few cases in which Hammerstein was caught napping. Covent Garden engaged Tetrazzini, and the story of her being spirited away grew out of an open visit to Mexico. At Covent Garden, Tetrazzini's success was sensational. The story is that she had had little publicity and that society stayed away from her opening night. Even the first-line music critics were not there. But at the end of the first act of "Traviata" people began rushing to telephones to call their friends, and by the time the third act began all the right people were present and primed for enthusiasm. As soon as he heard of this event, Hammerstein sent a messenger to London with what Madame Tetrazzini calls "a white paper"—that is, a contract with blanks left for her to fill in her salary. She wrote in twenty-five hundred dollars a performance—an astounding sum for the time, but Hammerstein was justified in paying it. She was his one great star in the old tradition.

For all that he was a figure, Hammerstein drew no publicity to himself. He merely used himself as a signboard for what he had to sell. This was easier to do in his time than in ours, since he lived before the days of intimate confessions, tabloid gossip, and publicity in which the religion of any public man is at least as important as the amount of candy he eats and his handicap at golf. Yet I think that even today, when he would be the pet of Broadway reporters, Hammerstein would escape self-exploitation. He had a genuine passion for solitude; he boasted that he was never seen on the street with a companion and was furious if anyone accosted him on his walks. His marriage, his divorce, and his second marriage were all known through the press, but they remained private events; his relations with his children came out only when his extravagance or his delight in litigation brought them into the foreground. He seemed to live without the benefit of society; although he was not stingy, he had no house and gave no parties, because a house and parties would mean that he would have to have people about him. At the height of his career his sons created a luxurious suite of rooms for him over the Manhattan Opera House; he moved in by the simple process of depositing his hat, slept there two nights, and returned to his garret. He had no stenographer; his office was on the front steps of the Victoria.

Men who are so hostile to society are usually absorbed either in themselves or in their work; Hammerstein was absorbed in both. For the first, he was a great egotist, not a profound one. His belief in himself was largely hostility to other people. He said, "I was never grateful to anyone in my life. I do not remember anyone who ever did anything for me without a selfish object," and he imagined that his own calling was "to use my God-given gifts to afford other people pleasure." He despised Carnegie and Rockefeller because they gave only "their idle wealth," while he gave something he knew to be much more precious: "I am giving my mind and my very life . . . my talents—genius, if you will, for I have it." He went to no one for counsel and rejected all advice; "my own taste and judgment are my sole arbiters, and if they are wrong all is wrong." He backed his own taste even against his own interest, hissing a singer at one of his own houses on one occasion and on another dissuading people from buying seats to see a show he had himself produced because it was so bad. He said he was afraid to go to heaven because they would have a chorus there he had not picked.

His passion for the opera may not have been greater than his passion for himself, but it was purer. Certainly he wanted the opera to make him rich and famous, but he plowed fame and fortune into the ground again to enrich the yield of the next year. He wanted nothing for himself. And this, I think, accounts for the exceptional circumstance that he became a dominating personality—one of the dozen or two persons who are "inspirations" to others—in spite of his failure. If you begin drawing out the separate threads of his life, you see that in the ordinary sense he was not a success. The fabric falls to pieces the moment the bright spectacular threads are taken out. He did not destroy the Metropolitan opera, he did not conquer London, he did not produce twenty operas simultaneously all over the United States, he did not die rich. I think he wanted to do all of these things, but he wanted more to do the one thing which he did do—that is, create grand opera on a scale that was actually grand. He gave off the exhilarating air of success because he was happy, because he had endless energy, and because he seemed to himself to be dictating his own course. And I think he was considered a success by Americans, even in the limited commercial way, because through the greater part of his life he thought in millions and actually disposed of hundreds of thousands. Great sums of money passed through his hands—and this may be nearer the American ideal of success than merely dying rich.

On the night that the Manhattan opened—the night he knew to be the successful climax of his life—Hammerstein took a street car from 34th Street to 42nd Street, ate, alone, an oyster stew at Childs, then went up to the cubbyhole in the loft of the Victoria where he had two chairs, a narrow bed, a cheap table, a hat-rack, and a piano. Rolling himself a cigar in his little machine, he was perfectly happy living over his satisfaction in his work. His religion of grand opera was not meant to bring him any other pleasure; it did not include anything grandiose for himself.

ISABEL BUTCHART

The modesty of Isabel Butchart, who, having escaped the invasions of celebrity-hunters, writes that as to her biography she has practically none, prevents us from learning, except by inference, the background of her literary work. She is best known in England as a contributor to *Country Life* of articles similar to, and including, that on Margaret Baxter, and of a number of poems, some of which have been collected and published in *Songs for a Day* (1916) and *A Faggot of Verse* (1930). In her only other book, *Other People's Fires* (1924), from which the present piece is reprinted, we learn, further, that her life was gravely scarred by losses in the War; that her mind has ranged widely over literature and art and responded sensitively to congenial, usually feminine, souls here and there; and that one of her special and most intense satisfactions consists in sharing, without too many companions, the warmth and light of another's literary hearth. "If you gave me the choice," writes Miss Butchart, "between a book with a good fire in it and one full of gay life, I would choose the former, if the fire were a solitary one after my own heart, with only the ghostly owner to bear me company, while I, too, shed mortality for the time being and sat beside it." She thus draws up her chair beside Mrs. Pepys, and Jane Austen, and Wilson, Elizabeth Barrett's inseparable maid, beside even St. Augustine, and Isaiah, and three "dear dead ladies" of Japan.

"Margaret Baxter" is a particularly deft little reconstruction of the life of a seventeenth century lady, dwarfed in her own day and obscured ever since by the formidable figure of the great Nonconformist preacher and divine, Richard Baxter (1615-91), her husband, who devotedly set down their Puritan love-story in the *Breviate*. The opening and the closing of this old book mark the beginning and the ending of the biography. Very closely akin, as the sketch is, to the "Lives of the Obscure" of Virginia Woolf (*The Common Reader*, 1925), it shows what can be done by a searching, sympathetic mind in evoking from the scantiest materials a forgotten human being.

MARGARET BAXTER

Now this was all that I knew about Richard Baxter: that he wrote *The Saints' Everlasting Rest* and many other theological works, and that at the age of forty-seven he married Margaret Charlton, a young girl "of strangely vivid and great wit with very sober conversation."

The spindle side is always the more interesting side of a family to me, and the queens-consort of England ten times more thrilling than the kings, and Margaret's youth and strangely vivid wit roused in me a passionate curiosity that her husband's fame could never alone have kindled.

So I went to the Picton Reading Room in Liverpool, and obliging little boys ran nimbly up spiral staircases in front of ceiling-high book-shelves and brought me twenty-five huge volumes of Baxter his works, and piled them round me until nothing but the crown of my embarrassed hat could have been visible. Each of the twenty-five heavy volumes was in small print, and the work of many lifetimes seemed around me, but the one short book on his wife was not there. Yet interest grew. What did the lonely child do while her husband spent (surely) every hour of every day on these five-and-twenty monuments to his piety and learning? Did her vivid wit in the end burn itself out in silence? Or was there love between the strangely assorted pair? We have many books about "the great lovers" of the past—more books than lovers—yet there is often more consolation to be found in the story of lowlier lives, every new discovery of quiet and unwearied love strengthening our wistful hope of immortality. "*Love is a great Thing: yea, a great and thorough Good; by Itself It makes everything that is heavy light: and It bears evenly all that is uneven.*"

So I waited another year until I found myself for the first time in the most satisfying place this side Heaven—the Reading Room of the British Museum. And they brought me Baxter's *Breviate* of the life of his wife. I opened the old book, printed in 1681, the year of Margaret's death, and written "for the good of

Readers and the honour of God's grace in her," and even the British Museum faded away.

They were born, those two, in the same county, Shropshire, within three and a half miles of one another, "but she of one of the chief families of the county, and I but of a mean Freeholder (called a Gentleman for his ancestor's sake)."

During Margaret's early girlhood her mother's castle was besieged by the Parliamentary soldiers, stormed and taken. Margaret saw the fighting, the killing of many of their servants, and the dead bodies lying on the ground, and this was the beginning, her husband thinks, of that "diseased fearfulness," or nervousness, from which she suffered all her life.

Little is said of Margaret's father, who had evidently died some time before the storming of the castle. Her mother, later, removed to Kidderminster, partly to listen to the edifying sermons of the popular Mr. Baxter, then rector of the parish. And there, too, of course, came sixteen-year-old Margaret, ruffling it bravely.

"In her vain youth, Pride and Romances and Company suitable thereto did take her up, and an imprudent *rigid* governess . . . had done her hurt by possessing her with ill thoughts of strictness in religion."

She found the poverty and "strictness" of the people of Kidderminster very tedious, "glittering herself in costly Apparel and delighting herself in her Romances."

There came a very dangerous illness when all despaired of her life, and after that, as she slowly struggled back to health, her "conversion," of which Baxter gives many details and would probably have given more but for her "strange silent keeping her case to herself . . . and exceeding injury to her peace." Then followed the most unhappy period of Margaret's life, a time of deep, unconquerable depression. And "she still had a concealing temper which made it never the easier within."

She was swept out of her depth in her newly found religion, doubting her own sincerity. Yet her intense unhappiness puzzled me. It was partly physical, partly spiritual, and partly—what? What was the secret grief in the background? Was she unhappy at home, I wondered? Or was the learned Mr. Baxter beginning to trouble her young heart? It was not until nearly the end of the book that I found the possible answer to my question.

"Ever since her sickness 1659 she hath lived in an ill-conceited fear for the overthrow of her understanding, which greatly hurt her. It was because she had an aunt long so, deceased, and her Parents were naturally passionate, and her spirits over-quick, and her blood thin and mobile, and though wisdom hid it from others in her converse, she felt the trouble of her own mind in things, as aforesaid . . . and so lived in constant fear, which tended to have brought on her what she feared. But her understanding was so far from failing that it was higher and clearer than other peoples; but like the treble strings of a Lute, strained up to the highest, sweet, but in continual danger."

Of Baxter's wooing we know nothing. He tells us curtly that for adequate but unstated reasons he will give no details. But he does tell us of the torrent of disapproval that bore down on the lovers. Margaret was too young for him. Margaret was too wealthy. And had not Mr. Baxter always opposed the marriage of the clergy, holding that the cares of wedded life were incompatible with the vocation of a priest?

But Baxter, by this time, had been ejected and separated from his "Pastoral Charge" as a result of the Act of Uniformity, so that the last reason ceased to have any weight, he explained. And there was no question of marrying a wealthy Margaret. She must leave behind her most of her fortune, only keeping what would make her his equal in financial matters. Moreover, she must promise not to encroach on the hours he set apart for writing and his "ministerial works." Thus Richard, crushingly—and married her. She would be about nineteen at the time.

It is here that the sensitive reader holds his breath, fearing quiet tragedy. But Baxter must have been a more suitable husband for a nervous highly-strung girl than one would have imagined.

"When we were married her sadness and melancholy vanished; counsel did something to it, and contentment something; and being taken up with our household affairs did somewhat. And we lived in unviolated love . . . sensible of the benefit of mutual help."

I like that little touch about "counsel." I hope he petted her as he administered it. My mind's eye (possibly a vulgar orb) sees her perched on his knee, as with many a "firstly" and "lastly" he points out the foolishness of fretting secretly. I think Margaret was never quite so unhappy again. She was fragile and haunted by headaches all her stormy life, she passed through many dangers—among them the Great Plague and the Great Fire—which increased that "diseased fearfulness, against which she had little more free will or power than a man in an Ague or Frost against shaking cold," but her troubles were never lonely ones again.

But hers was no clinging, dependent nature.

"All the operations of her soul were very intense and strong: strong wit, strong love, and strong displeasure."

But "anger she had none—or little made it known."

"Her household affairs she ordered with so great skill and decency as that others much praised that which I was no fit judge of. I had been bred among plain mean people and I thought that so much washing of Stairs and Rooms, to keep them as clean as Trenchers and Dishes and so much ado about cleanliness and trifles was a sinful curiosity and expense of servants' time, who might the while have been reading some good book. But she that was otherwise bred had somewhat other thoughts."

It is a pleasant picture—Margaret's spotless home, in days when living was often rude and rough. And possibly her maids were better pleased to scour and dust for their young mistress than to follow the master's theological arguments down the page, with exploring forefinger.

I gave up my theory of Margaret as a lonely young wife. She not only settled her own affairs but she arranged those of her husband, with a capability at which the unpractical man could only marvel. As he had been ejected from his parish he had to preach and teach when and where he could. Margaret hired this room and that—once she even had a room built for him—she went here and went there with him, moving from house to house without a murmur, until "out of tender regard for my health she took for us this most pleasant and convenient house in Southampton-Square."

"Among other troubles that marriage exposed her to, one was our oft necessitated removals, which to those that must take houses . . . and fit them and furnish them, is more than for single persons who have no such clogs or cares . . . and the women have most of that sort of trouble. But she easily bare it all. . . . When I was carried to the common gaol, for teaching, as aforesaid, I never perceived her troubled at it: she cheerfully went with me into Prison, *she brought her best bed thither;* and did much to remove the removable inconveniences of the Prison. I think she had scarce ever a pleasanter time in her life than when she was with me there."

"*Love is a great Thing: yea, a great and thorough Good; by Itself It makes everything that is heavy light: and It bears evenly all that is uneven.*"

Yet each was a little hard on the other at times. It was a real grief to Margaret that her husband, in his increasing deafness and ill-health, was sometimes tempted to relax his efforts of preaching and teaching, and she did not hide her disappointment. And he on his part sometimes thought her dread of insanity "but a passionate fanciful fear . . . not considering how great tenderness in all our discourse she needed; though I remember nothing else that ever I showed impatience to her in."

They disagreed, too, though amicably enough, on the subject of borrowing money, Baxter maintaining that one should do good with one's money as far as one's means allowed, but that one should not exceed them. Margaret argued that one ought to borrow money for charitable purposes if one could offer good securities. And she borrowed right and left.

"There are some things charged on her as faults . . . that she busied herself so much about Churches and works of Charity and was not content to live privately and quietly . . . that she was wasteful and imprudent in leaving me so much in debt.

"To that I answer, Let anyone consider . . . what she did, and he will not wonder at her debts. It was not to pamper her own body; she used mean clothing and a mean diet for her own person. . . . I doubt not but some of these accusers will say, '*Why open you all this? Were you not the Master? . . .*' Perhaps love and grief will make me speak more than many will think fit. . . . But I am not ashamed to have been much ruled by her prudent love in many things. . . . For my constant pains and weakness and ministerial labours forbade me the care of outward things . . . and her apprehension of such things was so much quicker and more discerning than mine."

Strangely enough, he blames her more for her reticence than for her debts.

"My dear Wife was faulty indeed in talking so little of Religion in company. . . . But her Religion lay in *doing* more than in talk."

She proved this by "her costliest obedience."

"It cost her not only her labour and Estate but somewhat of her trouble of body and mind. For her knife was too keen and cut the sheath. Her desires were more earnestly set on doing good than her tender mind . . . could well bear."

Margaret died in 1681.

"These near nineteen years I know not that we ever had any breach in point of love, or point of interest, save only that she somewhat grudged that I had persuaded her for my quietness to surrender so much of her Estate to a disabling her from helping others as much as she earnestly desired."

I had found out what I wanted to know. I closed the old book, written "in some passion indeed of love and grief but in sincerity of truth," and gave it back into the keeping of the British Museum.

VIRGINIA WOOLF

Of all the authors represented in this book—indeed, may we not add, of all living writers in English?—none equals Mrs. Virginia Woolf in sheer virtuosity. Her most successful books of fiction—*The Voyage Out* (1915), *Jacob's Room* (1922), *Mrs. Dalloway* (1925), *To the Lighthouse* (1927), *Orlando* (1928), *The Waves* (1931)—defy exact classification, save in their author's own mind. *Orlando*, for instance, bears the sub-title, *A Biography*, yet it sweeps its subject through a breathless career from the Age of Queen Elizabeth to the year of its publication. Her other "biography" is *Flush* (1932), the story of the familiar cocker spaniel of Elizabeth Barrett Browning. Her two series of prose pieces entitled *The Common Reader* (1925 and 1932)—and it is rather the *un*common reader, one fears, who is agile enough to catch all her bright shafts and follow her swift mental twistings —are usually called, for want of a more precise term, essays. Yet, sharing the same high intelligence, the same mastery of words, and the same subtlety of comprehension as her so-called novels, they give us a variety of original and complex effects that amaze while they delight.

Mrs. Woolf, born in London in 1882, was the third of four children of the distinguished nineteenth century critic, philosopher, and biographer, Leslie (later Sir Leslie) Stephen, by his second marriage. Through his first marriage to the younger daughter of W. M. Thackeray, the family was related to the Macaulays, Trevelyans, Darwins, Maitlands, Symondses, Stracheys, and other scholarly Englishmen; and many of these ties were strengthened by friendship. The Stephen home, where Mrs. Woolf obtained her education, was a gathering place of the most eminent writers of the day; and after their parents' death, when the two sons and two daughters moved to a small house in the Bloomsbury quarter of London, they became the nucleus of a no less brilliant company of their contemporaries. Among this Bloomsbury Group were Clive Bell, vigorous leader of contemporary art, whom the elder sister, Vanessa, married; and Leonard Woolf, editor, publisher, and political economist, whom Virginia Stephen married in 1912. Also there were the novelist, Edward Morgan Forster; John Maynard Keynes, economist and politician, and his wife, Lydia Lopokova, the celebrated dancer; and Duncan Grant, and Roger Fry, and, probably most influential of all in literature, Giles Lytton Strachey. It was quite the liveliest band of intellectuals in contemporary England, each member of which was a notable pioneer in his respective field. Their unifying spirit has been sympathetically set forth as "a belief in Reason, and a conviction that the pursuit of Truth and a contemplation of Beauty are the most important of human activities"; their chief distinction, that "they have acted upon it to an extraordinary extent. No subject of conversation has been taboo, no tradition accepted without examination, and no conclusion evaded. In a hypercritical society, they have been indecent; in a conservative society, curious; in a gentlemanly society, ruthless; and in a fighting society, pacifist. They have been passionate in their devotion to what they thought good, brutal in their rejection of what they thought second-rate, resolute in their refusal to compromise." At the center of this group was Mrs. Woolf, who, in addition to authorship, has given her efforts to fine printing, beginning with a small hand-press and ending with the publishing house, the Hogarth Press, which she and her husband direct.

The modern reader could not fail to recognize "Miss Ormerod" as the work of Virginia Woolf, but he would search in vain for its model or parallel. Here is an intelligent, rather masculine, Victorian woman with an independent mind and a bold scientific purpose belying both her sex and her time—"pioneer of purity even more than of Paris Green"—whom the author, herself independent and bold and intelligent, must have found most congenial to describe. Moreover, Eleanor A. Ormerod (1828-1901) was prominent enough as an entomologist to merit a full-length biography, yet obscure enough to "the common reader" to give him the delight of a fresh discovery and Mrs. Woolf, who relishes out-of-the-way figures, the challenge that seems always to evoke her subtlest powers. She reveals her subject's career with sympathy and vivid concreteness in a sequence of brief, fragmentary episodes, beginning with a childhood scene and ending with an impersonal announcement of her death. Like the blobs and splashes of color in a pointillist painting, these seeming scraps of narrative and description are all found, when at last the mind has the time and perspective to take them in, to fit together by an invisible joinery like the sharp-cut and well-polished mosaics they really are. Like all novel expression in art, it is hard to grasp the first time at the customary rate of reading. Technically, too, this is not a method to be imitated wantonly; but its minute study will well repay the effort.

MISS ORMEROD[1]

THE TREES stood massively in all their summer foliage spotted and grouped upon a meadow which sloped gently down from the big white house. There were unmistakable signs of the year 1835 both in the trees and in the sky, for modern trees are not nearly so voluminous as these ones, and the sky of those days had a kind of pale diffusion in its texture which was different from the more concentrated tone of the skies we know.

Mr. George Ormerod stepped from the drawing-room window of Sedbury House, Gloucestershire, wearing a tall furry hat and white trousers strapped under his instep; he was closely, though deferentially, followed by a lady wearing a yellow-spotted dress over a crinoline, and behind her, singly and arm in arm, came nine children in nankeen jackets and long white drawers. They were going to see the water let out of a pond.

The youngest child, Eleanor, a little girl with a pale face, rather elongated features, and black hair, was left by herself in the drawing-room, a large sallow apartment with pillars, two chandeliers, for some reason enclosed in holland bags, and several octagonal tables, some of inlaid wood and others of greenish malachite. At one of these little Eleanor Ormerod was seated in a high chair.

"Now, Eleanor," said her mother, as the party assembled for the expedition to the pond, "here are some pretty beetles. Don't touch the glass. Don't get down from your chair, and when we come back little George will tell you all about it."

So saying, Mrs. Ormerod placed a tumbler of water containing about half a dozen great water grubs in the middle of the malachite table, at a safe distance from the child, and followed her husband down the slope of old-fashioned turf towards a cluster of extremely old-fashioned sheep; opening, directly she stepped on to the terrace, a tiny parasol of bottle green silk with a bottle green fringe, though the sky was like nothing so much as a flock bed covered with a counterpane of white dimity.

[1] Founded upon *The Life of Eleanor Ormerod*, by Robert Wallace Murray. 1904.

The plump pale grubs gyrated slowly round and round in the tumbler. So simple an entertainment must surely soon have ceased to satisfy. Surely Eleanor would shake the tumbler, upset the grubs, and scramble down from her chair. Why, even a grown person can hardly watch those grubs crawling down the glass wall, then floating to the surface, without a sense of boredom not untinged with disgust. But the child sat perfectly still. Was it her custom, then, to be entertained by the gyrations of grubs? Her eyes were reflective, even critical. But they shone with increasing excitement. She beat one hand upon the edge of the table. What was the reason? One of the grubs had ceased to float: he lay at the bottom; the rest, descending, proceeded to tear him to pieces.

"And how has little Eleanor enjoyed herself?" asked Mr. Ormerod, in rather a deep voice, stepping into the room and with a slight air of heat and of fatigue upon his face.

"Papa," said Eleanor, almost interrupting her father in her eagerness to impart her observation, "I saw one of the grubs fall down and the rest came and ate him!"

"Nonsense, Eleanor," said Mr. Ormerod. "You are not telling the truth." He looked severely at the tumbler in which the beetles were still gyrating as before.

"Papa, it was true!"

"Eleanor, little girls are not allowed to contradict their fathers," said Mrs. Ormerod, coming in through the window, and closing her green parasol with a snap.

"Let this be a lesson," Mr. Ormerod began, signing to the other children to approach, when the door opened, and the servant announced,

"Captain Fenton."

Captain Fenton "was at times thought to be tedious in his recurrence to the charge of the Scots Greys in which he had served at the battle of Waterloo."

But what is this crowd gathered round the door of the George Hotel in Chepstow? A faint cheer rises from the bottom of the hill. Up comes the mail coach, horses steaming, panels mud-splashed. "Make way! Make way!" cries the ostler and the vehicle dashes into the courtyard, pulls up sharp before the door. Down jumps the coachman, the horses are led off, and a fine team of spanking greys is harnessed with incredible speed in their stead. Upon all this—coachman, horses, coach, and passengers—the crowd looked with gaping admiration every Wednesday all through the year. But today, the twelfth of March, 1852, as the coachman settled his rug, and stretched his hands for the reins, he observed that instead of being fixed upon him, the eyes of the people of Chepstow darted this way and that. Heads were jerked. Arms flung out. Here a hat swooped in a semi-circle. Off drove the coach almost unnoticed. As it turned the corner all the outside passengers craned their necks, and one gentleman rose to his feet and shouted, "There! there! there!" before he was bowled into eternity. It was an insect—a red-winged insect. Out the people of Chepstow poured into the high road; down the hill they ran; always the insect flew in front of them; at length by Chepstow Bridge a young man, throwing his bandanna over the blade of an oar, captured it alive and presented it to a highly respectable elderly gentleman who now came puffing upon the scene—Samuel Budge, doctor, of Chepstow. By Samuel Budge it was presented to Miss Ormerod; by her sent to a professor at Oxford. And he, declaring it "a fine specimen of the rose under-winged locust," added the gratifying information that it "was the first of the kind to be captured so far west."

And so, at the age of twenty-four Miss Eleanor Ormerod was thought the proper person to receive the gift of a locust.

When Eleanor Ormerod appeared at archery meetings and croquet tournaments young men pulled their whiskers and young ladies looked grave. It was so difficult to make friends with a girl who could talk of nothing but black beetles and earwigs—"Yes, that's what she likes, isn't it queer?—Why, the other day Ellen, Mama's maid, heard from Jane, who's under-kitchenmaid at Sedbury House, that Eleanor tried to boil a beetle in the kitchen saucepan and he wouldn't die, and swam round and round, and she got into a terrible state and sent the groom all the way to Gloucester to fetch chloroform—all for an insect, my dear!—and she gives the cottagers shillings to collect beetles for her—and she spends hours in her bedroom cutting them up—and she climbs trees like a boy to find wasps' nests—oh, you can't think what they don't say about her in the village—for she does look so odd, dressed anyhow, with that great big nose and those bright little eyes, so like a caterpillar herself, I always think—but of course she's wonderfully clever and very good, too, both of them. Georgiana has a lending library for the cottagers, and Eleanor never misses a service—but there she is—that short pale girl in the large bonnet. Do go and talk to her, for I'm sure I'm too stupid, but you'll find plenty to say—" But neither Fred nor Arthur, Henry nor William found anything to say—

". . . probably the lecturer would have been equally well pleased had none of her own sex put in an appearance."

This comment upon a lecture delivered in the year 1889 throws some light, perhaps, upon archery meetings in the 'fifties.

It being nine o'clock on a February night some time about 1862, all the Ormerods were in the library; Mr. Ormerod making architectural designs at a table; Mrs. Ormerod lying on a sofa making pencil drawings upon grey paper; Eleanor making a model of a snake to serve as a paper weight; Georgiana making a copy of the font in Tidenham Church; some of the others examining books with beautiful illustrations; while at intervals someone rose, unlocked the wire book case, took down a volume for instruction or entertainment, and perused it beneath the chandelier.

Mr. Ormerod required complete silence for his studies. His word was law, even to the dogs, who, in the absence of their master, instinctively obeyed the eldest male person in the room. Some whispered colloquy there might be between Mrs. Ormerod and her daughters—

"The draught under the pew was really worse than ever this morning, Mama—"

"And we could only unfasten the latch of the chancel because Eleanor happened to have her ruler with her—"

"—hm-m-m. Dr. Armstrong— Hm-m-m—"

"—Anyhow things aren't as bad with us as they are at King-hampton. They say Mrs. Briscoe's Newfoundland dog follows her right up to the chancel rails when she takes the sacrament—"

"And the turkey is still sitting on its eggs in the pulpit."

—"The period of incubation for a turkey is between three and four weeks"—said Eleanor, thoughtfully looking up from her cast of the snake and forgetting, in the interest of her subject, to speak in a whisper.

"Am I to be allowed no peace in my own house?" Mr. Ormerod exclaimed angrily, rapping with his ruler on the table, upon which Mrs. Ormerod half shut one eye and squeezed a little blob of Chinese white on to her high light, and they remained silent until the servants came in, when everyone, with the exception of Mrs. Ormerod, fell on their knees. For she, poor lady, suffered from a chronic complaint and left the family forever a year or two later, when the green sofa was moved into the corner, and the drawings given to her nieces in memory of her. But Mr. Ormerod went on making architectural drawings at nine p.m. every night (save on Sundays when he read a sermon) until he too lay upon the green sofa, which had not been used since Mrs. Ormerod lay there, but still looked much the same. "We deeply felt the happiness of ministering to his welfare," Miss Ormerod wrote, "for he would not hear of our leaving him for even twenty-four hours and he objected to visits from my brothers excepting occasionally for a short time. They, not being used to the gentle ways necessary for an aged invalid, worried him . . . the Thursday following, the 9th October, 1873, he passed gently away at the mature age of eighty-seven years." Oh, graves in country churchyards—respectable burials—mature old gentlemen —D.C.L., LL.D., F.R.S., F.S.A.—lots of letters come after your names, but lots of women are buried with you!

There remained the Hessian Fly and the Bot—mysterious insects! Not, one would have thought, among God's most triumphant creations, and yet—if you see them under a microscope! —the Bot, obese, globular, obscene; the Hessian, booted, spurred, whiskered, cadaverous. Next slip under the glass an innocent grain; behold it pock-marked and livid; or take this strip of hide, and note those pollulating lumps—well, what does the landscape look like then?

The only palatable object for the eye to rest on in acres of England is a lump of Paris Green. But English people won't use microscopes; you can't make them use Paris Green either—or if they do, they let it drip. Dr. Ritzema Bos is a great stand-by. For they won't take a woman's word. And indeed, though for the sake of the Ox Warble one must stretch a point, there are matters, questions of stock infestation, things one has to go into—things a lady doesn't even like to see, much less discuss, in print—"these, I say, I intend to leave entirely to the Veterinary surgeons. My brother—oh, he's dead now—a very good man—for whom I collected wasps' nests—lived at Brighton and wrote about wasps—he, I say, wouldn't let me learn anatomy, never liked me to do more than take sections of teeth."

Ah, but Eleanor, the Bot and the Hessian have more power over you than Mr. Edward Ormerod himself. Under the microscope you clearly perceive that these insects have organs, orifices, excrement; they do, most emphatically, copulate. Escorted on the one side by the Bot or Warble, on the other by the Hessian Fly, Miss Ormerod advanced statelily, if slowly, into the open. Never did her features show more sublime than when lit up by the candour of her avowal. "This is excrement; these, though Ritzema Bos is positive to the contrary, are the generative organs of the male. I've proved it." Upon her head the hood of Edinburgh most fitly descended; pioneer of purity even more than of Paris Green.

"If you're sure I'm not in your way," said Miss Lipscomb, unstrapping her paint box and planting her tripod firmly in the path, "—I'll try to get a picture of these lovely hydrangeas against the sky— What flowers you have in Penzance!"

The market gardener crossed his hands on his hoe, slowly twined a piece of bass round his finger, looked at the sky, said something about the sun, also about the prevalence of lady artists, and then, with a nod of his head, observed sententiously that it was to a lady that he owed everything he had.

"Ah?" said Miss Lipscomb, flattered, but already much occupied with her composition.

"A lady with a queer-sounding name," said Mr. Pascoe, "but that's the lady I've called my little girl after– I don't think there's such another in Christendom."

Of course it was Miss Ormerod, equally of course Miss Lipscomb was the sister of Miss Ormerod's family doctor; and so she did no sketching that morning, but left with a handsome bunch of grapes instead–for every flower had drooped, ruin had stared him in the face–he had written, not believing one bit what they told him–to the lady with the queer name, back there came a book, *In-ju-ri-ous In-sects*, with the page turned down, perhaps by her very hand, also a letter which he kept at home under the clock, but he knew every word by heart, since it was due to what she said there that he wasn't a ruined man–and the tears ran down his face and Miss Lipscomb, clearing a space on the lodging-house table, wrote the whole story to her brother.

"The prejudice against Paris Green certainly seems to be dying down," said Miss Ormerod when she read it.–"But now," she sighed rather heavily, being no longer young and much afflicted with the gout, "now it's the sparrows."

One might have thought that *they* would have left her alone–innocent dirt-grey birds, taking more than their share of the breakfast crumbs, otherwise inoffensive. But once you look through a microscope–once you see the Hessian and the Bot as they really are–there's no peace for an elderly lady pacing her terrace on a fine May morning. For example, why, when there are crumbs enough for all, do only the sparrows get them? Why not swallows or martins? Why–oh, here come the servants for prayers–

"Forgive us our trespasses as we forgive them that trespass against us. . . . For thine is the Kingdom and the power and the glory, for ever and ever. Amen–"

"*The Times*, ma'am–"

"Thank you, Dixon. . . . The Queen's birthday! We must

drink her Majesty's health in the old white port, Dixon. Home Rule—tut—tut—tut. All that madman Gladstone. My father would have thought the world was coming to an end, and I'm not at all sure that it isn't. I must talk to Dr. Lipscomb—"

Yet all the time in the tail of her eye she saw myriads of sparrows, and retiring to the study proclaimed in a pamphlet of which 36,000 copies were gratuitously distributed that the sparrow is a pest.

"When he eats an insect," she said to her sister Georgiana, "which isn't often, it's one of the few insects that one wants to keep—one of the very few," she added with a touch of acidity natural to one whose investigations have all tended to the discredit of the insect race.

"But there'll be some very unpleasant consequences to face," she concluded—"Very unpleasant indeed."

Happily the port was now brought in, the servants assembled; and Miss Ormerod, rising to her feet, gave the toast "Her Blessed Majesty." She was extremely loyal, and moreover she liked nothing better than a glass of her father's old white port. She kept his pigtail, too, in a box.

Such being her disposition it went hard with her to analyse the sparrow's crop, for the sparrow, she felt, symbolises something of the homely virtue of English domestic life, and to proclaim it stuffed with deceit was disloyal to much that she, and her fathers before her, held dear. Sure enough the clergy—the Rev. J. E. Walker—denounced her for her brutality; "God Save the Sparrow!" exclaimed the Animal's Friend; and Miss Carrington, of the Humanitarian League, replied in a leaflet described by Miss Ormerod as "spirity, discourteous, and inaccurate."

"Well," said Miss Ormerod to her sister, "it did me no harm before to be threatened to be shot at, also hanged in effigy, and other little attentions."

"Still it was very disagreeable, Eleanor—more disagreeable, I believe, to me than to you," said Georgiana. Soon Georgiana died. She had however finished the beautiful series of insect diagrams at which she worked every morning in the dining-room and they were presented to Edinburgh University. But Eleanor was never the same woman after that.

Dear forest fly—flour moths—weevils—grouse and cheese flies—beetles—foreign correspondents—eel worms—ladybirds—wheat midges—resignation from the Royal Agricultural Society—gall mites—boot beetles—announcement of honorary degree to be conferred—feelings of appreciation and anxiety—paper on wasps—last annual report—warnings of serious illness—proposed pension—gradual loss of strength—finally Death.

That is life, so they say.

"It does no good to keep people waiting for an answer," sighed Miss Ormerod, "though I don't feel as able as I did since that unlucky accident at Waterloo. And no one realises what the strain of the work is—often I'm the only lady in the room, and the gentlemen so learned, though I've always found them most helpful, most generous in every way. But I'm growing old, Miss Hartwell, that's what it is. That's what led me to be thinking of this difficult matter of flour infestation in the middle of the road so that I didn't see the horse until he had poked his nose into my ear. . . . Then there's this nonsense about a pension. What could possess Mr. Barron to think of such a thing? I should feel inexpressibly lowered if I accepted a pension. Why, I don't altogether like writing LL.D. after my name, though Georgie would have liked it. All I ask is to be let go on in my own quiet way. Now where is Messrs. Langridge's sample? We must take that first. 'Gentlemen, I have examined your sample and find . . .' "

"If anyone deserves a thorough rest it's you, Miss Ormerod," said Dr. Lipscomb, who had grown a little white over the ears. "I should say the farmers of England ought to set up a statue to you, bring offerings of corn and wine—make you a kind of Goddess, eh—what was her name?"

"Not a very shapely figure for a Goddess," said Miss Ormerod with a little laugh. "I should enjoy the wine though. You're not going to cut me off my one glass of port surely?"

"You must remember," said Dr. Lipscomb, shaking his head, "how much your life means to others."

"Well, I don't know about that," said Miss Ormerod, pondering a little. "To be sure, I've chosen my epitaph. 'She introduced Paris Green into England,' and there might be a word or two about the Hessian Fly—that, I do believe, was a good piece of work."

"No need to think about epitaphs yet," said Dr. Lipscomb.

"Our lives are in the hands of the Lord," said Miss Ormerod simply.

Dr. Lipscomb bent his head and looked out of the window. Miss Ormerod remained silent.

"English entomologists care little or nothing for objects of practical importance," she exclaimed suddenly. "Take this question of flour infestation—I can't say how many grey hairs that has grown me."

"Figuratively speaking, Miss Ormerod," said Dr. Lipscomb, for her hair was still raven black.

"Well, I do believe all good work is done in concert," Miss Ormerod continued. "It is often a great comfort to me to think that."

"It's beginning to rain," said Dr. Lipscomb. "How will your enemies like that, Miss Ormerod?"

"Hot or cold, wet or dry, insects always flourish!" cried Miss Ormerod energetically sitting up in bed.

"Old Miss Ormerod is dead," said Mr. Drummond, opening *The Times* on Saturday, July 20th, 1901.

"Old Miss Ormerod?" asked Mrs. Drummond.

ROBERT M. COATES

"Young people should not forget that literature is something that is still going on," said an eminent publisher in commending to the editor of this anthology the Profiles of *The New Yorker*. "They are likely to stumble on it almost anywhere, and might even write it themselves." This counsel will not be needed by readers who have become acquainted with the sketches of living men and women which that brisk weekly has printed. These brief biographies, often little more than expanded interviews, make no pretense to be full, but aim to depict, as their name implies, the salient features of interesting contemporaries. They have offered during the past ten years a standing challenge to young writers in the special field of the short biography.

The Profile of Helen Keller was contributed to *The New Yorker* of January 25, 1930, by Robert Myron Coates, author of *The Outlaw Years*, a study of the Mississippi River bandits of the early nineteenth century (1930), and of two novels, *The Eater of Darkness*, a mystery burlesque (1927), and *Yesterday's Burdens* (1933); translator of André de Hevesy's *Life of Columbus* (1928); editor of several anthologies; and book critic in 1930-32 for *The New Yorker*. Mr. Coates was born at New Haven, Connecticut, in 1897 and is a graduate, B.A., 1919, of Yale University. He served as student air pilot in the U. S. Navy in 1917-18. After college he lived for five years in Paris, where his literary work began. He resides at Gaylordsville, Connecticut.

Mr. Coates gives us here the now familiar story of a celebrated woman with fresh emphasis upon the problems and personality which made her famous. The points he lights up are, of course, selected with the greatest freedom. The style is colloquial and in the best sense popular. A few of the broader assertions, such as the opening one, may be overdrawn by a journalist's love for the striking; a few of the details, like the subject's street address, are trivial. But the author fulfills one of the first requirements of writing—he is interesting.

BLIND . . . DEAF . . . DUMB

A PROFILE

WITHOUT question, one of the major events of the year 1904, at least as far as the general public was concerned, was the graduation of Helen Adams Keller from Radcliffe College. A few doctors and students in the field of her affliction had been watching the history of her progress for years, but outside this narrow circle there were few who had ever even heard of the young lady, and to all the others the news of her achievement, breaking suddenly, had about it something of the qualities of a miracle.

Here was a girl—an American girl too!—blind, deaf, dumb: she had learned to talk; she had found the use of her intelligence, and had used it to such good purpose that she had earned a B.A. degree in an American institute of learning, "with," it was stated, "especial mention for her excellence in English Literature."

The accomplishment had, of course, its aspects of lasting importance. It demonstrated finally that the deaf, dumb, and blind need not necessarily, by reason of the curtailment of their senses, be classed as idiots, as the law had for so long termed them. It implied that by better training methods all persons so handicapped might be given a normal education.

But in general people gave little consideration to the remoter implications in what she had done. To them, Helen Keller was unique and marvellous. Her feat was felt to be heroic, superhuman: contemplating it, they experienced the same vicarious elation as when an American girl swims the Channel.

Newspapers printed stories about her on the front page. The *Ladies' Home Journal* presented her autobiography. In the next few years, her books—*Optimism, The Story of My Life, The World I Live In*—were published, and sold widely. She lectured; wherever she went, crowds gathered to gaze curiously at her. She bought a house at Wrentham, Massachusetts, with some sort of agrarian experiment in mind; reporters crowded after her. The officials at Radcliffe, who had shown no special anxiety to get her into college, expressed themselves as proud of her. Society took her up; she dined out, she went on yachting cruises.

But she had a stubbornness of intention through it all. Andrew Carnegie asked if it were true that she was a Socialist. She said she was. He said he ought to spank her. Later, he offered her an annuity of twenty-five hundred dollars. She declined, but he said he would let the offer stand for a while, "on probation." The Queen of Rumania invited her to join a movement whereby the blind-deaf were to be segregated in a little community of their own, to be called (appropriately enough to a lady whose pen name was Carmen Sylva) by the Latin name of "Vatra Luminosa": in English, Luminous Hearth. Helen Keller refused to have anything to do with it; the Queen was hurt, and never wrote to her again.

She hurt a good many people's feelings—people in whose plans she felt she detected a pitying or patronizing attitude toward the blind-deaf. Her point of view was diametrically opposite. She was opposed to segregating, coddling. She believed that the unfortunates should be taught to rely as much as possible on themselves. She was convinced that what she had done, others could do, and she felt that a great part of her own struggles had been in combating the eleemosynary attitude, the refusal on all sides to regard her, within her limitations, as a normal human being. "My whole desire has been to have my own door key," she said, "and go and come like people who can see."

Perhaps she was wrong in this. Certainly she has proved her point in her own case, but the philosophy is that of the strong for the weak. Her own capacities are far greater than the average: it may be that there were others, weaker-willed and weaker-witted, who needed more supervision than she, in her youth at least, seemed willing to allot them.

But that was her opinion, and she stuck to it, and people went away with that baffled resentment of those whose charitable gestures have been put aside. There was a backwash of criticism following her fame; magnified reports of her wealth, her grand life, made it easier to characterize her as hardboiled. As a matter of fact, the Wrentham experiment lost money from the start;

after several years' struggle the farm was sold. Illness, in the end, forced her to accept the Carnegie annuity. Continued after his death, it is still her chief source of income.

She was born, a normal child, in Tuscumbia, Alabama, on June 27, 1880. Her father, Arthur Keller, was a prominent man in the community, the editor of the *North Alabamian* and the owner of a large estate. He was, however, in the condition typical of many Southerners at the time: he was land-poor. Consequently when, at the age of nineteen months, an illness left Helen blind, deaf, and dumb, there was little he could do about it. The disease had been diagnosed as brain fever; according to the common theory of the time, it was believed to have left her an idiot.

She grew into childhood, wild and unruly–giggling and chuckling to express pleasure; kicking, scratching, uttering the choked screams of the deaf-mute to indicate the opposite. It was not until the Cleveland administration, in 1888, appointed her father district marshal of Alabama, with a salary of six thousand dollars a year, that he had money enough to provide expert care for the child. He wrote to the Perkins Institute at Boston, and a young teacher, Miss Anne Sullivan, was sent down to be Helen's companion and teacher. When she arrived, Helen was eight years old, but practically it was the beginning of all life for her. The two have been inseparable companions ever since.

The blind children at Perkins Institute had made a doll for Miss Sullivan to give to Helen Keller. She began her training with that. She would put the doll in Helen's hand, take it away; then she would spell "d-o-l-l," by the symbols of the "hand-manual" alphabet, into the child's palm. Finally, she would hold one hand open, and with the other hand she would move Helen's fingers to spell "d-o-l-l" into the palm again. Then, she would give her the doll to play with.

Because her illness had come at so early an age, it must be remembered, Helen Keller was to all purposes as if she had been born blind, deaf, and dumb. She had no conscious remembrance of ever having heard a sound, seen a light, uttered a word. She had no idea of the mental process, accepted unthinkingly by all of us, through which names represent things; she hadn't the faintest conception of the intricacies of language. Except for the difference in intelligence, the thing was like teaching a dog—but one who could neither see nor hear—to perform a complicated series of meaningless tricks, each at a different hand-signal. Nevertheless, she finally got the idea. By the end of a month, she had learned (since she had never even seen her fingers, it was purely by muscle-memory) to spell a few simple words: "c-a-n-d-y," "a-p-p-l-e," "s-p-o-o-n," and so on.

Then began the even more difficult job—that of teaching her the idea of an alphabet. Gradually, by spelling words, by repeating single letters over and over again, her conception of names as entities was broken down, and the idea of individual letters, out of which words could be built, was substituted. It required, on the part of Miss Sullivan, a tremendous patience and resourcefulness; on the part of the child, a philosophical spark that seems almost miraculous. It took three years, but by the time that she was eleven, Helen Keller knew the alphabet, both by palm-manual and Braille raised type, and could read and write.

By now, Miss Sullivan was convinced that she had in her charge an exceptional child, and when the rumor reached her that somewhere in Sweden a dumb child had been taught to talk, she decided to try it on Helen. The method she devised was based on the classification of all sounds as nasal, labial, and guttural. Accordingly, the child was taught to place her thumb on the speaker's throat, the first two fingers on the lips, and the third at the side of the nose. In this way she learned first to recognize the various sounds, and then to pronounce them. The first sentence she learned to speak was: "I am not dumb now." It is one of those simple statements to which circumstances can give an epic quality. Since then, in lectures, and recently in movie-tone, the two women have demonstrated the process of instruction hundreds of times. Always the climax, when Helen repeats in her queer, laboring voice, "Ah-eee ammm nnnot ha-dummm nnnowoo!" is infinitely moving.

The rest of her training went rapidly. By the time she was in her teens she had caught up with the normal scale of education; she entered Radcliffe at the age of twenty. Anne Sullivan went with her, spelling lectures into her hand, reading lesson assignments aloud while Helen fingered her lips. They were never parted. Anne Sullivan fell in love with John Macy, the poet and critic, and was married to him. The three moved to Wrentham together, to live. Later, Mrs. Macy and her husband separated. She remained with Helen.

They live now [1930] at 93 Seminole Avenue, in Forest Hills. The house is their own; they bought it with the proceeds of the sale of the farm at Wrentham. Mrs. Macy herself is now past sixty, and her own eyesight is failing: some fifteen years ago, Miss Polly Thomson, a young Scotch girl, with considerable experience among the blind, joined the family, to manage the household and the business affairs.

Although her present life seems almost like retirement after the blaze of notoriety of a quarter-century ago, Helen Keller is still a very busy woman. Soon after she left college, the American Foundation for the Blind was formed. It was one of the few organizations with whose aims she felt herself to be in sympathy, and she has worked to help it ever since, lecturing, campaigning for legislation to help the blind. She has a considerable daily mail to attend to—not only business letters, but also those more random communications which every celebrity receives. Curiously, she seems to have more appeal for men than for women. More men than women come to her lectures; more men write to her. An inventor, suddenly seized with the idea that this blind-deaf woman must be terrified by the machines, offers to guide her through a factory; the captain of an ocean liner sends her a little compass, its points marked in Braille type; a traveller, viewing the Pyramids, writes to Helen Keller about them.

She is now forty-nine years old. Her hair is graying; in figure she is stocky rather than tall. Her profile has a sharp, Grecian elegance, but seen full, her face is a little wider, the features more heavily formed, than from the side view one might expect. Her eyes are blue, and have none of the lack-lustre look usual to the blind. When she talks, they take on animation; they gaze at you with what seems a seeing glance.

She likes to talk, to be with people. With friends, she puts her fingers on their lips and "reads" their words. It is only necessary to enunciate clearly for her to understand. She repeats each sentence after them, to make sure. Her own speech is difficult to understand only as would be that of a foreigner a little uncertain of his accent. She lingers on certain consonants as a Spaniard might, and the voice comes with a breathing sound, as if she had to force the utterance. She still calls Mrs. Macy "Teacher," and she is still studying with her. "You swallow your words," Teacher will say, and Helen, with a little frown of concentration, reads the words after her: "Ee-you soowalllowoo ee-yourr worrrdz." Her gestures, as she speaks, have a curious, curbed vehemence.

She talks bookishly. Never having heard a voice, she has never learned the easy vocabulary of ordinary intercourse. To express her ideas, she falls back on the phrases she has learned from books, and uses words that sound stilted, poetical metaphors. "Mine is a reasonably happy life. I have the immeasurable fires of the mind for light," she will say, as one would remark, "I have a good time on the whole." It is perhaps because of this habit of phraseology that many people attribute to her a sentimentality of outlook which neither her life nor her writings would justify.

Thus, she has no illusions as to the various sixth senses which are often, with awe, attributed to the blind. She lays no claim to being able to tell colors by touch, and she admits to a very poor sense of direction. Recent tests by Doctor Frederick Tilney, the neurologist, and a group of Columbia professors, indicate that, fundamentally, her senses of touch, taste, and smell are hardly better than the average.

She has, however, developed a certain acuteness in interpreting these perceptions. She can tell, by the sense of smell, whether she is entering a church, a house, a public building; similarly, passing a shop door, she can often tell what goods are sold there, by their odor. She can feel the vibrations of various instruments, and distinguish the rhythm of the music, by touch. The poet, Carl Sandburg, is an old friend of hers, and she enjoys his visits especially because he brings his banjo and plays old folk tunes for her; she touches the rim of the instrument with her fingertips and "reads" the melodies. No matter how her friends may try to hide it, she can tell when one is cross, or nervous, or gay, by the almost imperceptible differences in the way their hands touch hers. But she often goes wrong in other things: for years, Mrs. Macy has been trying to explain to her that radiators do not give out light, and she has never got the matter straight yet. To her, light and heat are still the same.

Her whole life has been a struggle to come as near to self-reliance as her limitations would permit. Camping last summer at a lake near the Canadian border, she insisted on having ropes strung along the paths and out into the water, so that she could walk and swim by herself. At home, she is almost completely independent. She dresses and undresses herself. Her desk is her own; she types her own manuscripts, keeps them in order. She washes dishes; she eats unaided; afternoons, she walks back and forth in the garden at the side of the house, with no one but Hans, the Great Dane dog, for company.

She is essentially gay, spirited, sturdy. Inevitably, she must know moments of the most intolerable depression, and the blacker in that no sight nor sound can penetrate to distract her. Such moods she hides. She permits no one to pity her. On the other hand, she must have depths of meditation, of philosophical enjoyment, which we who live so much closer to the surface can never know. As for the more trivial pleasures, she has them, too. She plays solitaire, using cards with raised markings; she plays checkers, on a board whose squares are dug out in hollows to receive the pieces. She "listens," by the touch of her fingers, to the radio; sometimes she goes to the theatre, with Mrs. Macy or Polly Thomson along to spell the action into her hand as the play progresses.

This last enjoyment, however, always has its aftermath. Always, after a show, she dreams, fitfully and tormentedly, trying vainly to picture the progress of the drama she has been told about, but can never see.

BONAMY DOBRÉE

Bonamy Dobrée, born in 1891, has had two distinct careers: one in the army, the other in letters. After a schooling at Haileybury, he attended the Royal Military Academy at Woolwich and was commissioned in the Royal Field Artillery in 1910, from which he resigned in 1913. At the outbreak of the War, August 1914, he rejoined the corps and served with distinction in France and Palestine with the rank of Major. Then in 1920 he went to Cambridge University, became captain of the Fencing Team, and took a B.A. degree in the following year. From 1921 to 1925 he resided abroad and wrote the first of the masterful little books that have now become indispensable to students of the ages of Dryden and Pope, *Restoration Comedy* (1924) and *Essays in Biography* (1925). He was a lecturer at the University of London in 1925-26 and, after gaining the degree of M.A. at Cambridge, held the post of Professor of English in the Egyptian University, Cairo, 1926-29. By this time he had produced the beautiful and scholarly Nonesuch edition of the works of the dramatist Vanbrugh and a brief biography of Sarah Churchill, Duchess of Marlborough (1927); a brilliant Introduction to the World's Classics *Congreve* (1928); *Restoration Tragedy*, a companion to his first volume, and *The Lamp and the Lute*, a group of essays on modern writers (1929). In 1929 he was decorated with the Order of the British Empire. Since then, giving himself more fully to study and writing, Mr. Dobrée has collaborated on *The London Book of English Prose* (1931), edited, with a Life, *The Letters of Lord Chesterfield*, written lives of William Penn, John Wesley, and Giacomo Casanova, and, in *A Variety of Ways* (1932) and *As Their Friends Saw Them* (1933), added a dozen more charming biographical studies in his favorite literary period. To a recent volume called *Post-Victorians* he contributed one of the best criticisms we have of Lytton Strachey. His wife, Valentine Brooke-Pechell, is also a writer. They live at Harleston, Norfolk.

While Mr. Dobrée's work is founded upon the soundest modern scholarship and literary taste, its chief distinguishing marks are brightness and brevity. He is never long and, to the alert reader, never dull. In addition to these virtues, he brings to the writing of biography a technical ingenuity and address matched only in the work of Virginia Woolf. "One of the best technical rules to follow," says André Maurois, "in order to avoid showing the life of the hero as too squarely built is to allow the reader to see him through the eyes of friends and enemies who judge him differently." Accordingly, the seven "imaginary conversations" which make up the little book, *As Their Friends Saw Them*, take place each between two friends of the subject in question, two friends whose temperaments clash sufficiently, beneath the fine polish of their eighteenth century speech, to add a fascinating sparkle to the dialogue. Indeed, the talkers reveal not only the principal affairs in the life of their subject but some of their own experiences. Thus we are not allowed to forget, amid the stately prose and gracious manners, that it is the author of *Gulliver's Travels* and the author of *The Beggar's Opera* through whom we read the life of the author of *Love for Love* and *The Way of the World*. The occasion and the dialogue are, of course, imaginary, but the author's mastery of the subject certifies that they are true to life. As Mr. John Sparrow said in reviewing this book's expository counterpart, *A Variety of Ways*, "The scholar may find the essays slight and ask for more facts; it is their merit that they may stimulate exactly the same desire in the general reader."

WILLIAM CONGREVE

A Conversation between Jonathan Swift and John Gay, at the house of the Duke of Queensberry near London. June, 1730.[1]

SWIFT. She had his portrait built in wax? With its chair set ready at table?

GAY. And its doctor to swaddle it against the gout!

SWIFT. What a piece of work is a man! Faith! Congreve's fancy itself could scarce have whelped so gross an absurdity, which indeed smacks more of Jonson's chimerical satire than of his own sprightlier wit. Beware, Gay, beware! See what comes to those who bask in the sunshine of high ladies. But today men of letters are only lapdogs, or yelpers to be shut away in distant deaneries. We are taught the lesson of humility; it is well to learn it early.

GAY. I listen to your Reverence: I take example.

[1] It is not generally known that Swift paid a last flying visit to England in 1730; it has, indeed, been universally ignored by his biographers, and is here made public for the first time.

SWIFT. Imp! Incubus! I will deliver you into the hand of Pope; you will vanish as the autumn butterfly, and White's shall know you no more. But tell me, what is this tattle about his will?

GAY. "He gave what little wealth he had. . . ."

SWIFT. Don't quote me; tell!

GAY. . . . to my Lady Marlborough, except a trifle, a year's coach-hire, which he left to the sloe-eyed Bracegirdle.

SWIFT. What of that? She mothered him all his last years, and a man may surely pay for his dinners on his death-bed?

GAY. 'Tis just for that the nice moralists of the town blame him, and dub him indelicate. But her Grace has purchased herself a handsome necklace, and devised him a monument in the Abbey.

SWIFT. And a wax-work in her dining-room. What would they have had him do with his money but endow his private Bedlam?

GAY. They say Anne Bracegirdle would have put it to better uses.

SWIFT. And so they would have had him more indelicate just by blaring to the world what it wishes to believe true, and what the lady, veraciously or not, studiously declares to be false.

GAY. Ah! how she must have made an anchorite waver when she first played Angelica and Millamant, thirty years ago now, when, alas! I was too young to be there: but I do not repine, for Congreve did not see young Mrs. Cibber as Polly Peachum, so swift, so clear. They say Bracegirdle was ever tender-hearted to the poor: was she always so cruel to Congreve?

SWIFT. Need we ask? Must the respectable harpies of the world always lick their lips over secrets they cannot probe? In apprehension how like a God, in nostril how like a beast! Is there nothing but the aching senses? Are there not other pains to make men cry for ease?

GAY. For my part, I believe her chaste. You remember "pious Selinda"?

> "Would she could make of me a saint
> Or I of her a sinner."

SWIFT. Yet would he so readily have been a sinner?

GAY. Come, very Reverend Doctor, Congreve was no monster of purity, and knew the universal way of cheating time.

SWIFT. Gay, will you always be a child? Have you not learnt that for every man there comes a time when time will not be cheated? I did not say that Congreve had never sinned.

GAY. But that he feared fruition for the emptiness it would reveal?

SWIFT. Indeed, he had read Suckling too much, though he made Millamant quote him only to ignore his warning.

GAY. Yet I remember those words in *Love for Love:* "Uncertainty and expectation are the joys of life. Security is an insipid thing, and the overtaking and possessing of a wish discovers the folly of the chase. Never let us know one another better: for the pleasure of the masquerade is done, when we come to show our faces." But much later he still loved Anne Bracegirdle; he lived in the same street with her that he might see her the more often, though God forbid that I should attach any scandal to that, as some have done; but yet . . . perhaps the good time had once been, and, who knows? the heart may yearn for what the mind rejects.

SWIFT. You also have learnt that wisdom? But then, we are all tongue-lolling foxes, and the grapes are eternally out of reach, the grapes, that is, we know to be the sweetest.

GAY. Yet Congreve tasted so many, from the plaudits which greeted *Incognita*, even though he knew it for but a graceful trifle, to the better deserved ones which rewarded his plays, till Jeremy Collier came to sour them, and obscure the clear heavens with his stinking, sulphurous smoke.

SWIFT. Collier! A born hedge-parson, cluttered up with the silly jargon of the schools, weighed down by the names of the Fathers of the Church, which he wore ridiculously as a savage wears a necklace of oyster shells, believing them to be pearls. The rabble loved him, and thought the thunder he tried to steal from the prophets was authentic; but a pack of curs, if loudly enough hallooed will always leap at a stag to drag him down, if only because he is the nobler beast. Indeed, Collier was nothing but a heap of farmyard filth, crawling with the worms of envy and dull ambition, who soiled the names of virtue and learning by having them in his mouth, while he brawled and blustered like a fishwife who thinks herself better than her worthier neighbour because she can spell out her book.

GAY. Yet his satire stung.

SWIFT. His satire! He bawled like a bull of Bashan. For all the logic he had learnt he could not reason, so none could reason with him. For me, a man who can think at all can do so without logic, which gives only the appearance of wisdom, and deludes a man into believing he has wit because he can stutter a syllogism. As though truth could be caged in a triangle, one, moreover, of which we shall never find the base.

GAY. True. If you prick out the things about which you may reason, and declare you are only to argue one way, you can scarcely fail always to be right. Which is contrary to nature, though since it flatters man, it is agreeable to what he calls truth. Perhaps that was why Congreve reasoned so ill with Collier.

SWIFT. He did not reason ill, but he used a feather to tickle a pachyderm. Thus all his airiest foolery, such as pretending he had not meant Jehu when he said Jehu, was taken for serious argument, and so was thought by the coffee-houses to be nothing but silly evasion. He was too delicate.

GAY. Even in his satire?

SWIFT. What talk is this you make of satire, my gentle, jesting Gay? Congreve had not the daring to be a satirist, who must be like Milton's eagle which has purged and unscaled its long-abused sight, to look unblinking into the whitest heat of hell. He who, as he said, could not look at a monkey without mortifying reflections, could never steadfastly behold mankind for fear of discovering the ape.

GAY. You talk of him as though he had been a child.

SWIFT. Indeed, I think that for me he was always something of a child, even when his belly would not let him see his toes, and his eyes grew blear with cataract. He was, you see, my junior at Kilkenny, in—do not smile to hear me name so long ago—in '80 or '81, and he followed me to Trinity, where he soon o'ertopped me in height as he did in scholarship. But when I conjure him up in my mind it is of those early years that I think, for when the brain begins to weary, it is the pictures earliest imprinted upon it that remain, the later ones that grow cloudy and dim and faded.

GAY. Almighty Jove! And last year saw *A Modest Proposal!*

SWIFT. I remember him so well in Ireland, before the Revolution drove us both from that land given over to the villainies of Rome, and the cowardice of the worst and most cheating of the Stuarts. How active he was, for mere sport flinging his lithe body over yawning ditches, his handsome face flushed, and his eager eyes shining with delight, as when he fished out some darling passage of Juvenal, or happened upon a rare piece of Horatian wisdom. But I lost him while I was with Sir William Temple, and when I saw him again he was already in the grasp of his premature infirmities, his work behind him, as though his flame had been too bright to last, and his oil had burned itself out.

GAY. From the time I knew him he seemed eternally dwelling in the days that had been, as if he were always saying:

> "For though the present I regret,
> I'm grateful for the past."

But he was ever delicious, ever thoughtful for others, our unreproachful poet; yet at his warmest he seemed distant and elusive, so that even when he shook hands, it was the rather like a friend waving from the end of a street at the moment when he slips around the corner.

SWIFT. He was an *honnête homme*, as you fashionable feathers say. It gave me pleasure to be able to assure him his place in 1711, when Harley came in and the Kit-Cats went out, for I was glad to make a worthy man happy. He cared too little for business ever to make a great place, thus not enough to lose a trifling one.

GAY. You think he asked little of life?

SWIFT. Too little, as though he were lastingly afraid of failure, like a child that dares not ask its mother for a toy, for fear it should be refused the plaything.

GAY. Plaything? It was just as such, I thought, that he could not regard life, as far from asking too little of it, he always appeared to me to ask too greatly. His plays seem, in all their most wonderful scenes, to breathe a wish for an existence so exquisite, for beings so lovely in their persons, so delicate in their minds, that in despair he gave over creating them as patterns for mankind to imitate.

SWIFT. It is true he always hated fools.

GAY. Not hate, dear Dean; there was too much pity in his periods to let hate live. But he took no delight in his fools, just because, as you say, he did not want mankind to be monkeys: and since he could not imitate man without making him smaller, he preferred to be silent, to beat up listeners for a concert, write a few verses, or an essay upon the Pindaric Ode. These he might pass around among his friends, for their delectation, and to hear his thoughts echo in their hearts.

SWIFT. Stuff! my angel. He ceased to write plays because the pit would not take *The Way of the World* to its heart. They told me that he came enraged upon the boards, and swore he would write no more for blockheads that could not feel his shafts.

GAY. Say, rather, for ears that could not hear his music. Or was it that his real answer to Collier was *The Way of the World*, whose triumph would have justified him in his own eyes, but whose failure sent him sadly away from the tribunal as a man discountenanced and wronged?

SWIFT. I do not know how far the story is true. No sensible man should gird at the judgments of a rabble, especially of the one that pretends to judge, for that is the most unworthy of them all.

GAY. Are some rabbles worthy then?

SWIFT. Those which the belly goads. Nature gives such wretches a right to howl and to hate. If you dislike a comedy or concert you may stay away, but you cannot for always absent yourself from the stew-pot.

GAY. But here the comedy stayed away from the mob. Small blame to Congreve if he preferred the conversation of the polished.

SWIFT. The polished! as though that were praise! my boots are polished! Nothing is worse for a man of wit than to consort with the progeny of the drawing-rooms, who air what they have heard of Aristotle or Rapin, and do men of genius the honour of using them as foot-rules. A beggar had as well judge of banking, as a man who has never written one of a book. A good book is a fiery thing, a petard placed under the feet of the unwary; but the drawing-rooms seek only for sweetmeats, or at most for a devilled bone.

GAY. He could afford to be prodigal of his sweetmeats.

SWIFT. Nay, I feared, and feared rightly, for Congreve, when he sought for friendship among those who should have been his enemies. For I tell you, Gay, we who write are like a small band of adventurers in some rude America, where certain chiefs may do us lip-service, it is true, but where all are ready whenever chance offers a favourable turn, to stab us in the back. We seek for truth, and there is nothing men hate more; we reveal the cancer, while they would cover it up; we burrow under foundations they would like to think secure, and our reward is ashy and bitter.

GAY. Do we not give them beauty?

SWIFT. There is an old song I remember my mother used to sing, very long ago now, "Beauty is but a painted hell," and men dread beauty because they scent the hell beneath. When they no longer fear it—for men soon grow to love what is familiar—they are jealous of it, and will defend it, as a woman does her man from the approaches of a younger girl. We are society's everlasting tempest, and the more polished a man is, the more he hates to be ruffled. We must not care if our fellows abhor us. Congreve tasted like gall to men; he should not have groaned at their being harsh to him. We cannot have both the Revolution Settlement and King James III; once blessedly dead, we may not wish to be dragged again to life.

GAY. Yet there was no gall in Congreve, so he gave what he did not possess, or rather, men mistook his sorrow. Just because he grew tired of portraying fools so gross that they should arouse compassion rather than mockery, a wistfulness towards men emanates from his work as perfume from the pink. Lady Wishfort's railings show him to be more of a poet than do his Pindaric

Odes, though there he was more concerned for right building than for his feeling: but I would say too that there was as much poetry in the folly of old Foresight as in the haunting melody of his songs.

SWIFT. *Love for Love* is indeed his best work; there his learning —he showed how much he brought to it in his *False and Imperfect Citations*—leavened the loaf of the human lumpishness he drew. Then his learned sock was on, and, 'faith, in that play he is more like Jonson than in any other, more, that is, his true son than in *The Old Bachelor*, where he was but his slave and mimic. He had read much, I think, in Marston and in Brome . . .

GAY. And in Cowley.

SWIFT. . . . but it was not for that that I, more than anyone else, loved his work. I loved it as I loved the man, which I did for his honesty and his good-will, his sturdiness of humour and his tolerance in judgment.

GAY. You would not give him satire; will you give him gentleness?

SWIFT. Gentleness? No, I will not give him satire, but I cannot deny him the wish.

GAY. He declared it in the prologue to *Love for Love*, yet, as though Fate were to underline the denial of his wish, that was his best-liked play. Indeed he laughed at no foolishness but that which no man would own to, and the sentiment is as sweet as the rose. Who more generous than Valentine, more steadfast than Angelica? But in *The Way of the World*, as in his life, he seemed afraid of his own tenderness, as though it were something so fragile that it would break if handled; and he set palings about it, as Millamant did to secure her conjugal affections.

SWIFT. No one has written such prose as he did in those passages, so incisive, so clear.

GAY. Clear indeed; even Dryden could not but admire it . . .

SWIFT. Dryden!

GAY. . . . but it is the clarity of a rippling stream that reflects, not imbibes, the sunlight, to prison it in a lucent box.

SWIFT. A pity his plots were always so tedious or forced.

GAY. He should have stolen them, as Shakespeare did; and I

remember his avowing an envy for Terence, who had his fables from Menander, and could apply his ingenuity to the choice of his words. But *The Mourning Bride* had dignity.

SWIFT. Ay, the dignity of a cripple that will not walk too fast for fear of showing how ill his limbs unbend. It was fustian stuff, that "resistless moan," as poor Dick Steele ridiculously called it.

GAY. You detract from his writings?

SWIFT. What are a man's books to the man himself? It was the latter that I loved.

GAY. Who did not? He quarrelled with none.

SWIFT. Except once with Jacob Tonson, that fretting devil of Whiggery, God knows over what trifle: but the split was of short duration. He had that good-nature for liking men some only give to corpses, which can no longer hurt them, nor wrestle with them in the market-place. Yet he regretted his friends too, and wept for Garth and Rowe.

GAY. I thought he did not seem much to mourn the death of Mr. Addison.

SWIFT. He did not love Addison, he did not know Addison; nobody knew Addison. Who should? He hedged himself about with reserves, till he himself could not break through his own fences without powerful support from Burgundy and brandy. I had much to forgive him, but forgiveness was worth while. When Harley, St. John, and I ruled, he would scarce salute me in the street, though he and Steele had once formed a regular triumvirate with me. He was a prey to the party-spirit he decried and strove against. Congreve was never such: he was simplicity itself compared with Addison, whose soul was a labyrinth which he wished to appear as smooth and innocent as a lawn.

GAY. Thus Mr. Pope could dedicate his *Iliad* to Congreve, but could never have done so to Mr. Secretary Addison?

SWIFT. Congreve avoided strife, and Addison, though he may not have wished it, found himself ever in the centre of yapping puppies. Even when Pope snubbed Philips, or Dennis, Addison received some of the mud that was flung; and when in his grave, Steele and Tickell squabbled over him. He was too much a party man.

GAY. They say the dean of St. Patrick's . . .

SWIFT. I belonged to no party. I merely allied myself with the honester men.

GAY. Does any man ever do otherwise? We give the name of party not to the cage into which the beasts are driven, but to the beasts which tumble over one another in the cage, kicking up the dust until they all become the same sad colour, and not easily to be distinguished.

SWIFT. Except those that roar louder than the others. But I am now past the hot tempers and unwisdom of tampering with men. I would better my fellows, even though they are not worth the expense of a paragraph, but my paths are not those of the great. Macheath sits upon the Treasury chest, and who knows what Polly pilfers among the guineas; but the wretches in prison —and what a prison!—are still robbed of their ha'pence, and half-naked, struggle like famishing animals when a bone is thrown them. For these we work, to these we minister; but some day, I pray God not far hence, I shall join Stel—I shall join Congreve in the Elysian Fields, and act once more our old Kilkenny. Will *you* mourn for me, Gay?

GAY. Don't, I beseech you! Why are you so cruel?

SWIFT. Ay, for a week: Arbuthnot will grieve a day, and Pope with St. John maybe a little longer. What matter? Once I was young, and Congreve was younger: he did well to go before me, as he was wise to give up the struggle for vain rewards when I had scarce begun. Good-bye, Gay. Tomorrow I go to Ireland. It was good to speak of Congreve; it would have been better to remain silent. We like to be stroked, but caresses when applied to half-closed wounds end but by opening them again. Nay, let me be: do not clutch my arm. And call no one; for I have lately thought that when we finally depart, it is well that none should see us go.

F. L. LUCAS

Frank Laurence Lucas and Bonamy Dobrée are among the young Englishmen represented here who survived active service in the War to become competent biographers. If Mr. Dobrée's special literary sphere is the Restoration and Augustan drama, Mr. Lucas's is the Elizabethan and Jacobean. Yet he has contributed valuable studies also on Greek and Roman tragedy and on certain eighteenth and nineteenth century poets. Now, in his latest volume, from which the present biography is taken, he ranges luminously and charmingly over the literature of France and England together.

Fellow, Librarian, and Lecturer at King's College, Cambridge, Mr. Lucas brings a rich experience and a scholar's instinct to his work. He was born in Yorkshire in 1894 and was educated at Rugby and Cambridge (M.A.). During the War he served in France in the Royal West Kent Regiment and in the Intelligence Corps, was wounded, gassed, and mentioned in despatches. Before and after the War he won several prizes and medals at Cambridge, including the Chancellor's, which Lytton Strachey had won in his day, and in 1920 became a Fellow of King's. His principal books are *Seneca and His Tragedy* (1922), *Euripides and His Influence* (1924), *Authors Dead and Living* (1926), *The Collected Works of John Webster*, edited (1927), *Tragedy* (1927), *Eight Victorian Poets* (1930), *Studies French and English* (1934), and his anthologies of Crabbe, Beddoes, Tennyson, and D. G. Rossetti. He has published, as well, three novels, two plays, a book (with his wife) of travel in Greece, and four books of poetry, including a translation into English verse of the *Medea* of Euripides.

To such an endowment of learning and imagination as this list implies must be added gifts of wit, grace, and sensibility which fuse into a remarkably balanced and felicitous prose style. The following life of Dorothy Osborne (from *Studies French and English*) illustrates how the short biography may serve all the purposes of the critical essay without departing from its narrative course. It shows, too, how one's enjoyment of literature and life may be increased by a specialized study of such out-of-the-way matter as the intimate letters of this delightful young woman of the seventeenth century.

DOROTHY OSBORNE

THE PERFECT LETTER-WRITER

"Jamais toute la morale d'un pédagogue ne vaudra le bavardage affectueux et tendre d'une femme sensée pour qui l'on a de l'attachement."—ROUSSEAU.

WE ARE in the year 1648. General Cromwell is rising steadily to power in England; beyond the Channel, Cardinal Mazarin is already seated on the neck of France; Louis XIV is a neglected little boy of ten; Charles I lies prisoner in the Isle of Wight, in the keep of Carisbrooke; and from an inn in that island a party of young travellers is just setting out—two youths and a girl. At the last moment one of the young men turns round, goes back into the inn, and there writes something with a diamond on the window-pane. It is a sentence from the Bible, from the *Book of Esther*, "And Hamman was hang'd upon the Gallows he had prepar'd for Mordecai." That done, he hurries after his companions. A moment later someone notices the writing. Its meaning is as transparent as the glass it is written on: "Hamman" is Colonel Robert Hammond, Governor of the Isle of Wight for the Parliament, and gaoler of King Charles. This insolent young devil of a Cavalier has been quoting Scripture very much to his purpose. There is a hue and cry; horsemen go clattering off; the three young people are brought back and led before the Governor himself. "Which of you did this?" Before the real culprit can answer, the girl, his sister, has broken in: "I did." A woman?—that is different; even in the England of the Civil War all chivalry has not perished with the Cavaliers. Probably with a smile, the Governor let his prisoners go.[1] The incident was closed—no, not quite; not finally closed until, just half a century later, in Westminster Abbey the last flagstone was lowered into place above the body of Sir William Temple, the builder of

[1] It throws an odd light on "Progress" to reflect that in the Germany of 1933 she would probably have been paraded round the town with her head shaved and a placard round her neck, before being sent to five years' imprisonment.

the Triple Alliance and Privy Councillor of Charles II, laid now to his rest beside Dorothy Osborne, the wife of forty years.

But the course of this love that had so long to run, was far from running smooth at first. William Temple was just twenty when he watched the woman's wit of Dorothy Osborne, herself twenty-one, thus save her brother in the Isle of Wight. That day, if she set one prisoner free, she made another. How the lovers' acquaintance had first begun, we do not know; but a long period of trouble was still to pass before it ended happily in marriage. "The accidents for seven years of that amour," writes Temple's sister, Lady Giffard, "might make a history, and the letters that passed between them a volume." At this moment Temple, the son of Sir John Temple, Member of Parliament for Chichester, Master of the Rolls and a Privy Councillor for Ireland, was just going abroad to travel after two not very profitable years at Emmanuel College, Cambridge, where he had found tennis and other occupations more amusing than Dr. Cudworth's "harsh studies of logick and phylosophy." "I have heard him say," continues his sister in her Memoir, "if it had bin possible in the two years time he past there to forgit all he had learn't before, he must certainely have done it." Dorothy Osborne, on her side, came of a northern family which had settled in Essex in the mid-fifteenth century. At the close of the sixteenth her great-grandfather, John Osborne, six times Member of Parliament, husband of a niece of the famous scholar Sir John Cheke, and father of twenty-two children, bought Dorothy's future home, Chicksands Priory in Bedfordshire, a dissolved monastery of Gilbertines. Her mother, Dorothy Danvers, was a sister of Sir John Danvers, the future regicide who at the age of twenty married Magdalen Herbert, mother of ten children, including the poet; so that George Herbert and Dorothy Osborne were cousins of a kind. Her father, Sir Peter, had been Lieutenant-Governor of Guernsey for twenty-one years when the Civil War broke out; then, when the island declared for the Parliament, he maintained Castle Cornet for the King. After holding out for three years, cheated of supplies by the royalist Governor of Jersey and sickened with empty promises by the Court, he was superseded and withdrew to St. Malo. Thither Dorothy and her brother were now travelling to join the old Cavalier, when they fell in with Temple, whose father was a member of the hated Parliament. The lovers were crossed from the first, like another Romeo and Juliet, by the factions of their parents. Further, each family thought it could make a better match elsewhere. So that Temple, lingering on enchanted ground at St. Malo, was soon sent packing on his travels by a stern message from home. But it was too late. A sympathy, stronger than fathers or brothers or any worldly considerations could ever break, had already sprung up between the handsome, passionate, egotistical youth with his brown curling hair, and the "stately" young woman whose oval face with its long, straight nose and great dark eyes, full at once of humour and melancholy, still gazes from the portrait at Broadlands. They were parted now; but down the long Paris road he carried with him the memory of their days together, and of the lonely little house on the isle of Herm, by Guernsey, that they had seen from their ship sailing to St. Malo; as Dorothy was to remind him years afterwards in one of her most charming passages: "Do you remember Arme and the little house there? Shall we go thither? That's next to being out of the world. There we might live like Baucis and Philemon, grow old together in our little cottage, and for our charity to some ship-wrecked strangers obtain the blessing of dying both at the same time. How idly I talk; 'tis because the story pleases me—none in Ovid so much. I remember I cried when I read it. Methought they were the perfectest characters of a contented marriage, where piety and love were all their wealth, and in their poverty feasted the gods when rich men shut them out. I am called away—farewell."

What happened in the next few years remains obscure. At some point the lovers came to regard themselves as plighted; though Temple laughingly wagered ten pounds against Dorothy's constancy, to be paid him on the day she married someone else. He stayed in France two years (1648-50), saw Dorothy again in London, was sent abroad by his anxious father to the Low Countries for another fifteen months (1651-2). Meanwhile, since 1649,

she had been living mainly at home, in a quiet broken only by the indefatigable efforts of her brother Henry to get her married. Perhaps she had faded in Temple's memory. After a letter from Breda in March 1652, there followed a silence of nine months; but at last, as the year drew to its close, word came to Chicksands announcing the wanderer's return to England. On Christmas Eve Dorothy sat down and wrote in answer the first letter we still possess, beginning: "Sir,—You may please to let my old servant [*i.e.* lover], as you call him, know that I confess I owe much to his merits . . . ; but for the ten pound he claims, it is not yet due, and I think you may do well to persuade him (as a friend) to put it in the number of his desperate debts, for 'tis a very uncertain one."

With this reference to Temple's old wager against her constancy opens that correspondence, containing some eighty letters of hers and one of his, which covers the period of exactly two years and a day till the lovers were wed at Christmas, 1654. There are no more delightful letters in English. Love-letters—and indeed letters in general—are a province of literature for which no spectacled Aristotle has yet laid down the laws. But we may have views about them; as we shall see, Dorothy herself had. The writing of letters is an applied art which turns into a pure one, when they lose their original purpose; the readers for whom they are written come to die, the matter they express grows obsolete and immaterial, and yet by charm of manner alone they may still enthral an eavesdropping public for which they were never meant. The embroidery preserves the dress, when the stuff itself is long threadbare with the years. True, the subjects are not always ephemeral; a Pliny may watch Vesuvius engulfing five cities, a Sévigné see Fouquet on his trial. But these are lucky chances; good letters remain immortal though they chronicle the smallest beer, and describe merely the visits of cousins and the maladies of aunts. Nor is this simply because time gives back with interest the value it at first takes away from little things, so that hairpins grow precious in a thousand years and we would give its weight in gold for a laundry-bill of Augustus; it is because the real interest of good letters is one that years cannot lessen—the

attraction of human personality. To preserve the charm of some character with vivid responses to life—that is their achievement. A diary like Pepys's may be even more intimately revealing; but how many books are there in the world like his? Besides, a good correspondent, like a good conversationalist, is better when addressing others than in soliloquy; and we may little guess how charming people can be, until they try to charm. The art of letters is, indeed, the most social and one of the most civilised of literary forms. It stands nearer even than sermon or moral essay to the art of life. The eighteenth century knew its value; and it does small credit to our modern culture that we have so suffered it to decay. To combine sensitiveness and good sense; to be spontaneous yet delicate, natural without vulgarity and negligent without slovenliness; to show at once gaiety and grace; to possess a mind of one's own, a style of one's own, one's own way of seeing and describing life's brief trifles—that was the eighteenth-century ideal of conversation; and those seem to me, in all ages, the essentials of good letter-writing.

Small wonder, then, that women, with their keener sense for the graces of life, should have excelled since the days of Héloïse in this branch of literature, so that it is dominated by figures like Dorothy Osborne, Madame de Sévigné, Madame du Deffand, Madame d'Epinay, Mademoiselle de Lespinasse, Lady Mary Wortley Montague, Maria Edgeworth, Elizabeth Barrett Browning and Jane Welsh Carlyle (both of whom write so much better than their more famous husbands). Even their most successful male rivals, like Horace Walpole and poor Cowper winding his worsted, have sometimes been markedly feminine. I have noticed the same thing in my own experience; and I have certainly known women who, with that remarkable power their sex sometimes shows of withstanding any amount of education, could only spell precariously, and yet wrote far better and more vivid letters than some very distinguished writers, alive and dead.

This is not simply, I think, because women tend by nature to have more grace, as men more strength; or because they have a greater need, and a greater wish to please. They have tended also, ever since civilisation allowed many of them a good deal of

DOROTHY OSBORNE

From the original portrait at Broadlands

leisure, to have their originality and their natural spirit less worn down than men, whether in the mill of education or on the grindstone of active life. It is easier for hands unroughened by labour to keep their lightness of touch. This is not merely a vague generalisation; it has been noticed in widely different ages and countries what a natural command women may possess over their native tongue in its most living and unpedantic purity. It was remarked under the Roman Republic; it was remarked again in the France of Louis XIV, by Vaugelas: "Il vaut mieux consulter les femmes," says he, "et ceux qui n'ont pas étudié, que ceux qui sont bien savants en la langue grecque et en la latine." A century later Diderot is even more downright: "C'est que le bon style est dans le cœur; voilà pourquoi tant de femmes disent et écrivent comme des anges, sans avoir appris ni à dire ni à écrire, et pourquoi tant de pédants diront et écriront mal toute leur vie, quoiqu'ils n'aient cessé d'étudier sans apprendre."

Here lies part of the charm in the letters of Dorothy Osborne; but only part. Letters need more than style; particularly love-letters. For these last are apt to be dull reading; theirs is at once the most eternal and the most ephemeral of all subjects. They have indeed two essential themes—the facts of the situation and the feelings of the lovers; and the facts have all the more need to be vivid since the feelings, however thrilling for the persons concerned, tend to be so monotonous for everyone else. The cooing of turtles is agreeable; but exciting it is not. Accordingly love-letters are the better for a love that does not run smooth, but has to fight its way through alarms and despairs, surprises and vicissitudes. The feelings, too, need variation. One remedy is to quarrel; but there are less drastic methods: lovers can easily —none more easily—be scolded or mocked, tantalised and teased. In a word, the two great dangers of love-letters are sentimentality and boredom; the two great safeguards, with these as with other letters (and with everything else in life), are gaiety and grace.

So much for the art of letter-writing; it is time to return to Dorothy Osborne, whose romance we have delayed almost as long as her obdurate relatives. Certainly in these love-letters struggles with circumstance are not wanting. Her brother Henry in particular (not the same brother, it seems, as was with her in the Isle of Wight—that was probably a younger one called Robin) set his face violently against her marrying Temple, whom he disliked and despised as being an adventurer and an atheist; although it looks almost as if the real crime of Dorothy's lover was his love for her, and her brother's real motive a passionate jealousy. Eight years her elder, he was intensely possessive in his feeling: "he is much of your sister's humour," writes Dorothy to Temple, "and many times wishes me a husband that loved me as well as he does (though he seems to doubt the possibility on't), but never desires that I should love that husband with any passion, and plainly tells me so. He says it would not be so well for him, nor perhaps for me, that I should; for he is of opinion that all passions have more of trouble than of satisfaction in them." (This seems rather a flimsy excuse.) "But, seriously," she goes on, "I many times receive letters from him, that were they seen without any address to me or his name, nobody would believe they were from a brother; and I cannot but tell him sometimes that, sure, he mistakes and sends me letters that were meant to his mistress, till he swears to me that he has none." It is a curious coincidence that the equally devoted sister of Temple here referred to, the future Lady Giffard, was destined, after losing her husband in the first month of her marriage, to spend most of her life with her brother as almost a second wife to him. Meanwhile, at all events, Henry Osborne gave Dorothy no peace; until, if she ever read Webster (as she certainly read Shakespeare), she must have found the relations of the Duchess of Malfi with her brother, Duke Ferdinand, painfully like her own. He lectured her, he tried to intercept her lover's letters (only to be defeated by the trusty carrier's stout denials that he had any), he besieged her with rival suitors, he lost his temper with her for rejecting them. "I could tell you such a story ('tis too long to be written) as would make you see (what I never discover'd in myself before) that I am a valiant lady. In earnest we have had such a skirmish, and upon so foolish an occasion, as I cannot tell which is strangest. . . . All the people that I had ever in my life refused were brought again upon the stage, like Richard III's ghosts, to reproach me withal; and all the kindness his discoveries could make I had for you was laid to my charge. . . . Well, 'twas a pretty lecture, and I grew warm with it after a while; in short, we came so near an absolute falling out, that 'twas time to give over, and we said so much then that we have hardly spoken a word together since. But 'tis wonderful to see what curtseys and legs pass between us; and as before we were thought the kindest brother and sister, we are certainly the most complimental couple in England." Nine months later the battle is still raging: "He renounced me again, and I defied him, but both in as civil language as it would permit, and parted in great anger with the usual ceremony of a leg and a courtesy, that you would have died with laughing to have seen us."

Unhappy as she was, it will be seen that she had a very saving sense of humour. In the same way though as weary of her suitors as any Penelope–she "would live in a hollow tree to avoid them" –she manages to get as much amusement as any Portia out of them too; alternately laughing at them because they are so ridiculous, and teasing her lover with them because they are so attractive. The most engaging is Henry Cromwell, son of the Lord General, described by the grim Mrs. Hutchinson as a "debauched ungodly cavalier"; he is kept busy getting Dorothy Irish greyhounds on which her heart is set; and when his father dissolves the Parliament in April 1653, she cannot resist reminding Temple with a smile: "if I had been so wise as to have taken hold of the offer was made me by H. C., I might have been in a fair way of preferment." What would the Protector, one wonders, have made of this ironic daughter-in-law? But an even grander suitor is Sir Justinian Isham, Bart., of Lamport, whom she generally refers to as "the Emperor" on the strength of his Christian name; a county magnate, Solomon and Daniel in one, with four grown-up daughters. She promises Temple, by way of consolation, to put in a good word for him with one or other of these young women, in case she becomes their step-mother. But it was as well for Sir Justinian she did not. "Oh, my conscience! we should all have joined against him as the common enemy, for those poor young wenches are as weary of his government as I could have been.

He gives them such precepts as they say my Lord of Dorchester gives his wife, and keeps them so much prisoners to a vile house he has in Northamptonshire, that if once I had but let them loose, they and his learning would have been sufficient to have made him mad without my help; but his good fortune would have it otherwise, to which I'll leave him." Justinian's learning had indeed led him into one unlucky composition not meant for his mistress's eye. "Lord! what would I give that I had a Latin letter of his for you, that he writ to a great friend at Oxford, where he gives a long and learned character of me; 'twould serve you to laugh at this seven year." The worst of her faults, as there described by this seventeenth-century Sir Willoughby, was "a height (he would not call it pride) that was, as he had heard, the humour of my family; and the best of my commendations was, that I was capable of being company and conversation for him." Not that this sage could not also be gallant: hearing Dorothy had an ague, he forthwith had one himself, "so natural a sympathy there is between us." But at last finding even agues unavailing, Sir Justinian turned elsewhere: "it was not mine, it seems, to have an emperor; the spiteful man, merely to vex me, has gone and married my countrywoman, Lord Lee's daughter. What a multitude of willow garlands shall I wear before I die! I think I had best make them into faggots this cold weather, the flame they would make in a chimney would be of more use to me than that which was in the hearts of all those that gave them me, and would last as long."

Other wooers as provokingly went and died. "Never anybody had such luck with lovers; what with marrying and what with dying they all leave me. Just now I have news brought me of the death of an old rich knight that has promised me this seven years to marry me whensoever his wife died, and now he's dead before her, and has left her such a widow, it makes me mad to think on't: £1,200 a year jointure and £20,000 in money and personal estate, and all this I might have had if Mr. Death had been pleased to have taken her instead of him. Well, who can help these things? But, since I cannot have him, would you had her! What say you? Shall I speak a good word for you?" The old knight

DOROTHY OSBORNE

From the original portrait at Broadlands

cousin Franklin used to have the fault of "kissing his wife before company, a foolish trick that young married men, it seems, are apt to; he has left it long since, I suppose." Yet she cannot resign herself to face such a falling-off. "I could be infinitely better satisfied with a husband that had never loved me, in hope that he might, than with one that began to love me less than he had done." And she grows bitter in her contempt for marriages that are mercenary and loveless from the first. Her neighbour, Lady Grey de Ruthin, is engaged to a Mr. Yelverton: " 'tis the most troublesome, busy, talking little thing that ever was born; his tongue goes like the clack of a mill, but to much less purpose. . . . You would wonder to see how tired she is with his impertinences, and yet how pleased she is to think she shall have a great estate with him. . . . Two or three great glistering jewels have bribed her to wink at all his faults, and she hears him as unmoved and unconcerned as if another were to marry him." That so many marriages end in tears is mainly, she thinks, the women's fault; seeing that they usually show themselves more quarrelsome within their own families than men. Even when a husband is unsatisfactory, his wife can and should at least save appearances (we shall meet again this curiously strong dread in Dorothy of public ridicule); "as a kinswoman of ours that had a husband who was not always himself; and when he was otherwise, his humour was to rise in the night, and with two bedstaves tabour upon the table an hour together. She took care every night to lay a great cushion upon the table for him to strike on, that nobody might hear him, and so discover his madness. But 'tis a sad thing when all one's happiness is only that the world does not know you are miserable." But this view of the wifely duty of providing cushions does not prevent her having a high standard for husbands. She has indeed drawn a full-length portrait of her ideal, in a letter which can compare for wit and style with any of the Characters in Earle or Overbury:

"There are a great many ingredients must go to the making me happy in a husband. First, as my cousin Franklin says, our humours must agree; and to do that he must have that kind of breeding that I have had, and used that kind of company. That is, he must not be so much of a country gentleman as to understand nothing but hawks and dogs, and be fonder of either than his wife; nor of the next sort of them whose aim reaches no further than to be Justice of Peace, and once in his life High Sheriff, who reads no books but statutes, and studies nothing but how to make a speech interlarded with Latin that may amaze his disagreeing poor neighbours, and fright them rather than persuade them into quietness. He must not be a thing that began the world in a free school, was sent from thence to the university, and is at his furthest when he reaches the Inns of Court, has no acquaintance but those of his form in these places, speaks the French he has picked out of old laws, and admires nothing but the stories he has heard of the revels that were kept there before his time. He must not be a town gallant neither, that lives in a tavern and an ordinary, that cannot imagine how an hour should be spent without company unless it be in sleeping, that makes court to all the women he sees, thinks they believe him, and laughs and is laughed at equally. Nor a travelled Monsieur whose head is all feather inside and outside, that can talk nothing but dances and duels, and has courage enough to wear slashes when everybody else dies of cold to see him. He must not be a fool of no sort, nor peevish, nor ill-natured, nor proud, nor covetous; and to all this must be added, that he must love me and I him as much as we are capable of loving. Without all this, his fortune, though never so great, would not satisfy me; and with it, a very moderate one would keep me from ever repenting my disposal."

By the greatness of such expectations she irritated all the young men at a country house in Kent into "a custom of expressing anything that is nowhere but in fiction by the name of 'Mrs. O—'s husband.' . . . They laugh to hear me say that one unkind word would destroy all the satisfaction of my life, and that I should expect our kindness should increase every day, if it were possible, but never lessen. All this is perfect nonsense in their opinion; but I should not doubt the convincing them if I could hope I should ever be so happy as to be

Yours."

Was she disappointed? A little, we must believe; but not, perhaps, essentially. She was a realistic young woman as well as a romantic one. In that lies part of her charm. For the purely romantic character and the purely realistic are equally chilling in their opposite ways. In one respect, indeed, she will slightly shock her more romantic admirers. She is inflexibly resolved not to wed Temple in the teeth of the whole world's disapproval: "I confess that I have an humour will not suffer me to expose myself to people's scorn." She is prepared to keep her faith to him; to refuse all the matches her friends can find her, all the wealth the world can give; but she will not be "esteemed a ridiculous person," making a love-match in a cottage "to satisfy a giddy humour." She does not want praise. She does not fear anger. But she flinches at contempt.

There are even times when she takes a touch of primness. She finds extremely shocking the idea of a woman loving before she is loved. She will launch out into little sermons that yet possess a strange charm in their half-childish gravity and the sudden laughing apology that cuts them short: "what think you, might I not preach with Mr. Marshall for a wager?"; or again: "One would think it were I that had heard the three sermons and were trying to make a fourth; these are truths that might become a pulpit better than Mr. Arbry's predictions. But lest you should think I have as many worms in my head as he, I'll give over in time." All the same, she means what she says. She has even a morbid sense of guilt at moments about their passion as "but a refined degree of madness," which reason and religion should have better controlled. And she is outraged at her brother's suggestion that Temple is an infidel: "it must suppose one to be a devil in human shape."

And yet in religion she herself finds not so much joy, as a rather wistful comfort in a bleak and bitter world. Behind all her gaiety lies a confirmed sadness about life, based both on reason and temperament. She has learnt not to expect overmuch on earth, where with so much sorrow goes so little joy "that one may see 'tis merely intended to keep us alive withal." Strengthened as this strain in her must have been by her unhappy youth, it is clear, I think, that she was born with it; "my mother, I remember, used to say I needed no tears to persuade my troubles, and that I had looked so far beyond them that, were all the friends I had in the world dead, more could not be expected than such a sadness in my eye." She is not "apt to hope." Good fortune comes to her "like the sun to the inhabitants of Greenland" who, when it goes, look for six months of night to follow.

Little wonder, then, if under the strain of loneliness and persecution, with her mother dead and her father dying, her courage broke at one moment and she begged Temple for his own sake to give her up. "She's happier by much," she writes of a frivolous friend at this time, "than I shall ever be, but I do not envy her; may she long enjoy it, and I an early and a quiet grave, free from the trouble of this busy world, where all with passion pursue their own interests at their neighbour's charges; where nobody is pleased but somebody complains on't; and where 'tis impossible to be without giving and receiving injuries. You would know what I would be at, and how I intend to dispose of myself. Alas! were I in my own disposal, you should come to my grave to be resolved; but grief alone will not kill."

Happily she possessed in Temple a lover with the essential gift of knowing when not to take his mistress at her word; or at least the determination not to do so now. He would not hear of renunciations—would she, in her heart, ever have forgiven him if he had? For genuine as was her despair, no less genuine was the passion for him that she keeps half veiled beneath a mixture of mockery and modesty, mischief and reticence. "Love is a terrible word," she will write back, when he has seized ardently on some unguarded phrase of hers, "and I should blush if anything but a letter accused me on't. Pray be merciful and let it run 'friendship' in my next charge." Yet she lives for his letters. "Your last letter came like a pardon to one upon the block"; or "never anyone was so defeated as I was to find none"; or "I chid my maid for waking me in the morning, till she stopped my mouth with saying she had letters for me. I had not patience to stay till I could rise, but made her tie up all the curtains to let in the light; and amongst some others I quickly found my dear letter that was first to be read, and which made all the rest not worth the reading." As for writing to him: "nothing that is paper can 'scape me, when I have time to write, and 'tis to you." One night her brother and a friend are talking by the fire and "amongst other things (which I did not at all mind) they fell into a discourse of flying; and both agreed that it was very possible to find out a way that people might fly like birds, and despatch their journeys so: I, that had not said a word all night, started up at that, and desired they would say a little more in it, for I had not marked the beginning; but instead of that, they both fell into so violent a laughing, that I should appear so much concerned in such an art; but they little knew of what use it might have been to me."

And so in the end such fondness and persistence triumphed,[2] and Dorothy Osborne came, without need of wings, to her lover's arms at last. Adversity dogged her to the close: she caught smallpox just before her marriage should have taken place, and with it lost her beauty; but on Christmas Day, 1654, she and Temple were wedded in St. Giles'-in-the-Fields.

For us it is not quite such a happy ending; for with it end her letters also, except for a few stray ones of minor interest. But before we leave her correspondence, a word may be said of its merely literary qualities; for every time I read her, I am struck afresh by these. They matter less, indeed, than the personality they reveal, one of the most lovable in all literature; but her character we learn once for all, her gift of language is a perpetual surprise. Enough has been quoted to show her power; but it is worth concentrating for a moment on this matter of pure style, and her ideas about it. These are definite enough. "In my opinion these great scholars are not the best writers (of letters, I mean); of books perhaps they are. I never had, I think, but one letter from Sir Justinian, but 't was worth twenty of anybody's else to make me sport. It was the most sublime nonsense that in my life I ever

[2] There is an entry in her brother's diary, belonging to the period just after she had yielded to Temple's absolute refusal to give her up, which makes pleasantly ironic reading: "Jan. 13, Friday morninge. I came to Chicksands before dinner. I found Mr. Temple here and my sister broke with him, God be praised."

read; and yet, I believe, he descended as low as he could to come near my weak understanding. . . ." "All letters, methinks," says she, "should be free and easy as one's discourse; not studied as an oration, nor made up of hard words like a charm. 'Tis an admirable thing, to see how some people will labour to find out terms that may obscure a plain sense. Like a gentleman I knew, who would never say 'the weather grew old,' but that 'winter began to salute us.' I have no patience for such coxcombs, and cannot blame an old uncle of mine that threw the standish [inkpot] at his man's head because he writ a letter for him where, instead of saying (as his master bid him) that 'he would have writ himself, but that he had the gout in his hand,' he said that 'the gout in his hand would not permit him to put pen to paper.' "

Certainly she practised her own theory. But her writing is not simply honest English; in her lighter vein she often recalls the vivid prose of Elizabethan comedy, until one feels at moments as if she had been brought into the world, not by Sir Peter Osborne, but by Shakespeare, at some date between Beatrice and Rosalind. She complains, for instance, of her goldsmith's utter lack of invention: "What a strange fellow this goldsmith is, he has a head fit for nothing but horns. . . . It makes me think of the fellow that could paint nothing but a flower-de-luce who, when he met with one that was so firmly resolved to have a lion for his sign that there was no persuading him on't, 'Well,' says the painter, 'let it be a lion then, but it shall be as like a flower-de-luce as e'er you saw.' " Surely this touches Bottom! Similarly in her serious moods she has a literary quality that echoes the wistful quietness of Traherne, or of Izaak Walton, whose *Angler* came out in this same year 1653. One such passage is well known, in which she describes "a common that lies hard by the house, where a great many young wenches keep sheep and cows, and sit in the shade singing of ballads"; but no less lovely is her picture of a summer evening's loneliness: "Last night I was in the garden till eleven o'clock. It was the sweetest night that e'er I saw. The garden looked so well, and the jasmine smelt beyond all perfume. And yet I was not pleased. The place had all the charms it used to have when I was most satisfied with it, and, had you been there,

I should have liked it much more than ever I did; but that not being, it was no more to me than the next field, and only served me for a place to roam in without disturbance."

I confess that to preserve these letters I would gladly sacrifice all the haystacks and wagon-loads of theological and political controversy which that quarrelsome age produced, including the prose of Milton himself.[3] Real grace like this is so rare a thing in English prose, as compared with French. It is extraordinary that the late Sir Walter Raleigh could write: "We have no one in English to compare with Madame de Sévigné for the combination of wit and tenderness. Dorothy Osborne was an exceedingly amiable and admirable lady, full of sound sense, but if you take away from her letters that flavour of antiquity that gives a heightened interest to all her allusions and to her descriptions of the life of the time, you would have to admit that there are a thousand writers of letters alive today who equal or excel her." We would admit no such thing. "Amiable lady—flavour of antiquity!" It is a judgement worthy of Sir Justinian in person.

But there is another wider issue that these letters raise. How enormously, one feels after reading them, culture matters up to a certain point! And beyond that point, how little! Dorothy Osborne's charm is essentially that of a very delicate and sensitive personality, taught to write by reading a few good books—the Bible, Shakespeare, Cowley, and her beloved Jeremy Taylor. French romances, like those of Mademoiselle de Scudéry, she also devoured; but how ill-read and ignorant she would be thought by many a modern miss! And yet how often do we meet today as good a writer and as attractive a human being? Are we surfeited, comes the misgiving question, with the good things, not only of the material, but of the intellectual world as well? Do we travel through the realms of gold in too American a fashion, with no time to digest a tenth of what we swallow, or are forcibly stuffed with? For this scantily educated young woman possessed all the

[3] This blasphemy when first published brought an indignant protest from an admirer of Milton's prose. I am afraid I am unrepentant. "Eagles mewing their mighty youth" are monstrous fine; but I would not give this charming human being for a wilderness of mewing eagles.

essential things—the secret of style, not only in letters, but in life. She had never heard of Botticelli; she very likely thought the sun went round the earth; and yet— It is a lasting wonder how little difference, beyond a certain point, the increase of knowledge seems to make. May not the modern educationalist have grounds for heart-searching here?

But there remains little more to tell of Dorothy Osborne from the point where her letters end and her married life begins. Her husband rose rapidly in the world of diplomacy. He concluded, with an unexampled quickness due to the impression of frank honesty he gave, the Triple Alliance between England, Holland, and Sweden—the first of that great series of coalitions which for the next century and a half were to curb the dominance of France, and in Pepys's judgement "the one good public thing that hath been done since the King came into England." He was a main instrument in that momentous wedding of Princess Mary to William of Orange. In his triumphs Dorothy Lady Temple shared, admired to the last for her letters and in her old age a trusted friend of Queen Mary; but, as she foresaw, life brought her its share of sorrow too. Seven of her children died in infancy. Her one remaining daughter, Diana, was carried off by smallpox in her youth. Her one remaining son, John, having risen to be Secretary at War under King William, threw himself a week later, his pockets filled with stones, from a boat that was shooting London Bridge, because he felt too deeply that he had ill advised the King. Her own death was hastened by sorrow for the Queen's (1695). So after forty years William Temple was left once more alone. There in the shades of Moor Park, where a new and very different love from his was springing up between his moody Irish secretary, Jonathan Swift, and young Esther Johnson, could he find after all, one wonders, in the long career he looked back on, any other piece of diplomacy that had really mattered so much to him as a girl's quick tact in the Isle of Wight, half a century before? For kingdoms pass, and treaties snap like rotten threads, and all our tortuous statecraft is only a cumbrous machinery to help make man's life worth living, only one precarious means to that elusive end; the best it can achieve is to keep alive a civilisation in which human beings as lovable as Dorothy Osborne can find, and be, and forget themselves.

NOTE. There are two excellent editions of Dorothy Osborne's *Letters*, by Judge Parry (1888; reprinted in *Wayfarer's Library* and *Everyman's Library*), and by G. C. Moore-Smith (1928). Admirable as the latter is for the student, the ordinary reader may, I think, get more enjoyment from the other with its modernised spelling and punctuation, which suits the essential modernity of Dorothy.

FOR FURTHER READING

IN THE MODERN SHORT BIOGRAPHY

In addition to authors represented in the present collection, whose complete works are listed in the separate notes, here are a few others:

ABERCROMBIE, LASCELLES, *Revaluations: Studies in Biography*, London, Oxford University Press, 1931.
BEERBOHM, MAX, "No. 2, The Pines," in *And Even Now*, New York, Dutton, 1921.
BEST, MARY AGNES, *Rebel Saints*, New York, Harcourt, Brace, 1925.
BISHOP, MORRIS, *A Gallery of Eccentrics*, New York, Minton, Balch, 1928.
BOLITHO, WILLIAM, *Twelve Against the Gods*, New York, Simon & Schuster, 1929.
CANBY, H. S., *Classic Americans*, New York, Harcourt, Brace, 1931.
COURNOS, JOHN, *A Modern Plutarch*, Indianapolis, Bobbs-Merrill, 1928.
COURTNEY, JANET E., *Freethinkers of the Nineteenth Century*, New York, Dutton, 1920; *Oxford Portrait Gallery*, London, Chapman, 1931.
DARK, SIDNEY, *Twelve Bad Men*, 1929; *Twelve Royal Ladies*, 1929; *Twelve More Ladies: Good, Bad, and Indifferent*, 1932, New York, Crowell.
FULFORD, ROGER, *The Wicked Uncles* [English title: *The Royal Dukes*]: *The Father of Queen Victoria and His Six Brothers*, New York, Putnam, 1933.
HAGBERG, KNUT, *Kings, Churchills, and Statesmen*, New York, Dodd, Mead, 1929; *Personalities and Powers*, London, Lane, 1930. Translated from the Swedish.
JAEGER, MURIEL, *Adventures in Living* [English title: *Experimental Lives*], *From Cato to George Sand*, New York, Morrow, 1932.
JOSEPHSON, MATTHEW, *The Robber Barons*, New York, Harcourt, Brace, 1934.
KEYNES, J. M., *Essays in Biography*, New York, Harcourt, Brace, 1933.
MACCARTHY, DESMOND, *Portraits I*, New York, Putnam, 1931.
MADELIN, LOUIS, *Figures of the Revolution*, New York, Macaulay, 1929. Translated from the French.
NEUMANN, ROBERT, *Passion: Six Literary Marriages*, New York, Harcourt, Brace, 1932. Translated from the German.
POWYS, LLEWELYN, *Thirteen Worthies*, New York, American Library Service, 1923.
ROEDER, RALPH, *The Man of the Renaissance*, New York, Viking, 1933.

ROGERS, CAMERON, *Gallant Ladies*, New York, Harcourt, Brace, 1928.
ROURKE, CONSTANCE M., *Trumpets of Jubilee*, New York, Harcourt, Brace, 1927.
SANDBURG, CARL, *Steichen the Photographer*, New York, Harcourt, Brace, 1929.
SABATINI, RAFAEL, *Heroic Lives*, Boston, Houghton Mifflin, 1933.
SITWELL, EDITH, *The English Eccentrics*, Boston, Houghton Mifflin, 1933.
STOWE, LYMAN BEECHER, *Saints, Sinners, and Beechers*, Indianapolis, Bobbs-Merrill, 1934.
TUCKER, B. R., *The Gift of Genius*, New York, Stratford, 1930.
WORTHAM, H. E., *Three Women*, Boston, Little, Brown, 1930.

ON BIOGRAPHY

ADAMS, J. T., "New Modes in Biography," and "Biography As an Art," in *The Tempo of Modern Life*, New York, Boni, 1931.
BOWERMAN, G. F., "The New Biography," in *Censorship and the Public Library and Other Papers*, New York, H. W. Wilson, 1931.
BRADFORD, GAMALIEL, "Psychography," in *A Naturalist of Souls*, Boston, Houghton Mifflin, 1917; "Confessions of a Biographer," in *Wives*, New York, Harper, 1926; "Biography and the Human Heart," and "Biography by Mirror," in *Biography and the Human Heart*, Boston, Houghton Mifflin, 1932; "Sainte-Beuve and Biography," in *The Saturday Review of Literature*, July 11, 1931.
BURDETT, OSBERT, "Experiment in Biography," in *Tradition and Experiment in Present-Day Literature*, New York, Oxford, 1929.
CANBY, H. S., "Biography and Truth," in *Current Literature*, April 6, 1931.
CARLYLE, THOMAS, "Biography" (1832), in *Critical and Miscellaneous Essays, II.*
CROSS, W. L., *An Outline of Biography From Plutarch to Strachey*, New York, Holt, 1924.
CROTHERS, S. M., "Satan Among the Biographers," in *The Cheerful Giver*, Boston, Houghton Mifflin, 1923.
DUNN, WALDO H., *English Biography*, New York, Dutton, 1916.
ELLIS, HAVELOCK, "An Open Letter to Biographers," in *Views and Reviews*, Boston, Houghton Mifflin, 1932.
FUESS, C. M., "The Biographer and His Victims," in *The Atlantic Monthly*, January 1932; "Debunkery and Biography," in *The Atlantic Monthly*, March 1933.
GOSSE, SIR EDMUND, "Biography," in *The Encyclopaedia Britannica.*
GUEDALLA, PHILIP, "The Missing Muse," in *The Missing Muse and Other Essays*, New York, Harper, 1930.
HARRIS, FRANK, "The Art of Biography," in *Confessional*, New York, Panurge, 1930.
HART, LIDDELL, "Neo-Georgian Biography," in *The Cornhill Magazine*, February 1934.
JOHNSTON, G. A., "The New Biography: Ludwig, Maurois, and Strachey," in *The Atlantic Monthly*, March 1929.

JOHNSTON, J. C., *Biography: The Literature of Personality*, New York, Century, 1927.

LEE, SIR SIDNEY, *Principles of Biography*, New York, Macmillan, 1911.

LONGAKER, J. M., *English Biography in the Eighteenth Century*, Philadelphia, University of Pennsylvania Press, 1931.

LUDWIG, EMIL, "Introduction," *Genius and Character*, New York, Harcourt, Brace, 1927.

MAUROIS, ANDRÉ, "The Modern Biographer," in *The Yale Review*, January 1928; *Aspects of Biography*, New York, Appleton, 1929.

MERRILL, D. K., *The Development of American Biography*, Portland, Me., Southworth Press, 1932.

METCALF, J. C., "English Biography," in *The Stream of English Biography*, New York, Century, 1930.

MUMFORD, LEWIS, "Biographies," in the front advertising section of *The Atlantic Monthly*, December 1929.

NICOLSON, HAROLD, *The Development of English Biography*, New York, Harcourt, Brace, 1928; "How I Write Biography," in *The Saturday Review of Literature*, May 26, 1934.

NOTESSTEIN, WALLACE, "History and the Biographer," in *The Yale Review*, March 1933.

PEARSON, HESKETH, *Ventilations, Being Biographical Asides*, Philadelphia, Lippincott, 1930.

PONSONBY, ARTHUR, "Biographies," in *Casual Observations*, London, Allen & Unwin, 1930.

SAINTSBURY, GEORGE, "Biography: Modern Developments," in *The Encyclopaedia Britannica.*

STAUFFER, D. A., *English Biography Before 1700*, Cambridge, Harvard University Press, 1930.

SYMONDS, A. J. A., "Tradition in Biography," in *Tradition and Experiment in Present-Day Literature*, New York, Oxford, 1929.

THAYER, W. R., *The Art of Biography*, New York, Scribner, 1920.

TRUEBLOOD, C. K., "Biography," in *Dial*, August 1927.

WARD, A. C., "Biography," in *Foundations of English Prose*, London, Bell, 1931.